Sexuality Education

SEXUALITY EDUCATION

Past, Present, and Future

Volume 4
Emerging Techniques and Technologies

Edited by Elizabeth Schroeder, EdD and Judy Kuriansky, PhD

Praeger Perspectives

Sex, Love, and Psychology

Westport, Connecticut
London

Library of Congress Cataloging-in-Publication Data

Sexuality education : past, present, and future / edited by Elizabeth Schroeder and Judy Kuriansky.
   v. ; cm. — (Sex, love, and psychology, ISSN 1554–222X)
   Includes bibliographical references and index.
   Contents: v. 1. — History and Foundations.
   ISBN 978–0–275–99794–6 (set : alk. paper) — ISBN 978–0–275–99796–0 (v.1 : alk. paper) — ISBN 978–0–275–99798–4 (v.2 : alk. paper) — ISBN 978–0–275–99800–4 (v.3 : alk. paper) — ISBN 978–0–275–99802–8 (v.4 : alk. paper)
   1. Sex instruction—History. I. Schroeder, Elizabeth. II. Kuriansky, Judith.
HQ56.S38634 2009
613.9071'273—dc22   2008051469

British Library Cataloguing in Publication Data is available.

Library of Congress Catalog Card Number: 2008051469
ISBN: 978–0–275–99794–6 (set)
      978–0–275–99796–0 (Vol. 1)
      978–0–275–99798–4 (Vol. 2)
      978–0–275–99800–4 (Vol. 3)
      978–0–275–99802–8 (Vol. 4)
ISSN: 1554–222X

First published in 2009

Praeger Publishers, 88 Post Road West, Westport, CT 06881
An imprint of Greenwood Publishing Group, Inc.
www.praeger.com

Printed in the United States of America

∞™

The paper used in this book complies with the Permanent Paper Standard issued by the National Information Standards Organization (Z39.48–1984).

10 9 8 7 6 5 4 3 2 1

To my 6-year-old son, Matthew, my heart and my inspiration. I love you, my guy, to the moon and back.
                    —Elizabeth Schroeder

For all the people in the world who deserve sexually healthy and happy lives, and to my mom, who taught me unconditional love, and my dad, who inspired me to "follow—and fulfill—your dreams."
                    —Judy Kuriansky

CONTENTS

FOREWORD

For more than two generations, sexuality educators have been championing the cause for understanding the importance of healthy sexuality and sexual expression in human development. It has been a rocky road, still under construction, filled with numerous detours, challenges and fraught with significant controversy due to powerful social and political forces. The continuation of this effort is essential as recent data at this writing, especially about young people, is extraordinarily alarming:

- 100 young people become pregnant every hour of every day in America;
- 50 young people give birth every hour of every day in America;
- 25 young people have a pregnancy termination every hour of every day in America;
- 425 young people contract a sexually transmitted infection every hour of every day in America;
- 2 young people become infected with HIV every hour of every day in America.

So as you can see, this is not some vague social problem floating around in our culture. What kind of society allows this to occur? Shouldn't we question ourselves? Shouldn't this make us tremble? Shockingly, our best thinking and our best doing in this great country of ours got us where we are today. We simply must do better. For these reasons I am grateful for the opportunity to write this foreword for *Sexuality Education: Past, Present, and Future*. This is a formidable set of volumes and will provide essential tools in meeting the enormous challenges facing us as we move through the twenty-first century.

As I began to write the foreword for this important set of books, I was encouraged by the possibility of change. The United States has elected a new president and congressional leadership on the promise of change. Specific to the themes in this four book set, our new president Barack Obama is the first candidate in our lifetime who has openly supported comprehensive sexuality education throughout his campaign. He has consistently embraced research and reason and has resisted strong conservative attempts to restrain scientific public discourse on sexuality issues through the life cycle. While the extent to which the new administration will support comprehensive sexuality education is yet to be seen, dialogue about this critical issue has already begun at important senior levels of government. I believe this essential dialogue will be informed by this rich and vital resource of books with contributions from national leaders in the sexuality field.

Sexuality Education: Past, Present, and Future covers a vast range of issues of great value to educators, student's, policymakers, researchers, and the general public. All of these groups now have access to a unique overview that has never before been presented together in this fashion, from tracing the early development of the field to bringing it forward toward the most progressive possibilities for the future. I am honored that my own work of 25 years on adolescent pregnancy prevention with the Children's Aid Society in New York is discussed in various chapters in this series. No other resource I have seen has made a more thorough and intensive examination of the evolution of sexuality education—allowing us to see what has existed, what has changed or remains the same, and what holds promise for the future. This deep and rich four volume set also addresses the invaluable yet often overlooked need for educational intervention which is evident in the voices of learners themselves. Whether we reach people through a formal classroom setting, or teach eager persons in a remote rural areas willing to walk miles and sit on a dirt floor to learn about these topics, or educate individuals through one-on-one interventions via the Internet or over the air waves—a key component is understanding what learners *need* and also *want*—to know about sexuality.

Volume 1 sets the stage for the issues and context of this valuable process. Volume 2 is an invaluable resource for all sexuality educators, researchers, health professionals, policymakers and legislators, as it offers diverse and provocative reports of what different populations in the United States—and around the world—seek to learn about sexuality and sexual expression and how they face similar issues about access to acquiring such life-enhancing education. Equally important are the contributions that help us distinguish differences in approach for diverse cultural populations, and knowing what is appropriate to teach learners of different ages in such groups. Volume 3 of this resource addresses this issue by describing programs with children and unique approaches with adolescents engaged in peer education efforts, while also highlighting the need for parents to receive support in their roles as sexuality educators of their own children. Also included in this volume is the recognition that age is not the only issue about which sexuality education initiatives must remain cognizant. Diversity, including learning style, age, developmental level, sexual orientation, and gender and relationship status, all affect the way in which sexuality information is conveyed and heard. Accordingly, this volume provides invaluable perspectives on the best practices to effectively reach the many diverse audiences sexuality educators serve.

What does the future of sexuality education hold? Answers will reveal themselves over time, but volume 4 presents readers with cutting edge information, programs, approaches, techniques, and resources that enable us to think about best practices and how sexuality education can—and should—take place. My own view on this is that orthodoxy has failed, so we must continue to develop nontraditional ways of teaching about sexuality, and to push through the resistance that attempts to censor the public discussion of sexuality and sexual expression. Only then will we truly consider nontraditional topics or relationships and make a difference in the way all people, young and older, learn about their sexuality—which is an essential and not well understood fiber in the fabric of their wholeness. Volume 4 thoroughly captures these notions.

In my book, *Lessons for Lifeguards*, I suggest that "effective programs do not happen by spontaneous combustion; someone has got to light the fire. Be incendiary in your efforts." I believe this four-volume set provides the fuel and other combustible materials to enable you to make a difference in your role as a sexuality educator, however you may define that role and with whomever you engage. As of this writing, I have worked 50 years with young people and their families. These extraordinary volumes reinforce why I continue to try to press ahead in our field.

Dr. Michael A. Carrera

ACKNOWLEDGMENTS

"Thank you, thank you. Appreciation is the thing to do. Thank him, thank her. For all the things you do for me, thank you."

These words came to Judy in the middle of yet another all-nighter while working on the Herculean task of putting together this set of books, and they represent the feelings of both of us. The phrase formed the basis of a song that Judy and her co-lyricist and fellow composer, Russell Daisey, wrote and then performed at peace charity concerts in Japan. The spirit of appreciation that inspired the song was so appropriate for the Japanese tradition of honoring—but also very appropriately inspired the process of putting together this set of volumes.

To say that putting together this four-volume set was tantamount to giving birth to quadruplets is an unbelievable understatement. True, it wasn't as painful, but the labor took a long time, many people contributed to and supported us throughout the process, and we are very proud of the outcome.

So, now, at this time of completion of this four-volume set with over 60 chapters and more then 100 authors, we are moved to recall that spirit of appreciation that was captured in Judy's song:

- Our appreciation goes to all the contributors to these volumes, some of whom are dear friends as well as colleagues. We honor the individuals they are and the work they are doing, which is contributing so much to others. Their hard work and commitment to educating professionals and the public about the need for sexuality education, and the wide range of what can be considered sexuality education, have been invaluable. Thank you so much.
- Our appreciation also extends to all those written about in these pages; may they be comforted and inspired by their contributions to the caring and hard work

reflected in these chapters, to ease—and prevent—sexually related problems and contribute to sexually well-educated and healthy lives for all.

• We are also deeply grateful to Praeger Publishing's Debbie Carvalko, Praeger Senior Acquisitions Editor, psychology and health, who championed this project and was always available with wise counsel, vision, and encouragement. We're also grateful to Elizabeth Potenza, Praeger Development Editor, and Apex CoVantage's Project Manager, Mary Cotofan, for their kindness, attention, and hard work, whom we e-mailed over the course of this project more, even on Sundays, than some members of our own families. We thank them all for their valued guidance, patience, and support throughout this project. We also extend gratitude to all the staff at Praeger and Apex CoVantage, who worked so diligently on this project.

In addition, from Judy:

I have deep appreciation for my wonderful and wise, creative and caring, friend and musical collaborator Russell, who was constantly there for me through so many all-nighters while I was writing my own chapters and editing others. He is truly an angel and a shining example of a consummate talent, great listener and sage advisor rolled into one. The same wisdom and championing is true of my mom, Sylvia, whom I cherish and to whom I owe so much for her constant love and devotion. She is also truly an angel. No words can ever express the depth of my appreciation and affection for her, but *her* words, "one thing at a time," were such good counsel for her daughter who is compelled to multitask 10 things at once. Yet her confidence, "I know you will get it all done," was also reassuring. Equally inspiring is her profound respect for sexuality education, especially—as she'll even describe in her sweet way—having grown up in a generation less open about such things. And then, just when the work was reaching a fevered pitch, two other angels appeared in the form of my Smith College interns—Amanda Calvo and Jennifer Arias—with their warm hearts, devotion, trustworthiness, enthusiastic spirit, varied talents, and brilliance beyond their years, not to mention their keen editing skills and willingness to try any format for a table or look up any detail on the Internet. The chapters they each contributed to are favorites, as every word is infused with their love, hard work, and good humor, like when reminding me to sleep or eat. I adore them and I am filled with pride for who they are and for the professionals they will become.

Another angel was there from the start, my coeditor, Elizabeth Schroeder, who is indeed a dream come true as a colleague and friend with whom to share such a task. Her excellent judgment, steadfast reliability, warm heart, terrific good-humor and great team spirit—not to mention her brilliantly written e-mails, which always served to uplift and amuse—set a new standard for a collaborator with such a broad "skill set" in a woman with such a pleasant personality mixed with a smart and organized brain. I am very blessed—and now very spoiled—to have worked with her on this project and look forward to many more in the future.

And from Elizabeth:

I would not have been a part of this project had it not been for Bill Taverner, director of education at Planned Parenthood of Greater Northern New Jersey's Center for Family Life Education. You are a most generous, wonderful colleague, Bill, and I value you immensely.

I also wish to thank Nora Gelperin, director of education and training at Answer, who provided instrumental research assistance for the series. Nora, you are a consummate professional, colleague, and friend who I can also now refer to as my coworker. I am so lucky to know you.

I was also fortunate to have had a wonderful graduate student from Montclair State University, Holly Den Bleyker, helping me with obtaining permissions, inputting edits, and lending her keen eye to a good number of the chapters. Holly, I will miss being able to avail myself of your amazing work!

Above all, I need to thank Dr. Judy Kuriansky. Readers should know that Judy originally had a supervisory role as the series editor but became so excited by and committed to the project that she joined as an equal coeditor, both generating her own content and securing much of it as well. This four book set honestly would not have happened without her, and her contributions—as an author of so many compelling, eye-opening chapters; as an editor with a creative, analytical eye; and as a brilliant thinker and brainstormer whose humor and collegiality really kept me going throughout this project—truly made the set the unique resource it is. Judy, I am honored to have worked with you on this and to now be able to call you friend. So what's our next project?

Finally, we both want to thank all the sexuality educators in the field—those who have done the work in the past, those who are doing the work today, and those who will do the work in the future. Whatever your role—university professor, school teacher or administrator, community-based educator, researcher, advocate, therapist or clinician, parent or other adult with children or young people in your life, or anyone else who knows how vital it is to learn about sexuality in its broadest definition throughout the life cycle—know that you are so important. Thank you for reading this set about sexuality education and for all you do for individuals, communities, society, and the world.

Judy Kuriansky and Elizabeth Schroeder

INTRODUCTION

Elizabeth Schroeder

Now is the accepted time, not tomorrow, not some more convenient season. It is today that our best work can be done and not some future day or future year. It is today that we fit ourselves for the greater usefulness of tomorrow. Today is the seed time, now are the hours of work, and tomorrow comes the harvest and the playtime.

—W.E.B. Du Bois, civil rights activist

Volume 4 of *Sexuality Education: Past, Present, and Future* concludes by helping the reader outside of the proverbial box when it comes to traditional ways of seeing sexuality education. This volume also offers some new (and what some can consider nontraditional) methods and venues for providing sexuality education, all of which are providing a springboard for the future of the discipline and the field.

A significant focus of this volume is the media and how the many types of media available to individuals today can be used in educational settings. Most sexuality educators have been taking steps over the years to integrate current media into their classrooms, moving beyond the simply narrated film-strips of the 1960s and 1970s to using clips from television shows and films their learners watch as catalysts for discussion about sexuality-related issues. Other educators use contemporary music videos or lyrics; others have students search the Internet and rate sexuality education sites. This volume provides an insider's look into unique methods for teaching about sexuality: how some countries have used popular media to teach the general public about sexuality through radio soap operas; how sexuality education has been provided to individual callers and listeners to a radio talk show; how video games can be used to teach about sexuality-related issues and messages (in particular, gender and sexism); how the Internet can be used in much more creative ways, and more.

This volume also pushes the proverbial envelope by acknowledging the needs of adult learners and the ways in which sexually explicit media created specifically with an educational goal in mind can be used to train sexuality professionals and to educate individuals and couples about sexual functioning and relationship issues. Other chapters provide examples of creative venues for sexuality education—for example, sex museums and adult retail stores— reminding the reader once again that teachable moments relating to sexuality are everywhere for people of all ages and stages in their lives, if they are open to continuing to learn.

The volume concludes with one proposition for the future of sexuality education and the fervent hope that, one day, the controversies and disagreements over the subject matter will end, the fear and the shame will be eradicated, and the idea of sexuality as an integral, valuable part of the human experience will be accepted by all.

Part I

SEXUALITY EDUCATION ON COLLEGE CAMPUSES

Chapter One

COED SEX ADVICE COLUMNS IN CAMPUS NEWSPAPERS: CONTRIBUTIONS TO COLLEGE SEXUALITY EDUCATION

Judy Kuriansky, Yvonne K. Fulbright, and Amanda Calvo

A sex advice column is a repeating feature article published in any of a variety of traditional and modern media outlets that delivers sexuality and/or relationship information and guidance to its reading audience. Such writings have been called "informal" curricula of sexuality education—in contrast to more "formal" community and school-based curricula—in providing a site for talking, learning, and debating sexuality issues (Gudelunas, 2005). The style and format can vary, for example, as free-flow first-person essays or in a question-and-answer format. Published for decades in print outlets (e.g., newspapers, magazines, and weeklies) and more recently in online formats worldwide intended by and for adults, lately such columns have appeared in college newspapers across the country, written largely by coeds with no formal sexuality education training. These college columns exploded into media focus in 2002, garnering attention for their forthrightness about sex topics to a coed audience eager for sexual discourse. Under the ensuing scrutiny, the columns and their authors were either hailed for delivering needed sexuality information or criticized as salacious. This chapter explores the role of such college sex advisers and the forum of college newspapers in sexuality education of today's youth population.

BACKGROUND

Columns about sexuality have appeared throughout the world, in countries like Canada, China, Sweden, and Great Britain as well as in various African nations. In the United States, syndicated columnist Ann Landers is typically credited with being the first to take on sexuality-related matters in the second half of the twentieth century, followed by the more formally trained Dr. Joyce Brothers, whose advice was also syndicated in newspapers nationwide. Over the years, scores of writers and aspiring journalists have taken on the role of "sex columnist." Even more recently, college students have claimed that specialty, penning columns about sexuality topics in their school newspaper.

Since its debut in the University of California at Berkeley's *Daily Californian* campus newspaper in 1997, the college sex column has been a controversial headliner, creating one of the greatest stirs in U.S. college journalism (Reimold, 2004). Published in a supposed safe haven for learning and debate—the college newspaper—these writings have been praised for their role in stimulating valuable sexual dialogue (even though controversial), in challenging societal perceptions around sexuality, and in taking on a taboo subject. Yet, they have also been severely criticized for presenting information about sex that is based on questionable true experience or professional knowledge, as well as for being raunchy, clumsy, heterosexist and offensive and, therefore, not belonging in a college newspaper (Kolhatkar, 2005; Park, 2002). Given their wide readership by a population that is not well educated about sexual matters, these offerings constitute an influential outlet for information and models of attitudes and behavior about sexuality.

"Sex columns are the principal chroniclers of students' social lives. They are a barometer of students' sexual sentiments. They are a recorder of their friskiest trysts and oddest fetishes. And they exist as the most influential documentation related to modern student sex imparted by the students themselves," said Dan Reimold, a Scripps Howard Teaching Fellow at the University of Ohio. A PhD candidate at the E. W. Scripps School of Journalism, Reimold was heralded in a 2006 issue of *CO-ED* magazine as "the leading expert on the college sex columnist phenomenon."

Penned largely by female writers, sex advice columns have become increasingly popular in college communities, turning the sex scribes into instant celebrities on campus (Hoover, 2007). University papers often hold campus-wide contests to identify their next columnist, with one such campaign at Columbia University receiving 35 submissions (Grynbaum, 2004). The columns boost readership, with many papers running out of copies on the day the sex column is printed (Robbins, 2003). Reimold also discovered during his research that columns regularly received the highest number of hits on campus newspaper Web sites as well (Reimold, 2007).

College sex columns exploded as a cultural sensation in 2002. While some campus dailies have run columns like "Sex on Tuesday" and "Between the Sheets" for years, it took a *Chronicle of Higher Education* critique, inflamed by a Yale columnist's musings over whether to "spit or swallow" during fellatio, to catapult campus sexperts onto the media radar screen. In tracing the columns' popularity, media observers have pointed to TV shows that deal openly with sexuality, most notably HBO's *Sex and the City* series, with its role-model sex columnist character Carrie Bradshaw, played by Sarah Jessica Parker (Marklein, 2002). While the occasional college sex columnist sees her column as a stepping stone to a career in sex education or therapy, as did the second author, most are doing it just for fun or the writing experience. Also fueling interest in campus newspaper sex columns are the "sexploits" of young celebrities, covered in tabloids and on TV, like the photos of Britney Spears baring her private parts, professing an improbable virginity status, and pulling sexy stunts like lip-locking with pop singer Madonna at the MTV Music Awards. Adding to diminished taboos about sex in some societal sectors, young people have more confidence about airing their sex lives via public forums like sex columns. "Students think about sex. Therefore, students like to read about sex" (Allison, 2006). Many want to get in on the discourse, making their voices heard.

Given that abstinence-only sexuality education has dominated the U.S. government's stance for the past decades, the tone and topics of college sex columns can be regarded as rebellion against the lack of comprehensive sex education. Few opportunities exist on college campuses to get comprehensive education about sexuality (see chapter 2 in this volume), though an increasing number of campuses offer courses in women's studies or gender studies. And only a handful of schools currently offer graduate training in sexuality (a long-running program at New York University folded, as did one at the University of Pennsylvania, which was enveloped into a thriving program at Widener University). But, with one in four teen girls between the ages of 14 and 19 infected with a sexually transmitted infection (Centers for Disease Control and Prevention, 2008) and high numbers of college students sexually active, there is a dire need for students to be educated about sexuality and sexual health. With few outlets for sexuality education, it is not surprising that college sex columnists have become so popular and that youth turn to them for not only titillation but also for information. This content also makes their role that much more critical and the responsibility they bear that much greater. "I want to educate people," said Amber Madison (personal communication November 8, 2002), former columnist for *The Tufts Daily*. However, the question is: Are these sex columnists educating or just titillating, and how good a job are they doing?

THE COLLEGE SEX ADVISERS

While the exact number of such columns on all campuses throughout the country is unknown, a recent survey of 139 universities found that there were 78 campus columns where students could read a recurring article or e-mail a question about sexuality without revealing their identity (J. Daniels, personal communication, July 11, 2008). In 2003, it was estimated that about 10% of the approximately 1,200 members of the Associated Collegiate Press were publishing a sex column, and research showed that since 2004 sex columns had been running in 137 student publications at colleges and universities throughout the United States and Canada (Reimold, 2004).

Sex columns penned by coeds have appeared in small and large institutions around the country and in liberal, urban areas like New York City, as well as in more conservative states like Utah and in heartland America. Campuses that have had columns include Tufts, Johns Hopkins, Stanford, New York University, Boston College, and the University of Kansas, as well as many Ivy League schools, including Columbia, Yale, and Dartmouth. Other publications on some campuses provide even spicier material, like Vassar's *Squirm* and Harvard's *H Bomb*, a publication showing naked coeds (Miller, 2004). College-spun sex advice is available on most weekdays, from "Sex on Tuesday" in the *Daily Californian* at the University of California, Berkeley to "Wednesday Hump" at the *Daily Nexus,* University of California at Santa Barbara, and Thursday's "Sex in CINcity" at *The News Record* at the University of Cincinnati. Covering sex on college campuses has become such a sensation that university publications are hyping their columns, hoping to get wide distribution in an increasingly competitive news media world.

The vast majority of the columns are written by young people who have no formal training in sexuality or sexuality education (Marklein, 2002). Instead, they are authored by undergraduates who use personal beliefs, attitudes, values, opinions, and dating and sexual experiences to expound on vast topics like casual sex, self-pleasuring, styling pubic hair, selecting a vibrator, fetishes, pornography, sex with your ex, bondages, sadomasochism, erogenous zones, orgasm, sodomy laws, STIs, PDAs (public displays of affection), sex outdoors, the G spot, threesomes ("starting with a three-way kiss or tag-team kissing"), and group sex. Occasionally, a writer may call upon scholarly research or solicit outside expertise.

EXAMPLES OF TOPICS

The topics featured in college sex columns are surprisingly similar to questions that have been posed to veteran sexologists and mental health professionals working with the media (Kuriansky, 1996). Common topics include oral sex and how to spice up sex. Bold in taking on still somewhat taboo topics, columnists address often taboo topics like anal sex, which appears to have become a popular subject of student queries (both regarding health risks and how to do it painlessly). For example, UC-Berkeley's one-time columnist Rachael Klein was known for her "ass-play" commentary. Professor Kathy Greaves of "Ask Doctor Sex" at *The Daily Barometer* at Oregon State University notes that anal sex is second in popularity only to women's orgasm as subjects in the 5,000 questions she's gotten from her Oregon State students (K. Greaves, personal communication, December 12, 2002). Reimold (personal communication, July, 2008) discovered through interviews with 80 columnists that anal sex was among the most popular and definitely the most controversial subject tackled.

Many columnists are also dealing with their own personal issues and curiosities around sex-related matters. Outspoken college coed Meghan Bainum, who posed for a *Playboy* magazine feature about the coed sexperts, was worried that her behind was too big; the born-and-bred Kansan likened this to men worrying about their penis being too small when it's really six and a half inches—a perfectly average size when erect—saying, "I'm like everybody else obsessed that something's wrong with my body when I really need to be more confident" (M. Bainum, personal communication, October 14, 2002). Yale junior Natalie Krinsky heard her friend Amanda's tale of a wild make-out session in the back of a New York taxi and decided she wanted a similar hot PDA (public display of affection) with a "gangsta" and that it would make a good subject for her sex column in her college newspaper (N. Krinsky, personal communication, November 4, 2002). In what she called the "Tube Top Incident," where a drop of her tube top exposed her left breast, Boston College student Anna Schleelein (personal communication, December 17, 2002) feared that such a "wardrobe malfunction" (referring to the infamous Janet Jackson breast exposure at the 2004 Super Bowl halftime show) could lead her down a road into what she calls "the comically inept world of teen sex."

But some columns also address dating, as would be expected from a college sample concerned about intimate and casual sexual relationships. Often writing from a personal perspective, some columnists admit their own dating distress. "I had a lot of bad boyfriends," one adviser said, insisting on anonymity. "I'm not a person to be giving anyone relationship advice."

Some examples of topics tackled include:

Sex Toys

"Perhaps a purple, waterproof dildo that suctions to the shower wall wasn't exactly what Susan B. Anthony had in mind as a tool for female empowerment, but hey, whatever works, right?"—Marisa Picker, *The Diamondback*, at the University of Maryland

"You're having sex with a woman who finds that having an orgasm without clitoral stimulation is close to impossible. Hello vibrating cock ring with an attached clitoral stimulator. And there's no reason to rule out ones that have remote control." —Rachael Klein, *Daily Californian*, at UC-Berkeley

Masturbation

"Masturbating in a group-living situation does pose some problems, but where there is a will, there is a way."—Meghan Bainum, *Daily Kansan*, at the University of Kansas

Oral Sex

"You wouldn't put something in your mouth if you didn't know where it had been; why would you do that with your crotch?"—Rachel Klein, *Daily Californian*, at UC-Berkeley

"While a good cheese is easier to find than good oral sex, we don't deserve to eat good cheese if we can't appreciate it."—Sara Franklin, *The Tufts Daily*, at Tufts University

"Part of what makes writing this column so difficult is that I haven't ever gotten off from oral sex."—Miriam Datskovsky, *Columbia Daily Spectator*, at Columbia University

Spicing up Sex

Advice to women: "Be spontaneous. Have fun with costuming; be a school teacher or a nun and discipline your 'student' with a ruler. Buy a French maid's outfit or a Batman cape. Take control. Be dominant. Don't be afraid. You might discover you like to be spanked." "If you've been missing a spark in your sex life, adding a good pair of handcuffs or a spanking or two to your normal routine could be the way for you to put the sprinkles on your ice cream cone." And advice to men: "Blindfold your girlfriend and take her to a strip club."—Meghan Bainum, *Daily Kansan*, at the University of Kansas

Other popular topics include, communication, women masturbating and learning about their body, men learning about a woman's body, and giving good fellatio (tease, take time, include testicle stimulation)—subjects sexuality educators have covered with some audiences for years.

On Faking an Orgasm

"She's faking it. That's right. It's not hard. All we have to do is throw in an 'ooh' and a couple of 'aahs,' gyrate the hips and you guys think you're the Jedi Master."—Beth Van Dyke, *Daily Nexus*, at the University of California at Santa Barbara

On Group Sex

"You can sandwich a woman between two men with a penis in the vagina and the anus. Or, you can have one woman giving a man a blowjob while another woman pleases the man above the waist. Also, two women or two men could hook up while the other person sits back and enjoys the show."—Emily Chung, *Daily Californian*, at UCLA

On Sexual Emissions

"Granted, there is no polite way to wipe poo off the wall, but there are ways to deal with awkward situations in bed. Take, for example, the enigma of the wet spot ... you have to deal with the spot, on the spot, or you'll end up with a collection of crusty zones."—Mindy Friedman, *Daily Californian*, at UC-Berkeley

On Personal Dating Experiences

"I have never even hooked up with a younger guy. Is a relationship like that bad? Give the freshman guy a chance. You never know: he might be the next Ashton Kutcher."—Heather K. Strack, *Dartmouth Free Press*, at Dartmouth College

Many sex columnists are discovering their own sexual behavior preferences. "College is a time to explore kinks, put sprinkles on the cupcakes," Bainum says, admitting that she is turned on by bondage, spanking, and role-playing dominance and submission. "It's fun to be bossed around," she says, but is discouraged over whether she can find a partner to comply. As she says, "They try, but I've always been the dominant one, more in control." Proud that she gets into "a lot of cool things," Bainum makes lots of "booty calls" (a commonly used term to describe calling up someone and going over for casual sex). The wildest thing she's ever done is to "get it on" in an ex-boyfriend's grandfather's bed. Urination activity sounds "interesting" to her, as she can see why some people might like it and she isn't averse to try. Two years ago, when she was 19 years old, she tried out being a stripper. "I got the job, but it's a long story, and I decided to clean hotel rooms instead," she says, even though the experience gave her that coveted feeling of being in charge of her sexuality. She would also try same-sex behavior, saying, "I'd kiss a girl 'n stuff," reflecting on four or five attractive candidates and rationalizing, "It's like kissing a guy, just a set of lips on a person, something to do when you get drunk and can use it to turn guys on." Her perfect date would involve someone taking her to an awesome concert, getting drunk, staying up till 7 A.M. and having sex without inhibitions, not worrying about cellulite or acne.

Another 19-year-old adviser says she'd draw the line at anything painful, like needles, and she's unsure about having sex with a woman. As she says, "It's something I want to try at some time. . . what if I'm a lesbian and didn't know it?"

University of Wisconsin-Madison's former "Between the Sheets" columnist Caley Beals (personal communication, November, 2002) brags that she loves to break the rules. Touting exhibitionism in her column and recounting couples' debates over whether to do it in the stairwell of the chemistry building or the bathroom in Humanities, she says, "Doing it somewhere you shouldn't is one of the ultimate highs." One creative couple, she reported, stapled a poster to the wall in a library study room that said "Did it here with Durex." Construction sites are best, she concludes. Perhaps not surprisingly, her column garnered some negative reactions (Miller, 2004).

WHAT ABOUT THE "A" IN THE ABC METHOD?

A favorite topic of the college sex columnists is condoms. Many write about their use, where to get them on and off campus, how to use them, and the pros and cons of various styles. Few, however, address abstinence or promote it. UCLA's former columnist Teresa Chin once challenged her sexually adventurous readers to try a technique she guaranteed would knock their socks off: abstinence. Promising to rekindle the joys of oral sex, light groping, and necking, Chin ultimately retreated to propose an only-five-minute restraint period she called an "abstinence quickie" (T. Chin, personal communication, November, 2002). Abstinence promotion was the topic of only a small number of columns, but columnists did at times recommend various pre-intercourse activities, interestingly, as a way to refrain from full sex for awhile. Krinsky, for example, wrote about bringing 'the hand job' back into style, seeing it as a way for people to please their male partners and not have to feel pressured to engage in intercourse immediately (D. Reimold, personal communication, July 2008).

WHERE DO THEY GET THEIR SEXUALITY INFORMATION?

While sex columnists with graduate degrees, like Yvonne Fulbright (the second author formerly of NYU's "Sexpert Tells All"), Professor Kathy Greaves, and Melinda Myers (formerly of "Sexually Speaking" at California State University—Humboldt), have been noted for bringing formal training to their work and offering constructive advice, most are college students with no formal training. They draw from their own or peers' adventures, confessions, ruminations, gossip, and observations at drunken college parties. As one columnist said, there is no dearth of material from activities and events they observe or participate in on campus. Bainum shared, "At one party, I watched a hot guy with girls all over him, hitting on him and kissing him. I see a lot of sex going down in front of me."

A few advisers consult sexuality texts or Web sites for ideas and facts. Some write blatantly in the first person using a lot of self-disclosure, while others use the ambiguous term "you." The degree of self-disclosure varies. The first piece that a 19-year-old sophomore wrote for her school newspaper described the first time she got "fingered" when she was 14 years old and a sophomore in high school, although she says she did not have sex until she was 19 years old, with someone she cared about, and using birth control. Another columnist also revealed personal experiences, but admits she played up her favorite piece about flashing her breasts when her tube top fell down, "to make it funny to appeal to my target audience ... and to make others feel better that they're not the only one."

As one of the few with professional training, having earned a master's degree in human sexuality education from the University of Pennsylvania and as a doctoral student in health studies at New York University, the second author says that being on such a professional track influences her approach to her writing. Her campus column, which ran from 2001 through 2005, was also among the few to use a question-and-answer rather than commentary format, where she gave answers in an academic, straightforward way. She says, "The other college girls do exhibitionistic writing. I want to give the facts."

THEIR BACKGROUNDS

Most of the young advisers are female coeds, 19 to 21 years old, who are sophomores or juniors, except for Fulbright, a 27-year-old doctoral student with a master's in human sexuality education. They are pursuing different majors, including those in journalism seeking to gain experience in that field. (Bainum's project on fetishism for an advanced reporting class motivated her to beg the paper to let her write a column. The editors resisted until a new editor came on board and finally gave her the opportunity.) Others are majoring in liberal arts, like art history, American studies, Spanish, English, and theology. All report becoming curious about sexuality and becoming even more so through their role as sex adviser. After covering "the beat" (newspaper word for the topic a reporter specializes in), several are considering a future career in writing about sex or becoming sexuality educators.

The family backgrounds of the advisers are diverse. Some come from small conservative towns, one grew up on a farm, another on a commune, whereas others come from academic homes (e.g. one's father is a college professor). Parents variously approve or disapprove of their offspring's new venture.

Some columnists had sex for the first time at 16 years old, while the oldest and most professionally trained adviser was a self-professed "late bloomer" in that realm, having her first sexual encounter at almost 20 years old. Some college advisers realize over the course of their writing how much there really is to know about sexuality. One columnist asked the first author for advice about common questions she receives, for example, about the best ways to orally please a woman, what reaching climax feels like, and how to have more than one orgasm.

IMPACT OF BEING A PEER SEX ADVISER

Immersion in the subject of sexuality and, certainly, being a sexuality educator invariably changes one's personal life. Wearing the "sexpert" hat lends itself to being more open about sex, as well as less self-conscious or anxious about the subject. Others' perceptions are impacted, too (e.g., some people think that sex columnists are "kinky"). Men have also been known to feel either threatened or intensely challenged to prove their superior performance or to get insider information by wooing a sex columnist.

"Guys might ask a question but really be hitting on you," Fulbright says, describing an experience with a man who complained that his wife is against porn but that he got some porn tapes from his boss before handing Fulbright his business card. Another time, a roommate tried to fix her up but warned that the guy thought she'd be an "easy lay" given her career choice. "I like to surprise them that I'm not easy," she says, adding that as a blonde from Iceland she often has to dispel another myth—that Nordic goddesses are constantly "hot to trot."

Another adviser tells of being introduced to a guy at a party as a sex columnist, to which he responded, "I'll have you know I'm extremely good at giving oral sex" (she came back with "No, go away!"). Other guys who meet her are surprised, she says. "They end up saying, 'you're just a normal chick, that's cool.'"

Krinsky said that a male reader told her, "When that Natalie chick came out for 'swallow' I sure wanted to get some of that." Since his girlfriend refused to do that act, he was thinking of dumping her, buoyed by a pact with his buddies not to date any girl who doesn't go along with the columnist's preference.

Dealing with a boyfriend when you go public about your sex life isn't easy, as well, admits one columnist, who said anonymously, "He doesn't like the idea of so many guys thinking of me, and he gets teased by other guys.... But he knows it's something I want to do."

GENDER POINT OF VIEW: WOMEN OR MEN AS PEER SEX ADVISERS

The fact that vast majority of college sexperts are female raises gender issues about peer sexuality educators. While the female columnist for *The Tufts Daily* was inspired by the two males (a comic and a medical doctor/addiction specialist) who gave advice on the popular MTV show *Loveline*, she said, "I don't want to hear two men telling me what to do with my vagina ... The world needs women giving sex advice and women need to be told by women."

The fact that females are dominating sex columns should be no surprise, given the gender makeup of the field of sexology itself, which is dominated by women. Men represent a third (32.2%) of the sex educators certified by the American Association of Sexuality Educators, Counselors and Therapists (AASECT), with the vast majority of the membership (including therapists and related practitioners) of the professional organization being female (AASECT, personal communication, July 7, 2008). It is commonly maintained that male readers tend to prefer the female writer (Kolhatkra, 2005), although male sex columnist Brandon Bilinski from Clemson University said he signed up because he decided that "it was time for a male voice to be heard" (Bilinski, 2008). When writing his first column, he decided, "I could think of nothing more pertinent to men than pornography, so my first foray into the sex columnist world explained in detail the nuances between soft and hard core porn." He notes that, after receiving some good feedback (mostly from guys who thought reading about masturbation in a newspaper was funny), the newspaper editors decided that, while female writers presented good writing samples or were persistent, is was not essential to select a woman.

One columnist noted that females can get away with writing things men cannot and that men would be called male chauvinists for tackling many of the same topics that women address (Hoover, 2007). Some advisers reveal in their columns that women have more challenges than men in making decisions about sex. As one says, "Women just aren't as sexually satisfied as they should be…. They're higher at risk for getting STIs, and they don't have as much enjoyment in sex. It's just not fair!" As a result, her agenda is to empower women: "I want girls to be open, not slutty, so I want to get girls to masturbate and know the vagina is not a dirty place. And I want to get girls to use condoms." Another says, "Women want guys to give a shit about them having a good sexual experience" (Bainum, personal communication, 2002).

While some of the females insist that women take responsibility for sex (a valid point, professionals advise), as one said, "Find out what you like, find out what you don't, and take responsibility for letting him know both. Positive reinforcement is key. Draw him a map. Promise him a treat. Give him a cookie." Other columnists want guys to learn how to treat and respect a woman. "Just aim to please. Don't expect them all to come," says one. "Boys (note the not-so-feminist word), I can't stress this enough: pay attention…. Don't expect all girls' hot spots to be the same….Think of it like driving a car. You wouldn't use the same map to go to New York as you would to go to South Bend."

The sex column has been seen as one form of advancing a feminist agenda or poking fun at men. Male body parts are at times referred to in a not-so-professional but more slang way, for example, "Free Willy to breach his Marine World sanctuary" and "Let Mr. Salt Malt know you're down for a splooge slushy or two." One columnist wrote that homophobia can "make a dick flaccid faster than you can say, 'Sally saw Sammy's slim sausage swing sideways swiftly.'" Words used to refer to the male sex organ include "dode," "shloppy," and "puck."

It's these gender issues that lead Greaves, the instructor of an undergraduate human sexuality course, to wonder about whether the young advisers are perpetuating sex-role stereotypes. A sex adviser for 8 years for her campus paper at Oregon State University (a largely agricultural school with what she calls a "Bible-quoting" student body), who also took classes in public health and women's studies, Greaves (personal communication, 2002) says, "They tend to say that men are oversexed and women should be in control and decide when things happen, overgeneralizations that can be dangerous."

A MALE SEX COLUMNIST: HUMORIST OR SEXUALITY EDUCATOR

Brandon Bilinski is unique as a male writing a sex column for a college newspaper. Now 23, married, and living in California, Brandon wrote his "On the Prowl" column for *The Tiger*, an independent student newspaper, while at Clemson University in upstate South Carolina. He started out treating the subject humorously and in a light tone, partly because he had enjoyed creative writing since childhood (not surprisingly, he won second place for entertainment writing in a competition run by the South Carolina Collegiate Press Association for his first column). In that spirit of humor, he says "I made up things and I tried to think of the most outrageous topics. So I wrote an annotated history of dildos that was all made-up ideas about when and where in history they came from" (B. Bilinski, personal communication, July 2008).

Another reason for taking on a sex column was that, as a male, he "did not want to come across as a misogynist," since previous writers had all been female. Further, he wanted to avoid flack from home, which he got when he used his real name for his debut column. Friends of his parents in his small conservative town told them, "I can't believe your son is doing this. We thought you raised him better than that." (Brandon was surprised, since he thought that writing about where to get birth control and cheaper condoms was hardly raunchy.) He also didn't want to "burn any bridges" for his future, "since I didn't know then where I would go or what job I would get after graduation." So he decided to assume a pseudonym, "Orson Swelles."

As Orson Swelles, Brandon went "straight for the jugular of the prudish population" with articles on Internet porn (which, he points out, guys really responded to), Kegel exercises, and "giving dirty talk advice." This got "talk" on campus and on the newspaper online message board—especially since the former female writer had been tamer and focused on relationships. Some hate mail followed, making Swelles disappointed in the conservatism of his college. One girl wrote that if she had read his column before accepting the school, she would have gone elsewhere.

One article that he notes that was particularly informative was about fetishes. A "furry," he explained, "is a person who gets sexually aroused by images of anthropomorphic animals having sex (usually because they believe they harbor the soul of an animal), and these people organize at furry events dressed in animal suits." But furries are old news, as the now computer expert explained: "The new fad around the web is the 'Mechy,' which involves machines and vehicles such as jets and tanks that are human-like and usually nude. Trust me when I say that you haven't seen weird unless you've seen a B-52 bomber having sex with an M1 Abram tank."

But, besides having fun with his columns, Brandon notes that he was also responsible and intentionally "tried to be educational." This was evident in his first column every year (he did it for three years of his five-year engineering science program), when he reviewed information that freshmen need to know about sexual health, working with the sexual health center on campus. Keeping the spirit of freshman orientation, the column focused on sexual health resources on campus, including on the value of getting tested and the low cost of doing so at the student health center (free HIV tests were offered for a week and at other times cost $7). Like a true sexuality educator, he pleaded with his readers, "Please, get yourself tested for these diseases if you have had sex with anyone that you did not know the sexual history of (or even if you haven't)." He adds information about HPV and its vaccine; says that females between 18 and 25 should get the shots to help prevent cervical cancer, and recommends talking to the school health department, "because they have many more answers than I do, and they are extremely helpful in this regard"; and urges females to see the resident nurse practitioner who is the head of the women's clinic, since "from what I've heard, she is many girls' best friend around campus."

"I've contributed a lot to sexual health on campus," he says, so much that he is upset that Clemson got an "F" on the Trojan Sexual Health report card, which rates 139 American universities on their efforts to promote sexual health on campus on the basis of questions on subjects like the availability of sexual health information, the publication of a sexuality column in the newspaper, if any, and one's ability to get tested for STIs. Bilinski (2008b) admitted that "maybe the student body isn't as well informed about sexual health as it should be" and appealed to his classmates to break the top 20 on the report card, writing that "the next time you are sexually active, think about USC being 84 spots ahead of us and strap on a free condom or take your birth control pills as a small step in doing what you can for the proud tradition of this fine university."

AN EXPANDED VIEW OF SEXUALITY—
FROM SINGULAR TO PLURAL

In response to the current generation, a new trend in sexuality education on college campuses is the recognition of not just sexuality, but "sexualities." This expanded term includes people who identify with various orientations and choices and even those who deliberately don't want to be defined or limited by any specific term. At some women's colleges, it seems this movement is strong, as living and learning with other women gives students an environment in which to explore their identity. This openness is reflected in articles in publications on campuses like Smith College, one of the few remaining bastions of women-only higher learning. Once a haven for conservative young women in black sheath dresses and pearls, the Seven Sister college became a sowing ground for free thinkers, women's movement founders, and radical feminists like Gloria Steinem and Betty Freidan in the 1960s and emerged with a reputation for nurturing assertive, expressive, exploring young women. Nestled in the community of Northampton, Massachusetts, itself known for its artsy residents, the college now hosts a diverse student body that some say is symbolized by gender-neutral bathrooms. The diversity of writers is evident in two writers for the independent campus newspaper, the *Sophian*.

On one hand, Smith student Jessica Lee writes her sex column as a heterosexual female who loves partying, drinking, and sex. She writes, "Anyway, the reason why I bring up Jamie Foxx's fine, soft, silky, smooth aria, which is apparently about how he wants to stick his penis in his woman in all sorts of new and exciting ways, is that it calls to my mind the Smithie's sex life. Un—pre—dick!—table. Well, maybe this just describes the consequences of the adventurous nature of my sexuality" (Lee, 2008). Yet, determined to improve the way Smithies present themselves around men, Lee challenged her fellow female students: "to what degree of crapulence is it deemed socially acceptable to place a guy's hand under your shirt and your own down his pants?" The answer: just not in the middle of a party, and most certainly not when you haven't even exchanged names (Lee, 2007).

On quite another note, Smith junior Alexandra Bregman submitted an article to the *Sophian* called "Sex and the Smithie," about gender and heteronormativity, to address this broader term of "sexualities." As she writes, "Welcome to Sex and the Smithie, resplendent with all the colors of the rainbow.... The intense combinations of females interested in females, males-males, females-pansexual, female-to-male (F to M), 'queer,' etc., left me astonished and puzzled by the vastness Smith had exposed me to. Smith is not a 'lesbian' school; it's an everything school" (Bregman, 2008).

Openly gay students are increasingly becoming campus columnists. Chad Callaghan, an openly gay male, took over for Natalie Krinsky at the *Yale Daily News*. Occasionally, he assumes a metrosexual role, speaking from a female perspective, but mostly his columns address topics like the role of Facebook (a social networking Web site) in making it easier for gays to meet each other; the struggle of straight men in facing homosexuals; gay and heterosexual love triangles; and his personal journey. For example, he writes, "Being me and being gay are inextricable at this point in my life. My sexual identity and my psychological development are irreparably intertwined. If I hadn't gone to prom with a girl because there was no one else to go with ... if I hadn't polished my own perception of sexual identity so that I could confidently come out ... if I hadn't been forced to formulate heteronormative bonds with Catholic school prep boys, I wouldn't be me. My sexuality makes me more psychologically mature, politically savvy and socially aware. And of course I'm more sexually liberated. Gay men, like blondes, do have more fun. Seriously, you straight guys should try it some time. You're totally missing out" (Callaghan, 2006).

A SPRINGBOARD TO A BROADER
ROLE AS SEXUALITY EDUCATORS

Several college sex columnists have gone on, postgraduation, to take their role as sexuality educator much more seriously. Fulbright is currently the sex columnist for Foxnews.com, which involves writing two columns a week, making guest expert appearances on online and Fox Channel shows, and posting weekly Q&A blogs. Currently working on her seventh book, she is a blogger for the Huffington Post, an editor for the American Association of Sexuality Educators, Counselors and Therapists' newletter "Contemporary Sexuality," and a postdoctoral fellow at the University of Iceland, where she is writing a number of journal articles on youth access to sexual and reproductive health services. She has also drafted a curriculum for teaching health educators effective sex education strategies for her native country and is a featured expert on sex education sites like CherryTV.com and SexHealthGuru.com.

Also, Amber Madison, 23 years old at this writing, the former sex columnist for *The Tufts Daily* newspaper, is seeking to address voids in the American sexuality education system. Like other budding sex educators, Madison needed to "piece together" her college program in sexuality, double majoring in community health and American studies. She wrote her honors thesis on sexuality education programs, finding, like the experts who have investigated the subject, that comprehensive sexuality education is the best approach but that it is sorely lacking because the government provided funding only for abstinence-only programs, which do not work. Madison went on to write *Hooking Up: A Girls' All-out Guide to Sex and Sexuality* (2006), which was endorsed by noted sexuality education leaders like a former president of Planned Parenthood Federation of America and Guttmacher Institute president and CEO Sharon L. Camp. Madison's new Web-based television show, launched in July 2007, offers programs on sexual health topics like the use of condoms, the HPV vaccine, masturbation, and signs of an abusive relationship. She also helped promote a pro-choice organization, Choice USA, founded by renowned activist and author Gloria Steinem and other feminist leaders, by donating signed copies of her book (Choice USA, 2007). "Sexuality education is very needed," says Madison (personal communication, 2008). "But instead of addressing concrete issues like how to wear a condom, you have to work with emotional issues and deal with sexuality holistically."

AN AWARD FOR SEXUAL HEALTH REPORTING

A new campaign by condom manufacturer Trojan is encouraging college sex writers to be more responsible sexual health educators. Clearly, reaching the college audience is a commercial coup for a condom manufacturer, but the condom company's project has had a positive impact on the role these cub reporters are playing in promoting the sexual health of their peers. Just as

Bilinski touts the value of his campus health center and writes about their student-friendly services, Trojan is encouraging similar student responsibility. In describing Trojan's "Evolve" campaign vice president of marketing Jim Daniels (2008) noted, "College students are truly in a position to help shape this nation into a sexually healthy society, and can communicate about the need for accurate information to their peers, school officials, health professionals, as well as their broader community." Daniels explains that the campaign is branded "Evolve" to indicate that "society's attitudes, policies, and thinking about sexual health and condoms need to evolve—from the idea that sex is unhealthy or something to be policed to acknowledgment that it is a natural expression and intrinsic to our overall well-being." The company has partnered with the National Sexuality Resource Center's Campaign for Sexual Literacy to offer the Trojan Evolve Student Journalism Award to "recognize students' efforts on sexual health reporting within their college newspaper or online media outlet." The grand prize was a $2,000 cash prize and a trip for two to San Francisco, where the winner was honored at the 2008 Champions for Sexual Literacy annual dinner.

As proof of the seriousness of the issue, the company cites statistics that are important to all sexuality educators: that each year Americans experience more than 3 million unintended pregnancies, 19 million sexually transmitted infections (STIs), and more than 1 billion acts of unprotected sex among single adults. Sixty-five million Americans live with an incurable STI. Yet, despite the proven effectiveness of latex condoms in preventing unintended pregnancy and the transmission of disease, single sexually active Americans between the ages of 18 and 54 use them in only about 25 percent of their sexual encounters (http://www.trojancondoms.com/EvolveInMotion.aspx).

A COLUMN CLEARLY CONSTRUCTED
BY THE HEALTH CENTER EXPERTS

Some columns currently written in college newspapers are targeted to sexuality information and education. "Ask the Sexpert" in the *Daily Princetonian* is written in a question-and-answer format by a team of peer sexual health educators and fact-checked by University health professionals. As such, the column is intentionally oriented toward sexuality education. One column, for example, addressed this question from "Testing":

> "What STI testing does the University offer? How much does everything cost?" The answer: "Dear Testing, It's great that you're asking about STI testing. It's important to get tested if you are sexually active at all, and as long as the STI has a test, there are health professionals at UHS who will test you for it. You can make an appointment with Women's and Men's Health Services, or you can go to urgent care if you feel you need to be seen immediately. If you are on the student health plan, all

STI testing at UHS is free. If not, there is a charge for most tests, which vary in cost. It is likely, however, that you will be able to get at least a partial refund from your insurance provider. I cannot stress how important it is to get tested for STIs. The myth that you don't have to worry about STIs if you're not having vaginal intercourse simply is not true. Remember that STIs are transmitted through the sharing of bodily fluids and/or mucous membrane contact. So anal sex, oral sex or even naked dry humping can put you at risk for contracting an STI. Though condoms are wonderful, even they don't protect completely against every STI. So be careful and get tested." Signed, "The Sexpert." (www.dailyprincetonian.com/archives/2007/04/12/arts/18057.shtml)

CONTROVERSY

The approach and topics of the college columns have drawn criticism from peers, parents, professionals, media, and officials—perhaps not unexpected, since the topic of sexuality still generates controversy and since the tone and topics are often racy. The columns' often graphic contents have been criticized for being one-sided, failing to give sound advice, reinforcing stereotypes, and being offensive, inappropriate, and irresponsible. Some parents and alumni are aghast and concerned that the columns encourage sexual experimentation, pushing young people beyond their comfort zones (Hull, 2004; Kolhatkar, 2005), as reflected in statistics about the number of college students engaging in sexual behavior. Some columnists have been criticized for their "naughty sex chronicles," for being "sluts with a pen" (Allison, 2006), and for writing in a "breezy, all-knowing tone," with their "pseudo-diaries" attacked for sensationalizing their sex lives in drawing upon personal experiences (Kolhatkar, 2005). Some schools' alumni and parents have reacted with angry phone calls. Papers have received e-mails of outrage from readers, as well. Northern Arizona University even held a meeting with the student newspaper board to discuss its newly launched sex column in 2004 (Miller, 2004). Some argue that the same subjects are covered over and over again, from year to year and publication to publication (Kolhatkar, 2005), while others claim that such criticism is unfair, given that much of the content is new to each class of undergraduates (Allison, 2006).

Greaves, a member of the American Association of Sexuality Educators, Counselors and Therapists, regrets that the college columnists do not have more formal training in sexuality and therapy. She worries that the less-educated young writers can sway other students to fall in line uncritically with whatever they write. Fulbright, too, worries about the professionalism of the advice. "Everyone thinks they can be a sexuality expert," she says. "It trivializes the credentials of people in my field and what we are trying to do." There's danger in college kids not knowing what's "good" advice, she points out.

While the advisers claim to be complimented and appreciated by readers, they admit to receiving some negative feedback. One received some e-mails that called her "immature," demanding: "What makes you think you're a sex expert when you're only 19?" Some editors claim they leave their writers alone, but some sex advisers say they struggle with editors, including over what constitutes acceptable terminology for print. As one adviser said, "I tried to use the word 'pussy' once, but they didn't want me to."

Parents of the writers themselves have also not always approved. Schleelein, who calls herself "daddy's little girl," says her dad chooses not to read her column. "He doesn't want to confront the idea of me as a sexual person."

Perhaps the most intense battle the young writers face is for freedom of speech. Twenty-one-year-old Kelsey Blackwell said she was thrown to the forefront of fire over First Amendment issues after an article she wrote about condoms was accompanied by a photograph of a banana covered by a greenish-bluish condom with (accurately) a bubble at the tip. The Southern Utah University junior, a communications major and Spanish minor hoping for a summer fashion magazine internship, was doing her job as a staff reporter for the *University Journal* when she agreed to write a story about the obstacles obtaining condoms on campus. Only one student sent a letter complaining that the graphic was "offensive and did not represent the school well," she reported (K. Blackwell, personal communication, November 2002), but school officials reacted more strongly to the piece's "poor taste and bad judgment" and set up an advisory steering committee. In defense of their right to a free press, a political science student, Mark Justice, formed a group, the Students Association for Free Expression, supported by the Student Press Law Center and the Society for Professional Journalists. The controversy was played out in the local press with one paper, the *Daily Spectrum*, opposed, and the *Salt Lake Tribune* coverage more positive, while the church-owned *Deseret News* did not mention the issue.

Justice (personal communication, December 2002), who hoped to go to law school, said, "The worst thing they [the administration] can do is kick me out of school. We must be heard or watch democracy be crushed. They got money, but we got truth." Upset that an administration would feel it has the right to dictate content and act out of fear of economic backlash from conservative donors, Justice maintains that such repression negates "cultural pluralism and everything America stands for."

Though Blackwell grew up in conservative Utah, her family was "open about sex" (her dad had several heart-to-hearts with her about boys starting when she was in the 9th grade), empowering her to bring about change with the power of her pen in the face of a "ridiculous" controversy where "the morals and values of a dominant religion are held as standards for others not of that religion." "Controversy is a good thing," she says, "though the banana jokes every day on campus are getting old."

In another conservative hub across the country, Schleelein faced similar fire for writing about sex at Boston College, which is run by Jesuits. "They're not too happy with me," she said, after writing only four columns." But the newspaper is not funded by the college, so there's not much they can do." A priest asked her, "What will you tell your children?" (her answer: "I'll say I wrote for the school newspaper"); his next question was, "What if you want to run for public office?" (her answer: "It's not my interest, and, anyway, I used to work for Planned Parenthood"); his comment: "I hope you'll stop doing this" (her reply: "I appreciate your concern").

Peers also protest. While some older male admirers e-mail her, saying that they wish she had been around when they went to college, others accuse her of being a "horrible model of behavior" and warning her to "repent now and save your soul." Despite the criticism, the Ithaca-born young woman stayed at the Jesuit school because of its good law school, which she hopes to attend. She wishes her detractors would see beyond the explicit to her satire and messages urging responsibility.

Fulbright, based at the more liberal NYU, with its diverse student body, faced the least protest. "One staff person wrote an e-mail with a complaint about fantasy, saying I gave irresponsible advice mentioning sex in public because you could get arrested, but I didn't think I should play the moral police," she says. When she notified the newspaper of the complaint, staff was apparently thrilled, thinking it would boost circulation.

The columnists claim they are not the ones promoting sex. As Boston College's Schleelein wrote in her column, "Sex and the Univer-City," "They took 6,000 of us who are in our sexual prime and crammed us into a dorm room where there's nowhere to sit except on the bed. Members of the opposite—or same, of course—gender are but a single flight of stairs away, and often right next door."

GETTING MEDIA COVERAGE: SEXUALITY EDUCATION GOES PUBLIC

The raw and sometimes raunchy public exposure in print of their own and their peers' sexual adventures and awakenings has made the sex columnists budding celebrities, not only on their campuses but in major media, with features in outlets ranging from the *New York Times* to the *Today* show. Columnists became instant "stars" and were written about in *Cosmopolitan* and *USA Today* and interviewed on major television shows. The *Today* show on NBC-TV interviewed Fulbright from NYU's *Washington Square News* and Krinsky from the *Yale Daily* in October 2002. A handful landed speaking engagements and found career opportunities. For example, Krinsky got an agent and published a "chick lit" fiction novel, *Chloe Does Yale*, which some claimed was a thinly disguised memoir as it follows the story of a Yale junior, Chloe Carrington, who writes a stirring column, "Sex in the (Elm) City" for the *Yale*

Daily News. Jessica Beaton, the sex columnist for Johns Hopkins' *News-Letter*, got an offer to write an "Ask College Girl" column for *CosmoGirl* magazine.

A number of current and former columnists also are featured on the Web site of *Elle* advice columnist E. Jean Carroll, askejean.com. But not all the advisers are comfortable being covered by the media. One columnist was afraid that if she were more public, she would get letters from prisoners.

RECOMMENDATIONS

Given the valuable role coed sex columnists can play on campuses, the following recommendations can be offered:

- Prior to launching a sex column, a newspaper should conduct a survey on students' needs and behavior.
- An adviser or advisory board should help provide information about sexuality and review columns for accuracy.
- Columnists themselves should seek out reliable sources of sexual health information, incorporating research to back up their facts in addition to their opinions and including quotations from experts and professionals in the field of human sexuality.
- University health services and campus counseling centers should collaborate with the campus sex columnists to explore how the column can be best used as a sexuality education tool and forum for coeds. It has been pointed out that students today bring to campus more serious personal problems than ever before (Behnke, 2008).
- University staff and administrators should consider how a college sex column can be a resource and support the inclusion of more courses on comprehensive sexuality education in the curriculum.

DISCUSSION AND CONCLUSIONS

College publications are playing a major role in sexuality education, for better or worse. Many are replete with sex talk, fostered by the popularity of columns written with attitude and candor. Besides being titillating, they are pushing back boundaries to allow more open discussions about sexual mores and relationship rules, as well as sexual health. Even if the writer intends merely to entertain, the messages have an impact on many readers who turn to them for values and education about various sexual behaviors, as well as for permission and thrills. While sometimes criticized, this trend has proven itself an influential form of campus entertainment and also a source of sexual information. College sex columns have become publicized and politicized, making them not just an important phenomenon in student journalism but a reflection of youth attitudes and behavior, what sexuality educators need to know about youth, and what youth need to know about sexuality education. Given modern technology, coeds expressions about sexuality have already moved beyond printed newspapers to other formats, particularly blogs; one such blog even reviews college sex columnists (www.ivygateblog.com/tag/sex-columns/).

Despite criticism from various fronts, many columnists' peers react positively, feeling validated during their sexually charged undergraduate years and regarding the sex columnist as a voice of their generation. It can be argued that the rise in college sex columnists is partly a result of the dearth of information and guidance on sex and relationships. With many American secondary schools focusing on abstinence-only-until-marriage curricula, students come to college uninformed or misinformed. The columns represent an important forum for talking about, learning about, and debating sexuality-related issues.

Since its debut in 1996, the college sex column has expounded on a variety of sex topics and garnered much attention on campus and across the country. While heavily criticized for their lack of professionalism, unreliability of information, and salacious style, these columns have stimulated sexual dialogue, taking on sexual taboos and sometimes providing valuable information about sexual health to which students may otherwise not have access, thereby presenting opportunities to educate peers about sexuality.

ACKNOWLEDGMENT

Much gratitude to Deborah Schoenblum, MSW, for being exceptionally helpful in doing initial research on this subject.

NOTE

Some sex columnists in this chapter were interviewed for a magazine column that was previously published.

REFERENCES

Allison, J. (2006, November). Carrie Bradshaw 101: The rise of the college sex columnist *CoEd Magazine*. Retrieved January 2, 2009, from http://www.juliaallison.com/articles/2006/11/college_sex_columnists.html#more

Behnke, S. (2008). The unique challenges of campus counseling. *Monitor on Psychology, 39,* 88–90.

Bilinski, B. (2008). On the prowl. *The Tiger.* Retrieved July 4, 2008, from http://media.www.thetigernews.com/media/storage/paper863/news/2008/04/18/Timeout/On.The.Prowl-3334174.shtml

Bregman, A. (2008). Sex and the Smithie: It's not just us. *Sophian.* Retrieved July 14, 2008, from http://media.www.smithsophian.com/media/storage/paper587/news/2008/04/24/Opinions/Sex-And.The.Smithie.Its.Not.Just.Us-3353583.shtml

Callaghan, C. (2006). Mr. Fishburne, I'm not taking the red pill! *Yale Daily News.* Retrieved July 11, 2008, from http://www.yaledailynews.com/articles/view/19311

Centers for Disease Control and Prevention. (2008). National Health and Nutrition Examination Survey. Retrieved July 11, 2008, from http://www.cdc.gov/nchs/nhanes.htm

Choice USA. (2007). Author Amber Madison donates for Choice. Retrieved December 23, 2008, from http://www.choiceusa.org/index.php?option=com_content&task=view&id=251&Itemid=92

Daniels, J. (2008). Trojan Brand Condoms. Retrieved July 3, 2008, from www.trojancondoms.com/ArticleDetails.aspx?ArticleId=1

Gudelunas, D. (2005). Talking taboo: Newspaper advice columns and sexual discourse. *Sex and Culture: An Interdisciplinary Quarterly, 9*(1), 62–87.

Grynbaum, M. M. (2004, February 18). Columbia sex column hits news stands. *The Harvard Crimson Online.* Retrieved January 4, 2009 from http://www.thecrimson.com/article.aspx?ref35745

Hoover, E. (2007). The new sex scribes. *Chronicle of Higher Education.* Retrieved January 7, 2009, from http://chronicle.com/free/v48/i40/40a03301.htm

Hull, D. (2004, September 20). Sex talk on campus: Columnists don't shy away from explicit advice. *Mercury News.* Retrieved September 20, 2004, from http://www.mercurynews.com

Kolhatkar, S. (2005, November). College newspapers discover the sex column. *Atlantic Monthly.* Retrieved July 9, 2008, from www.theatlatantic.com/doc195711/sexcollege

Kuriansky, J. (1996). *Generation sex; America's hottest sex therapist answers the hottest questions about sex.* New York: Harper.

Lee, J. (2007). Are you done yet? *Sophian.* Retrieved July 8, 2008, from http://media.www.smithsophian.com/media/storage/paper587/news/2007/10/18/O pinions/Are-You.Done.Yet-3045446.shtml

Lee J. (2008). Are you done yet? *Sophian.* Retrieved July 8, 2008, from http://media.www.smithsophian.com/media/storage/paper587/news/2008/03/13/O pinions/Are-You.Done.Yet-3270349.shtml

Marklein, M. S. (2002, November 14). Casual sex, in newsprint. *USA Today,* D9.

Miller, S. B. (2004, February 27). College students bring "pillow talk" out into the public square. *Christian Science Monitor,* p. 1.

Park, M. Y. (2002, October 17). Parents turned off by students' sex columns. Retrieved October 17, 2002, from www.foxnews.com/story/0,2933,65891,00.html

Reimold, D. (2004). Sexual, revolutionary: The start of the first U.S. college newspaper sex column. *American Sexuality Magazine.* Retrieved October 6, 2007, from http://nsrc.sfsu.edu/MagArticle.cfm?SID=27CAEAD920CF89B9F8BB5D9F6A50EB7A&DSN=nsrc_dsn&Mode=EDIT&Article=608&ReturnURL=1

Reimold, D. (2007, Spring). Carnal knowledge: The explosion of sexual expression and experimentation in the contemporary campus media. *College Media Review, 44*(4), pp. 4–11.

Robbins, A. (2003, March). Meet the new "sexperts." *Cosmopolitan,* pp. 206–9.

Chapter Two

SEX WEEK AT YALE: MORE THAN JUST A "SEX EDUCATION"

Eric Jay Rubenstein

Health, wealth, and *love* share an intimate relationship with one another. Success in any one vital area will positively affect the other two. In fact, to improve in a certain area, sometimes you must first focus on and improve another area. For example, you can increase your success in love by maintaining or improving your wealth as well as your health. People who are healthy, fit, and energetic in social situations project a higher replication value and thus are more likely to connect with and attract those around them.

The Mystery Method: How to Get Beautiful Women into Bed, Mystery, p. 21

All three of these brain networks—lust, romantic attraction, and attachment—are multipurpose systems. In addition to its reproductive purpose, the sex drive serves to make and keep friends, provide pleasure and adventure, tone muscles, and relax the mind. Romantic love can stimulate you to sustain a loving partnership or drive you to fall in love with a new person and initiate divorce. And feelings of attachment enable us to express genuine affection for children, family, and friends, as well as a beloved.

Why We Love: The Nature and Chemistry of Romantic Love, Helen Fisher, p. 78

It [sex] is as religious a subject as a discussion on belief in God. It is only through sexual congress that a soul is brought into this world, that a man and woman merge as one, as they were before creation, and it is one of the few mystic experiences of life in which most of us share.

Kosher Sex, Rabbi Shmuley Boteach, p. 46

Truth is, the sexual revolution isn't over. Now we need a sexual evolution, and lots of education....My cure is the Three R's to rule your sex life: Respect (for yourself and others), Responsibility (you control your thoughts and acts, they don't control you), and the Right to Say Yes or No...the 4 T's: Trust, Talking, Touch, Taking Time....Then there's the Five F's: freeing up Feelings, facing Fears, accepting Fantasies, expressing aFFection, and having Fun.

Generation Sex: America's Hottest Sex Therapist Answers the Hottest Questions about Sex, Dr. Judy Kuriansky, pp. 3–4

What do a pick-up artist, an anthropologist, a rabbi, and a sex therapist—all quoted above—have in common? All of these widely known individuals—famous in their own right for their knowledge and teaching on love, sex, intimacy, and relationships—participated in a biannual, multidisciplinary sex education program at Yale University appropriately called *Sex Week at Yale*. Along with many of their peers, these experts spoke to large and small audiences at the university on topics common to sex education programs (e.g., abstinence, which is the only way to definitively prevent pregnancy and sexually transmitted diseases) as well as topics uncommon to sex education programs (e.g., the emotional effects of sex in relationships and sex as it relates to spirituality and religion). With speeches, seminars, and events on subject matter ranging from the biological to the spiritual, from the psychological to the historical, from the academic to the secular, *Sex Week at Yale* explored all aspects of love, sex, intimacy and relationships, challenging students to think critically about these issues and to reconcile their beliefs on these topics in their own lives.

This chapter describes *Sex Week at Yale*, recounts its development, history, and future, and offers guidelines for sex educators to conceptualize and organize similar events. It also recounts the author's personal story and lessons learned in being the founder of this pioneering event.

WHO AM I?

For purposes of full disclosure up front, I should provide some details about myself, my background, and my credentials. I am not a sex therapist, nor am I an educator in the traditional sense of the word. My experience with sex education comes from my experience in founding and planning *Sex Week at Yale* in 2002 and 2004 while I was an undergraduate student at Yale University and my intimate involvement in planning the subsequent iterations of the event in 2006 and 2008. As the founder of *Sex Week at Yale*, I have become a sex educator of sorts, in having to become familiar with a vast amount of sexual material and deem which is appropriate to be presented in an academic setting. In doing this, I also developed relationships with many of the leading contemporary educators and thinkers on the subjects of love, sex, intimacy, and relationships; I have read many of these leader's articles and books on these topics, and I have debated these thinkers on such topics, developing a deeper understanding in the process. By no means does this make me an authority on such matters of sexuality; however, even though I do not have a formal training in sexuality education, I consider myself well versed in such subjects after my intense experiences and prolonged involvement in organizing these sex education events, interacting with sexuality experts, and becoming particularly knowledgeable in all content and logistics related to *Sex Week at Yale*.

In terms of my formal education, I have a bachelor's degree in psychology with a focus in behavioral neuroscience from Yale University and a master's degree in business administration with a focus in international business from Temple University. Regarding my personal history and family background, I am the oldest of five children and was raised in a conservative household in which sex and sexuality were not topics of discussion. During my formative years, I grew up in a little-known conservative town called Fort Myers, located on the gulf coast of Florida. Politically, I would consider myself in the center but leaning to the right. Suffice it to say, while growing up I never would have expected to one day plan an internationally acclaimed, week-long program dedicated to the exploration and education of sex and sexuality. Ironically, the circumstances in which I decided to plan the event (described in the section of this chapter titled History of *Sex Week at Yale*) were not predetermined by me.

Instead, the role came about by a series of events. In college, I was involved in a number of activities. I frequented the gym; played intramural sports; attended talks by professionals, including politicians, businessmen, and actors; cofounded (with other students) the Yale Undergraduate Business Society; and occasionally attended classes at the campus Hillel (part of the network of Jewish student groups on campuses internationally). As will be explained later, the concept of *Sex Week at Yale* began to develop in the time between my freshman and sophomore years. The resulting event became a large part of my education and, in many ways, continues to provide lessons for me to this day.

The following is the story of the unique week I developed, including background describing what the event is and why a program like this is necessary in college (and particularly at Yale). This chapter also gives a history of the event, including its evolution over its four iterations, a discussion of the controversy it engendered, and suggestions on planning similar events in the future.

WELCOME TO YALE

Yale is a school where students, in my experience, though intellectually advanced in many ways, have not had as much experience in relationships and, as a result, with sex in comparison to students entering other colleges. This observation is supported by how students have commented on their experience at Yale. For example, in her 2002 *Yale Daily News* article about *Sex Week at Yale*, Yale student reporter Marissa Kellogg says, "As usual, Yalies will talk about sex this week instead of actually getting it. But this time they're getting professional help" (Kellogg, 2002). In fact, Yale students' inexperience with relationships, when coupled with their unyielding intellectual curiosity, laid the groundwork to allow for serious conversations about the topics of love, sex, intimacy, and relationships on campus. This was my thought when I was developing the idea for the week-long event.

Yale is a particularly ideal place to hold an event like *Sex Week at Yale* because of the administration's policy on sex education. The importance of sex education in preventing unplanned pregnancy and sexually transmitted infections is noted, and thus freshmen are required to attend a mandatory sex education talk by the campus Peer Health Educators. However, this talk does not put sexuality education into the greater context of a relationship. While Yale should be applauded for this effort to keep students safe by providing them necessary information they may not have received otherwise, separating safe sex education from the greater context of a relationship leaves out the details describing when and how these safe sex practices should be implemented. It is the understanding of these simple details that separates those who eventually practice what they learn from those who know the practices but do not put them to use. I intended *Sex Week at Yale* to fill this void.

The events presented at *Sex Week at Yale* were meant to go further than simply discussing topics of safe sex and abstinence alone. Instead, *Sex Week at Yale* integrates sex into the greater context of life by discussing the business, politics, religion, psychology, sociology, and history of sexuality, among the many other dynamics of sex and relationships. As such, *Sex Week at Yale* engages students and challenges them in a way no other program has in the past.

At many colleges, an event like *Sex Week at Yale* may not be possible for political, religious, or logistical reasons. For example, students at some schools who are conservative by upbringing might not be receptive to a discussion of love and sex. Since the Catholic Church does not recognize contraception as an allowable practice, Catholic schools might not allow discussions of contraception on their campuses. Or, there might not be available experts on love, sex, intimacy, or relationships near one's school; though some people educated on these topics can be found in almost any area of the country (i. e., one such resource to find experts is the American Association of Sexuality Educators, Counselors and Therapists which can be found online at www.aasect.org).

This is not to say that other programs already existed at other schools, for example, at New Jersey's Montclair State University's Body Awareness Week, and at the 40-hour course on human sexuality at Rutgers at the Robert Wood Johnson Medical School in New Jersey (see http://www.umdnj.edu/umcweb/

marketing_and_communications/publications/umdnj_magazine/hstate/ sprsm98/sexweek.html), and a program at the University of North Carolina (the differences are discussed later in this chapter). But students and educators at Yale and other universities agree, at least anecdotally, that the structure of sex and relationship education offered during the *Sex Week* is more developed at Yale than at other campuses, and is particularly effective.

Evidence of this includes the fact that, since *Sex Week at Yale* began, a number of other schools have contacted the organizers of *Sex Week at Yale* and expressed interest in holding a *Sex Week* on their campus. One such school that successfully—based on attendance—built a sex education program based on the *Sex Week at Yale* model is Northwestern University, which held its own *Sex Week* in 2007 and again in 2008 (http://groups.northwestern.edu/ feminists/events.htm; http://groups.northwestern.edu/sexweek/). This program held lectures, seminars, educational fairs, movie screenings, and plays on topics as diverse as the business of sex, sexual technique, ethics, and biology (a full schedule can be found at http://groups.northwestern.edu/sexweek/ images/final4.jpg). Due to the diversity of topics and the range in the delivery of those topics, I certainly agree that the organizers of *Sex Week at Northwestern* did a terrific job in executing the *Sex Week at Yale* model.

For years, I have believed that the *Sex Week at Yale* approach to sex and relationship education can be adapted to other schools and forums. It is for this reason I add a section at the end of this chapter describing considerations in planning a *Sex Week* event. The impact of *Sex Week at Yale* is fascinating and encouraging for sex educators and students everywhere and is discussed in detail in the pages that follow.

WHAT IT IS: SEX ED IN COLLEGE IS MORE THAN JUST A SEX EDUCATION BECAUSE . . .

Sex Week at Yale has pioneered a new way of approaching sex education. One lesson sex educators can learn from *Sex Week at Yale* comes directly from my own lessons in planning the week. My advice is this: Do not limit yourself with boundaries in your definition of sex education. This is an affirmation to which I know certain sex educators subscribe. To believe that sex education is the education of sex alone is stifling, limiting, and a disservice to those you are teaching. In my view, sex education should not be just about the education of sex alone, but should be life education, which is limitless. This is consistent with the belief of many experts who subscribe to sex education as a part of life skills education. This lesson is one I have learned well in planning *Sex Week*.

Sex Week is more than sex education. "Sex education" in college is often stale and heavily weighted, not surprisingly, at educating students about safer sex practices. At some schools, like at Yale, sex educators hold mandatory lectures teaching students about sexual health and safe sex practices. These lectures are not-for-credit classes, but are considered supplementary educational curricula organized by campus organizations (such as the Yale Peer Health Educators, or the Sexual Health Awareness Group at Cornell) (see http://www.yale.edu/uhs/med_services/student_health.html; http://sao.cornell.edu/SO/search.php?igroup=728).

In contrast, limited or no education about sex is provided at many campuses at all. For example, the University of Miami is quoted by Bert Sperling (of Sperling's Best Places, which conducted a study for Trojan Brand Condoms, which is further discussed later in this chapter) as having "absolutely no evidence of a Separate Sexual Health Awareness Program...which is just as bad as not having a program at all" (http://media.www.thehurricaneonline.com/media/storage/paper479/news/2007/10/04/News/Um.Gets.An.f.On.Sex.Ed.Report.Card.For.Sexual.Awareness.Program-3011262.shtml). According to students at Vanderbilt University I recently spoke with, Vanderbilt is another school that does not offer extracurricular sex education opportunities. Still, Vanderbilt offers for-credit classes on reproductive biology (a biology class) and a class called "Porn and Prostitution" (a history class). These classes are limited in scope and even limit enrollment, making them unavailable to all students.

I agree that safer sex education is important and necessary and that intellectually challenging courses on specific subject matters are critical in the university setting. But sex education has largely not evolved into a more robust curriculum. To me, this is disappointing. In my view, to have the greatest impact, sex education has to be incorporated into a more integrated conversation that puts sex into the larger context of relationships and life in general.

One example of an individual who recognized this void—though not at the undergraduate but rather at the medical school level—is Dr. Richard Cross of Rutgers University. Cross, who was teaching public health at what is now UMDNJ-Robert Wood Johnson Medical School (RWJMS), has said, "The faculties of medical schools were very good at presenting the facts, but weren't adequately teaching the intangibles: ethics, attitudes, beliefs, values, subjects like human sexuality and death and dying" (Iozzia, 1998).

In 1967, Cross decided to bridge this educational void through informal round-table discussions about sexuality between himself and the school's entire second-year student body of 16 students. In the years since, the discussion has grown into what is now a required 40-hour, five-day "Human Sexuality" course. The course, now affectionately known on the Rutgers campus as "Sex Week," started as a two-day event and expanded to be a three-day event until, in 1973, it was expanded into a full week of lectures, small-group interactions, films, and panel discussions (Iozzia, 1998).

In terms of for-credit university curricula on other campuses, the most widely taught classes are those describing the biological mechanics of sex and reproduction alone. A simple Google search of "biology of sex and reproduction college class" yields 138,000 hits, many of which are links to descriptions of college classes on the exact topic—the biology of sex and reproduction. As this Google search suggests, sex taught methodically through biology courses is quite common. Less common are courses on more complicated topics involving emotions and the sociological and psychological consequences of love and intimacy. Even when these more involved subjects are approached in the classroom, they often are given by the women's studies department and lesbian, gay, bisexual, and transsexual studies departments at universities. This in turn makes them less available to the general school population due to class size limits and restrictions on who can take the classes based on major and seniority. Because such classes are targeted to specific majors in specific departments, classes like these represent an isolationist approach, meaning they do not educate the masses of students on campus and do not integrate different disciplines of thought into the education on the manifestation of sex in society (e.g., teaching the psychological and sociological consequences of sex along with the biological or historical). Such sexuality education courses in the context of life skills are important to all students and have their place in a college education.

EXAMPLES OF CLASSES AT YALE INCLUDE...

Yale is one of the schools that does have classes that address issues related to sexuality. Selections from Yale's 2007–2008 course catalogue and one class taught by noted sex educator Dr. Ruth in 2004 and again in 2007 are described in this section (http://students.yale.edu/oci/search.jsp). The offerings demonstrate a restricted choice in topics, and these classes severely restrict enrollment, leaving an educational void available for *Sex Week at Yale* to fill.

Gender, Race, and Law in Early America (History Department)

The intersections of race, gender, and law in early American society during the colonial and revolutionary periods. The role of the courts and legislatures in regulating issues such as sex and sexuality, marriage and divorce, violence and crime, speech and slander, and citizenship and property.

Genders and Sexualities in Victorian Literature and Culture (English Department)

Nineteenth-century British discourses of eroticism and desire as reflected in Victorian literature, social history, popular culture, science, and law. Connections with emergent and shifting notions of gender and sexuality; intersections with race, class, and colonialism.

Biology of Gender and Sexuality (Biology Department)

A critical examination of current biological thinking about gender differences and their origins; male-female sexual dimorphisms and their variations; the continuum from essentialism to constructionism; the mental and cognitive aspects of sexuality; theories of eroticism and sex-object choice; physiology of sexual responses; and genetic factors in the biology of behavior.

Biology of Reproduction (Biology Department)

Introduction to reproductive biology, with emphasis on human reproduction: development and hormonal regulation of reproductive systems; sexuality, fertilization, and pregnancy; modern diagnosis and treatment of reproductive and developmental disorders. A segment on social and ethical issues is included.

Love and Attachment (Department of Psychology)

Although romantic and early parental love are clearly distinctive developmental periods, an examination of those elements shared in common—the perception of an altered mental state, intrusive thoughts and images associated with a heightened awareness of the other, and a complex behavioral repertoire aimed at eliciting a reciprocal response—may provide a useful vantage point for considering the evolution and neurobiology of love and its range of normal and psychopathologic outcomes.

Personal Fulfillment and Intimacy in the Contemporary American Family (Residential College Seminar—counts toward humanities requirement credit)

The infamous sex educator, radio, and television personality Dr. Ruth Westheimer (better known as simply Dr. Ruth) has taught a number of courses at Yale over the years as well (Gibbons, 2007). I had the privilege of taking one of these classes in the 2003–2004 school year titled "Personal Fulfillment and Intimacy in the Contemporary American Family" (Bit, 2004). This class was cotaught with two Yale professors, a psychiatrist and a historian. This class was different than most because it dealt with concepts of intimate and personal, very uncommon subject matter in my experience for a college class. In crossing this boundary between the traditional and modern, Dr. Sledge, the psychologist who cotaught the class, said about the class, "It helps students analyze not only the information swirling around them but their inner feelings and emotions"

(Von Hoffmann, 2004). Further, Sledge said, "One of the things that helps people know what they want to do is knowing what other people do, and talking about it makes that information more accessible and helps them in making their own decisions" (Von Hoffmann, 2004). By having professors from different educational specialties and including a celebrity sex educator, this class most closely aligned with *Sex Week at Yale*'s goal of integrating disciplines in order to give a more robust education on the topic of sex and relationships.

WHAT IS *SEX WEEK AT YALE*?

Sex Week at Yale is an interdisciplinary sex education program designed to pique students' interests through creative, interactive, and exciting sex educational programming. This programming includes, but is not limited to, talks by the nation's most widely known sex educators and therapists, as well as by professors, writers, relationship coaches, executives in the entertainment and media industries, and adult-entertainment stars. It is inclusion of all these types of experts that makes *Sex Week at Yale* unique and controversial (which will be discussed later in this chapter).

Sex Week brings together those experts on love, sex, intimacy, and relationships from different perspective and fields to speak with students on a practical as well as theoretical level. The fact that these experts come from different fields, backgrounds, and experiences creates an exciting and educational atmosphere for students to learn about life, love, and sex. Few such campus-wide events, for example, include people representing the "business" side of sex or the adult sex industry. Introducing students to different elements of industries that use images of sex, love, intimacy, and relationships to promote and sell goods and services teaches students valuable lessons about the power of sex as an image, not only as a biological, sociological, and psychological phenomenon.

On an academic level, bringing together the professional (defined as sex educators, therapists, authors, business people, adult-entertainment professionals, and others who use sex or the idea of sex to make a living) and academic worlds of sex, love, intimacy, and relationships bridges a critical gap in the study of psychology, sociology, and biology with the study of other subjects like economics, marketing, and film, thereby creating a truly interdisciplinary event. My goal in founding *Sex Week at Yale* was to create this bridge between the academic and the professional worlds while providing students with crucial insight into universal ideas that are often not taken seriously in a public context. These ideas refer to those related to love and sex—topics that are not commonly discussed in academic settings due to the common perception that they are inferior to traditional subjects or somehow inappropriate for critical and academic discussion. Bridging professionals from outside the ivy-gate with academic approaches to the same controversial subjects affords students the opportunity to better understand what sex is and allows them to define for themselves how sex relates to love and intimacy in their own lives.

The week goes beyond just lectures, to include events that get students to actually participate and challenge the way they think about love, sex, intimacy, and relationships. This is done through fashion shows, concerts, dinners, and dating services. By including these events, *Sex Week at Yale* gets more students actively involved, participating in and talking about what is going on in the real world.

Offering these more diverse experiences and topics makes students on campus start talking about sex and relationships at the very start of *Sex Week at Yale*. Because the topics are so broad, so close to students' lives, and so controversial, such open talk happens even for those who might not ordinarily reflect on the subject or talk about it openly.

WHY IS THERE A NEED FOR SEX EDUCATION IN COLLEGE?

Sexuality education is insufficient in the United States and even in other countries (Weaver et al., 2005). The reason for this is three-fold. The first reason can be found in the political and religious history of our country. The second reason can be blamed on people's fear of what would happen if people talked about sex openly. The third reason is the self-fulfilling absence of education and understanding, caused by the spiral of sexual ignorance in society.

From an historical perspective, in the 1600s, the Puritans left Europe in search of a morally pure land to raise their families away from sin and moral corruption. Arriving in the new world, they began a religiously conservative society that served as the foundation for the America we know today. It is from these conservative religious foundations that American social policy and attitudes—written and unwritten—were formed (Godbeer, 2002).

Despite the influx of cultures and peoples that America has attracted since the first Puritans landed on this continent, the principles set forth by these first settlers continue to pervade America's social landscape. These principles include those related to marriage and divorce, the freedom to choose a romantic partner, and the punishment of sex outside of marriage (Godbeer, 2002). In those early times, education about sex and relationships was confined to religion and the home. Not until the 1900s did the idea of sex education beyond the home come into existence in the United States (Rosow & Persell, 1980; Strong, 1972). Still, it is from the early times of the settlers that more contemporary approaches to sexuality have persisted, including fear-based attitudes toward sex and sexuality, the tradition of just not talking about the subject, and a guilt-stricken culture (Godbeer, 2002).

Sex education in those early times was largely restricted to the home; yet, only a limited amount of sex education occurred then. Such restriction has even persisted into the present times (Westheimer & Lopater, 2002). Our country has had several policies on sex education at a governmental level, some of which are inherently flawed and have been proven less effective (Hoff et al., 2000; McKeon, 2006). In the ensuing national debate, programs that focus on abstinence only—"just say no" to sex—and do not allow discussion of contraception as a form of sexual health and a safer way to prevent pregnancy and disease than oral sex and coitus interruptus (also known as the "pullout" method) have rallied the most political support. Programs focusing not only on sexuality, sexual health, sexually transmitted diseases, and reproduction but also life skills are more appropriate and effective in my view and from my experience on my college campus. In fact, research has shown that abstinence-only approaches have not been effective to lessen the problems of unwanted pregnancy and sexual diseases in youth (McKeon, 2006).

In my opinion, most of these government policies supporting abstinence-only sex education were put into place to prevent an open and exhaustive conversation on sexuality education due to a fear of the religious or social consequences that such an education might cause. Fear of what would happen if people talk about sex openly has limited the conversation about sex at all levels of development. In restricting what is taught in schools, these programs appear to put the burden of teaching children about important and life-shaping topics on parents; however, the real burden ends up falling back on the children themselves to protect themselves, although they are ill equipped to do so.

In fact, while parents are expected to teach their children about love, sex, intimacy, and relationships, they are largely undereducated in these areas, uncomfortable or incapable of speaking about these issues themselves. Yet, I ask, can we honestly expect parents to be the best source of sex and relationship education for our children, with divorce rates at historical highs; abuse, murder, and self-destructive acts permeating society; and high-profile professionals in business, politics, and entertainment under scrutiny for questionable and troublesome sexual behaviors? More importantly, should we expect parents to be the best and/or only source of education on sex and relationships for kids?

The result of this situation is problematic. Parents, for the most part, are not teaching their kids effectively about these topics. They do not integrate these topics into an education at an early enough age; for example, parents may talk to their young kids about relationships with friends but not about romantic partners. When children become adolescents, parents may talk about relationships with romantic partners but not about sex. When children are teenagers, parents may talk about sex but not about love and intimacy. When children are in high school, parents may even mention love and intimacy but not explain adequately what love and intimacy are and why they are important in romance. Thus, young people are never prepared to cope with their life choices and experiences.

The education parents provide is not supposed to be solely through what parents say to their children but also in how they model these ideas, attitudes, and behaviors through words and actions in their own relationships. Most parents are not aware of how they model behavior about sex and relationships and do not think about it enough to change their behaviors for their own sake and the sake of their children. In my view, if we expect children to learn from the modeling of relationships parents are supposed to provide, we should be ashamed that we are such poor providers of that modeling for our kids.

This situation begs the question: Is this informal education children receive from their parents enough? It is hard to argue that this informal education children are "receiving" at home is enough given that:

> Every year, one million U.S. teenage women become pregnant, more than half a million have a child, and three million teenage men and women acquire a sexually transmitted disease.
>
> More than nine in ten American adolescents experiment with sexual behaviors.
>
> By the time they turn age 20, more than three-quarters of American young women and young men have had sexual intercourse. (Haffner, 1995)

Since most children do not learn about these topics from their parents in a meaningful way, the result is that children and students learn through the means most available to them, that is, from peers, their own sexual experimentation, and various pornographic materials they can get their curious and hormone-driven hands on. On playgrounds, at slumber parties, and in locker rooms, curious children and teenagers discuss, experiment with, and debate these fascinating topics. In fraternity houses, dorm rooms, and study sessions, college students pick up pointers and influence each other about these topics.

Given the magnitude of the effects of risky sexual practices today, clearly, more should be done in the way of sexual education, yet what has concerned me is the method by which students are actually receiving their education on the topic. Children are sent to high school for a formal education in math, science, and literature; meanwhile, they are expected to pick up an education on social and interpersonal skills and on love and relationships (which hugely affect their lives and well-being) through informal experience. To think that an education on love and relationships is supposed to come from observation and experience, and an education about intimacy and sex from informal conversation and experimentation, is upsetting, to say the least. In addition, when there is any formal education being provided at school or in religious settings, the programming is severely limited and does not integrate the topics into a more useful and educational conversation.

Since sexuality education is not provided adequately at home or in school, the need for this education persists when teens go off to college.

WHY IS THERE A NEED FOR *SEX WEEK AT YALE*?

Though Yale students are similar to students at other schools across the country, on some levels they are also unique. Students are admitted to Yale for their academic and extracurricular achievements, not necessarily for being superior in their social aptitude. Often, Yale students have put aside romantic relationships in deference to academic and other pursuits (like social service projects) during middle and high school, purposefully to excel on those levels. It is this social inexperience, coupled with intellectual aptitude and curiosity, that makes Yale a terrific setting for a *Sex Week*.

Yale's sex education policy, defined by the administration, does provide students with exposure to safer sex practices—an approach that shows their awareness of the sexual inexperience on the part of students and acknowledgement of their potential sexual behavior at this age. For this, they can be commended. For example, condoms are readily available for students for free in the dorms and at the health center, and peer health educators[1] are available for free consultation and advice on campus, as are professionals at the campus student health center (http://broadrecognition.blogspot.com/2006/10/yale-1-sex-school.html). Yale even has a mandatory hour-long lecture (called the "Connections Workshop") for all freshmen to attend when they enter the school, where safer sex practices are discussed and contraceptives are described and made available for students to look at and touch. Thus, every student entering the school is given a brief remedial education on safe sex and abstinence. In my view, this is very commendable. Also responsible and commendable is that Yale's peer health educators always emphasize that abstinence is the only definitive way to prevent unwanted pregnancy and disease. This shows that they are not promoting sex but rather educating students in ways to be healthy if they choose to make sex with a partner part of their lives. What's more, Peer Health Educators are trained by professionals at the Student Health Center to talk to their peers (fellow students) about topics ranging from proper sexual technique to contraception, and are available to students, as are the professionals at the Student Health Center whenever approach voluntarily.

Through providing these services, the Yale administration is responsibly recognizing that freshmen may not be sexually aware, and goes the extra mile to provide that lecture on safe sex and abstinence. What the school doesn't provide is a context for this discussion and a forum for a larger discussion on sex and relationships. The school is doing right in identifying that students need at least a formal sit-down lecture on safe sex and abstinence, but what they overlook is the reason why students need that lecture. In my opinion, the reason is that a large portion of the student population has not been in relationships and/or sexual situations before. Still, a conversation about love, intimacy, and relationships remains absent from the conversation.

Sex Week at Yale bridges this void. By bringing scholars and professionals from all different fields and backgrounds, *Sex Week at Yale* creates an integrative weeklong curriculum from which students can learn. *The Week* provides a forum for conversation about love, sex, intimacy, and relationships, thus integrating sex into a broader conversation and challenging students to learn from professionals and one another.

HISTORY OF *SEX WEEK AT YALE*: THE EVOLUTION OF AN IDEA

In the spring of 2000, I was asked by the leadership of Yale's Hillel—part of the previously mentioned network of Jewish student groups on campuses internationally—to attend a leadership conference that coming summer, with the intent of grooming me for student leadership. At this event, students pondered ways to get Jewish students more involved with the Jewish community on campus. While some students believed that dipping *matzah* (unleavened bread) in chocolate was an intriguing enough event to capture Jewish students' interest in their religion and culture, I believed something drastically different was necessary.

I was convinced that if we wanted students to get involved, we had to host events that were universal, unique, stimulating, and even provocative. Events had to be held at all venues on campus and could not be limited to classrooms alone. These thoughts were consistent with my view of sex as a universal topic to which everyone can relate, which everyone is interested in, and about which people are insecure and ignorant, especially in the context of religion. The result of this line of thought led me to the creation of what came to be called *Kosher Sex Week at Yale*.

The first iteration of this idea of *Kosher Sex Week* derived from my involvement in the leadership seminar at the Hillel summer workshop at one particular discussion where the prescribed topic of conversation explored ideas concerning how to get Jewish students involved in Hillel who otherwise would not have been involved. It was my idea that *Kosher Sex Week* would be a week of events concentrating on the idea of sex and sexuality in the Jewish religion. Through talks and events, *Kosher Sex Week* would be a way for Jewish students to come together and tackle a challenging subject in a way they had never experienced before.

After a month and a half of my planning, professors and students alike were interested in launching such a program. By this time, I had spoken with professors and leaders of various students groups, and everyone seemed interested in the event. Now it was necessary for me to bring everyone together, explain the vision for the week, and begin planning the event. At the first meeting, the student head of Yale's Peer Health Educators (Jacqueline Farber '03) followed by Professor Bill Summers of the Medical School and undergraduate biology department, questioned why the week could not take a broader form as a campus-wide event. With the Hillel rabbis' silent approval, we made the decision right then that *Sex Week*, an event with universal appeal, should not be limited to any one student demographic, such as Jewish students. This decision changed the fate of *Kosher Sex Week*, and the first form of *Sex Week at Yale* was born.

In 2002, *Sex Week* took form for the first time as *Campus-Wide Sex Week*. Planned by the coordinated effort of Yale Hillel, Yale Peer Health Educators, the Women's Center, and the Lesbian, Gay, Bisexual, Transgender Student Cooperative at Yale, Jacque Farber and myself took the lead in planning the events, which included student panels, a faculty lecture series, a Valentine's Day dinner, guest speakers, a celebrity panel, and a film festival featuring classic films concerning ideas of love, sex, intimacy, and relationships. During the planning of the week, one student formally represented each of the student groups involved in the planning, and other students from those student groups joined the organization committee as ancillary coordinators of events. The week differed from the iterations of *Sex Week at Yale* that followed in one obvious and important way. *Campus-Wide Sex Week* was a campus-centric event. The core of the event was talks by Yale professors and students speakers. The faculty lectures were used to round out an academic side to the week with talks about biology and literature and such, while the student talks focused on safe sex and relationships.

In this sense, in my view, the week was limited, and we made some mistakes. As organizers, we tried to be too politically correct and remained too academic in our selection of events. While we reasonably hosted a diversity of events directed at specific audiences (e.g., Jewish students, women, and bi-, trans-, and homosexuals), we thought diverse content alone would be enough to draw students to events (lectures on love, sex in religion, the biology and psychology of transgender). What we found was that the diversity of the content was not enough if the topics were not entertaining as well as being educational. For example, we found that a professor's lecture titled "The History of the Vibrator" was extremely well attended, while another professor's lecture, titled "History and Theory of Romantic Love in European Culture," as well as the talk already mentioned on transgender issues, titled "The Anatomies of Sex: Theme and Variation," were not well attended. The latter seemed too consistent with the more academic and dry content of the already offered course curriculum. This point was noted in the 2003 *Atlantic Monthly* article about *Sex Week at Yale*, written by noted journalist, author, and 1968 Yale graduate Ron Rosenbaum (see Appendices 2.1–2.4 for the full schedules from Campus-Wide Sex Weeks).

After evaluating the strengths and weaknesses of the event after its conclusion, we decided to reconstruct aspects of programming so that the focus of the week would more adequately appeal to students and would fit the trials and tribulations of the daily life of today's academic youth. That meant the focus of the week had to shift from abstract issues related to sex and intimacy to a focus on topics students could relate to—topics that would help students reconcile their beliefs about love, sex, intimacy, and relationships.

To do this, we realized that students needed to be challenged not only with theoretical and academic issues but with practical, worldly issues that they deal with everyday: issues of morality, law, media, marketing, love, intimacy, business, and, of course, sexual technique and sexual health. Furthermore, students needed to be challenged not only in the classroom but also in smaller, more intimate forums and in more interactive and interesting events.

We, the organizers, decided that not only is the week meant to provide a forum for the discussion of sex, but it also is meant to provide a forum to discuss if sex is an appropriate topic for discussion. By challenging students to think about issues related to sex, they are, in turn, forced to think about everyday issues they come into contact with in their own lives daily.

SEX WEEK AT YALE: AN INNOVATIVE SEX EDUCATION PROGRAM

The point of *Sex Week at Yale* is to challenge students to think critically about sex and sexuality by exposing them to a diversity of programs on the subject. The week is meant to be an overall experience, not just a series of talks. By hosting exciting, dynamic speakers and by encouraging students to attend parties, dinners, and informal gatherings, *Sex Week* captivates students' minds and allows them to ask questions and express their views openly in a safe and inquisitive environment. *Sex Week at Yale* is meant to challenge people to think about sex and allow them to define what sex means to them.

We wanted to address today's problems because we decided that students are not always afforded the opportunity to explore their beliefs and opinions about sex openly and safely. On campus, it is easy to find a forum for discussion about science or politics, but there is no widespread forum that encourages students to feel comfortable discussing sexuality. Students may be socially conditioned to joke around about sex, but sex is not a joke and should not be taken lightly as a topic for conversation. Drawing students in by making the subject of sexuality interesting and entertaining is key to getting students involved and learning. Whether students realize it or not, *Sex Week* allows them the opportunity to explore their beliefs and opinions about sex and challenges them to think about sex seriously. To give students this chance to explore sex openly and safely is to provide true sex education.

A further innovation that *Sex Week at Yale* has brought to sexuality education on campus is the integration of topics related to sex, but not just the technical aspects of sex or relationships. Inclusion of discussions on the spiritual, psychological, sociological, historical, and political, as well as biological, fronts brings sex into a greater context than talks on safer sex and relationships alone provide. For example, during *Sex Week at Yale* in February 2008, along with safer-sex talks, there were diverse talks not elsewhere covered in a college curriculum, including the business approach of how Trojan Brand as a company markets condoms; the history of pornography; sex and spirituality; the art of the "pick-up" (how to successfully attract the opposite sex); and the brain functioning involved in love and attachment. A full schedule of this *Sex Week at Yale* is in Appendix 2.4.

These talks were intended to present a variety of subjects to challenge students to think critically about sex in society and sex in their own lives. In a full week, about 15 events were offered, each with its own unique subject matter to add to the conversation. These went beyond talks about the more technical aspects of sex and the intricacies and pitfalls of relationships.

For example, from the first *Campus-Wide Sex Week at Yale*, I intended to spark students into some controversy and bring new perspectives about sexuality to light by bringing to campus a panel that included Rabbi Shmuley Boteach, known for his controversial book, *Kosher Sex* (1999), and Dr. Judy Kuriansky, the very popular host of a radio call-in advice show, *LovePhones*. Her radio show on Z100 radio in New York City was well known to many students, had higher ratings than shock-jock Howard Stern's show, and dealt with questions from young people about all aspects of sex, from betrayal by boyfriends to bondage and body image, as chronicled in her books *Generation Sex* (1996) and tips about dating in *The Complete Idiot's Guide to Dating* (Kuriansky, 2002). Boteach stirred the audience with his ideas about sex being consistent with orthodox religion. And Kuriansky led the students in a live interactive session about the new trend of what's called "tantric sex," where high states of ecstasy can be reached through intimate connection without sexual contact or intercourse, as presented in her book *The Complete Idiot's Guide to Tantric Sex* (Kuriansky, 2004). The students in the session came away with new ideas about sex from both speakers and energized by the active participation in Dr. Judy's session, which was experiential rather than just a typically didactic academic format, and which left many students wanting to talk long after the session was over to get more information. This conversation was carried into a dinner whereby Dr. Judy continued to talk to the students about the topic, offering a unique opportunity for interaction between the students and an expert.

SEX WEEK AT YALE BEYOND THE CLASSROOM

To extend the *Sex Week at Yale* mission and education beyond Yale's ivy-covered gates, *Sex Week at Yale* established a website in 2004 (www. sexweekatyale.com) and published a magazine in 2006 and 2008 (described below), and in 2008 a documentary about *Sex Week at Yale* was produced by students involved with the week. All of these modes of communication are a carefully thought-out way to spread the message that *Sex Week at Yale* represents outside of Yale's classrooms, and more into the general public.

In this effort to bring the *Sex Week at Yale* experience outside of Yale, in February 2006, nearly 25,000 copies of *Sex Week at Yale: The Magazine* were distributed among 18 of the country's best-known universities, including all schools in the Ivy League (Agapakis, 2006). Asked why a nationally distributed magazine accompanied the week of *Sex Week* events, the 2006 *Sex Week at Yale* director and magazine publisher said, "We wanted to bring the experience outside of just Yale. . . . It would even be a shame if it [*Sex Week at Yale*] were limited only to Yale because it's just that good" (Agapakis, 2006). The magazine in both 2006 and 2008 included contributors who participated in *Sex Week at Yale* in each of those years in addition to contributors who did not speak at *Sex Week at Yale* in either year. Among the 2006 magazine's notable contributors who both wrote for the magazine and spoke at *Sex Week at Yale* was sex and relationship author Ian Kerner, who wrote an article entitled, "Thinking Outside Her Box: A Primer on Sexual Cliteracy." Another such contributor to the 2008 magazine was University of Washington professor Pepper Schwartz. The Seattle-based sociologist, sexologist, and 1974 Yale graduate wrote an article for the *Sex Week at Yale* magazine in 2008 entitled, "Debunking the Top Ten Modern Sex Myths." Other notable contributors to the magazine include Jim Griffiths, president of the Playboy Entertainment Group; John Gray, Ph.D., author of *Men Are from Mars, Women Are from Venus*; Ron Louis and David Copeland, authors of *How to Succeed with Women*; and columnists from such publications as *Cosmopolitan*, *Men's Health*, and *Maxim*.

In February 2008, *Sex Week at Yale*'s press release announced the production of *Sex Week at Yale: The Documentary*. The release stated, "The documentary will trace *Sex Week* from inception to realization, including interviews with students and faculty" (http://www.sexweekatyale.com/2008_release. pdf). A trailer is currently available on the *Sex Week at Yale* website at www. sexweekatyale.com, and the documentary will be available on the website as soon as it is released. The *Sex Week at Yale* documentary is yet another way for the concept and message of the *Week* to reach more people in entertaining and informative ways in an effort to educate, excite, and challenge.

WHEN IS *SEX WEEK AT YALE*?

Sex Week at Yale is held during the week of Valentine's Day every other year (semiannually), since February 2002. The timing is perfect for logistical and social reasons. For example, Valentine's Day was determined as the appropriate time for the event since everyone knows that "love is in the air" at that time, so there is already an inferred association with love and sex. Also, around this time, students are ready for a break from the long and cold New Haven winter. Logistically, the middle of February is halfway between the beginning of the spring semester and spring break. Since there are few midterms during Valentine's Week and little else exciting is happening on campus at that time, *Sex Week* was expected to be welcome and well attended. Socially, at this time, people are thinking about love and romance as Valentine's Day approaches. Due to Yale's particular dating scene (or lack thereof), many Yalies embrace a distraction from the holiday that forces them to think about lost love or simply the lack of romantic love in their lives. Thus, Valentine's Week was seen as the perfect week to hold *Sex Week at Yale* as it becomes a chance to warm hearts and minds during a very chilly and mentally (and sexually) taxing time of year at Yale.

We decided to hold the week every other year to allow for two classes of students to graduate and two new classes to enter the school. Therefore, half of the students on campus have already experienced the event and will be excited that it is happening again, and the other half will be excited to experience the event for the first time. A biannual plan also gives the organizers the essential amount of time to train new students to run the event and to spend time planning to completely reinvent the event—which is critically important to its overall success.

HOW THE EVENT IS RECEIVED

Sex Week at Yale has gotten more attention and recognition than anyone involved anticipated. From conservative critics to international media acclaim, the event draws extensive attention. But does the event achieve its goal to challenge students to think critically about love, sex, intimacy, and relationships? A simple Google search finds a plethora of articles, many of which are written by students for campus newspapers, but others from mainstream media, which discuss the Week, question the Week's meaning, and, finally, discuss the events and topics the Week presented. These are discussed in more detail in this section.

On Campus

The Students

The students' response to the event is always mixed, though I consider this positive because it means students are seriously thinking about the topics the Week presents. An overwhelming majority of students attend events and really enjoy themselves and tell the organizers that they learn from the experience. Many students become quite engaged and ask speakers difficult and penetrating questions in true Yale form. Another group of students comes to events intent on hearing what speakers have to say in order to challenge and refute the speaker's ideas and/or line of work—a process which is typical of the type of students Yale attracts, who like to confront authority and state their own opinions.

I consider even these critiques positive because it means students are seriously thinking about the topics the Week presents. In my view, stirring up campus talk is exactly what *Sex Week* is supposed to do. *Sex Week* not only brings out those with sexual experience and those who want to be entertained but also attracts students who are critical, and another group: those who are seeking answers to their real problems. With all these reactions, the week can be considered a success, since students are interacting with the speakers, being challenged, and learning from the exchange.

For example, in a February 2004 *Yale Daily News* article, the student-run campus daily newspaper, Yale student journalist Michael Katz '04 quoted Yale student Josh Ehrlich '07, who expressed appreciation for the opportunity to talk frankly about sexual issues. "I went to a religious Jewish high school and we didn't have open sexual discussions," Ehrlich said. "It's important to be laid-back (or more accepting) when talking about sex, and this week has been important for that" (Katz, 2004). But Katz also noted the more vocal response the Week evoked in fellow classmates. In his article, Katz wrote:

> Other students expressed surprise in reaction to the discourse that *Sex Week* has provoked. "I knew Yale was a very liberal campus," said Nate Pocksta '07. "[But] I was surprised to see people's willingness to engage with presenters. I know you wouldn't see this at Princeton or Harvard." (Katz, 2004)

A more recent article written during the 2008 iteration of *Sex Week at Yale* and published by Bloomberg News, quoted Yale student Jordan Garner as saying:

> When I first found out about *Sex Week*, I was with my parents," said Jordan Garner, a biology and religious studies major who plans to pursue a graduate degree in religious studies. "They freaked." The organizers include "something for everyone," Garner said. "I have a lot of Christian friends, and they say they're really proud of this." (Randall, 2008)

An interesting example of the effectiveness of *Sex Week* in getting students to think critically about sexuality and how it relates to themselves and others is evident in another *Yale Daily News* article and a rebuttal in the same publication. In the February 16, 2004, edition, Yale student Taylor Larson '04 wrote:

> In my opinion, the implicit message of *Sex Week at Yale* has undermined its attempt to present a balanced collection of opinions regarding sexuality. Engaging in sexual-

ity as essentially about individual gratification and entertainment is a choice available to all Yale students, but it is far from clear that this is the best approach to take.
Hopefully the leaders of *Sex Week* will be able to add more balance to the tone of
their initiative in the future." (Larson, 2004)

In rebuttal, Nick Seaver '07 wrote three days later:

Larson's criticism of individual sexuality seems more rooted in cultural stigma than
in any sort of logical method. In my opinion, sexuality should not be repressed, be
it individually or in a relationship. I appreciate the concern for saving sexual intercourse for marriage, but this certainly should not rule out sexual alternatives to
intercourse before marriage. *Sex Week* did exactly what it was supposed to: it brought
sexual issues that are not often spoken about, like masturbation and sex toys, into a
public forum. (Seaver, 2004)

This exchange clearly reveals how *Sex Week* evoked a dispute about sex before marriage. In my view as organizer, this debate proves that *Sex Week at
Yale* is achieving its goals. The fact that two students took the time and effort
to organize and write their thoughts in a public forum proves the power of
such an event. Both students wrote well-thought-out commentary, making
valid points. Though I would like to see *Sex Week at Yale* receiving only praise
in the press, my interest is in challenging students (and the public, through
the media) and getting them to think critically about sex in their lives. The
published exchange in our campus newspaper between students Taylor and
Nick shows that students are being challenged and challenging each other.
Real learning does not have to take place in the classroom alone; to me, this is
where *Sex Week at Yale* gets the formula right.

The Speakers

"The more people talk about sexuality, the better," Summers said. "Sexuality's a vague
concept to pin down. Where do I fit in? Am I normal? How do I understand these
feelings, and how do I integrate them into how I see the world? Our culture doesn't
tell us much about the sexual aspect of the world. (Kellogg, 2002)

Like Professor Bill Summers who is quoted above—the same professor
who favored expanding *Kosher Sex Week at Yale* into a broader event—speakers
often are thrilled to get involved with *Sex Week at Yale*, to share their knowledge, and to learn from Yale's students. For instance, Logan Levkoff, a sex
educator and spokeswoman for Trojan—the condom unit of Princeton, New
Jersey-based Church & Dwight Co.—said in an interview after one of two
events she participated in during *Sex Week at Yale* 2008, "Yale's *Sex Week* is
pretty much the foremost for its distinct, provocative format" (Randall, 2008).
And, just before her talk in 2004, Betty Dodson, known as the godmother of
masturbation, said, "I'm so glad to know that they have sex at Yale" (Del Mar
Galindo, 2004). Clearly she was pleased to participate and spread her message
to the Yale class.

But there are also hurdles to overcome in booking speakers. This happened in the case of Betty Dodson, whom I first called to invite in the fall of 2003. While she wanted to speak at the event, she insisted on being paid. Students for a Sexually Aware Campus (the student group I created to run the event after the 2002 event) had a very limited budget and so could not afford to pay any speakers. Dodson's prominence in the field of sexuality and her outspoken style made her a particularly desirable speaker. Thus, I was committed to convincing her to speak. After a few phone conversations, Dodson finally agreed to speak at the event without pay, saying, "You've seduced me into coming." You can imagine my amusement at this choice of words. Whether it was my persuasive skills and excitement over the event or the draw to speak to a Yale audience, speakers agreed to attend the event even for no honorarium and had a great time in doing so.

At *Sex Week*, Dodson spoke at a Yale's Women's Center venue to an audience of about 65 students, mostly female. She spoke about masturbation and sexual exploration. Yale student and Yale newspaper journalist Maria Del Mar Galindo wrote in the *Yale Daily News,* "Dodson—who answered questions for 45 minutes after she had concluded her talk—began the open dialogue about sex that various guests, including a rabbi and a pornography star, continued to encourage during the week" (Del Mar Galindo, 2004).

The size of Betty Dodson's event was characteristic for events in 2004. The largest turnout for an event we had was a panel with participants Joe Francis (the founder of the *Girls Gone Wild* video series, in which females gleefully expose their breasts), Devinn Lane (an adult entertainment Wicked Pictures contract girl), and Dr. Susan Block (sex therapist, HBO television personality, and '77 Yale University graduate), moderated by Joey Reynolds (WOR 710 radio personality, the original radio "shock jock"). About 300 students attended.

By 2008, *Sex Week at Yale* had grown such that 300 students or more attended half of the week's talks. For example, "About 300 students crowded a lecture hall to hear Ruth Westheimer, known as 'Dr. Ruth' from her 1980s television show. Students giggled in the aisles as the 4-foot-7 (1.4-meter) sex expert talked about masturbation and body image and encouraged students to pursue sex studies" (Randall, 2008).

Even critics of the week see value in the week and are impressed by the breadth of the week's talks and events. Dawn Eden, author of the book *The Thrill of the Chaste*, spoke in 2008 as part of a panel entitled, "Sex and Spirituality." Dawn spoke again the next night at an event sponsored by the Yale Christian Fellowship, which was not officially part of *Sex Week at Yale*'s events and which I believe was chosen by both Dawn and the Yale Christian Fellowship as a sign of protest against *Sex Week*, since her message is against sex outside marriage and anything that can be perceived to promote such activity. The fact that someone is willing to take part in the *Sex Week at Yale* event on one evening and protest it the next night is what I find especially inspiring about the *Sex Week at Yale* event itself.

On her blog, Dawn wrote, "That there was a chastity advocate at all [i.e., herself] during *Sex Week*...was indeed impressive" (http://www.dawneden. com/2008/02/lux-be-lady-championing-chastity-at-sex.html). In that same blog entry, Dawn wrote, "with the exception of my appearance on the panel, *Sex Week* notably omitted any respectful discussion of the most obvious context for sex: marriage and children" (http://www.dawneden.com/2008/02/lux-be-lady-championing-chastity-at-sex.html). Dawn makes a good point that a talk about marriage and children might be interesting, but in response I would say that many of the week's talks include discussions about marriage and children. What makes the concept of *Sex Week at Yale* interesting is that one talk does not necessarily have to address a topic for conversation about other topics to come up.

This means that many topics lead the conversation into different topic areas. For example, love, sex, marriage, chastity, and romance are ideas so interrelated that a discussion about biology and relationships in one talk can turn into a conversation in the audience about marriage, and a conversation with an adult entertainment star in another panel can turn into a conversation about relationships in general, as happened during *Sex Week at Yale* in 2008. During a talk delivered by noted anthropologist and author Helen Fisher and sexologist Logan Levkoff entitled, "The Chemistry and Communication of Love: What Makes That Special Someone So Special," a conversation turned from the main topic to a discussion about how humans are designed to be serial monogamists—meaning humans are biologically designed to have loving relationships long enough to bear and raise a child. In this discussion, students questioned how marriage could be a pillar of society if biology does not support the established precept. As another example, during a presentation entitled "The Great Porn Debate," which was moderated by ABC-TV reporter Martin Bashir and filmed by *Nightline* and aired on the ABC-TV network, students asked adult entertainment stars Ron Jeremy and Monique Alexander what their parents think about their involvement in such a profession and how being involved in pornography affects their ability to have a romantic relationship. In response, Monique Alexander mentioned a recent conversation with her grandmother in which her grandmother congratulated her on her professional success and her success in becoming a financially independent woman (http://abcnews.go.com/nightline/faceoff/altindex).

In further support of the importance to diversify the *Sex Week* events by adding opinions that challenge people to think critically about their beliefs and actions, this particularly flattering excerpt appeared on another blog entry written by conservative participant Dawn Eden. Evidently, Eden appreciated us (as organizers) for our evenhandedness:

> One pleasant surprise of the evening was that *Sex Week* founder Eric Rubenstein was there from the start despite his own event's going on in the other room—and he stayed for my entire talk and Q&A. Since our interactions at the "Sex and Spirituality" panel had been heated on both sides (and I do regret having erupted at him and current *Sex Week* director Joe Citarrella during the event), it was with some surprise that I saw how gracious and genuinely interested he was. He spoke with me and Yale Christian Fellowship campus minister Greg Hendrickson afterwards and solicited our advice on how to make the next *Sex Week* more balanced. (http://www.dawneden.com/2008/02/if-lux-could-thrill-giving-sex-week.html)

Eden's reaction affirmed that *Sex Week at Yale* should include interesting and challenging talks on all aspects of relationships—just what the week intends to do.

The Administration

The college administration recognizes the *Sex Week* event as legitimate and protects students' rights to freedom of speech and expression by allowing the event to exist. The school, furthermore, recognizes the student group that runs the event as registered and in good standing and, in doing so, allows *Sex Week at Yale* events on campus so long as rooms are booked in advance and certain precautions are put in place to ensure the events are safe (such as having security at certain particularly large events). The administration does not, however, have any role in planning the event. They simply give their quiet approval by allowing the event to take place. In an article published by *Bloomberg News*, author Tom Randall wrote:

> Yale allows students to use classrooms and equipment, as it does for other campus organizations, and doesn't pay for the activities, university spokesman Tom Conroy said. (Randall, 2008)

One quote in an article in the *Harvard Crimson* from 2008 does actually mention that the Yale administration supports the week's activities:

> The college's administration said it supports the week's activities. Yale is happy to let the students have the intellectual freedom to create events that are meaningful for them, said P. Gila Reinstein of the Yale Office of Public Affairs. "We stand ready to assist the students." (Lee, 2008)

The Critics and the Controversy

Although *Sex Week at Yale* draws praise from a diverse student population at Yale, and speakers enjoy their involvement and think very highly of the event, and the media find the event worth recognition, *Sex Week at Yale* is not without critics and controversy. For example, the following was written in the *Yale Daily News:*

> "It used to be that if people wanted to discuss sex, they read [Plato's] 'Symposium' or 'Works of Love' by Kierkegaard," said Sarah Longwell, Senior Program Officer for the Collegiate Network. "At Yale, you would expect them to do that. Instead, [the University hosted] a fast-food version of discussion of these questions." The Collegiate Network is composed of representatives from 80 conservative college publications from across the nation, including the Yale Free Press and Light and Truth. Between March 10 and April 1, the organization conducted extensive research into each nominated university. Nikki McArthur '05, editor of the Yale Free Press, nominated Yale's *Sex Week* for the award in late February. She characterized the event as "pretty immature." (Katsuyama, 2004)

With regard to the award mentioned in the above article, *Sex Week at Yale* was nominated for, and eventually won, the, albeit, dubious award presented by the Collegiate Network— the "Polly Award," (http://www.isi.org/cn/pollys/04/pollyyale.aspx). According to the Collegiate Network's website, "These awards for the worst campus outrages are given each year to universities to remind the public that political correctness, curricular decay, and violations of academic freedom and free speech remain an unfortunate reality throughout much of higher education" (http://www.isi.org/cn/pollys/polly04.aspx). Though this award is designed to publicly recognize universities for holding events and allowing activities that the conservative Collegiate Network disapproves of, the fact that Yale won 1st place on the Polly Award's award list in 2004 for hosting *Sex Week at Yale* shows that the *Sex Week at Yale* message reaches far beyond Yale's campus, meeting the goal of the *Sex Week at Yale* staff. After Yale was awarded the Polly Award, I was quoted as saying, and still agree with the statement that:

> "I was pleased to find that people were recognizing the event, because it's worth the recognition," Eric Rubenstein, BK '04, coordinator of this year's *Sex Week*, said. "I think it's outrageous, and that's why people are drawn to it, but it's outrageous in a positive way." (Miller, 2004)

The worst critics of *Sex Week at Yale* seem, in my view, to be those who do not even attend the event at all, like those who awarded the Polly Award to us for *Sex Week at Yale* University. Usually these critics admit their lack of attendance. This was also the case of a Yale student in 2008 who was interviewed by Fox News and who was critical about the existence of the week as a whole and of specific events in particular. Usually the events most criticized are the ones involving representatives from the adult entertainment industry.

We, the organizers of *Sex Week at Yale*, were fortunate enough in 2008 to have one such critic speak at *Sex Week at Yale* as a guest. Below is an excerpt from an article written by a reporter from *Bloomberg News* who attended the event. The report quoted the highly conservative and aforementioned participant and critic of *Sex Week*, Dawn Eden:

> Detractors include some participants, such as Dawn Eden, a panelist this weekend and author of the book "The Thrill of the Chaste." She said the week promotes premarital sex and endorses unhealthy images of sexuality. She objected to a porn debate between adult-film stars Ron Jeremy and Monique Alexander, to be moderated by ABC television's "Nightline" host, Martin Bashir.
>
> "This is how they [the organizers] get out the word, by having juicy events featuring porn stars and sexologists?" Eden said in a telephone interview. "I think that is very damaging, physically, psychologically and certainly spiritually." (Randall, 2008)

Though Ms. Eden did not attend any events other than her own, I believe she did learn more about the week and recognized the positive effect the week can have. An event of such magnitude and subject matter cannot be expected to go without critics. Engaging critics simply broadens the conversation and furthers the mission of the week.

Hosting adult entertainment stars always receives criticism. To these critics, I like to point to an article they likely did not come across in their literature reviews on *Sex Week at Yale*, since it was published by *Hustler* Magazine in 2004 (the article can be found on the *Sex Week at Yale* website, www.sexweekatyale. com). Referring to a talk given by adult entertainment star Devinn Lane, Yale graduate Chris Rovzar wrote:

> Soon, almost in spite of themselves, the viewers began to ask the porn star questions about her ethics, raising her daughter and the nature of feminism in the industry. Lane supplied them with thoughtful, intelligent answers. (Rovzar, 2004)

In my view, this demonstrates the value of including such adult industry players in *Sex Week*, which exists to facilitate these sorts of conversations. Who better to ask about the complexity of relationships than an adult entertainment star who has to consider a multitude of complications in all the relationships in her life? Who better to ask about sex than someone who has sex for a living? Just as speaking with someone who has chosen to abstain from having sex—like Ms. Eden has done—can be educational, so can speaking with someone on the other side of the spectrum. And as Dr. Judy notes in her column she wrote for the *New York Daily News* Web site in 2004:

> No need to worry that talking about it makes kids go out and DO it, though, as research on my call-in radio advice show proved. Said one Yale senior, a veteran of both *Sex Weeks*, "I sure learned to talk more openly about it, but it didn't lead to any more action." (Kuriansky, 2004)

This counters criticism that *Sex Week at Yale* promotes sex by holding programs in which students talk about sex. In her same article, Dr. Judy also wrote about *Sex Week at Yale* that, "Attendees expressed surprise to surrealism, but mostly widespread welcome for newfound openness about sex" (Kuriansky, 2004).

In the Media

Over the four iterations of the week (2002, 2004, 2006, and 2008), thousands of students attended *Sex Week at Yale* events, hundreds of publications across the world published articles about *Sex Week at Yale*, and numerous television and radio new stations covered and/or featured the event on their shows. Publications that have published articles concerning the event are varied and include, but are not limited to *The Atlantic Monthly*, the *New York Times*, *The Wall Street Journal*, the *New York Daily News*, *Newsweek*, the *New Yorker*, *Hustler*, *Bloomberg News*, the *Associated Press*, the *National Review*, the *Christian Science Monitor*, the *Washington Post*, the *Providence Phoenix*, the *New Haven Register*, the *New Haven Advocate*, the *Vanderbilt Torch*, *Daily Vanguard*, *The Tufts Daily*, *Cornell Review*, not to mention the *Yale Daily News* and the *Yale Herald* among others.

Most media coverage included mention of the week and its purpose, along with mention of a few of the week's events. This unbiased coverage contrasts with the conservative press, which questions the legitimacy of an event like *Sex Week at Yale*, especially the fact that such an event could take place at an academic institution of such prestige and import. Additionally, conservative press criticized the event itself, as was described in the *Critics and the Controversy* section described above. More positive coverage includes Yale's number one ranking in the first-ever publication of the *Trojan Sexual Health Report Card*. The survey, first released in September 2006 by the makers of Trojan brand condoms and Sperling's Best Places, was the first survey that graded the sexual health of colleges and universities across the country and ranked them (http://www.bestplaces.net/docs/studies/SexualHealth.aspx). In talking about why Yale was chosen as number one in the study, Bert Sperling, the president of Sperling's Best Places (the research firm that compiled the report) was quoted by the *Yale Daily News* as saying, "Yale did very well across the board." He continued, "It was far and away the number-one spot, especially when we looked at, for instance, the extra events and programs that are available, like *Sex Week at Yale*" (Macbeth, 2006).

The *Yale Daily News* noted that the report card recognized "the resources the University offers to students facing a sexual-health crisis, the birth-control measures it makes available to students, the helpfulness of Yale's website and special events like *Sex Week at Yale* in granting the top honor" (Macbeth, 2006). The same article continued:

> For most students, *Sex Week at Yale* may simply be an excuse to attend humorous lectures or participate in unconventional, even titillating workshops. But for the evaluators of Trojan's Sexual Health Report Card, the event represents much more: a valuable effort to increase understanding of the importance of safe sex on campus. *Sex Week* was one of the most important features in Yale's sexual-health arsenal that helped it earn the top ranking in Trojan's recent survey, Sperling said. (Macbeth, 2006)

Lastly, the article made the significance of Yale's place on the report card clear when compared to other notable institutions: "Yale was the only school to achieve A grades in all seven categories on which the 100 colleges and universities in the study were judged and a grade-point average of 4.0—no other school scored above a 3.6. Princeton, the sixth-ranked school, earned a 3.4, and Harvard, which came in 43rd place, was awarded a 2.1" (Macbeth, 2006).

The report card itself ranked the top five universities, according to rank as shown in Table 2.1.

Table 2.1 shows the rankings and individual category scores for the seven categories across which schools were graded. The report card shows that *Sex Week at Yale*'s notability reaches far beyond the university itself. To Sperling's Best Places and Trojan, this is not just because the event takes place at Yale, and is not simply because of whatever risqué content the week has originated. The week is recognized for its import in the world of sexuality education, and this is certainly an accomplishment not to be overlooked.

Still, the reason why *Sex Week at Yale* is covered by the majority of media sources is not because the week is important in raising sexual and relationship awareness but because the event is risqué and takes place at Yale University. *Sex Week* is definitely a unique, one-of-a-kind sex education event. This is even truer because the event takes place at Yale. At most other schools, an event like this would be overlooked or thought of as rather plain. The Rutgers event is one proof of this, and the Northwestern event is another. In fact, the Northwestern event did receive limited press but was not nearly as recognized as the *Sex Week at Yale* event even though the event was modeled directly after the event at Yale. Also worth noting is that Northwestern ranked 42nd on the 2008 recent Trojan Sexual Health Report Card (http://www.trojancondoms. com/assets/pdfs/2007_SHRC.pdf).

So why does *Sex Week at Yale* receive such recognition? First, the fact that the event is at Yale somehow attracts the media and rallies their attention. Because the event is at the notable Ivy League institution, the *Sex Week at Yale* becomes extraordinary, unique, and daring. Founded in 1701, Yale is the third oldest institution of higher education in the country (the oldest being Harvard

Table 2.1
Sexual Health on College Campuses: The Trojan® Sexual Health Report Card

Rank	School	Score	Web site	Condom avail.	Contra-ception	HIV & STI testing	Sexual assault services	Advice column, Q&As	Lecture, outreach programs	City	State
1.	Yale University	4.0	A	A	A	A	A	A	A	New Haven	CT
2.	University of Iowa	3.6	A	A	A	A	B	A	C	Iowa City	IA
3.	University of Michigan–Ann Arbor	3.6	A	A	A	A	B	C	A	Ann Arbor	MI
4.	Stanford University	3.6	A	A	A	A	A	D	A	Stanford	CA
5.	Oregon State University	3.4	B	A	A	C	A	A	B	Corvallis	OR

and the second oldest being the College of William and Mary) and has been recognized in the past for interesting sex-related news; for example the controversy over five orthodox Jewish Yale students who refused to live in coed dorms (Glaberson, 1997) and the infamous Porn n' Chicken Society (Stein, 2001). Adding to the media frenzy is the fact that the event's pedigree provides legitimacy for sex to be taken as a serious topic, capturing wide attention more than the content itself.

In addition, the event garners attention outside of the Yale campus because it is truly dynamic, challenging, unique and different in content and design. It tackles dynamic and challenging topics in unique and stimulating ways, making it intellectually penetrating in its own right. Furthermore, the event does an excellent job of what it is trying to do: challenging people to think critically about sex and relationships and their place in our lives. The attention itself is proof that the week is unique and worth recognition. Further, added proof of the Week's success is that such attention has been sustained across four iterations of the event spanning almost eight years.

CONSIDERATIONS IN PLANNING A *SEX WEEK*

The success of *Sex Week at Yale* proves that a program of such scope is possible and lays the groundwork for similar programs to be planned in other formats. Still, when planning a *Sex Week*, considerations beyond the mission of the week are many and cannot be ignored. One must consider who is planning the event, the target audience, the events and speakers, the times and locations of the events, and the funding and marketing.

Planning a *Sex Week* takes a lot of patience, persistence, and creativity. There are many different routes that can be taken in creating a successful *Sex Week*. With *Sex Week*, the potential is unlimited, given a whole world of entertainment and education to draw from. The following sections of this chapter describe factors that need to be considered when planning a *Sex Week* and describe the pitfalls that might be encountered along the way.

Phase I: Generating Ideas and Organizing Thoughts

Sex Week, like most things in life, begins with an idea. A mental foundation must be built with a vision and mission for the event. In the case of *Sex Week*, the mission has been drawn out and defined: a week during which students, professors, and professionals can come together and explore love, intimacy, and sex in a meaningful manner designed to reconcile the three. The way this mission is carried out (the vision) has more flexibility and is really the creative and challenging part of the week, as there are infinite possibilities for events and structure.

Though the possibilities are limitless, a vague structure is useful to follow when shaping events and ideas. Every idea, for instance, should be considered on two fronts: academic and entertainment. Ideally, these two seemingly contradictory considerations should be fused in each event, making each event both entertaining and educational. Ideally, each event should entertain and challenge not only the audience but also the speaker, teaching each an important lesson about life, love, intimacy, and/or sex.

The events should reflect or explore certain genres or themes of sexual education. By this I mean every aspect of sex, intimacy, and love should be covered in as many different ways possible. A talk about intimacy is just as necessary as the chance to experience firsthand intimacy when sharing a meal with speakers or seeing a movie where intimacy is clearly a main theme. The genres and themes should thus form a fusion of different ideas on love, sex, and intimacy throughout the week by means of attending a number of different events.

Phase II: Organizing the Week

What specific events you want to plan, when and where the events should take place, and the funding and marketing of the week are all unique to the school and part of the country you are in and what is available. Large schools will have different resources than smaller schools. Knowing your school, as well as the neighborhood, is of particular importance for the success of the week. Take advantage of the resources near you that are available to you. You will find these to be invaluable as you plan your event.

At Yale, as mentioned earlier, there is a framework for sex education in that every freshman has to attend a sex education talk at the beginning of their Yale career. This talk, and similar talks that take place throughout the year, are delivered by the Peer Health Educators, whose group and talks are supported by the university. Thus, at Yale, there was a precedent whereby talks about sex were allowed before *Sex Week at Yale* even began. Other universities, as those in the Midwest and the South, might not have this administrative reception thus, different actions would have to take place in the organization of the week.

The Planners

Planners of the event can range from a single individual to a conglomerate of student and professional organizations. As long as the people involved are interested and vested in the project, the planning should go fairly smoothly.

At Yale, for instance, organizationally, we have planned the event a few different ways as the event has developed over years. In the beginning, different student groups co-sponsored the event, which increased awareness on campus and created diversity in the programming at a time when the event had no history or track record. In later years, we created a single student group with faculty advisors to facilitate the organization of the event. As time has passed, that student organization's relationship with Yale's administration has also developed such that the administration is consulted during the planning process. This is fairly significant because the administration, though they have always approved of the event's existence, now takes a more formal part in the event's planning by making sure everything is being planned according to school policy.

Planners have to be organized and motivated since planning an event like *Sex Week at Yale* takes significant energy and time to be done professionally. Not all events, however, have to be, or can be, just like the *Sex Week at Yale*. Smaller events can be just as significant. In fact, I encourage individual talks and lectures throughout the year. The more students are challenged to think critically about how they are and should be living their lives, the more they will refine their beliefs and act on them.

An example of an individual event that can have a big impact is an event I held after *Sex Week at Yale* in 2004. In April 2004, I held a follow-up event to *Sex Week* because the girls from Toys in Babeland who spoke at the *Sex Week at Yale* event in February wanted to return to campus as part of a national speaking tour they were undertaking. The talk they planned for the event was entitled "G-spotting" and was a discussion of female sexuality, specifically, the biology and history of the Grafenburg spot, which is a center of female arousal.

I expected 20 to 30 students to show up to the "G-spotting" event. Since many rooms at Yale are available in the evening, I chose not to book a room and sent a simple e-mail a day before the event to announce the event. To my surprise and delight, as the speakers were setting up for the talk, more and more students arrived for the talk. Next thing I knew, more than 150 students crowded the hall and we had to scurry to find a larger lecture hall to accommodate so many students. Before the event began, I stood up and spoke briefly about *Sex Week at Yale*, telling stories about planning the event and, in an effort to find someone to organize the event in 2006, I mentioned that there was no one to plan *Sex Week at Yale* once I graduated later that year. I passed around a paper for students to sign if they had interest in organizing *Sex Week at Yale* 2006. When the paper was returned to me, more than 60 students' names and contact information were on the paper.

The "G-spotting" event turned out to be a highly interactive and interesting talk, with students asking intelligent questions and receiving intelligent responses. After the event, a dozen or so students approached me, thanking me for planning *Sex Week at Yale* and the "G-spotting" event they had just experienced. Furthermore, students expressed sincere intent in planning *Sex Week at Yale* two years later.

After receiving a number of e-mails from students interested in running the event in 2006, I held a meeting to help me decide who would be the most capable candidates. Unfortunately, the evening's weather was atrocious, with the rain making me question whether it was worth even me showing up for the meeting. Reluctantly, I trudged across campus to meet my potential successor. One particular student at the meeting asked informed questions about the more intricate business related aspects of the event. Since I wanted to find a successor in a student with a mind for business and who would be structured in organizing the event, luckily, I found what I was looking for in this student. To my excitement, he sent me an unsolicited email confirming his interest. Thus, in hosting a talk outside of the *Sex Week at Yale* event, I had not only done a service by educating students, but I had found my successor to plan the next *Sex Week*.

Funding and Marketing

In terms of funding, each *Sex Week* might be different and unique. Some events will not need any money, as professors and local professionals will speak for free and flyers can be distributed and posted to attract students. Other events will need funding to provide transportation for speakers if no local speakers are available, or if a special speakers is necessary (like an adult industry star) who lives outside the area.

At some schools, student groups can apply for funding to pay for flyers and speakers' transportation. If the school does not offer money to student groups to put on events, perhaps they allow student groups to design t-shirts or other memorabilia to sell them on campus to raise revenue. If this is not a possibility, student groups might be able to sell tickets to events. Funding does not have to be complicated, but is necessary at times to hold a successful event. If rooms need to be booked and paid for, money is necessary to make sure these bills are paid.

At Yale, it is the culture of the school that all events are free. Therefore, funds could not be raised by selling tickets to events. Consequently, we have resorted to appeals to student organizations to obtain funding predominantly in our beginning years, and subsequently, we have solicited corporate sponsorship. Whatever your budget is, you need to be creative about raising funds to cover event costs.

In terms of marketing, we at *Sex Week at Yale* have used banners, posters, table tents, e-mail, and advertisements in the school's newspapers. We have also launched a website, which we also advertise on campus. Word of mouth is probably the most effective strategy for spreading the word about the week. Talk to friends and get people involved in the planning to get the campus excited and involved. To help facilitate conversation about the week, we printed t-shirts and hats for distribution on campus. It was amusing to me when I first started seeing the shirts worn by students working out at the gym. This was one of the signs that the event was gaining traction.

The Events

The events you choose should be tailored to your audience. If your audience has a lot of experience with sex education, you have more flexibility with what topics can be covered at your event. If your audience needs sex education as a base for further discussion, then sex and relationship education should be the event's focus. In the latter case, once students have a base-level education in sex and relationships, the next time the event is held, more liberty can be taken to plan events more loosely tied to that core educational necessity.

If the week you are planning is targeting a particular group of people, the events can have a bent toward that group's sexual health and interest. *Sex Week at Yale*'s target audience is Yale undergraduate students. The week could just as easily target just homosexual students, just religious students, or just men or women. For each of these groups, different speakers are appropriate; such audiences will gain more from different programming if the programming is targeted.

Sex Week at Yale has taken the approach of providing a broad-based sex and relationship education curriculum. By bringing in experienced speakers of diverse backgrounds and experience, students receive the benefit of a cross-training in sex and relationship education. And, as mentioned earlier, *Sex Week at Yale* becomes "life education" by challenging students to think critically about how other people are affected by their decisions and how those decisions impact their lives beyond just sexuality.

It is interesting to observe the different audiences that events at *Sex Week at Yale* attract. Most events result in an almost even gender distribution with an equal number of male and female attendees. Some events attract particular groups of students more than others, but even events at which you would expect particular types of students to be attracted—e.g. religious, liberal, sexually active, homosexual, sexually inactive, irreligious, ethnic, or sheltered—still draw a variety of students. For instance, at a talk about female sexuality, the crowd is usually evenly coed with an equal number of male as female students attending; however, the female portion of the crowd is usually imbalanced with a greater portion of attendees who are women's studies majors. It is also interesting to note that professors and graduate students often attend events and gain as much if not more from the discussion. Often, professors and graduate students approach speakers after events and have lengthy conversations about topics of mutual interest. Seeing professors engage speakers further justifies the legitimacy of the event.

Event Logistics

Logistically speaking, the number of events that can realistically fit into a week-long schedule needs to be considered, as does the number of events per day. Within these constraints, a balance of genres and themes needs to be achieved so that no one theme overwhelms the week. For example, there should not be too many talks about sexual technique on one day, and these should not be overrepresented in the week. Thus, ideally, no one topic—whether business, media, entertainment, sexual technique, health, intimacy, or love—should be over- or underrepresented or have too strong or too weak a presence in the week.

This holds true if planning a week of events or only a few events. Constraints still remain, and similar details must be attended to. These details include: choosing dates, booking speakers, booking rooms, marketing on campus, final preparation, execution, and follow-up.

Choosing Dates

The choice of a date to hold the event is important because the timing shapes the character of the event. *Sex Week at Yale* takes place during Valentine's Week for reasons mentioned earlier including that Valentine's Week is neither an exam week nor is it a very popular week for holding other events on campus. For presumably similar reasons, the University of North Carolina also holds their event during Valentine's Week. Their event is focused directly on sexual health and is sponsored by several campus organizations along with their Counseling and Wellness Services who co-sponsor events specifically inspired by National Sexual Responsibility Week. The University of North Carolina's Sexual Responsibility Week includes events such as those shown in Table 2.2.

Other schools have one-off events that target reducing risky behaviors prior to breaks from school. Recognizing that promiscuous behavior might take place over spring break, Rutgers University as well as Hamline University held events just prior to students leaving for their exotic vacation locales (Brookhart, 2008; Shelman, 2008). At these events, discussion of safe sexual behavior is discussed and condoms are distributed to students.

Table 2.2
Examples of Events at the University of North Carolina's Sexual Responsibility Week

---

Tuesday, 5 P.M. to 7 P.M.

- "Sex and Chocolate" night. What is condom fishing? What is sex trivia? Stop by the SRC to find out. Win prizes and enjoy free food.

Wednesday, 11 A.M. to 1 P.M.

- Pit-sitting with condomgrams and more goodies. Write a message in honor of someone you love or respect for the rest of the campus to see.

Thursday, 7 P.M. to 8 P.M., Toy Lounge in Dey Hall

- Panel Discussion and Q&A on a variety of sexual health and relationship topics, with panelists representing the LGBTQ Center, UNC Pharmacy at Campus Health Services and the UNC student body.

Vouchers for a free oral HIV test at Campus Health Services will be available (Hamby, 2007).

Whether your event is going to be designed to limit sexually risky behavior or to broaden people's understanding of what sex and relationship issues they might encounter, time of year is important to a program's design and success.

Other issues to consider when choosing a date include: How much time will it take to organize the event? What is happening on campus on or around the date of your event? When are exams? Will students be able to attend or will they be studying?

Perhaps just after the excitement of the start of school dies down is a good time to host a fun and interesting event. Just before final exams is a good time when students have free time and are not studying. If you are in the northeast, weather will influence students' activities and moods, while if you are in a warm climate, weather will likely not be a factor in choosing a date. However logistics for getting speakers to and from campus considering potential weather restraints (snow, rain, plane delays) should be of concern.

Depending on your event concept, it will take longer or shorter to plan your event. If you have to register a student group in order to host your event, a semester might go by before you can even hold your event. Use this time wisely to fill out paperwork and begin planning your event. If you are working with a student group already registered, plan at least a couple months to call speakers, organize marketing, and book rooms. If you are planning a whole week of events, an entire semester or more can be put to good use organizing speakers, transportation for speakers, booking rooms, marketing and exciting campus about the event.

One final consideration regarding when the event should take place is the time of day and the day during the week your event is. My recommendation is to plan certain times for certain types of events and then try and fit everything into the schedule you have drawn up. Things may need to be shifted, but if you have a game plan and good reasons for doing things on certain days or at certain times, you can shift events around to fit into a schedule you can live with, and/or you have a tool to work with when trying to convince people to do things the way you see them being done.

For example, events at Yale typically take place between 4 P.M. and 5 P.M. or between 7 P.M. and 8 P.M. because dinner is from 5 P.M. until 7 P.M. in the school dining halls and events typically are planned not to conflict with dinner. Sundays are difficult days to hold events because students are exhausted from the week and use Sunday to catch up on their studies. This contrasts with the middle of the week when students are very busy but eager to attend extracurricular events in between classes and other planned activities.

Booking Speakers

Booking speakers can be as easy as finding a number in the yellow pages of a local expert and calling them to book an appearance, or as difficult as contacting friends of friends to get in touch with a particular person who knows a famous speaker and can get you in touch.

Anyone who is articulate and who has something interesting and/or significant to say can be a speaker. Booking professors on campus is usually easy and is certainly great for adding value to your event. The health center and religious organizations on campus can be terrific resources, as well.

If you want to get more exotic with your speaker lineup, the internet is a great resource for finding contact information for potential speakers and doing background research to learn who the people are so you can convince them to speak. I cannot stress enough that if you go this route, it is critical to know whom you are calling/contacting and why you are contacting that person specifically. Many people can talk about sex and relationships, but, if you are targeting notable individuals, it is crucial to have a reason to be inviting them specifically.

Before you begin inviting speakers, you should have chosen a range of dates to hold your event (as mentioned above). When talking to the speaker, check if those dates are available, and if the dates are available, make sure the times you prefer are good for that person. Most speakers in my experience are straightforward and cooperative. If you have any trouble, try and convince the speaker that you are doing certain things for their benefit: be sincere, and say you are doing things a certain way to help the week run more smoothly and, in doing so, to help them look good. People will listen to you seriously and consider what you have to say if you have good reasons and are sincere in what you are saying. Also, when dealing with speakers, you will get a feeling for who you can work more flexibly with, and whom you need to work around. Businessmen, for instance, often have tight schedules and have certain times they can do things and other times they cannot. Some sex therapists, however, have a more flexible schedule. So long as everyone knows well beforehand when the event is going to take place, you can call them back later and set up specific dates and times more easily.

Booking Rooms
Once dates and times are locked in, and usually after speakers have been booked, rooms can be arranged. Booking rooms at Yale goes through the Registrar's Office. It is always good to book rooms in advance to make sure they will be available, and to do this through whatever campus organization is standard for your school.

Marketing on Campus
Marketing on campus can take many forms. These include the following:

Printed Materials
Posters, banners, table tents, and other printed materials are always good for getting the word out about events. A word of advice when using

printed materials: Know what dimensions and content are allowed and/or required printed materials on campus. At Yale, for instance, posters that are posted in shared public areas on campus have to be a certain size and can be no larger. Knowing these rules saves a lot of headache and extra hardship.

Word of Mouth

Word of mouth is always an effective marketing tool. Talk to as many people as possible and build excitement for the event. If you are excited about the event, people will feed off of your excitement!

Promotional Items

T-shirts, baseball caps, and other promotional items—all with your logo—can add flavor to the marketing of the event by doubling up as printed and word-of-mouth marketing items. T-shirts, calendars, door hangers, and other promotional items are all interesting and (most importantly) tactile. Anything you have to handle that can promote the week makes the marketing interactive and will help people remember the event more by inspiring memory through multiple senses. Funding for these items can be raised through sales or sponsorship, as discussed in the section above titled *Funding and Marketing.*

Internet and E-mail

In this technological age, websites are a great way to spread the word of your event, as is e-mail, Facebook, and YouTube. Websites offer remote access to information about the events in case posters are not handy. E-mail and texting are now a highly accessible and simple form of communication, especially for college students. Take advantage of these modes of communication.

Advertisements

If you really are interested in getting the word out widely, consider advertisements in school and/or local newspapers. Some campus publications will put your events in their calendars for free (such as the *Yale Bulletin*), which is always something worth taking advantage of. Other publications will require payment unless you can convince them to do it for no fee (such as getting a reporter to cover the event in the local school publications, like the *Yale Daily News* and *Yale Herald,* or convincing the newspaper to sponsor the advertisement themselves).

Final Preparations

Once your dates and times are set, speakers and rooms are booked, and people know about the event, it's time to take care of last-minute items. Make sure speakers know how to get to the school and have contact numbers to call if they have questions. Make sure rooms are confirmed and talk to people to make sure people are going to attend the event. Make sure computers are booked and audio/visual is applied for and set up if speakers are going to be presenting via that fashion. The devil is in the details, and details can be easy to overlook if you are not paying attention.

Execution Week of the Event

Make sure everyone is where they are supposed to be. Make sure you have water bottles for speakers so they can have a drink during the event. Make sure you are a gracious host and that both the speakers and the audience are taken care of. The execution is a part which many people remember, so make sure things go smoothly so your event is remembered in the best light.

After the Event: Follow-up

Be sure to thank speakers for attending. Additionally, if you plan on having more events, make sure there will be people available to plan the event and start the process all over again to hold another successful event.

THE FUTURE OF *SEX WEEK AT YALE*

I expect that *Sex Week at Yale*, though quite mature at such a young age, will continue to grow and evolve. I say that the event is quite mature because it has grown so much that I do not know how it can possibly be more diverse and interesting in the future than it has been in the past. With the help of myself and past directors of the event, future organizers will have to come up with new creative ways to keep the event fresh. This will be difficult given the success the event has had and the diversity and caliber of events already held.

The Week has already extended its message beyond Yale through two different editions of *Sex Week at Yale: The Magazine* as well as through the significant press coverage it has gotten (e.g. on network television), the popularity of the *Sex Week at Yale* website (www.sexweekatyale.com), and the documentary about *Sex Week*. All these prove that the messages of *Sex Week at Yale* certainly reach beyond the Ivy Gates inside which it was born.

Ideally, *Sex Week at Yale* will become a forum for educators and professionals to challenge one another as much as the week succeeds in challenging students to think critically about sex and relationships in their own lives. *Sex Week* recognizes that you cannot tell people what to believe and expect them to believe it. You have to engage people in the conversation and challenge them to explore thoughts and ideas on their own. It's through the struggle that people define their beliefs and shape their ideas.

Hopefully future directors of *Sex Week at Yale* will further the week's mission in 2010 and beyond by finding even more creative ways to spread *Sex Week*'s message. *Sex Week at Yale* 2008's assistant director will be directing the event in 2010 and already has ideas in mind for the direction and focus of the event. My hope in founding this event is that the message of *Sex Week at Yale* spreads more widely to other campuses and to the public: that students, professors, and educators alike are inspired and encouraged by the open discussion of a variety of issues related to sexuality, and that other sites plan similar programming for all to learn from, to share, and to enjoy.

APPENDIX 2.1

2002 Schedule—*Sex Week at Yale*

Sunday, February 10

9:30 P.M. Safer Sex Study Breaks
Peer Health Educators

Monday, February 11

7 P.M. The Anatomies of Sex: Theme and Variation
Professor William Summers, Professor of Biology and Women's and Gender Studies at Yale University
9:30 P.M. Secrets of Great Sex
Peer Health Educators

Tuesday, February 12

7 P.M. History and Theory of Romantic Love in European Culture
Professor Linda-Anne Rebhun, Professor of Anthropology at Yale University
8:30 P.M. Intimate Sanctity: Sexuality, Pleasure and the Idea of the Holy
Rabbi Ilan Haber, Yale Hillel campus rabbi
9:30 P.M. How to Be a Better Lover
Peer Health Educators

Wednesday, February 13

5 P.M. The History of the Vibrator
Professor Naomi Rogers, Professor of Women's and Gender Studies at Yale University
7:30 P.M. Sex: Why Wait?
Student Panel
9:30 P.M. How to Hook Up at Yale
Peer Health Educators

Thursday, February 14

5 P.M. Slifka's Sexy Dinner
7:30 P.M. Kosher Tantric Sex: Learning from the Kabbalah and Eastern Mysticism

Rabbi Shmuley Boteach, author of *Kosher Sex*
Dr. Judy Kuriansky, sex therapist and host of Z100 radio call-in advice
  show *LovePhones*

Friday, February 15

3 P.M. College Sex 101b
  Faculty Panel

Saturday, February 16

12 P.M. Sex Fest 2002 movie series
9 P.M. Live music concert

Sunday, February 17

3 P.M. Selling Sex: Where Do You Draw the Line?
  Dr. Susan Block '77, sex therapist and HBO personality
  Al Goldstein, founder of *Screw Magazine*
  Nancy Slotnick, relationship coach, founder of www.cablight.com, and
    founder of Drip Café in New York City
Moderated by Joey Reynolds, radio personality

APPENDIX 2.2

2004 Schedule: *Sex Week at Yale*

Monday, February 9

8 P.M. Sex Toys 101
  Rebecca and Claire from Toys in Babeland
  Berkeley Bagel Bar

Tuesday, February 10

4 P.M. *One Woman's Illustrated Sexual Revolution*
Women's Center
  Betty Dodson, sexologist and author

Wednesday, February 11

3:30 P.M. Sex in the Age of Terrorism: How to create peace without and
  peace within
  Berkeley Masters Tea
  Dr. Judy Kuriansky, sex therapist and host of Z100 radio call-in advice
    show *LovePhones*
7 P.M. Dessert and book signing with Rabbi Shmuley Boteach, Slifka Center
7:30 P.M. Sexuality vs Sensuality: How the Male Libido has Extinguished
  Female Eroticism in the Modern Age
  Rabbi Shmuley Boteach, author of "Kosher Sex"
Slifka Center

Thursday, February 12

4 P.M. Sex, Entertainment, and the Media
  Joe Francis, founder of Girls Gone Wild!
  Devinn Lane, Wicked Pictures contract girl
  Dr. Suzan Block '77, sex therapist and HBO personality
Moderated by Joey Reynolds, radio personality
LC102
5 P.M. Red and White themed dinner, Slifka Center
8 P.M. Girl Talk: Mr Right vs. Mr Right Now
  Nancy Slotnick, relationship coach, founder of www.cablight.com, and
    founder of the Drip Café in New York City
LC102
KKG girls only
Night: *Porn Party!* sponsored by Wicked Pictures at Sig Ep

Friday, February 13

4 P.M. History of the Vibrator
  Naomi Rogers, Professor of Women's and Gender Studies at Yale Uni-
    versity
Women's Center
12:30 P.M. *Private Lunch with Devinn Lane,* Wicked Pictures contract girl

Saturday, February 14

4 P.M. Sex at Yale: Theory and Practice
Saybrook Master's Tea
  Dr. Susan Block '77, sex therapist and HBO personality
Night: Got a Valentine? Party
Image Night Club

APPENDIX 2.3

2006 Schedule: *Sex Week at Yale*

Monday, February 13

4 P.M. The Art of Mackin': Develoing Some Semblance of Game at Yale
  Tariq Nasheed, dating specialist and guest of Conan O'Brien and Jay Leno
    LC102

Tuesday, February 14

4 P.M. Sex and Love in the Age of the Booty Call: Can Girls View Sex the
  Way Guys Do?
  Ian Kerner, Ph.D., sex therapist and New York Times best-selling author
8 P.M. Homosexuality and Religion: Why Homosexuality Is Viewed as a
  Threat to Christianity

Professor Ludger Viefhues, former Catholic Priest and professor of religion and women's and gender studies at Yale University

Wednesday February 15

4 P.M. Everything You've Been Too Embarrassed to Ask about Sex
Patty Brisben, CEO of Pure Romance, Inc.
9–11 P.M. Pure Romance Party at Alchemy Lounge
Girls' night out

Thursday, February 16

4 P.M. Dating 101: How to Get the Girl/Guy You've Always Been After
Ron Louis and David Copeland, dating experts and authors of *How to Succeed with Women*
8 P.M. Ten Commandments of Pleasure: Sex in Relationships
Dr. Susan Block '77, sex therapist and HBO personality
9–11 P.M. Dating Workshop

Friday, February 17

4 P.M. The College Striptease
Miyoko, former Playboy TV host
8 P.M. Brynne Lieb Lingerie Show
11 P.M.–1 A.M. Lingerie show after party

Saturday, February 18

4 P.M. The Real Porn in the Morn: A Panel
Panel with *Pirates* star *Jesse Jane;* director *Joone;* Samantha Lewis, president of Digital Playground; and First Amendment attorney *Gregory A Piccionelli, Esq.*
8 P.M. For the Love of the Boy
Frank Terry's irreverent musical comedy
10:30 P.M.-1 A.M. Jesse Jane Party at Toads

APPENDIX 2.4

2008 Schedule: *Sex Week at Yale*

Sunday, February 10

8 P.M. Life, Love, Sex, Death, and Other Works in Progress…A Multi-Chakra Extravaganza
Stevie Jay, an entertainer known for his "cosmic variety show" *Life, Love, Sex, Death & Other Works in Progress*
SSS 114

Monday, February 11
Relationships
4:30 P.M. Myths and Misconceptions about Sex and Relationships

Pepper Schwartz '74, Ph.D., Professor of Sociology at University of Washington in Seattle, Washington

LC 101

7:30 P.M. Sexually Speaking

Dr. Ruth Westheimer, sex therapist and radio and television personality

Slifka Center

Tuesday, February 12

What a Girl Wants

4 P.M. The Female Orgasm

Logan Levkoff, sex therapist

LC 102

7:30 P.M. Everything You've Always Wanted to Know about Sex (and sex toys!)

Patty Brisben, founder and CEO, Pure Romance, Inc.

Davies Auditorium

9–11 P.M. Girls' Night Out, with Patty Brisben!

Center St. Lounge

Wednesday, February 13

Seduction

4:30 P.M. Seduction: How to Get the Girl You've Always Wanted

Matador, from VH1's *The Pick-Up Artist*

LC 102

7:30 P.M. The Mystery Method: Ladies Want Him, Guys Want to Be Him

Mystery, from VH1's The Pick-Up Artist

SSS 114

Thursday, February 14

Love

4:30 P.M. Mating Intelligence: Sex, Relationships, and the Mind's Reproductive System

Glenn Geher, professor at SUNY and Director of SUNY New Paltz's Evolutionary Studies Program

Scott Barry Kaufman, author of The Role of Creativity and Humor in Mate Selection

LC 101

7:30 P.M. The Chemistry and Communication of Love: What Makes That Special Someone So Special

Dr. Helen Fisher, Research Professor of Human Evolutionary Studies and Anthropology at Rutgers University

Logan Levkoff, sexologist, relationship expert, TV personality and advice columnist

LC 102

Friday, February 15

The *Sex Week at Yale* Fashion & Lingerie Show: AIDS Awareness Benefit, $5
Suggested Donation

All proceeds will be donated to various AIDS research and awareness organizations

Cocktail hour, 6 P.M.

Show starts 7 P.M.

LoRicco Ballroom

216 Crown St

8:30 P.M. The Great Porn Debate

Moderated and televised by *Nightline* (ABC), with host Martin Bashir

   Ron Jeremy, adult-entertainment star

   Monique Alexander, Vivid Entertainment contract girl

   Craig Gross, Pastor of xxxchurch.com

   Donnie Pauling, former producer of pornography

LoRicco Ballroom

216 Crown St.

Saturday, February 16

Vivid Day

4:30 P.M. The Business of Pornography: How Vivid Made It Mainstream

   Steven Hirsch, cofounder and cochairman of Vivid Entertainment

WLH 119

7:30 P.M. Panel discussion and Q&A with Vivid's adult superstars

   Vivid Girls *Monique Alexander* & *Savanna Samson*, with acclaimed director *Paul Thomas*

Law School Auditorium

10:30 P.M. Skull & Boned Party @ The TOAD

Toad's Place

Sunday, February 17

Sex and Spirituality

4 P.M. Sex & God: Saybrook Master's Tea

   Dr. Susan Block '77, sex therapist and HBO personality

Saybrook Master's House

6 P.M. Sex and Spirituality: A Panel Discussion

   Dawn Eden, social and religious commentator and author

   Dr. Judy Kuriansky, sex therapist and host of Z100 radio call-in advice show *LovePhones*

   Dr. Susan Block '77, sex therapist and HBO personality

   Stevie Jay, an entertainer known for his "cosmic variety show" *Life, Love, Sex, Death & Other Works in Progress*

WLH 119

Monday, February 18

Safe Sex

4 P.M. Eroticizing Safe Sex: Make It Fun!
Peer Health Educators
LC 101
7:30 P.M. Evolve: America's Sexual Health Problem and What Trojan's Doing about It
David Johnson, Group Product Manager, Trojan Condoms
WLH 119
9:30 P.M. An open forum with *Sex Week* Director *Joe Citarrella* and team
Sex Week is a controversial event. Come share your thoughts with us.
WLH119

NOTE

1. Yale's Peer Health Educators are a group of undergraduate students trained to provide information on substance abuse, HIV/AIDS, risk reduction, and safer sex practices, covering such topics as abstinence, contraception, sexually transmitted diseases, and sexual assault. Their greatest accomplishment is the annual *Connections Workshop,* held during orientation for all incoming freshmen; however, programs and presentations are available for special student groups, cultural centers, fraternities, sororities, and any other interested parties within the Yale and New Haven communities. Source: http://www.yale.edu/uhs/med_services/student_health.html

REFERENCES

ABC News. Retrieved June 4, 2008, from http://abcnews.go.com/nightline/faceoff/altindex

Agapakis, M. (2006, February 13). Yale University magazine to debut at Dartmouth. *The Dartmouth.* Hanover, NH.

Bit, K. (2004, January 16). Yale students find related seminars arousing. *Yale Herald.* New Haven, CT.

Boteach, S. (1999). *Kosher sex.* New York: Broadway Books.

Brookhart, H. (2008, March 12). Students 'leied' for safer sex. *Daily Targum.* Retrieved June 4, 2008, from http://media.www.dailytargum.com/media/storage/paper168/news/2008/03/12/University/Students.leied.For.Safer.Sex-3264085.shtml

Del Mar Galindo, M. (2004, February 13). Innately intimate? Sure, sex is an act, but should it be more? Has *Sex Week* forgotten the fundamentals?. *Yale Daily News.* New Haven, CT.

Eden, D. (2008, February 21). If *lux* could thrill: Giving *Sex Week* a chaste kiss-off. Retrieved June 4, 2008, from http://www.dawneden.com/2008/02/if-lux-could-thrill-giving-sex-week.html

Eden, D. (2008, February 19). *Lux* be a lady: Championing chastity at "Sex Week." Retrieved June 4, 2008, from http://www.dawneden.com/2008/02/lux-be-lady-championing-chastity-at-sex.html

Fisher, H. (2004). *Why we love: The nature and chemistry of romantic love.* New York: Henry Holt.

Gibbons, D. (2007, June). It's wonderful to be Dr. Ruth. *Thrive, 1,* no. 25. Retrieved June 4, 2008, from http://www.nyc-plus.com/nyc25/itswonderfultobe.html

Glaberson, W. (1997, September 7). Five Orthodox Jews spur moral debate over housing rules at Yale. *New York Times.*

Godbeer, R. (2002). *Sexual revolution in early America.* Baltimore: Johns Hopkins University Press.

Haffner, D. W. (1995). Facing facts: Sexual health for America's adolescents. New York: Sexuality Information and Education Council of the United States.

Hamby, T. (2007, February 12). Week targets sexual health. *Daily Tar Heel.* Durham, NC. http://media.www.dailytarheel.com/media/storage/paper885/news/2007/02/12/University/Week-Targets.Sexual.Health-2711413.shtml

Hoff, T., and Greene, L. (2000). *Sex education in America: A view from inside the nation's classrooms.* Menlo Park, CA: Kaiser Family Foundation. Available online at http://www.kff.org/

Hoff, T., Greene, L., & Davis, J. (2003) *National survey of adolescents and young adults: Sexual health knowledge, attitudes, and experiences.* Menlo Park, CA: Kaiser Family Foundation. Available online at httl://kff.org/

Intercollegiate Studies Institute. (2004). Retrieved June 4, 2008, from http://www.isi.org/cn/pollys/04/pollyyale.aspx

Intercollegiate Studies Institute. (2004). Retrieved June 4, 2008, from the World Wide Web: http://www.isi.org/cn/pollys/polly04.aspx

Iozzia, B. (1998). Sexual Healing. Retrieved June 4, 2008, from http://www.umdnj.edu/umcweb/marketing_and_communications/publications/umdnj_magazine/hstate/win98/endpage.html

Isaacs, C. (2007, October 4). UM gets an "F" on sex ed report card for sexual awareness program. *The Miami Hurricane.* Miami, FL.

Katsuyama, N. (2004, April 5). Sex week "wins" outrage award. *Yale Daily News.* New Haven, CT.

Katz, M. (2004, February 12). Dr. Judy talks sex in times of terror. *Yale Daily News.* New Haven, CT.

Kellogg, M. (2002, February 12). *Sex Week* to stimulate Yalies: Campus groups sponsor a week of discussion on love, intimacy, and sex. *Yale Daily News.* New Haven, CT.

Kuriansky, J. (1996). *Generation sex: America's hottest sex therapist answers the hottest questions about sex.* New York: Harper Paperbacks.

Kuriansky, J (2002). *The complete idiot's guide to dating.* (3rd edition) New York: Penguin Group (USA).

Kuriansky, J. (2004). *The complete idiot's guide to tantric sex.* (2nd edition) New York: Penguin Group (USA).

Kuriansky, J. (2004, February 16). *Sex Week at Yale* and love at the Week. *New York Daily News.*

Larson, T. (2004, February 16). *Sex Week at Yale* lacks balancing viewpoints. *Yale Daily News.* New Haven, CT.

Lee, J. (2008, February 22). Yale grants self one week of fun. *Harvard Crimson.* Cambridge, MA.

Macbeth, C. (2006, September 26). Univ. earns clean bill of sexual health. *Yale Daily News.* New Haven, CT.

Maggie. (2006, October 20). Yale: the #1 sex school? Retrieved June 4, 2008, from http://broadrecognition.blogspot.com/2006/10/yale-1-sex-school.html

McKeon, B. (2006). Effective sex education. Retrieved June 4, 2008, from http://www.advocatesforyouth.org/publications/factsheet/fssexcur.pdf

Miller, M. (2004, April 2). *Sex Week* wins dubious distinction. *Yale Herald.* New Haven, CT.

Mystery. (2007). *The Mystery Method: How to get beautiful women into bed.* New York: St. Martin's Press.

National Center for Education Statistics (1999). *Community service.* Institute of Education Sciences, U.S. Dept. of Education, Washington, DC. Retrieved June 4, 2008, from http://nces.ed.gov/quicktables/result.asp?SrchKeyword=community+service&Topic=All

Northwestern University College Feminists. Retrieved June 4, 2008, from http://groups.northwestern.edu/feminists/events.htm

Northwestern University College Feminists. Retrieved June 4, 2008, from http://groups.northwestern.edu/sexweek/

Randall, T. (2008, February 15). Porn stars, Dr. Ruth, "freaked" parents: It's *Sex Week at Yale.* Bloomberg News. Retrieved June 4, 2008, from http://www.bloomberg.com/apps/news?pid=20601109&refer=home&sid=aNB5lQm.eKlE

Rosenbaum, R. (2003, January/February). *Sex Week at Yale*: In which academics ponder "webcam girls," hermaphrodites, demonic-male chimps, the history of the vibrator, and "sex with four professors." *Atlantic Monthly.* Retrieved June 4, 2008, from http://www.theatlantic.com/issues/2003/01/rosenbaum.htm

Rosow, K., & Persell, C. H. (1980, Fall). Sex education from 1900 to 1920: A study of ideological social control. *Qualitative Sociology, 3,* no. 3, 186–203.

Rovzar, C. (2004, August). *Hustler.* Retrieved June 4, 2008, from http://www.sexweekatyale.com/files/Condensed%20Media%20Coverage%20Packet.pdf

Seaver, N. (2004, February 19). *Sex Week* fulfilled purpose. *Yale Daily News.* New Haven, CT.

Shelman, J. (2008, March 16). Putting the brakes on spring break recklessness: A rash of alcohol-related deaths leads Hamline University to offer quick lessons in responsibility. *Star Tribune.* Minneapolis-St. Paul, MN.

Sperling's Best Places. Sexual health on college campuses: The Trojan® Sexual Health Report Card. Retrieved June 4, 2008, from http://www.bestplaces.net/docs/studies/SexualHealth.aspx

Stein, J. (2001, April 29). The chicken was delicious. *Time Magazine.* Retrieved June 4, 2008, from http://www.time.com/time/magazine/article/0,9171,999838,00.html

Strong, B. (1972, Summer). Ideas of the early sex education movement in America, 1890 1920. *History of Education Quarterly, 12,* no. 2, 129–161.

Students for a Sexually Aware Campus. Retrieved June 4, 2008, from http://www.sexweekatyale.com/2008_release.pdf

Trojan Brand Condoms. (2007, September 10). Trojan Brand Condoms ranks U.S. colleges and universities in second annual Sexual Health Report Card. Retrieved June 4, 2008, from http://www.trojancondoms.com/assets/pdfs/2007_SHRC.pdf

Von Hoffmann, K. (2004, March 26). Life after Yale: Can college couples survive? *Yale Herald.* New Haven, CT.

Weaver, H., Smith, G., & Kippax, S. (2005, May). School-based sex education policies and indicators of sexual health among young people: a comparison of the Netherlands, France, Australia and the United States. *Sex Education, 5,* no. 2, 171–188.

Westheimer, R., & Lopater, S. (2002) *Human sexuality: A psychosocial perspective.* Baltimore: Lippincott Williams & Wilkins.

Yale Health Plan. Retrieved June 4, 2008, from http://www.yale.edu/uhs/med_services/student_health.html

Part II

MULTI-MEDIA AND SEXUALITY EDUCATION

Chapter Three

BLAME OR ACCLAIM? THE ROLE OF THE MEDIA AS TEEN SEXUALITY EDUCATORS

Jane D. Brown and Sarah N. Keller

Adolescents in the United States today have unprecedented access to an array of media, including television, movies, music, magazines, and the Internet. Most spend much more time with the media then they spend with their parents or in school. Much of the content they attend to includes messages and images about sexual attraction, romantic relationships, and sexual behavior. Very little of this content includes any information about sexuality or health (Hust, Brown, & L'Engle, 2008).

Other potential agents of sexual socialization in the culture, including parents, schools, and religions, are remarkably reticent or punitive about teens' sexual behavior. In this context, the media are important sources of sexual information and norms for their attentive teen audiences. A growing body of social scientific research documents the role the media play in the sexual socialization of adolescents, as well as points to strategies for enhancing the positive effects of the media on adolescents' sexuality.

DO THE MEDIA "CAUSE" TEENS TO HAVE SEX?

Parents, educators, and scholars have long been concerned about the possible effects of the media on teens' sexual behavior. Interest increased in the 1990s during the "culture wars" and as the proliferation of media and competition for audiences increased the frequency and explicitness of sexual portrayals. In the late 1990s, with encouragement from Congress, the National Institutes of Health issued a call for proposals to investigate the effects of the media on adolescents' sexual behavior. A number of large-scale longitudinal studies were funded, and some of the initial findings are now available. These studies built on a growing body of previous smaller scale content analyses, cross-sectional surveys, and a few experiments that suggested that the media do affect teens' sexual attitudes and behaviors (for comprehensive reviews, see Escobar-Chaves, Tortolero, Markham, & Low, 2004; Huston, Wartella, & Donnerstein, 1998; Strasburger, 2005; Ward, 2002).

One NIH-funded longitudinal study of a nationally representative sample of 12- to 17-year-olds, conducted by Collins, Elliott, Berry, Kanouse, Kunkel, and Hunter (2004), concluded, after controlling for a number of other factors, that early exposure to sexual content on television "hastens" initiation of sexual intercourse on average by about six months. In further analyses of the same data set, Martino et al. (2006) found that adolescents who listened to music considered to contain more "degrading" sexual content were more likely to initiate intercourse and to progress to more advanced levels of noncoital sexual activity two years later than those teens who were listening more to music with nondegrading sexual content, suggesting that the kind of music a teen is listening to also matters.

Brown, L'Engle, Pardun, Guo, Kenneavy, and Jackson (2006) undertook a longitudinal study in North Carolina called the Teen Media study, which found that early adolescents, ages 14–15, who had heavier sexual media diets across four media (music, movies, television, and magazines) were twice as likely as those with lighter sexual media diets to have initiated sexual intercourse by the time they were 16 years old. The relationship was stronger for white than black adolescents after controlling for other factors that could affect either exposure to the media or sexual behavior, including closeness to parents and perceptions of peers' sexual behavior.

Both of these studies were innovative in that they linked individual teens' actual media exposure with their sexual behavior over time. We will learn more as the findings of the other large studies become available. Although these studies have helped establish that there is something going on, there is more to know about how this process works, for whom, and under what circumstances.

Theoretical Challenges: Who, When, and How?

It is increasingly clear that the media-sexual behavior link is a complicated process in which selection, attention, interpretation, and sometimes even resistance to media content, as well as other contexts, are important factors. Social-demographic identities, such as gender and race or ethnicity, personality characteristics, and other socialization contexts affect which media are selected, which content is paid attention, to and to what extent content is incorporated into a teen's everyday life and sense of sexual self (Steele & Brown, 1995). Media use and effects do not occur in isolation and are affected by the teen's family configuration and interactions (e.g., do older siblings choose what's on? does the family have rules about content exposure and time spent with the media?), as well as peers (e.g., do friends use and discuss the same media?). Further study of these and other potential mediators and moderators of the relationship between media exposure and teen sexual behavior would be helpful both in furthering our theoretical understanding of the process of media effects and in guiding the design of media interventions for sexual health.

Gender, Racial and Ethnic, and Other Social Identities

One of the core developmental tasks of adolescence is the development of a sense of self in relation to others and the culture. Gender and race or ethnicity are two key components of identity that affect both which media content is chosen and how it is interpreted. The digital revolution has resulted in an amazing array of channels of television, movies, and music that are available on computers and portable devices that allow for increasing selectivity in media choices. Even before the digital revolution, it was as if boys and girls live in different media worlds, as girls tend to choose more relationship-oriented content and boys choose sports and action-adventure (Hust & Brown, 2008). Boys, for example, are much more likely to attend to pornography on the Internet than girls (Malamuth, 1996; Peter & Valkenburg, 2006). This matters because boys and girls may be getting very different views of sexuality in the content they choose.

Race and ethnicity also affect media selection and use. In the Teen Media study, Brown and Pardun (2006) found that blacks and whites and male and female adolescents had only 4 of a list of 150 current television shows in common. The majority of black teens, both boys and girls, regularly watched shows that featured black casts, whereas white girls and boys rarely watched shows with black casts and tended to choose gender-stereotypical fare. In 2002, for example, the TV show with the largest number of teen girl viewers was *American Idol*—a show that chose a new singing star from amateur contenders. Teen boys, meanwhile, were watching *World Wrestling Entertainment* and National Football League (NFL) games (*Teen Media Monitor*, 2003).

Although Collins et al. (2004) found similar patterns for blacks and whites, Brown et al. (2006) found that for black teens the strength of the link between media exposure at 12 to 14 and sexual behavior two years later disappeared when perceptions of parental expectations and peers' sexual behavior were taken into account. They speculated that the effect of the media may occur earlier for black children both because blacks on average reach sexual maturity earlier than whites and because the media blacks attend to is more sexual than the media white teens typically use. Given the currently high rates of teen pregnancy among Hispanic youth, it is vitally important to learn more about the media as a sexual socialization agent in their lives, as well.

Involvement/Attention/Interpretation

It has long been assumed that the media have more of an effect on users who are more involved or identify with media characters. This is a basic prediction of Social Cognitive Theory (Bandura, 1986). Some have speculated that the media may serve as a source of "sexual super peers"—sexually active characters with which adolescents may identify and seek to emulate (Brown, Halpern, & L'Engle, 2005). But assessing involvement and identification are difficult, especially in survey designs across multiple media. We know even less about how depictions of sexuality are understood by adolescents from different backgrounds, at different developmental stages, or with different sexual experience.

In one attempt to try to put some of these pieces together, L'Engle, Brown, and Kenneavy (2006) conducted cluster analysis with the Teen Media sample of 1,017 adolescents (14 to 16 years old). Four distinct clusters of sexual self-concepts were identified. The *Virgin Valedictorians* (16% of the sample) were less interested in sex and instead focused on school and their families. They watched less television, were the most likely to see media depictions of sex as unrealistic, and were the least likely to want to be like media characters. *Curious Conservatives* (29%) were interested in sex and had a cautious and informed approach to sexual relationships. They loved music and magazines and liked to talk with their friends about what they were listening to and reading. More than half (53% in 2002) were watching reality dating shows on television. These teens were most likely to identify with the teens they saw on television and in teen magazines such as *Seventeen* and *Teen People*.

Silent Susceptibles (26%) wanted increased sexual activity and seemed likely to seize the opportunity for sexual intercourse with little consideration of the consequences. More than half intended to have sexual intercourse in the next year, although very few had discussed AIDS and STDs with romantic partners. These teens were video- and computer game players and relatively frequent viewers of explicit sexual material (more than one fourth had watched X-rated movies). *Sexual Sophisticates* (29%) were relatively well informed about sex, confident about sexual relationships, and the most likely to have had sexual intercourse (more than half [53%] had had sex before age 15). These teens were frequent media users and attended to more adult and sexually laden content. More than one-fourth (27%) reported going to Internet porn sites; 45% had watched X-rated movies. This group had the strongest desire to be like people they saw in the media and thought the teens presented in the media were realistic.

These four profiles suggest very different patterns of media use and sexual behavior and introduce a range of factors that may modify the relationship between teen's media use and sexual behavior. Further study should focus on those factors that may increase or decrease the possibility of negative effects of the media on adolescents' sexual behavior. Sexual health educators might use these clusters to segment audiences and tailor media messages to speak exclusively to each segment.

The Difficulty of Establishing Causality

If we think about a teen's sexual development from an ecological perspective, it is clear that the media is only one of a number of possible contexts in which a teen will learn about norms and expectations for sexual behavior. Most teens are learning about sex in a mixture of ways. Some teens are able to talk with their parents about sex, some are getting sexuality education at school, some rely on their friends, and some adhere to religious principles. In fact, the media are a rather distant context in relation to parents, friends, and schools for most young people. It may be most appropriate, however, to think of the media as permeating all these other contexts. Teens' interactions with their friends and parents and schools both influence and are influenced by the media. Given that these other contexts are also influenced by mass-media depictions of sexual behavior and affect attention to and interpretation of media content, it is very difficult, if not impossible, to assess the unique influence of the media with traditional survey research designs.

The selectivity and complexity of typical media use have led some methodologists to argue that the standard longitudinal survey research design is inappropriate for establishing the media as the cause of unhealthy behaviors, even though it is the prototype for epidemiological research. In media research, there is rarely a true "control" group that has not been exposed to some media content, and it is impossible to control for all other possible factors that might influence either media selection or the health behavior or both. Given these inherent problems, it may be most fruitful, both theoretically and practically, to put more energy into conducting interventions that focus on factors that may decrease the potentially negative effects of the media on youth. These interventions should take a solution-oriented rather than a problem-oriented approach, manipulating exposure to media that focus on positive outcomes and reduced risk rather than current media fare that probably contributes to unhealthy sexual behavior (Robinson & Sirard, 2005).

INTENTIONAL USE OF THE MEDIA FOR SEXUALITY EDUCATION

The media have been used effectively to promote sexual and reproductive health in other countries for decades (Singhal & Rogers, 1999). The media may be especially useful for teaching young people about sexual and reproductive health practices—for precisely the same reasons they are influential in promoting sexually risky behaviors. Teens may find the media a less embarrassing way to learn about sexuality than talking with a parent or other adult, and messages can be presented in the media teens use frequently by media characters they admire and wish to emulate. A few media-based campaigns in the United States do suggest that the media could be used in the promotion of sexual health and pregnancy prevention. Five kinds of media-based strategies for sexuality education are worth pursuing: sexual health media campaigns, entertainment-education, media literacy education, media advocacy, and new media.

Sexual Health Media Campaigns

Traditional mass-media campaigns typically employ a range of media to distribute health messages, typically with a combination of informational and emotional appeals. One of the most impressive trials of a safer sex televised public service announcement (PSA) campaign occurred recently in Lexington, Kentucky, with Knoxville, Tennessee, as a control city. The Two-City Safer Sex campaign used 10 television PSAs, developed through intensive formative research (40 sets of focus groups), to increase safer sexual behavior among high-sensation-seeking and impulsive-decision-making at-risk young adults. The TV ads were released on paid and public airtime (with a 1:1 match of donated to paid airtime negotiated with the stations) during shows known to be popular with the target audience, determined by baseline surveys. Independent, monthly random samples of 100 individuals were surveyed in each city for 21 months as part of an interrupted time series design. Eighty five to 96% of the audience reported seeing one or more PSAs during the 21-month campaign, varying over the month audience members were surveyed. Analyses indicated a significant 5-month increase in condom use, condom-use self-efficacy, and behavioral intentions among the target group in the campaign city, whereas there were no changes in the comparison city. Overall effects were estimated to be a 13% increase in safer sex acts (Zimmerman et al., 2007).

Another promising effort came from a coalition of MTV and the Kaiser Family Foundation (KFF) called "It's Your Sexlife.org." In 2002, MTV and KFF sponsored a year-long campaign focused on HIV/AIDS, other sexually transmitted diseases (STDs), and unintended pregnancy. The campaign included special programming, public service messages, and a comprehensive sexual health Web site for youth. A survey in 2003 of MTV viewers (16–24 years old) found that of those who had seen the campaign, three-fourths were more likely to take a relationship seriously and were more likely to use a condom if having sex. Two-thirds said they were more likely to talk to a boyfriend or girlfriend about safer sex and were more likely to wait to have sex (Kaiser Family Foundation, 2003). The campaign continued as "Think MTV," with special programming on MTV, public service messages, and a comprehensive sexual health Web site for youth (see www.think.mtv.com).

Also encouraging was a campaign, "Talk to your kids about sex: Everyone else is," conducted in 20 counties in North Carolina (using radio, TV and billboard ads). The campaign was designed to promote parent-child communication and researchers found a positive association between campaign exposure and parents' self-reported frequency of talking to children about STDs, teen pregnancy, and contraception (DuRant, Wolfson, & Lafrance, 2006). Paid TV PSAs were aired in 22 of these counties, radio PSAs were aired in 21 counties, and billboards were displayed in 6 counties over a period of 9 months. The counties experienced anything from no exposure to exposure to all three types of media. To assess the impact of the campaign, a sample of 1,132 parents of adolescents was administered a postexposure telephone survey. Exposure to each component of this mass-media campaign was associated with parents recently having talked to their adolescent children about sex and parents' intention to talk to their children during the next month.

Entertainment-Education

The entertainment education (E-E) strategy involves incorporating an educational message into existing popular entertainment content to raise awareness, increase knowledge, create favorable attitudes, and, ultimately, motivate people to take socially responsible action in their own lives. Despite the introduction of new media technologies, such as the Internet, television remains the primary medium for entertainment education in the United States. Over the years, the E-E strategy has been applied in a variety of ways and has raised a number of social and health issues in entertainment programming, including substance abuse, immunization, teenage pregnancy, HIV/AIDS, cancer, and other diseases.

Embedding sexual health messages in entertainment programming has been found to be especially effective at persuading audiences to seek and use contraceptives, to limit the size of their families, and to postpone sexual behavior in a number of countries around the world (Singhal & Rogers, 1999). The advantage of entertainment-education over traditional media campaigns is that the complexity that surrounds sexual issues (relationships, values, love, parents, regret) can be explored in entertainment media in much more depth, with more nuance and with less preachiness than are found in the typical public service announcement. In the United States, the technique also has been effective, but more limited, given the difficulty of working with a highly commercialized media free from government control.

Two groups (the Kaiser Family Foundation in partnership with Advocates for Youth and the National Campaign to Prevent Teen and Unplanned Pregnancy) have been most effective in working with the U.S. entertainment media to get responsible sexual health messages in media content that adolescents or their parents see. Since the 1990s, the National Campaign to Prevent Teen and Unplanned Pregnancy has generated pregnancy prevention-related programming that has reached more than 300 million teens and parents on all six TV networks and top cable outlets, in national magazines and on leading Web sites. The Campaign encouraged media producers to explore the motivations behind adolescents' decisions to either wait to have sex or to use protection if they do have sex and to get teens to engage in conversation about their own decision making. Entertainment media already tailored to different teen audience segments (e.g., younger girls, urban teens) were used to approach these issues in ways that are most relevant to the targeted teen audience segment.

The Campaign also developed innovative ways of increasing the teen audience's involvement with the material. After one episode of a show and a public service announcement that promoted the Campaign's Web site, viewers were encouraged to answer questions that challenged them to relate what happened in the show to their own lives. The Campaign then shared the responses with other teens and with network executives so that they could see the kind of response a show about teen sex, relationships, and pregnancy engendered in their audience. The Campaign learned that regular viewers care a lot about what their favorite characters do, and when these "super-peers" begin dealing with sex and pregnancy, viewers react and talk about it.

Rigorous evaluation of the effectiveness of such efforts has been sparse but promising. One evaluation found that exposure to a 3-minute discussion on the television program *ER* increased viewers' awareness of emergency contraception by 17 percentage points, and a 1-minute discussion of HPV (human papillomavirus) increased viewers' awareness by 23 percentage points. The show also stimulated viewers to talk with friends and family about the topics (Brodie et al., 2001). A study of adolescent viewers of a *Friends* episode in which a pregnancy resulted from condom failure found that up to two-thirds learned that condoms can fail, and another third learned about condom's efficacy in preventing pregnancy (Collins, Elliott, Berry, Kanouse, Kunkel, & Hunter, 2003). The *Friends* study also illustrates a potential problem in working with the media to promote healthy behavior. Sometimes, in the interest of drama, the healthy message may not be as clear as desired.

Several efforts have combined traditional mass-media campaigns with embedded storylines in existing programming. U.S. media giant Viacom and the San Francisco-based Kaiser Family Foundation launched one of the most ambitious HIV/AIDS media campaigns ever conducted in this country, in which they use the tools honed by Madison Avenue and Hollywood to fight the epidemic. The "KNOW HIV/AIDS Campaign" produced public service announcements and print and outdoor advertising worth $120 million. Viacom issued a directive to the producers of its television shows to include storylines in their popular dramas and comedies that would raise AIDS awareness and encourage prevention, testing, and counseling. An in-house report showed that one component of the campaign, called "Rap It Up," on BET and other networks that target African Americans, influenced self-reported awareness and intentions to practice safe sex among the 18–24-year-old target audience (Kaiser Family Foundation, 2004).

Research has shown that such efforts are more successful if the messages are simple, are presented by characters and on shows that young people like, and are frequent and sustained over time (Keller & Brown, 2002).

Media Literacy Education

Another promising strategy for media-related sexuality education is media literacy. Media literacy education typically focuses on increasing awareness of how media content is produced and packaged. Media literacy is a relatively new approach to helping young people make good decisions about their health. The assumption is that such education can help adolescents become more critical of what they see and hear and become less likely to engage in the unhealthy behavior promoted in the media. Although media literacy education has been practiced in other countries, such as Canada, Great Britain, and Australia, for three decades or more, it is just now gaining a foothold in the United States. The movement has spawned two national organizations that advance media education training, networking, and information exchange through professional conferences and media list-serves: National Association for Media Literacy Education (NAMLE) and Action Coalition for Media Education (ACME).

A few studies have established that media literacy training increases critical thinking about the media and affects attitudes about health issues (e.g., alcohol and tobacco use, body image, and violence) (Austin & Johnson, 1997; Moore, DeChillo, Nicholson, Genovese, & Sladen, 2000; Piran, Levine, & Irving, 2000; Robinson, Wilde, Navracruz, Haydel, & Varady, 2001). It is not clear at this point, however, how much media education is necessary, when it should start, how long it should last, or what components are most important. One recent study, however, has shown that even one media literacy training session can increase early adolescents' skepticism toward advertising and that taking an emotional rather than a fact-based approach may be most effective with middle-schoolers (Austin, Chen, Pinkleton, & Johnson, 2006). Another study found that the greater the knowledge about the persuasion techniques used in cigarette advertising, the less likely teens were to smoke cigarettes

(Primack, Gold, Land, & Fine, 2006). Media literacy interventions focused on the norms of sexual behavior presented in the media may be helpful in reducing the impact of the media's portrayals on adolescents.

Media Advocacy

Even if, or perhaps especially because, resources for media interventions are limited, media advocacy—the use of news media to keep a social issue on the policy and public agenda—should be used to maximize campaign effectiveness beyond paid media. Gaining and keeping sexual health issues on the media's agenda can be an important tool. Press coverage is often called "uncontrolled publicity" by public relations professionals, since news reports about an organization or its issues have the advantage of being free, reaching a large audience, and enjoying third-party credibility; at the same time, it is less controllable. News coverage of health issues can be an important factor in setting the agenda for policy change and can influence individual decisions, as well as community-wide decisions, (Laugesen & Meads, 1991; Pierce & Gilpin, 2001; Wallack, 1994). One study of the impact of news coverage of tobacco risks found that such coverage increased adolescents' perception of smoking risks and lowered recent smoking behavior (Smith et al., 2008). Media advocacy may be best targeted toward generating events and highlighting issues likely to increase and sustain news attention. News pegs created in partnership with local TV or radio stations can also be used to highlight embedded messages in entertainment programming or other paid media efforts.

New Media

New media technologies are expanding perhaps more rapidly than public health advocates can figure out how to use them. Newer media technologies include text messaging on cell phones, blogs or chat rooms on Web sites, information received via iPods, and social networking sites like Facebook or MySpace on the Internet, where many users can simultaneously create and communicate on the same Web pages. It is clear that young audiences are frequent users and often seek sexual health information on Web sites and even on cell phones. In one study, two in five young people (41%) reported that they had changed their behavior because of health information they found online, and almost half (49%) had contacted a health care provider as a result (Ybarra & Suman, 2006). The Internet is also, unfortunately, a source of sexual risk. Studies have shown that sex partners who meet online engage in higher risk sexual behaviors and are therefore at high risk of STDs (Bolding, Davis, Sherr, Hart, & Elford, 2004; McFarlane, Ross, & Elford, 2004).

Nonetheless, the Internet (and other new communication technologies) provides a valuable opportunity to engage audiences in online sexual health education (Ross, 2002; Ross, Tikkanen, & Manson, 2000). Several independent randomized control trials showed that teens reported increased HIV knowledge, intentions to practice safe sex, and reduced condom failures in response to Computer-Assisted Instruction (CAI) programs (Evans, Edmundson-Drane, & Harris, 2000; Kienee & Barta, 2006; Roberto et al., 2008).

One program, "Reducing the Risk," involved a computer-based intervention designed to change perceived threat, perceived efficacy, attitudes, and knowledge regarding pregnancy, STD, and HIV prevention in rural adolescents. The intervention, which was guided largely by the extended parallel process model, was implemented and evaluated in nine rural high schools. The extended parallel process model, developed by Witte, Myer, and Martell (2001), asserts that individuals are not likely to change their health behaviors unless they perceive a health threat that is both personally relevant and severe and also perceive a recommended solution to be effective and easy to do. A large group (889) of ninth-graders was randomly assigned to treatment and control. Each student completed a survey before and after completing the computer-based instruction (either Reducing the Risk or a tutorial on another, unrelated subject). Students in the treatment group outperformed students in the control group on knowledge, condom self-efficacy, attitude toward waiting to have sex, and perceived susceptibility to HIV. These results suggest that computer-based programs may be a cost-effective and easily replicable means of providing teens with basic information and skills necessary to prevent pregnancy, STDs, and HIV (Roberto et al., 2008).

Another study evaluated a computer-delivered, theory-based, individually tailored HIV risk-reduction intervention (Kienee & Barta, 2006). The intervention content and delivery were based on the Information-Motivation-Behavioral Skills Model of Health Behavior Change and used Motivational Interviewing techniques (Becker, Maiman, Kirscht, Haefner, & Drachman, 1977). Participants completed a baseline assessment of their level of HIV prevention information, motivation, behavioral skills, and behavior, attended two brief computer-delivered intervention sessions, and completed a follow-up assessment. When compared to the control group (a nutrition education tutorial), participants who interacted with the computer-delivered HIV/ AIDS risk reduction intervention exhibited a significant increase in risk reduction behavior. Specifically, participants reported that they more frequently kept condoms available and displayed greater condom-related knowledge at a 4-week follow-up session; among sexually active participants, there was a significant increase in self-reported condom use (Kienee & Barta, 2006).

Downs et al. (2004) conducted a longitudinal randomized study to evaluate the impact of "What Could You Do?" an interactive video intervention, on 300 urban adolescent girls' (a) knowledge about sexually transmitted diseases (STDs), (b) self-reported sexual risk behavior, and (c) STD acquisition.

The video provides a cognitive rehearsal session where teenagers can apply generic points they have learned to actual situations. When the teenager chooses a low-risk behavior for the girl in the video (refraining from sex or using a condom), the video then shows the boy trying to pressure her while the girl remains steadfast in her decision. When a high-risk option is chosen, no reinforcement is provided. All teens are eventually directed to a portion in the video where the girl chooses to bring a condom with her and refuses to have sex without it. Self-reports revealed that those assigned to the interactive video were significantly more likely to be abstinent in the first 3 months following initial exposure to the intervention, and experienced fewer condom failures in the following 3 months than were controls. Six months after enrollment, participants in the video condition were significantly less likely to report having been diagnosed with an STD.

Lightfoot, Comulada, and Stover (2007) evaluated a computerized version of Project LIGHT (Living in Good Health Together), an interpersonal intervention targeted at high-risk adults and adolescents with a track record of increasing condom use. The computerized version was found even more effective than the in-person version. Adolescents in the computerized intervention were significantly less likely to engage in sexual activity and reported significantly fewer partners after three months than were controls. Although these sexuality education efforts were assessed only in small groups, they could be disseminated via DVDs or Web sites on a large scale.

Several promising efforts using even more interactive technologies to address sexual risk include Trojan's "Evolve Campaign," a television and Internet campaign designed to increase the social acceptability of condoms. The campaign's public service announcements have been viewed more than 100,000 times on YouTube, and www.trojanevolve.com attracted more than 400,000 unique visitors in its first six months. In the TV commercials for Trojan condoms, women in a bar are surrounded by anthropomorphized, cell-phone-toting pigs. One shuffles to the men's room, where, after procuring a condom from a vending machine, he is transformed into a head-turner in his twenties. When he returns to the bar, a fetching blond who had been indifferent now smiles at him invitingly. The campaign had more than 48,000 friends on MySpace and many more on Facebook. Despite this apparent success, TV networks CBS and Fox rejected the condom ads nationally—and ABC and NBC affiliates refused to air them locally in Pittsburgh, Pennsylvania.

In another effort to engage the new technologies as sexuality education tools, the San Francisco Department of Public Health developed a text-messaging service, SexInfo, which answers commonly asked questions such as what to do if a condom breaks. The service was inspired in part by the way fans can text their vote for their favorite contestant on the "American Idol" television program. SexInfo—which costs about $2,500 a month to administer—aims for the text-messaging process to take about one to two minutes, with most messages ending with the phone number that users can call for more information. Urban youth can also use the service to send in reports of partners who may be infected, partners who may be cheating, or concerns about unprotected sex by using single digits to alert the health department and solicit advice. If a cell phone user sends the text message "sexinfo" to one of two phone numbers set up by the health department, the system sends back a reply asking the user to choose one of several categories that matches his or her question. Preliminary data showed that 4,500 callers used the service during its first 25 weeks, and 2,500 of the messages led to referrals and requests for more information. The most popular call requests were A1 (what to do if a condom broke); C3 (to find out about STDs); and B1 (if you think you're pregnant). The health department conducted surveys in 2006 of a convenience sample of 322 patients ages 12–24 at clinics to which SexInfo users were most commonly referred. Those who were more at risk for STDs were more likely to be aware of the campaign; overall, 11% of respondents reported awareness of the campaign (Levine, McCright, Dobkin, Woodruff, & Klausner, 2008).

New York's Department of Health and Mental Hygiene also launched a Web site that enabled people with sexually transmitted diseases (STDs) to send anonymous e-mail warnings to their partners to help slow a rise in new infections. It also offered information about getting tested and treatment (Honan, 2008). The site (www.InSpot.org), which then became available in nine states and three cities internationally, used the E-Card model to send messages like "I'm So Sorry" to notify people that they may have been exposed to a disease.

LESSONS LEARNED

Experts recommend that, to be successful, media campaigns conduct formative research with the target audience; use theory as a conceptual foundation; segment the audience; tailor messages; promote interpersonal dialogue; use media channels with a broad reach; and conduct process and sensitive outcome evaluation (Noar, 2006; Perloff, 2003; Randolph & Viswanath, 2004; Rogers & Storey, 1987; Salmon & Atkin, 2003). A few of the concepts that are most crucial in media-based sexual health education are highlighted here.

Use Theory to Design Sexuality Education

Many of the media-based sexuality education efforts discussed in this chapter were explicitly based on communication, persuasion, or health education theories—KNOW HIV/AIDS, the Two-City Safer Sex project, It's Your Sex Life, *Friends* episodes on condom use, *ER* episodes, and the CAI modules (Collins et al., 2003; Evans et al., 2000; Downs et al., 2004; Kiene & Barta, 2006; Lightfoot et al., 2007; Roberto et al., 2008; Zimmerman et al., 2007).

It seems clear, for example, that young people need to have self-efficacy to engage in safer sexual practices and that social support can improve self-efficacy. These are two psychosocial variables that media interventions can address. Self-efficacy, or behavior-specific confidence, is a construct related to behavior change by many common health educational theories, including the Social Cognitive Theory, the Health Belief Model, and the Transtheoretical Model (Bandura, 1977; Becker et al., 1977; Prochaska, Norcross, & DiClemente, 2001). Naar-King, et al. (2006) conducted a path analysis to determine the constructs of the Transtheoretical Model for HIV interventions and found that *self-efficacy* completely mediated the relationship between stage of change and unprotected intercourse acts. *Social support* specific to reducing risk was associated with increased self-efficacy. Such results point to the potential of sexuality education that simultaneously boosts self-efficacy and social support specific to practicing safer sex. Many health education theories, such as Social Norms Theory, indicate that social support for behavior change increases the likelihood of individual change in response to a media message or intervention (Lewis & Neighbors, 2004).

Segment, Involve the Audience, and Tailor the Messages

A shortcoming of some previous sexual risk-reduction interventions for adolescents has been the use of generic intervention strategies and messages directed toward the "average" teenager. Broad, nonspecific programming ignores diversity in sexual attitudes, behaviors, values, and circumstances. Recognizing and responding to key differences between group members is a core principle in effective public health programming; dividing a large heterogeneous target population into smaller, homogeneous subgroups that receive tailored communications increases the likelihood that people will respond positively to interventions (Maibach, Kreps, & Bonaguro, 1993; Slater, 1996). Norms also vary among groups of adolescents, and program planners should consider the gender, race, culture, and developmental status of targeted youth (D'Angelo & DiClemente, 1996).

Private marketing techniques have long demonstrated the value of audience segmentation and targeting through formative research—which needs to be replicated to the extent possible in sexual health campaigns (Zimmerman et al., 2007). The ultimate purpose of segmentation is to divide heterogeneous audiences into more homogenous subgroups whose preferences will be similar enough so that campaign messages will be maximally effective when targeted to that subgroup (Slater, 1996). Many variables can be used to segment, including race, gender, age, risk level, sensation-seeking attributes, and identity types, the Kaiser Family Foundation (2004) achieved success by specifically targeting African American youth with

"Rap It Up." Since few efforts have targeted very young teenagers, and because sexual risk behaviors begin in pre- and early adolescence, more media efforts need to be designed to speak to younger audiences with age-appropriate messages.

Interventions are more likely to achieve measurable effects if they steer clear of health belief and behavior areas that are already close to desirable levels at baseline. For example, the King County, Washington, condom promotion campaign was relatively ineffective in promoting condom efficacy—possibly because of the community's high level (75%) of condom use at baseline survey (Alstead, 1999). The Two-City Safer Sex campaign conducted focus groups with high-sensation seekers prior to designing messages and targeted those youth specifically (Zimmerman et al., 2007).

Other lessons for campaign design include the need to include local values and to foster audience participation. Effective campaigns typically include some kind of audience interactivity, either through formative research in campaign message design or in the dissemination of messages. Bushley, Cassel, Hernandez, Robinett, and Goodman (2005) showed the effectiveness in recruiting young women for an HPV cohort study through the use of a campaign designed specifically to address Hawaii's diverse culture. Alstead et al. (1999), among others, showed how audience involvement in campaign design and message delivery can enhance a project's effects.

Focus on New Behaviors

Similar to commercial marketing, where selling new purchases is easier than teaching lifestyle changes that involve abstention, health campaigns that promote something new, be it a condom, the HPV vaccine, or an HIV test, are more likely to be effective than those that ask users to stop doing something, like having sex or multiple partners (Snyder & Hamilton, 2002). The types of sexual health behaviors promoted by the campaigns discussed here ranged quite a bit, with some of the actions, including using a condom, talking with your child about sex, calling a hotline, text messaging a friend, or designing a slogan, being more concrete than others.

Ensure Adequate Frequency and Reach

No degree of targeting will achieve effects if the messages are not seen or heard. Snyder and Hamilton (2002) found that average exposure levels, that is, the percentage of a target audience that typically views or hears campaign messages, were surprisingly low (36–42%) in the health campaigns they reviewed. Recent campaigns have achieved higher saturation levels, such as the Two-City Safer Sex campaign, which achieved 85–96% exposure (Zimmerman et al., 2007).

While most health campaigns have used multiple channels, research has not effectively analyzed which channels are most effective for various audiences or whether more channels are better than fewer. In fact, recent evidence shows that significant changes can be achieved through single channels, such as television or radio (Palmgreen & Donohew, 2003; Reger, Wootan, & Booth-Butterfield, 1999). Since high exposure (both in reach and frequency) is important for effects, process evaluation should be conducted to document exposure levels midstream to maximize reach. One advantage of embedded message and media advocacy strategies is that most existing broadcast programs and news publications have high circulations; embedding health messages into mainstream shows or newspapers is one way to extend a campaign's reach. However, because, in such situations, control over content lies outside the campaign and because of the high cost of mainstream airtime and print placement, campaigns that operate in this way are usually limited to one-time messages or low repetition, limiting the frequency with which an audience views or hears a message.

Stay in for the Long Run

Study after study has shown that media impacts on sexual health risk behaviors are short-lived (Delgado & Austin, 2007; Zimmerman, 2007). Limited resources have severely hampered educators' ability to disseminate the kind of campaigns that might achieve longer term effects. Media advocacy offers one solution to public health's limited budgets. News coverage of risky behaviors may be particularly important during times of budget cuts (Chapman & Dominello, 2001). The news works both directly to inform the public about the items being reported and indirectly to shape notions of the importance of particular issues and events (Chapman & Dominello, 2001; Jernigan & Wright, 1996; Lemmens, Vaeth, & Greenfield, 1999). The news also provides various stakeholders with a particular perspective on relevant causal factors and possible solutions (Wakefield, Flay, Nichter, & Giovino, 2003). Media advocacy has thus become an important component of comprehensive public health communication programs (Jernigan & Wright, 1996; Russel, Voas, Dejong, & Chaloupka, 1995). By working directly with the producers of local news, advocates seek to influence the level of consideration afforded to specific concerns and their potential solutions and to counteract or reframe arguments proposed by opponents (Chapman & Dominello, 2001).

Use the New Media

Finally, new media technologies need to be explored more fully by sexual health educators. Internet, MP3, and cell phone technologies offer not only the potential for more cost-effective dissemination but also the ability to reach more diverse adolescent audiences (including young adolescents) in ways never before possible. Clinic waiting rooms offer one avenue for evaluating new technology interventions through randomized control trials, with the potential of using behavioral markers for documenting effects among patients.

Evaluate Outcomes

Given the difficulty of conducting randomized control trials of mass-media effects, more field experiments or quasi-experiments of interventions should be conducted, using time series analyses or pre/posttest control group designs (Delgado & Austin, 2007; Noar, 2006). Only one sexual risk intervention in the United States to our knowledge—the Two City Safer Sex Project—employed a field experimental approach (Zimmerman et al., 2007), and only the classroom-based computer-assisted instruction modules used randomized control trials (Downs et al., 2004; Evans et al., 2000; Kienee & Barta, 2006; Lightfoot et al., 2007; Roberto et al., 2008). Most campaigns, however, have been evaluated with less powerful designs—posttest only or one-group pre/posttest comparisons (DuRant, Wolfson, & LaFrance, 2006; KFF 2002, 2003, 2004; Kennedy, O'Leary, Beck, Pollard, & Simpson, 2004). Evaluation of media interventions is more feasible for local or regional campaigns than for national campaigns in which it is difficult to control exposure and to assess historical events and other social trends that may affect outcomes (Hornik, 2002). Previous studies typically have included typically less reliable self-report measures to document audience effects. Future studies should include more reliable measures, such as simple STD tests to assess safer sex behavior.

CONCLUSION

It is clear that the media are only one of a number of possible contexts in which adolescents learn about norms and expectations for sexual behavior. A variety of factors, including parental communication, peer norms, school-based curricula, religious principles, and community norms, influence teens' decisions about sexual behavior. We posit that the media may permeate all these other contexts and that teens' interactions with their friends and parents and schools both influence and are influenced by the media.

Given what we have described as a cyclical relationship between mass-media depictions of sexual behavior and individual, social, and familial contexts (affecting attention to and interpretation of media content), it is very difficult if not impossible to assess the unique influence of the media. In media research there is rarely a true control group that has not been exposed to some media content or had some interpersonal interaction about the media content. Thus, we have argued here that it may be most fruitful, both theoretically and practically, to put more energy now into conducting sexuality education efforts that focus on factors that may decrease the potentially negative effects of the media on youth. Health practitioners need to move beyond the research question of whether the media can have effects on sexual behavior and move directly to designing and implementing media-based interventions to promote healthy sexual behavior and reduce risk behavior among adolescents.

The media are important and powerful sexuality educators for many young people in the United States. Most media are not in the business of sexual health, however, so much of what youth see or hear in the media does not promote a sexually healthy lifestyle. A number of strategies exist that could improve the media's role as sexuality educator. Children and adolescents could be taught media literacy skills so that they will be more critical consumers of the sexual content in the media. Sexual health advocates could work with media producers to embed sexually responsible messages in the entertainment content adolescents attend to. Media-based sexual health campaigns could be developed for teens at high risk for engaging in sexually unhealthy behavior, and new media technologies could be used to reach teens with sexual health information and support for healthy behavior. Although much remains to be learned about the role of the media in the sexual education of youth, enough is known now to engage the media in the effort to raise sexually healthy young people.

REFERENCES

Alstead, M., Campsmith, M., Halley, C. S., Hartfeild, K., Goldbaum, G., & Wood, R. W. (1999). Developing, implementing, and evaluating a condom promotion program targeting sexually active adolescents. *AIDS Education and Prevention, 11*(6), 497–512.

Austin E. A., Chen Y C., Pinkleton, B. E., & Johnson, J. Q. (2006). Benefits and costs of Channel One in a middle school setting and the role of media-literacy training. *Pediatrics, 117,* 423–433.

Austin, E. A., & Johnson, K. (1997). Effects of general and alcohol-specific media literacy training on children's decision making about alcohol. *Journal of Health Communication, 2,* 17–42.

Bandura, A. (1986). *Social foundations of thought and action: A social cognitive theory.* Englewood Cliffs, NJ: Prentice Hall.

Becker, M. H., Maiman, L. A., Kirscht, J. P., Haefner, D. P., & Drachman, R. H. (1977). The Health Belief Model and prediction of dietary compliance: A field experiment. *Journal of Health and Social Behavior, 18*(4), 348–366.

Bolding, G., Davis, M., Sherr, L., Hart, G., & Elford, J. (2004). Use of gay Internet sites and views about online health promotion among men who have sex with men. *AIDS CARE, 16*(8), 993–1001.

Brodie, M., Foehr, U., Rideout, V., Baer, N., Miller, C., Flournoy, R., & Altman, D. (2001). Communicating health information through the entertainment media. *Health Affairs, 20*(1), 192–199.

Brown, J. D. (2000). Adolescents' sexual media diets. *Journal of Adolescent Health, 27S*(2), 35–40.

Brown, J. D., Halpern, C. T., & L'Engle, K. L. (2005). Mass media as a sexual super peer for early maturing girls. *Journal of Adolescent Health, 36*(5), 420–427.

Brown, J. D., L'Engle, K. L., Pardun C. J., Guo, G., Kenneavy, K., & Jackson, C. (2006). Sexy media matter: Exposure to sexual content in music, movies, television, and magazines predicts black and white adolescents' sexual behavior. *Pediatrics, 117,* 1018–1027.

Brown, J. D., & Pardun, C. J. (2004). Little in common: Racial and gender differences in adolescents' television diets. *Journal of Broadcasting & Electronic Media, 48*(2), 266–278.

Bushley, A. W., Cassel, K., Hernandez, B. Y., Robinett, H., & Goodman, M. T. (2005). A tailored multi-media campaign to promote the human papillomavirus cohort study to young women. *Preventive Medicine, 41*(1), 98–101.

Chapman, S., & Dominello, A., (2001). A strategy for increasing news media coverage of tobacco and health in Australia. *Health Promotion International, 16,* 137–143.

Collins, R. L., Elliott, M. N., Berry, S. H., Kanouse, D. E., & Hunter, S. B. (2003). Entertainment television as a healthy sex educator: The impact of condom-efficacy in an episode of Friends. *Pediatrics, 112*(5), 1115–1121.

Collins, R. L., Elliott, M. N., Berry, S. H., Kanouse, D. E., Kunkel, D., & Hunter, S. B. (2004). Watching sex on television predicts adolescent initiation of sexual behavior. *Pediatrics, 114*(3), e280–289.

D'Angelo, L. J., & DiClemente, R. J. (1996). Sexually transmitted diseases including Human Immunodeficiency Virus infection. In R. J. DiClemente & L. E. Ponton (Eds.), *Handbook of adolescent health risk behavior* (pp. 333–367). New York and London: Plenum Press.

Delgado, H., & Austin, B. (2007) Can media promote responsible sexual behaviors among adolescents and young adults? *Current Opinion Pediatric, 19,* 405–410.

Doniger, A. S., Adams, E., Utter, C. A., & Riley, J. S. (2001). Impact evaluation of the "Not Me, Not Now" abstinence-oriented adolescent pregnancy prevention communications program, Monroe County, New York. *Journal of Health Communication, 6,* 45–60.

Downs, J. S., Murray, P. J., de Bruin, W. B., Penrose, J., Palmgren, C., & Fischhoff, B. (2004). Interactive video behavioral intervention to reduce adolescent females' STD risk: A randomized controlled trial. *Social Science & Medicine, 59*(8), 1561–1573.

DuRant, R. H., Wolfson, M., & Lafrance, B. (2006). An evaluation of a mass media campaign to encourage parents of adolescents to talk to their children about sex. *Journal of Adolescent Health, 38,* 298–317.

Escobar-Chaves, S. L., Tortolero, S., Markham, C., & Low, B. (2004). *Impact of the Media on Adolescent Sexual Attitudes and Behaviors* (Grant # H75/CCH623007–01–1). Austin, TX: Medical Institute for Sexual Health.

Evans, A. E., Edmundson-Drane, E. W., & Harris, K. K., (2000). Computer-assisted instruction: An effective instructional method for HIV prevention education? *Journal of Adolescent Health, 26,* 244–251.

Farrelly, M., Davis, K. C., Haviland, M. L., Healton, C. G., & Messeri, P. (2005). Evidence of a dose-response relationship between "truth" antismoking ads and youth smoking prevalence. *American Journal of Public Health, 95*(3), 425–431.

Fishbein, M., Hall-Jamieson, K., Zimmer, E., Von Haeften, I., & Nabi, R. (2002). Avoiding the boomerang: Testing the relative effectiveness of antidrug public service announcements before a national campaign. *American Journal of Public Health, 92*(2), 238–246.

Honan, E. (2008, February 14). Web site allows anonymous warning of STD infections. New York: Reuters. Retrieved January 19, 2009, from http://www.isis-inc.org/news_articles2008.php

Hornik, R.C. (2002). Public health communication: Making sense of contradictory evidence. In R. C. Hornik (Ed.), *Public health communication: Evidence of behavior change* (pp. 1–19). Mahwah, NJ: Erlbaum.

Hust, S., Brown, J. D., & L'Engle, K. (2008). Boys will be boys and girls better be prepared: An analysis of the rare sexual health messages in young adolescents' media. *Mass Communication and Society, 11*, 1–21.

Huston, A. C., Wartella, E., & Donnerstein, E. (1998). *Measuring the effects of sexual content in the media: A report to the Kaiser Family Foundation.* Menlo Park, CA: Kaiser Family Foundation.

Jernigan D., & Wright, P. (1996). Media advocacy: Lessons from community experiences. *Journal of Public Health Policy, 17*, 306–330.

Kaiser Family Foundation. (2002). *Key facts: Teens online.* Menlo Park, CA: Kaiser Family Foundation.

Kaiser Family Foundation. (2003). *National Survey of Teens and Young Adults on Sexual Health Public Education Campaigns: Topline Results.* Menlo Park, CA: Kaiser Family Foundation.

Kaiser Family Foundation. (2004). *Assessing public education programming on HIV/AIDS: A national survey of African Americans—BET Rap It Up.* Menlo Park, CA: Kaiser Family Foundation.

Keller, S. N., & Brown, J. D. (2002). Media interventions to promote responsible sexual behavior. *Journal of Sex Research, 39*(1), 67–72.

Kennedy, M. G., O'Leary, A., Beck, V., Pollard, K., & Simpson, P. (2004). Increases in calls to the CDC National STD and AIDS Hotline following AIDS-related episodes in a soap opera. *Journal of Communication, 54*, 287–301.

Kienee, S. M., & Barta, W. D. (2006). A brief individualized computer-delivered sexual risk reduction intervention increases HIV/AIDS preventive behavior. *Journal of Adolescent Health, 39*, 404–410.

Kubey, R. Obstacles to the development of media education in the United States (1998) *Journal of Communication, 48*, 58–69.

Laugesen, M., & Meads, C. (1991). Advertising, price, income and publicity effects on weekly cigarette sales in New Zealand supermarkets. *British Journal of Addiction, 86*, 83–89.

Lemmens, P., Vaeth, P., & Greenfield, T., (1999). Coverage of beverage alcohol issues in the print media in the United States. *American Journal of Health, 89*, 1555–1560.

L'Engle, K. L., Brown, J. D., & Kenneavy, K. (2006, March). The sexual self-concept of middle adolescents. Paper presented at the Society for Research on Adolescence, San Francisco, CA.

Levine, D., McCright, J., Dobkin, L., Woodruff, A., & Klausner, J. (2008). SexInfo: A sexual health text messaging service for San Francisco youth. *American Journal of Public Health, 98*, 393–395.

Lewis, M., & Neighbors, C. (2004). Gender-specific misperceptions of college student drinking norms. *Psychology of Addictive Behaviors, 18*(4), 334–339.

Lightfoot, M., Comulada, W. S., & Stover, G. (2007) Computerized HIV preventive intervention for adolescents: Indications of efficacy. *American Journal of Public Health, 97*(6), 1027–1031.

Maibach, E. W., Kreps, G. L., & Bonaguro, E. W. (1993). Developing strategic communication campaigns for HIV/AIDS prevention. In S. Ratzan (Ed.), *AIDS: Effective health communication for the 90's* (pp. 15–35). Washington, DC: Taylor and Francis.

Malamuth, N. M. (1996). Sexually explicit media, gender differences, and evolutionary theory. *Journal of Communication, 46*(3), 8–31.

Martino, S. C., Colis, R. L., Kanouse, D. E., Elliott, M. & Berry, S. H. (2006). Social cognitive processes mediating the relationship between exposure to television's sexual content and adolescents' sexual behavior. *Interpersonal Relations and Group Processes, 89*(6), 914–924.

McFarlane, M., Ross, M. W., & Elford, J. (2004). The Internet and HIV/STD prevention. *AIDS Care, 16*(8), 929–930.

Moore, J., DeChillo, N., Nicholson, B., Genovese, A., & Sladen, S. (2000). Flashpoint: An innovative media literacy intervention for high-risk adolescents. *Juvenile and Family Court Journal, 51,* 23–33.

Naar-King, S., Wright, K., Parsons, J. T., Frey, M., Templin, T., & Ondersma, S. (2006). Transtheoretical model and condom use in HIV-positive youths. *Health Psychology, 25*(5), 648–652.

Noar, S. (2006). A 10-year retrospective of research in health mass media campaigns; Where do we go from here? *Journal of Health Communication, 11,* 21–42.

Noar, S. (2008). Effects of a televised Two-City Safer Sex mass media campaign targeting high sensation-seeking and impulsive decision-making young adults. Unpublished document. Lexington: University of Kentucky.

Noar, S., Clark, A., Cole, C., & Lustria, M. (2006) Review of interactive safer sex Web sites: Practice and potential. *Health Communication, 20*(3), 233–241.

Oakes, J. M. (2006). The effect of media on children: A methodological assessment from a social pathologist. Background paper prepared for Workshop on Media Research and Methods. Board on Children, Youth, and Families, National Research Council and Institute of Medicine, Washington, DC. Available at http://www.bocyf.org/030206.html

Palmgreen, P., & Donohew, L. (2003). Effective mass media strategies for drug abuse prevention campaigns. In Z. Slobada & W. J. Bukoski (Eds.), *Handbook of drug abuse prevention: Theory, science and practice* (pp. 27–43). New York: Kluwer Academic/Plenum.

Perloff, R. M. (2003). *The dynamics of persuasion: Communication and attitudes in the 21st century* (2nd ed.). Mahwah, NJ: Erlbaum.

Peter, J., & Valkenburg, P.M. (2006). Adolescents' exposure to sexually explicit material on the internet. *Communication Research, 33*(2), 178–204.

Pierce, J. P., & Gilpin, E. A. (2001). News media coverage of smoking and health is associated with changes in population rates of smoking cessation but not initiation. *Tobacco Control, 10,* 145–153.

Piran, N., Levine, M., & Irving, L. (2000). GO GIRLS! Media literacy, activism, and advocacy project. *Healthy Weight Journal, 14*(6), 89–90.

Primack, B. A., Gold, M. A., Land, S. R., & Fine, M. J. (2006). Association of cigarette smoking and media literacy about smoking among adolescents. *Journal of Adolescent Health, 39*(4), 465–472.

Prochaska, J. O., Norcross, J. C., & DiClemente, C. C. (1994). *Changing for Good.* New York: Morrow.

Randolph, W., & Viswanath, K. (2004). Lessons learned form public health mass media campaigns: Marketing health in a crowded media world. *Annual Review of Public Health, 25,* 419–437.

Reger, B., Wootan, M. G., & Booth-Butterfield, S. (1999). Using mass media to promote healthy eating: A community-based demonstration project. *Preventive Medicine, 29*(5), 414–421.

Roberto, A. , Zimmerman, R. S., Carlyle, K., Abner, E., Cupp, P. & Hansen, G. (2008). The effects of a computer-based HIV, STD, and pregnancy prevention intervention: A nine-school trial. Paper presented at the annual meeting of the International Communication Association, New York City. Retrieved October 10, 2008, from http://www.allacademic.com/meta/p12375_index.html

Robinson, T. N., & Sirard, J. R. (2005). Preventing childhood obesity: A solution-oriented research paradigm. *American Journal of Preventive Medicine, 28*(2S2), 194–201.

Robinson, T. N., Wilde, M. L., Navracruz, L. C., Haydel, K. F., & Varady, A. (2001). Effects of reducing children's television and video game use on aggressive behavior: A randomized controlled trial. *Archives of Pediatric Adolescent Medicine, 155,* 17–23.

Rogers, E. M., & Storey, J. D. (1987). Communication campaigns. In C. R. Berger & S. H. Chaffee (Eds.), *Handbook of communication science* (pp. 817–846). London: Sage.

Ross, M. (2002). The Internet as a medium for HIV prevention and counseling. *Focus: A Guide to AIDS Research and Counseling, 17*(5), 4–6.

Ross, M., Tikkanen, R., & Manson, S. (2000). Differences between Internet samples and conventional samples of men who have sex with men: Implications for research and HIV interventions. *Social Science and Medicine, 51,* 749–758.

Russel, A., Voas, R. B., Dejong, W., & Chaloupka, M. (1995). MADD rates the states: A media advocacy event to advance the agenda against alcohol-impaired driving. *Public Health Reports, 10,* 240–245.

Salmon, C. T., & Atkin, C. (2003). Using media campaigns for health promotion. In T. L. Thompson, A. M. Dorsey, K. I. Miller, & R. Parrott (Eds.), *Handbook of health communication* (pp. 285–313). Mahwah, NJ: Erlbaum.

SexInfo (2008). Retrieved April 24, 2008, from http://www.SexInfoSF.org

Singhal, A., & Rogers, E. M. (1999). *Entertainment-education: A communication strategy for social change.* Mahwah, NJ: Erlbaum.

Slater, M. D. (1996). Theory and method in health audience segmentation. *Journal of Health Communication, 1*(3), 267–285.

Slater, M. D. (2003). Alienation, aggression, and sensation seeking as predictors of adolescent use of violent film, computer, and website content. *Journal of Communication, 53*(1), 105–121.

Smith, K., Wakefield, M., Terry-McElrath, Y., Chaloupka, F., Flay, B., & Johnston, La. (2008). Relation between newspaper coverage of tobacco issues and smoking attitudes and behavior among American teens. *Tobacco Control, 17*(1), 17–24.

Snyder, L. B., & Hamilton, M. A. (2002). A meta-analysis of U.S. health campaign effects on behavior: Emphasize enforcement, exposure and new information, and beware the secular trend. In R. C. Hornik (Ed.), *Public health communication: Evidence for behavior change* (pp. 357–384). Mahwah, NJ: Erlbaum.

Steele, J. R., & Brown, J. D. (1995). Adolescent room culture: Studying media in the context of everyday life. *Journal of Youth and Adolescence, 24*(5), 551–576.

Strasburger, V. C. (2004). Children, adolescents, and the media. *Current Problems in Pediatric Adolescent Health Care, 34,* 54–113.

Strasburger, V. C. (2005). Adolescents, sex, and the media: Oooo, baby, baby—a Q & A. *Adolescent Medicine Clinics, 16*(2), 269–288.

Teen Media Monitor. (2003). Menlo Park, CA: Henry J. Kaiser Family Foundation.

Vandewater, E., & Lee, S. J. (2006). Measuring children's media use in the digital age: Issues and challenges. Background paper prepared for Workshop on Media Research and Methods. Board on Children, Youth, and Families, National Research Council and Institute of Medicine, Washington, DC. Available at http://www.bocyf.org/030206.html

Wakefield, M., Flay, B., Nichter, M., & Giovino, G. (2003). Role of media influencing trajectories of youth smoking. *Addictions, 98,* s79–s103.

Wallack, L. (1994). Media advocacy: A strategy for empowering people and communities. *Journal of Public Health Policy, 15,* 420–436.

Ward, L. M. (1995). Talking about sex: Common themes about sexuality in the prime-time television programs children and adolescents view most. *Journal of Youth & Adolescence, 24*(5), 595–615.

Ward, L. M. (2003). Understanding the role of entertainment media in the sexual socialization of American youth: A review of empirical research. *Developmental Review, 33*(3), 347–388.

Ward, L. M., Gorvine, B., & Cytron, A. (2002). Would that really happen? Adolescents' perceptions of sexual relationships according to prime-time television. In J. D. Brown & K. Walsh-Childers (Eds.), *Sexual teens, sexual media: Investigating media's influence on adolescent sexuality* (pp. 95–123). Mahwah, NJ: Erlbaum Associates.

Ward, L. M., & Rivadeneyra, R. (1999). Contributions of entertainment television to adolescents' sexual attitudes and expectations: The role of viewing amount versus viewer involvement. *Journal of Sex Research, 36*(3), 237–249.

Wellings, K. (2002). Evaluating AIDS public education in Europe: A cross-national comparison. In R. C. Hornik (Ed.), *Public health communication: Evidence of behavior change* (pp. 131–146). Mahway, NJ: Erlbaum.

Witte, K., Myer, G., & Martell, D. (2001). *Effective health risk messages.* Newbury Park, CA: Sage.

Ybarra, M. L., & Suman, M. (2006). Reasons, assessments, and actions taken: Sex and age differences in uses of Internet health information. *Health Education Research, 23*(3), 512–521.

Zimmerman, R. S., Palmgreen, P. M, Noar, S. M., Lustria, M. L. A., Hung-Yi, L., & Horsewski, M. L. (2007). Effects of a televised two-city safer sex media campaign targeting high-sensation-seeking and impulsive-decision-making young adults. *Health Education & Behavior, 34,* 810–826.

Chapter Four

SEX, SOAP, AND SOCIAL CHANGE: THE SABIDO METHODOLOGY FOR BEHAVIOR CHANGE COMMUNICATION

Kriss Barker

Anguach and Demlew are the main characters in an Ethiopian serial drama. They are a loving young couple with a bright future. But Demlew's mother, who doesn't like Anguach, begins to meddle and pushes a neighbor to seduce her son. He succumbs, sleeps with the neighbor, and is infected with HIV. Anguach is devastated, but forgives him, and cares for him until he dies. Although she is terrified that she might be HIV positive, Anguach gets tested and finds out that she is negative. Anguach eventually marries again (this time, a man without a meddling mother!) and lives happily ever after. Touching story—but did it have any impact?

This episode was one of 257 in a radio serial drama *Yeken Kignit* ("Looking over One's Daily Life"), produced between 2002 and 2004. *Yeken Kignit* is one of many serial dramas (commonly known as "soap operas") developed using the Sabido methodology for behavior change communication using the mass media. Unlike typical "soap operas," Sabido-style serial dramas are used to sell not sex or soap but, rather, social change.

The Sabido methodology, named for its creator Miguel Sabido of Mexico, has been proven to be highly effective in motivating positive behavior change in the numerous countries where it has been used. Miguel Sabido was vice president for research at *Televisa* (Mexican television) during the 1970s, 1980s, and 1990s. While at *Televisa*, Sabido developed a theoretical model for eliciting prosocial attitudinal, informational, and behavioral change through commercial television programming. He called this model "entertainment with proven social benefit." Between 1973 and 1981, Sabido produced six social-content serial dramas in Mexico.[1] During the decade when many of these Mexican soap operas were on the air, the country underwent a 34% decline in its population growth rate. As a result, the United Nations Population Prize was awarded to Mexico as the foremost population success story in the world.

In this chapter, we explore the Sabido methodology and the reasons why this theory-based approach to behavior change through this particular medium of communication has been so successful, particularly preventing HIV/AIDS and in ameliorating other reproductive health concerns. We also address the following:

- How do Sabido-style serial dramas differ from "soaps," and how does the Sabido methodology differ from other entertainment-education approaches in the way it addresses issues related to sexual health?
- Why do audiences worldwide, from the Philippines to India, from Mali to Ethiopia, and from Mexico to Bolivia, find these dramas irresistible—and much more than merely educating in an entertaining way?

ETHIOPIA: A CASE STUDY USING THE SABIDO METHODOLOGY FOR SEXUAL HEALTH

Ethiopia has the second largest population in Africa—79 million—and given its annual growth rate of 2.6 percent, its population is estimated to double in 29 years. Ethiopia's fertility rates are among the highest in Africa, at about six children per woman. In addition, of all African countries, only South Africa and Nigeria have more people living with HIV/AIDS than Ethiopia. In 2003, there were an estimated 1.5 million Ethiopians living with HIV/AIDS. Projections indicate that the number of Ethiopians living with HIV/AIDS will increase to between 7 million and 10 million by 2010 and that adult prevalence will be between 19 percent and 27 percent.

To respond to these issues, Population Media Center (PMC) produced a radio serial drama, *Yeken Kignit* ("Looking over One's Daily Life"), which was broadcast over Radio Ethiopia in 257 episodes between June 2, 2002, and November 27, 2004. *Yeken Kignit* addressed issues of reproductive health and women's status, including HIV/AIDS, family planning, marriage by abduction, education of daughters, and spousal communication.

Yeken Kignit was extremely popular. More than 15,000 letters poured in from inside and outside Ethiopia, and the media ran more than 100 stories on the show. Scientific research conducted by an independent research firm in Ethiopia showed that listeners included 47% of all the men in the country and 45% of all the women. But the impact went far beyond letters, news stories and a loyal audience. As shown in Figure 4.1, nationwide surveys conducted before and after the broadcast showed significant increases in the percentage of listeners who actually got tested for HIV. In fact, male listeners got tested at four times the rate of nonlisteners, and female listeners got tested at three times the rate of nonlisteners. The postbroadcast survey revealed that listeners had "fallen in love" with Anguach and followed her example of getting tested

Figure 4.1
Yeken Kignit (Ethiopia)

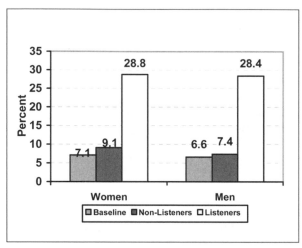

Percentage of Respondents Who Had Taken a Blood Test for HIV.

for HIV. There was also a more significant reduction in prejudice against those living with HIV/AIDS among listeners than among nonlisteners.

Why Was *Yeken Kignit* So Popular?

Sabido-style serial dramas are popular because they (1) are entertaining; (2) address issues of concern to the target audience; and (3) reflect real-life situations and lifestyles of members of the target audience. Extensive formative research is conducted to determine the key issues that will be addressed by the serial drama and to gather information about the characteristics, needs, and preferences of the target audience. This information is used to design the characters, settings, and story lines of the serial drama.

HOW DO SABIDO-STYLE SERIAL DRAMAS ACHIEVE SUCH IMPRESSIVE BEHAVIOR CHANGE RESULTS?

Relying on the formative research, the show's developers create characters for the serial drama that reflect the audience so that the show is in harmony with the culture. Through the gradual evolution of characters in response to problems that many in the audience also are facing, the serial drama can model the adoption of new, nontraditional behaviors in a way that generates no negative response from the audience. Because of the bonds that are formed between audience members and characters and because of the commonality of problems between characters and the audience, audience members tend to accept these changes, even though they may challenge some cultural traditions.

Most Important, Are These Results Replicable in Other Settings, Languages, and Cultures?

The Sabido methodology is adaptable to the individual values and cultures of each country where it is used. The process of formative research, which was developed by Sabido and Ana Cristina Covarrubias in 1974, provides culture-specific information to assist the writing and production team to design characters, settings, and storylines that are specific to each audience.

Research over the past 30 years has repeatedly demonstrated the effectiveness of the methodology. Since its inception in the 1970s and 1980s, the approach has been used in more than 200 health intervention programs in more than 50 countries in Latin America, Africa, and Asia, dealing mainly with reproductive health issues such as HIV/AIDS prevention, family planning, environmental health, teenage pregnancy prevention, and gender equality (Singhal, Cody, Rogers & Sabido, 2004).

THE SABIDO METHODOLOGY: AN EMPIRICAL AND REPRODUCIBLE APPROACH TO ENTERTAINMENT-EDUCATION

The design of the serial drama is critical to its potential success in terms of behavior change. Sabido-style serial dramas achieve results because they are developed using an empirical and reproducible approach to behavior change communication via mass media. In fact, every detail of a Sabido-style serial drama is developed according to a theoretical and empirical research–based formula in order to reinforce a coherent set of interrelated values that is tied to specific prosocial behaviors. The Sabido methodology is also a replicable methodology that, although formularized, is still adaptable to the individual values and cultures of each country where it is used.

One of the advantages of using serial dramas, rather than documentaries or single-episode dramas, is that they allow time for the audience to form bonds with the characters and allow characters to evolve in their attitudes and behavior at a gradual and believable pace in response to problems that have been well illustrated in the story line. Entertainment programs forge emotional ties to audience members that influence values and behaviors more forcefully than the purely cognitive information provided in documentaries.

Entertainment, whether via a nation's airwaves, popular magazines, or newspapers, is the most pervasive mass-media genre. It can also be extremely persuasive, influencing how we dress, speak, think, and behave. We are "educated" by the entertainment media, often unwittingly.

The major tenet of the Sabido methodology is that education can be compelling and educational. Sabido originally termed his approach "entertainment with proven social benefit," and, since then, many communication professionals and scholars have applied the term "entertainment-education" to the Sabido approach. However, the Sabido methodology is more than mere entertainment-education.

Let us begin by defining entertainment-education and then explain how the Sabido methodology differs from this approach.

Arvind Singhal, communication scholar as well as the Samuel Shirley and Edna Holt Marston Endowed Professor at the Sam Donaldson Center for Communication Studies at the University of Texas, El Paso, has been conducting research on the effectiveness of entertainment-education for more than 20 years. Singhal defines the approach as "the process of purposely designing and implementing a media message to both entertain and educate, in order to increase audience members' knowledge about an educational issue, create favorable attitudes, shift social norms, and change overt behavior" (Singhal and Rogers, 2002).

Singhal further defines entertainment-education as a "performance which captures the interest or attention of an individual, giving them pleasure, amusement, or gratification while simultaneously helping the individual to develop a skill or to achieve a particular end by boosting his/her mental, moral or physical powers." A common goal of entertainment-education programs is to entertain and educate audiences in order to catalyze social change in a socially desirable manner.

Entertainment-education comes in many different sizes and shapes:

- Single films and videos have been important in Asia and Africa, where they are shown from video vans as well as on national media.
- Variety shows are increasingly popular with youth in developing countries, and many of these programs engage young people directly in content and production (Kiragu, Van Hulzen-Sienche, Obwaka, & Odallo, 1998).
- Television and radio spots often include entertainment-education through short narratives or through use of familiar characters (Kincaid et al., 1996; Underwood, 2001).
- Locally, street theater, community radio, indigenous storytellers, drama contests, and community rallies with local performers incorporate and/or adapt national entertainment-education productions (Valente, Poppe, & Merritt, 1996).
- Many popular songs and music videos are inspired by the role-modeling techniques used in Sabido-style serial dramas.

Many of these entertainment-education programs have attracted large audiences and have had major effects on audiences' knowledge, attitudes, and behavior. However, although they certainly produce results, these various entertainment-education programs have not demonstrated the same magnitude of effects or cost-effectiveness achieved by Sabido-style programs, such as *Yeken Kignit*.

WHAT MAKES SABIDO-STYLE PROGRAMS SO DIFFERENT FROM OTHER FORMS OF ENTERTAINMENT-EDUCATION?

Successful use of the Sabido methodology hinges on two key factors: (1) use of the serial-drama format and (2) rigorous adherence to the theories underlying the methodology. Also, most entertainment-education programs are devoted to sending messages, whereas the Sabido methodology uses characters as vicarious role models to demonstrate the desired behaviors. The use of these vicarious role models is a critical element of successful application of the Sabido approach.

Format (Long-Running Serialized Drama)

First and foremost, the Sabido methodology requires the use of serial drama. In serial dramas, the story is carried over days and months, with story lines developing over time and characters remaining fairly constant. The fact that the serial drama continues with these characters for several months or years is an extremely powerful form of entertainment-education that can influence both specific health behaviors and related social norms. This is because:

- Serial dramas capture the attention and the emotions of the audience on a continual basis.
- Serial dramas provide repetition and continuity, allowing audiences to identify more and more closely over time with the fictional characters, their problems, and their social environment.
- Serial dramas allow time for characters to develop a change in behavior slowly and to face the hesitations and setbacks that occur in real life.
- Serial dramas have various subplots that can introduce different issues in a logical and credible way through different characters, a key characteristic of conventional soap operas.
- Serial dramas can build a realistic social context that mirrors society and creates multiple opportunities to present a social issue in various forms (Coleman & Meyer, 1990).

By modeling the process of change gradually, serial dramas are less likely to result in backlash or negative reactions by the audience, than are programs that try to bring about behavior change too quickly. Ideally, Sabido-style serial dramas should continue for at least 120 to 180 episodes (over the course of several years).

Serial dramas can present different perspectives and stimulate audience questioning that can lead to both individual health behavior change and to a change in social norms (Figueroa, Kincaid, Rani, & Lewis, 2002; Johns Hopkins University Center for Communication Programs, 1997; Kincaid, 1993; Kincaid, 2002; Netherlands Entertainment-Education Foundation [NEEF] and Johns Hopkins University, 2000; Singhal et al., 2004). As Piotrow states, "Of all the formats for entertainment-education programs which have been adapted, developed, tested, or contributed to, serial drama—on television where possible, or on radio when access to television is limited—has proven to be a highly effective format to promote long-term changes in health behavior and to influence the social norms that can reinforce such change" (Singhal et al., 2004).

Second, the Sabido methodology is based on various communication theories, each of which plays an essential role in the development of a Sabido-style serial drama (see Table 4.1). The application of these theories is critical to the success of the Sabido methodology in achieving behavior change.

Table 4.1
Theories Underlying the Sabido Methodology

Theory	Function in Sabido-Style Soap Opera
Communication Model (Shannon & Weaver, 1949)	Provides a model for the communication process through which distinct sources, messages, receivers, and responses are linked.
Dramatic Theory (Bentley, 1967)	Provides a model for characters, their inter-relationships, and plot construction.
Archetypes and Stereotypes (Jung, 1970)	Provides a model for characters that embody universal human physiological and psychological energies.
Social Learning Theory (Bandura, 1977)	Provides a model in which learning from soap opera characters can take place.
Concept of the Triune Brain (MacLean, 1973) and Theory of the Tone (Sabido, 2002)	Provide a model for sending complete messages that communicate with various centers of perception.

Source: Heidi Nariman (1993), Soap Operas for Social Change. Westport, CT: Praeger.

The table shows the different theories that guide the development of Sabido-style serial dramas and provide the methodology with a foundation for the structure and design of messages, settings, characters, and plots—a foundation that is based on formative research. The theories also provide a framework for articulating hypotheses for summative (evaluation) research on the impact of the program.

Communication Model: Shannon and Weaver, 1949

Modern communication theory is based on mathematical theorems developed by Claude Shannon, an engineer and researcher at Bell Laboratories, in 1948. Shannon's original theory (also known as "information theory") was later elaborated and given a more popular nonmathematical formulation by Warren Weaver, a media specialist with the Rockefeller Foundation. In effect, Weaver extended Shannon's insights about electronic signal transmission and the quantitative measurement of information flows into a broad theoretical model of human communication, which he defined as "all of the ways by which one mind may affect another."

The original model consisted of five elements, arranged in a linear fashion.

1. An *information source*, which produces a message.
2. A *transmitter*, which encodes the message into signals.
3. A *channel*, to which signals are adapted for transmission.
4. A *receiver*, which "decodes" (reconstructs) the message from the signal.
5. A *destination*, where the message arrives.

A sixth element, *noise,* is a dysfunctional factor and is defined as any interference with the message as it travels along the channel (such as static on the telephone or radio) that may cause the signal received to be different from the signal as originally sent. The components in this model are shown in Figure 4.2.

Shannon and Weaver's transmission model is the best-known example of the "informational" approach to communication. Although no serious communication theorist would still accept it, it has also been the most influential model of communication yet developed, and it reflects a commonsense (if misleading) understanding of what communication is. The major problem with Shannon and Weaver's model is that it fixes and separates the roles of sender and receiver. Human communication involves *simultaneous* sending and receiving (not only talking, but also body language and so on). In Shannon and Weaver's linear model, there is no provision for *feedback* (reaction from the receiver). Sabido adapted Shannon and Weaver's linear diagram and formed a communication circuit that depicted the circular nature of the communication process. He then applied this circuit to a serial drama. In the case of a commercial soap opera on television, the communicator is the manufacturer of a product, the message is "buy this product," the medium is the soap opera, the receiver is the consumer, and the response is the purchase of the product and television ratings (see Figure 4.3).

In the design of a social-content serial drama, Sabido left the communication circuit of a commercial serial drama intact; however, he added a second communicator, a second message, a second receiver, and a second response. These additions to the communication circuit did not impede the function of the first communicator, which is still the product manufacturer, as shown in Figure 4.4.

Dramatic Theory: Bentley, 1967

A second key element of the Sabido methodology is the use of melodrama. Melodrama is one of the five genres of theater (tragedy, comedy, tragicomedy,

Figure 4.2
Shannon and Weaver's Model of Communication

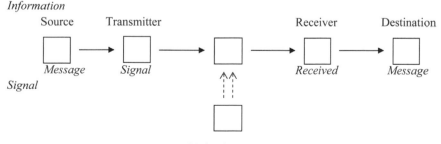

Source: Claude E. Shannon and Warren Weaver (1949). *The Mathematical Theory of Communication.* Urbana: University of Illinois Press.

Figure 4.3
Sabido's Circular Model of Communication

Source: Televisa, Institute of Communication Research, "Toward the Social Use of Soap Operas." Paper presented at the International Institute of Communication, Strasbourg, France, 1981.

farce, and melodrama) described by Eric Bentley in 1967. Among these genres, melodrama presents reality in a slightly exaggerated sense in which the moral universes of good and evil are in discord. Sabido, originally a dramatic theoretician himself, employed Bentley's structure of the melodrama genre as a basis on which to design characters and plots. "Good" characters in Sabido-style serial dramas accept the proposed social behavior, and "evil" characters reject it. Plots are then constructed around the relationships between good and evil characters as they move closer to or farther away from the proposed social behavior. Their actions encourage the audience to either champion or reject these characters accordingly.

The tension between the good and evil characters evoked by the melodrama places the audience between the forces of good and evil. But, in a twist on the typical audience role in melodrama, where audience members simply watch or listen to the battle between good and evil, Sabido inserted the audience into the heart of the action—by representing audience members through a third group, one that is uncertain about the social behavior in question. These "uncertain" characters are intended to be those with which the target audience most closely identifies. It is also these "transitional" characters who guide the audience members through their own evolution toward adoption of desired behavior changes.

Figure 4.4
Additional Circuit for a Social-Content Soap Opera

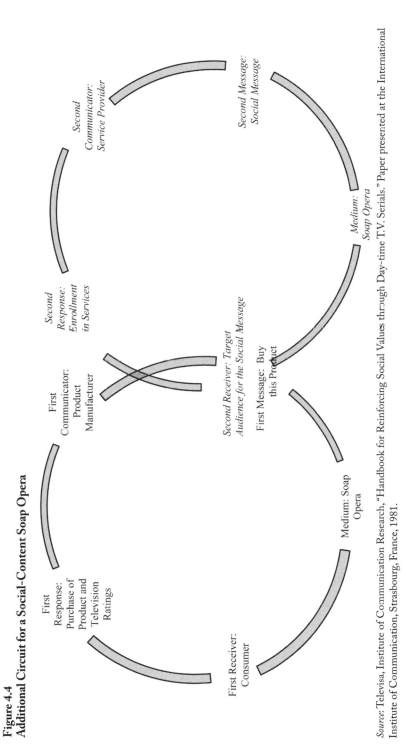

First Communicator: Product Manufacturer

Second Communicator: Service Provider

Second Response: Enrollment in Services

First Response: Purchase of Product and Television Ratings

Second Receiver: Target Audience for the Social Message

First Message: Buy this Product

Second Message: Social Message

Medium: Soap Opera

Medium: Soap Opera

First Receiver: Consumer

Source: Televisa, Institute of Communication Research, "Handbook for Reinforcing Social Values through Day-time T.V. Serials." Paper presented at the International Institute of Communication, Strasbourg, France, 1981.

Although the three groups of characters in Sabido-style serial dramas are exaggerated, as is the case in melodrama, they are modeled on real people within the target audience. Therefore, they reflect the perceptions these people might have regarding the social value and behavior being presented.

For example, in *Yeken Kignit*, "evil" is embodied in the negative character of the stepmother and in Demlew himself, who allows himself to be seduced. As in all good melodrama, the "evil" character (Demlew) is ultimately punished, here by contracting HIV. Anguach, his wife, is the "transitional" character and evolves from being uncertain about taking an HIV test to realizing the importance of knowing her sero-status. When she finally decides to take an HIV test, she draws the audience along with her, through role modeling.

Archetypes and Stereotypes—Theory of the Collective Unconscious: Jung, 1970

Jung's theory states that there are certain scripts or stories with familiar patterns and characters that people play out throughout history. These universal scripts or stories appear in myths, legends, and folktales around the world. Jung posited that these universal scripts or stories are the "archetypes of a collective unconscious" and share common characters such as "Prince Charming," "the mother," and "the warrior." Jung further suggests that these archetypes are expressions of a primordial, collective unconscious shared by diverse cultures (Jung, 1970). In *Yeken Kignit*, the mother-in-law character is based on an archetype of an interfering, scheming mother-in-law that is commonly satirized in Ethiopian culture.

Sabido-style serial dramas rely on extensive formative research to identify the culture- or country-specific versions of these archetypes and to identify local archetypes that represent the prosocial values (or the antithesis of these values) that will be addressed in the serial drama. If the formative research upon which the serial drama is based is done properly, the scriptwriters will be able to develop archetypical characters with which audience members will be able to identify. The formative research is used to develop a grid of positive and negative social values that these positive and negative characters will embody.

Social Learning Theory

Social Learning Theory, as articulated by Stanford University Professor of Social Science in Psychology Albert Bandura, explains how people learn new behaviors from vicariously experiencing the actions of others (Bandura, 1977, 1986). Bandura postulates that there are two basic modes of learning. People can learn either through the direct experience of trial and error and the rewarding and punishing effects of actions, or through the power of social modeling. Trial-and-error learning by direct experience is not only tedious but harmful when errors produce costly or injurious consequences. Consequently, many people short-cut this process by learning from the successes and mistakes of others. This shortcut, called vicarious learning or modeling, is a key tenet of Bandura's Social Learning Theory (Bandura, 1977).

According to Social Learning Theory, people learn not only in formal situations such as classrooms but also by observing models. In fact, the largest portion of learning to adapt to society takes place through such observational learning. The models used in this observational learning can be people in real life or characters in mass media (such as television or radio).

A key to the use of Social Learning Theory in Sabido-style serial dramas is the use of appropriate models that are visibly rewarded (or punished) in front of the audience in order to convert the values being promoted by the serial drama into behavior. Social Learning Theory postulates that positive rewards have a vicarious effect upon the observer (in this case, the audience) and can motivate audience members to practice similar behavior(s). Punishing a role model for practicing a socially undesirable behavior likewise provides a vicarious experience for the observer and can inhibit his or her practice of the same behavior. This adoption is called modeling because it is based on the role model's conduct. Through modeling, it is possible to acquire new forms of behavior and to strengthen or weaken certain behaviors. In Sabido-style serial dramas, characters "teach" audience members via modeling so that they are able to make a recommended response.

Sabido determined that three types of characters are fundamental to successful modeling by audience members. The first two types of characters are positive and negative role models. They embody positive and negative behaviors related to the social issues addressed in the serial drama (and are based on Jung's theory of archetypes and stereotypes, described earlier). These characters do not change during the course of the serial drama but are repeatedly rewarded or punished for their behaviors. The consequences of these positive or negative behaviors must be directly linked to the behavior in question; for example, a truck driver character that is practicing at-risk sexual behavior should suffer from a sexually transmitted infection or even contract HIV but should not be the victim of a traffic accident.

The third type of character is the "transitional character." These characters are neither positive nor negative but somewhere in the middle. These transitional characters play the pivotal role in a Sabido-style serial drama and are designed to represent members of the target audience. The transitional characters' evolution toward the desired behavior is like that which the audience members will use to model their own behavior change.

As mentioned previously, in *Yeken Kignit*, Anguach "teaches" audience members about the importance of getting an HIV test by struggling with whether or not to get tested herself. When she ultimately decides to get tested, audience members will model this behavior, as was shown by the results of the evaluation conducted at the end of the broadcast of the program.

Bandura also developed a related theory, Social Cognitive Theory, which explains that behavior change can occur only when an individual feels sufficiently empowered to change (Bandura, 1989). If an individual feels that the society, culture, religion, or his or her deity (or "Fate") dictates individual behavior and its consequences, there is little that communication can do to impact behavior change. For example, if a woman perceives that Fate has determined the number of children she will ultimately bear during her childbearing years, even a well-conceived family planning communication campaign will have little effect in motivating her to plan or space her pregnancies; she feels that this decision is not hers to make. In this case, the woman's perception of self-determination must be addressed first.

Bandura termed this perception of self-determination "self-efficacy." The more self-efficacy an individual perceives, the more likely that person will be to feel empowered to make decisions that affect his or her life and circumstances.

Triune Brain Theory: MacLean, 1973, and Theory of the Tone: Sabido, 2002

The Sabido methodology is based on conveying a holistic message that is perceived by audience members on several levels of awareness. Prior to his work at *Televisa*, Sabido was a theater director and dramatic theoretician. In his work in the theater, Sabido discovered that actors can have different effects on their audiences by channeling their energy through three different body zones. If actors focused their energy behind their eyes, the tone of the production would be conceptual. If the actor focused energy in the base of the neck, the tone of the production would be emotive. If the actor focused energy in the pubic area, the tone of the production would be primal (Sabido, 2002). Sabido instinctively understood that in order to motivate or persuade, it is necessary to provide a complete message that speaks to these three levels of perception.

Auditory senses are also tapped into. Sabido's "tonal theory" describes how the various tones that are perceived by humans can be used in drama. In this theory, the producer/director serves almost the same function as an orchestra conductor, who can evoke different tones from each instrument in order to create various harmonies or tones within the body of the music and thereby inspire different moods among the audience. Although the theory is quite complex, it can be summarized by saying that for Sabido, the "tone" is the human communication form to which the receiver gives a tone according to his or her own genetic and acquired repertoire, thus making the "tone" the foundation of human communication (Sabido, 2004). The theory has one main hypothesis: it is possible to change the tone of communication by hierarchically ordering its flow elements in a specific manner. This general hypothesis is organized into twelve subhypotheses, which allow us to take this abstract idea and apply it to day-to-day communication.

The producer/director uses various nonverbal elements of communication, including facial expressions, body language, lighting, music, sound effects, and tone of voice, to evoke different responses from the audience.

At first, Sabido lacked a theoretical explanation for what he was observing. He eventually discovered Paul MacLean's concept of the triune brain, which presents a model of human brain structure with three levels of perception—cognitive, affective, and predispositional (MacLean, 1973).

Thus, MacLean's theory gave Sabido the scientific basis he needed for focusing on the emotional (second) and the instinctive/impulse (first) zones as the basis for his serial dramas, with the third (cognitive) zone used primarily to reinforce the first and second zones' messages in the drama.

CONCLUSIONS

The world is facing unprecedented change, including the interrelated concerns of global warming, deforestation and species extinction, collapsing fisheries, fresh-water shortages, rising energy costs, rising food costs and food shortages, poverty, poor health, political unrest and instability, and inability of many of the poorer countries of the world to keep up with growing demand for schools and government services. An overriding element of many of these problems is the net growth in the world's population by 80 million per year. Unplanned and often unwanted childbearing is a major factor in the growth of the world's population by the equivalent of a new Los Angeles County every six weeks.

Changing social norms on issues as sensitive and personal as human reproduction is not easy. Human behaviors are often rooted in long traditions that may once have been adaptive but that no longer are. There is now, however, a great body of evidence, including the data given in this chapter, that change is possible.

Sabido-style serial dramas are one of the most cost-effective communication strategies for motivating behavior-change. The ultimate measure of cost-effectiveness is the cost per person among those who changed their behavior in a positive direction. Sabido-style serial dramas are highly cost-effective because of the huge audiences they attract and the strong impact they have on the public. In Ethiopia, *Yeken Kignit* cost just 4 U.S. cents to reach each listener. Cost per listener of a similar program in Tanzania was 3 cents per year. The annual cost per new adopter of family planning in Tanzania was 34 cents U.S., while the cost per person among those who reported that they changed behavior to avoid HIV infection as a result of hearing the serial was 8 cents.

In summary, the Sabido methodology for development of mass-media entertainment-education serial dramas is unique in that it is designed according to elements of communication and behavioral theories. These confirm specific values, attitudes, and behaviors that viewers can use in their own personal advancement.

NOTE

1. Between 1973 and 1981, Miguel Sabido produced six social-content serial dramas in Mexico.

- *Ven Conmigo* ("Come with Me") provided specific information about a study program offered by the Secretary of Public Education in 1975. Role models were used to motivate viewers to register for literacy classes.
- *Acompáñame* ("Accompany Me"), Sabido's second entertainment-education soap opera, broadcast from August 1977 through April 1978, contained a family planning message. Role models were used in this serial drama to motivate women to use contraceptive methods and to show wives how to negotiate contraceptive use with their spouses.
- *Vamos Juntos* ("Let's Go Together"), broadcast from July 1979 through March 1980, promoted responsible parenthood and the active development and integration of children in the family and in society. Role models were used in this program to teach parents about family integration behaviors and family life planning.
- *El Combate* ("The Struggle"), broadcast from April through September 1980, promoted an adult education program launched in several communities outside of Mexico City. Behavior models were used in this program to inform rural audiences how to dispel the myth that adults cannot go back to school.
- *Caminemos* ("Going Forward Together"), broadcast from September 1980 through April 1981, tackled the theme of sex education for adolescents. Role models in this program were used to model responsible sexual behavior for teenagers.
- *Nosotros las Mujeres* ("We the Women") ran from April to October 1981. Through the effective use of role modeling, this program was designed to counter traditions associated with machismo and to encourage women to become aware of their important role in the family and society.

In 1997–1998, Sabido produced one additional social-content serial drama before retiring from Televisa in 1998:

- *Los Hijos de Nadie* ("Nobody's Children") addressed the issue of street children. This program used role models to change opinions among audience members about the "silent conspiracy" surrounding the problem of street children in Mexico.

REFERENCES

Bandura, A. (1977). *Social learning theory.* Englewood Cliffs, NJ: Prentice Hall.
Bandura, A. (1986). *Social foundations of thought and action: A social cognitive theory.* Englewood Cliffs, NJ: Prentice-Hall.
Bandura, A. (1989). Social cognitive theory. In R. Vasta (Ed.), *Annals of child development, 6. Six theories of child development* (pp. 1-60). Greenwich, CT: JAI Press.
Bentley, E. (1967). *The life of drama.* New York: Atheneum.
Coleman, P. & Meyer, R.C. (1990). *Proceedings from the Enter-educate Conference: Entertainment for Social Change.* Baltimore: Johns Hopkins University, Population Communication Services.

Figueroa, M. E., Kincaid, D. L., Rani, M. & Lewis, G. (2002). *Communication for social change: An integrated model for measuring the process and its outcomes.* New York: Rockefeller Foundation and Johns Hopkins University Center for Communication Programs.

Johns Hopkins University Center for Communication Programs (1997). Working Paper No. 3, *Reaching men worldwide: Lessons learned from family planning and communication projects, 1986–1996.* Baltimore: Johns Hopkins University, Center for Communication Programs.

Jung, C. G. (1970). *Archetypes and the collective unconscious.* Buenos Aires: Editorial Paidos.

Kincaid, D. (1993). Using television dramas to accelerate social change: The enter-educate approach to family planning promotion in Turkey, Pakistan, and Egypt. Paper presented at the International Communication Association, Washington, DC.

Kincaid, D. (2002). Drama, emotion, and cultural convergence. *Communication Theory, 12*(2): 136–152.

Kincaid, D. L., Merritt, A. P., Nickerson, L., deCastro Buffington, S., deCastro, M. P. & deCastro, B.M. (1996). Impact of a mass media vasectomy promotion campaign in Brazil. *International Family Planning Perspectives, 2*(4), 169–175.

Kiragu, K., Van Hulzen-Sienche, C., Obwaka, E. & Odallo, D. (1998). Adolescent reproductive health needs in Kenya: A communication response—Evaluation of the Kenya youth initiative project. Cited in Singhal, M. J. Cody, E. M. Rogers & M. Sabido (Eds.) (2004)., *Entertainment-education and social change: History, research, and practice.* Mahwah, NJ: Lawrence Erlbaum Associates.

Kral, V. A. & MacLean, P. D. (1973). *A triune concept of the brain and behaviour, by Paul D. MacLean. Including psychology of memory, and sleep and dreaming; papers presented at Queen's University, Kingston, Ontario, February 1969, by V. A. Kral [et al. Toronto].* Published for the Ontario Mental Health Foundation by University of Toronto Press, Netherlands Entertainment-Education Foundation [NEEF] & Johns Hopkins University Center for Communication Programs (2000). Think big, start small, act now. In *Proceedings of the Third International Entertainment-Education Conference for Social Change.* Arnhem/Amsterdam, September 17–22, 23–24.

Sabido, M. (2002). *The tone, theoretical occurrences, and potential adventures and entertainment with social benefit.* Mexico City: National Autonomous University of Mexico Press.

Sabido, M. (2004). Personal communication.

Shannon, C. E. & Weaver, E. (1949). *The mathematical theory of communication.* Urbana: University of Illinois Press.

Singhal, A., Cody, M. J., Rogers, E. M. & Sabido, M. (Eds.) (2004). *Entertainment-education and social change: History, research and practice.* Mahwah, NJ: Lawrence Erlbaum Associates.

Singhal, A. & Rogers, E. (2002). A theoretical agenda for entertainment-education. *Communication Theory, 12*(2), 117–135.

Underwood, C. (2001). *Impact of the HEART campaign: Findings from the youth surveys in Zambia 1999 & 2000.* Baltimore: Johns Hopkins School of Public Health, Center for Communication Programs.

Valente, T. W., Poppe, P. & Merritt, A. P. (1996). Mass-media generated interpersonal communication as sources of information about family planning. *Journal of Health Communication, 1,* 247–265.

Chapter Five

LOGGING ON TO LEARN: A WEB-BASED SEXUALITY EDUCATION TRAINING PROGRAM

Emil Man-Lun Ng, Judy Kuriansky, Wing-Yan (Winnie) Yuen, Yee-Lun (Eilean) So, Tina Mo-Yin Ng, Shir-Ming Shen, and Bruce Cheung

Sexuality education is an important strategy for achieving a healthy sex life, which is an integral part of maintaining a healthy body and mind (Pan American Health Organization, 2000). This is particularly important for teenagers, given that contemporary youth are sexually more mature and active than were youth of earlier generations. Data from the World Health Organization have revealed a high rate of premarital sex and pregnancies in China and around the world; at present, about 15 million young women below the age of 20 get pregnant every year around the world, and 2 to 4 million women undergo unsafe abortions (Li, 2006). In Hong Kong, the situation is exacerbated by a decline in sexual knowledge among school-age young people, as revealed by a series of sexuality surveys conducted by the Family Planning Association of Hong Kong with youth and students over a decade (Family Planning Association of Hong Kong, 1997).

The lack of knowledge in a climate of more open sexual attitudes in the global contemporary society has indeed put young people at increased risk of sexually transmitted diseases, including HIV/AIDS. Given these facts, it is essential that young generations have access to proper knowledge about sex and that they have help with handling sex-related issues wisely. The question arises, then, how to best implement such sexuality education; for example, by using more traditional means (i.e., the school system or any available community centers) or by taking advantage of newer methods of communication. The latter has been attempted, taking advantage of the new modality of teaching using Internet and Web-based technologies, and is explored in this chapter through a pioneer effort to provide education for health professionals who can then pass this information on to the populations they serve in the public (Ng, 2001; 2004).

One of the most important venues for providing sex education to youth is school. While providing well-informed sex education programs at school is seemingly effective, well-trained teachers are in fact the key to success. However, a survey conducted in 2000 (Lee, 2000) revealed that two-thirds of primary school teachers admitted that they were not confident in answering questions related to sex.

Moreover, studies and clinical observations have shown that many men and women, as well as couples, in the general population suffer from sexual problems. While physicians and allied health professionals who play a major role in health care can offer first-line help to such people, it is not always the case that they have the necessary knowledge to recognize sexual dysfunctions and the basic educational, counseling and therapeutic skills to approach these problems. Many professionals still feel uncomfortable when dealing with sexual complaints and problems, and some even have idiosyncrasies when dealing with a patient's personal sexual aspects of physical disease (Coleman, 1996; Kaimola & Volkama, 2000).

These obstacles to public sex education suggest an urgent need to provide sex education training to teachers, physicians, and other health care professionals. Training courses for sex-health professionals have been conducted as part of undergraduate or postgraduate courses in Western countries, where promoting sexual health is more accepted than in Hong Kong or neighboring countries (Coleman & Haeberle, 1999; Haeberle & Gindorf, 1993). Pioneer training has been done in mainland China, where Western sex experts have conducted week-long sessions in American sex counseling techniques for medical doctors and health professionals. The results of these trainings have shown significant improvement in the participants' knowledge of sexual issues and attitudes toward sexual topics and their treatment (Hu, Kuriansky, & Shen, 2003; see also chapter 12 of volume 2 in this set). Certain limitations existed in applying this model in Hong Kong, given the lack of funding and qualified teachers to provide sex-health education, in addition to limited community involvement and initiative from policymakers. The need for such professional sex-health education programs and the promise of their effectiveness, as shown in other efforts, has led to the development of a new model to accomplish these aims, as described in this chapter.

SETTING THE STAGE FOR A NEW MODEL

At the turn of the millennium, new opportunities emerged for developing needed professional sex education programs in Hong Kong. Increasing health-promotion efforts by the government and by nongovernmental organizations (NGOs) to combat HIV/AIDS, sexual harassment, and sexual inequality, as well as to treat sexual problems, greatly raised public awareness on sexuality issues. This was enhanced by the fact that a major international conference on sexuality, the World Congress of Sexology, was held in Hong Kong in 1999 (Ng, Borrás-Valls, Pérez-Conchillo, & Coleman, 2000). Public awareness of sexuality was also heightened by media presentations on radio and television by the main author (Ng, 1993; Ng & Fan, 1996). As a result, the general public's views on human sexuality and the sexual rights of sexual minorities (e.g., homosexuals) also broadened. Additionally, the Education Department was reinforced to encourage sex education for teachers. All of these factors and events brought the issue of sexual-education training courses into heightened awareness on the part of several stakeholders, including local government, schools, teachers, and the public.

OPPORTUNITIES FOR E-SEX EDUCATION: DEVELOPMENT OF THE E-COURSES

Since the emergence of the first "virtual classroom" in the 1980s (Hiltz, 1986; Hiltz & Meinke, 1989) on the World Wide Web, e-learning technology has undergone rapid advancement and improvements and has allowed innovative teaching methods, such as the use of multimedia, to be carried out effectively in the virtual environment (Cuthbert, 2004; Belar, 2006). For example, an online sexuality-education course for health professionals was developed at the University of Sydney in Australia. This course was based on the PLISSIT model (which uses graduated steps, from granting permission and providing limited information and specific suggestions to requiring intensive therapy) with discussion boards and quizzes, and was found to provide useful flexibility in time, place, and resources for both students and instructors (Weerakoon & Wong, 2003). The challenges to extending distance learning of other subjects to sexuality education has been pointed out (Marega, 2005) in that teaching sexuality involves emotional intelligence (overcoming prejudices, developing positive attitudes, expression of feelings) more than just knowledge or intellectual processing. Therefore, such application requires creative use of technological multimedia to engage learners in emotional learning as well as pedagogy.

The effort addressed in this chapter took advantage of technology innovation and support from the World Association for Sexology and the Hong Kong Sex Education Association, as well as the School of Professional and Continuing Education of the University of Hong Kong (HKU SPACE) in collaboration with the Department of Psychiatry at the University of Hong Kong (HKU), to offer the first Web-based Certificate in Sex Education, in 2002 (Ng, 2001; Ng, Ng, & Cheung, 2004a). Once that first experience was successful, a postgraduate diploma in Principles in Sex Counseling and Therapy was also developed and offered in 2004.

Another important factor in the development of the present model was the decision to design the courses to be available on a part-time basis. This was deemed necessary because many people who would benefit from the course are already in careers as health providers and do not have the time or logistical ability to be present at a brick-and-mortar facility or at set, regimented times. These students include medical doctors, family planner, other health providers and people in full-time positions who wanted to change careers to become a sexuality educator.

The new mode of part-time Web-based courses provides convenient, comprehensive and professional programs built on the principles of sexuality education, sex counseling, and therapy, and aimed at meeting the needs of teachers, physicians, and allied health professionals from varied disciplines who want to obtain a high standard of sex-education training for themselves and then provide a high standard of sex education to their clients. Students in these programs were expected to develop positive attitudes and confidence in educating the public; to apply appropriate counseling skills; and to be comfortable in discussing sensitive issues, such as sexual health and related interpersonal issues, with clients. The aim of this chapter is to report our experience developing these courses and the results of running these Web-based sex-education and counseling courses in Hong Kong. The effectiveness of these courses was evaluated and provides a foundation for discussing future enhancement in Web-based sexuality education courses.

METHODS

Teachers and Examiners

Teachers were recruited from an international network of mental health professionals through several sources: references from professional organizations like the World Association for Sexual Health (WAS), the Asia-Oceania Federation for Sexology (AOFS), and the Hong Kong Sex Education Association (HKSEA); through local and overseas universities in countries such as Singapore, Taiwan, Germany, Canada, the United States, and the United Kingdom; and from personal contacts of the authors. Several criteria were imposed on the teacher-selection process. First, the teacher had to have international participation and experience in sexuality education, as well as expertise in particular topics of sexuality education that would be included in the course. Second, it was necessary that teachers be actively involved in teaching sexuality and in clinical and research activities in the field. Third, given that the target students would come from different ethnic groups and have different subculture backgrounds, teachers had to be sensitive to the students' cultures and problems that might arise in various service settings.

Professionals who became part of the teaching team included psychiatrist Roger Ho from Singapore; sexologist FangFu Ruan from Taiwan; sex educator Erwin Haeberle from Germany; psychologist Ka-Tat Tsang and sex educator Josephine Wong from Canada; clinical psychologist and sex researcher Judy Kuriansky (the second author) and sex educator William Granzig from the United States; sex educator Michael Reiss from the United Kingdom; and sociologist Yu-Xin Pei from mainland China. Local Hong Kong teachers included Emil Ng (the first author) and Atty Ching, founder of Teen AIDS, an NGO that promotes youth sex education and AIDS prevention. These teachers were responsible for performing duties that included writing the course materials assigned to them, conducting chat-room tutorials, and supervising course assignments and students' special projects. They were also encouraged to be present at in-person sessions, teaching, meeting with students, and participating in student group evaluations. Eminent local and international scholars were also invited to be advisers to the courses.

The teachers also served as examiners, but, for each course, a sex-education expert from an overseas university was appointed as an external examiner to oversee and advise on the standard, format, and marking of examinations questions on the basis of independent knowledge and experience running examinations in similar courses. These external examiners reviewed a random selection of the students' marked papers to ensure that they had been properly and fairly graded and would re-mark any paper about which there was any question, including discussing discrepant findings with the teacher.

Support Staff

A team of general educational and technological staff was provided by HKU SPACE. The educational staff consisted of educational administrators and their assistants, who took care of recruitment, quality control, and syllabus development. The technological staff included computer engineers and programmers, who were responsible for developing and maintaining the Web facilities for the course (Ng, Ng & Cheung, 2004b). A project officer was dedicated to keep track of the logistics; this person's responsibilities were to facilitate communication and coordination between teachers and students, to ensure that all materials were posted at appropriate times, and to inform all teachers and students about events, assignment deadlines, and assessment details.

Student Recruitment

Students were recruited through press releases and advertisements in local newspapers. All applicants for admission had to be age 21 or older, have a university degree, and work in a field related to sex education or counseling.

Course Contents

The Certificate in Sex Education

The Certificate in Sex Education is a one-year part-time program, conducted in English and supplemented with local vocabulary. The course content consists of theory and content about sexuality as well as a special project. The content and theory were delivered via an e-learning mode, which consisted of four compulsory modules: Sex and Health, Sexual Psychology, Sex and Society, and Sex Education. There were 7 to 12 chapters in each module. The online contents included course outline, discussion questions, recommended readings and online videos, written by local and overseas teachers. The written course materials were designed to be informative and reader-friendly, meaning they had to be clear and in readable chucks of paragraphs (consistent with Web-based materials) so that the eye could capture the concept easily. The modules and chapters taught in this course are listed in Appendix 5.1.

Upon completion of the theoretical component, students were required to complete an independent project, where they applied their knowledge to sex education. They could select a topic from the suggested list or a topic of their own choice.

The independent project was conducted under close and intensive supervision by one of the teachers. The projects were varied, for example, a teen counselor produced a flyer for teenagers about unusual sexual behaviors and ways to handle those impulses which was to be used in his sexual health clinic, and a physician wrote a paper addressed to policymakers about the importance of condom use for sex workers. Other topics included awareness about sexual abuse, information about AIDS education and counseling, and tips for parents about sex education. Two students participated in a research project, in collaboration with their American supervisor (second author Kuriansky) and their community health center, about the impact of SARS (Severe Acute Respiratory Syndrome) on people's feeling and relationships.

Postgraduate Diploma in Principles in Sex Counseling and Therapy

This was also a one-year part-time program conducted in English, supplemented with local vocabulary. The course was composed of two parts: theory and case study.

The theory learning consisted of six modules: Sex and Health, Sexual Psychology, Sex and Society, Sexual Dysfunctions and Treatment Modalities, Principles of Sex Counseling Skills, and Principles of Sex Therapy Skills. Each module had four to seven chapters. The modules and chapters taught in this course can be found in Appendix 5.2. These modules were delivered through e-learning mode, supplemented by regular face-to-face seminars, called "Sex Focus," for all the students. In these seminars, students presented their on-going work to the group. The seminar was led by the main teacher/course developer (Ng, also the main author of this chapter), but all teachers were also welcome and some came from far away to be present and participate. The second part of the program was based on case studies. For this part, students were individually supervised by a teacher. The diploma represents more advanced training; hence, priority was given to applicants who had satisfactorily completed the Certificate Course in Sex Education or its equivalent.

Course Assessments and Examinations

For both courses, the students' academic outcomes were measured by midterm examinations, in which they were required to complete a set of computer-generated, randomized multiple-choice questions in a classroom setting. Further, the students had to submit a report about their independent project (similar to the independent project done by students in the certificate course). These reports were given randomly to the external examiner for review of the standard and objectivity of grading.

The examination grading system was based on the mean total marks (scores) each student obtained from all the examinations in the course, with 100 as the maximum. A grade of "A" ("distinction") was given to those achieving 80 marks or above; a "B" grade ("credit") was given for achieving a score of 70–79; a "C" grade ("pass") was given for scoring 60–69; and scores below 60 were given a "fail" grade.

Course Learning Platform

The Web-based courses, delivered through the e-learning platform SOUL (SPACE Online Universal Learning), have the following characteristics, which made these e-learning courses more efficient:

1. Content Engineering: The courses contain user-friendly wizards that enable teachers to develop the e-course with systematic flow based on corresponding pedagogical approaches known as "task-based learning." The outputs conform to the common e-learning content packaging open standards. The embedded Total Quality Management (TQM) mechanism provides quality assurance in the e-course development by generating curriculum design reports, which can help teachers monitor and control the implementation process. Moreover, Content Engineering has built-in artificial intelligence and determining agents, which enable teachers to evaluate and improve the e-course by providing them with learner progress reports and recommendations.
2. SmartTutor: This feature is empowered by an artificial intelligence advisory agent and a personalized learning planner, so that personalized advice to learners can be provided. SmartTutor performs such feedback mechanism by collecting and analyzing collective information on learners' performances and learning difficulties, using data-mining techniques. The results of students' performance are then channeled back to the Content Engineering to drive the continuous improvement in the e-learning experience.

3. Personal Classroom: This function enables students to have interactive self-learning with the SmartTutor without connecting to the Internet. Offline study can be done by downloading the e-course and SmartTutor to a desktop or notebook computer. Personal Classroom also allows students to synchronize their learning profiles between online and offline learning sessions. Because the course materials can be downloaded and used offline, this system has Secure e-Course Exchange (eCX) technology to eliminate any unauthorized distributing and sharing of course materials. Thus, the copyright of e-courses is ensured.

THE LEARNING MODES

Online Lecture

These sex education courses for professionals were distinct in that they made full use of the capabilities offered by e-learning to overcome limitations of traditional courses of similar nature and objectives. To operate the software, the students first had to log on from the SOUL Web site (www.soul.hkuspace.org). After they had logged in, they could find online lectures notes for previous chapters and for the chapter being taught. After reading the online lecture notes, students had to complete a quiz at the end of each section of the lecture. Only students with satisfactory performance in those quizzes could proceed to the next chapter. An excerpt from an online lecture and sample quiz question (called "revision questions") is given in Table 5.1. The excerpt is from the second author's course on attraction.

Course materials were posted according to the timetable, giving students normally two weeks to complete a chapter. There were records of when students logged on to the SOUL and whether they had finished the chapters, making it possible for teachers to monitor students' attendance and performance closely. A glossary of vocabulary was also available for students to check for translation and explanation.

E-Tutorial

Besides online lectures, there was at least one two-hour e-tutorial per week for each chapter taught, through use of the chat-room function. The online tutorials were hosted by the teacher who developed the module and the discussion time was fixed according to their schedule. These tutorials allowed teachers and students to have an interactive discussion where students could ask questions on the topic.

E-Conference

Another feature that SOUL offered to enhance the efficiency and effectiveness of e-learning was a Web conference room which enabled teachers and students to post and respond to messages. When students were carrying out their projects or case studies, they could communicate in the Web conference

Table 5.1
Excerpt from Online Course Content and Quiz Question

What causes sexual attraction? There are several factors to explain sexual attraction.

---

1. Sociological theories. For example, the law of "contiguity" says that just merely being next to someone makes it likely you will interact and therefore could be attracted. This means you could get attracted to people who are next to you on a movie line or in the supermarket. Another explanation involves the similarity factor which maintains that the more <u>alike</u> you are to someone, the more likely you will <u>like</u> that person. Research has shown that those who filled out similar answers to a questionnaire rated each other as more likeable.
2. Biological/anthropological explanation. According to the theory of "sexual strategy," men seek to propagate themselves and so would seek a healthy, fertile female who can carry their progeny. Women seek a man who can create healthy babies and then protect her young, consequently choosing a male partner who is healthy, successful, and strong.
3. Behavioral theory. Social psychologist Donn Byrne formulated a "reinforcement theory" that we are attracted to people who give us more positive reinforcement (compliments, making us feel good); thus partner selections are affected by the number of reinforcements versus punishment.
4. Cultural factors. Countries have different rules and customs about attraction. In some cultures, parents still control mating, or pairings are based on social class.
5. Psychodynamics: we are attracted to people who reflect psychological needs, conflicts, and family dynamics that can often be traced to childhood

Revision Questions (Answer true or false to the following):

A. Sexual attraction can be caused by chemicals flowing in the body. T/F
B. Trust is often mentioned as the most important pre-condition for an intimate relationship. T/F
C. Passion is more important than intimacy in establishing a committed loving relationship. T/F
D. Men have fears of intimacy but women do not. T/F
E. Sexual attraction is affected by the values of the society in which a person lives. T/F

Source: Printed with permission of Judy Kuriansky, Ph.D., teacher/developer of this particular course content.

---

room. They could also communicate with their supervisors through e-mail. Students were expected to allocate their time and effort effectively to ensure that the theory learning and case studies were completed according to the assigned learning schedule.

E-Chat

Students also had an opportunity to participate in chat rooms. An example of e-chat is shown in Table 5.2. The table shows excerpts from e-chat between students and a tutor (the second author) on the course topic of synchronizing sexual desire.

Table 5.2
Chat-Room Excerpts from the Course on Synchronizing Sexual Desire

STUDENT 3: How is it possible to synchronize sexual desire with one's partner?

TUTOR: Synchronizing sexual desire requires several steps: (1) accept the potential changes; (2) explain what is going on with you; (3) tell each other what you need and desire at that time; (4) agree that you can take turns, where one week one person gets their sexual timetable more attended to, and the next week it is the other's turn; and (5) an amazing technique is to do what's called 10-minute connects. That means, even if you don't want sex, you assume a spoon position together and breathe at the same time.

STUDENT 4: Professor, how about massage? Should it always be done with the demand to have sex?

TUTOR: Massage should not be a demand for sex. A good technique is to take turns pleasuring each other to relax and please without expecting sex. Thus the couple learns that pleasure can come from many parts of the body, and they discover more erotic spots. The giver of a massage should first avoid touching sexual parts, to give the receiver more relaxation and less pressure. This is also the way to increase TRUST.

STUDENT 3: For my patients who have hysterectomies. During the recovery period, I always encourage a couple to touch each other without intercourse because the woman will feel the husband's love.

TUTOR: EXCELLENT! Yes, massage after very emotionally challenging surgeries is crucial. Hysterectomy, like mastectomy, is upsetting to the woman's feeling of femininity and massage makes her get more in touch with, and hopefully feel good about, her body. The same is true for men in the case of prostate cancer — which is an increasing problem for men. Non-demand pleasuring is key to intimacy and love.

Source: Printed with permission of Judy Kuriansky, Ph.D. tutor and teacher of this course.

Face-to-Face Monthly Seminars

In order to provide students with immediate feedback on skills application, monthly face-to-face seminars were organized. While video presentation or videoconferencing could also have served a similar function, regular face-to-face seminars were feasible since Hong Kong is geographically small and has good transportation networks between districts. These seminars, called Sex Focus, were held to complement the Web teaching and to help promote cognitive and affective aspects of learning, as well as psychomotor skills, in the Web-based learning system.

During these seminars, a wide variety of activities were conducted to help students develop both practical skills in and positive attitudes about conducting sex education and counseling. These included discussions, video presentations, case conferences and case management, emotional and attitudinal reappraisals, and sex counseling and sex therapy videotape demonstrations. A large variety of topics was covered, including sexual activities, sexual cases with organic problems, and sexual issues with social implications.

QUALITY ASSURANCE (QA)

Program Approval

The aim of the Quality Assurance (QA) process is to ensure that the academic standards of the course are compatible with the university standards and that the course is of high international caliber. The academic approval process is under the auspices of the Quality Assurance Committee. Initially, the proposal for the Certificate in Sex Education was discussed and endorsed at the divisional meetings. Then, the directorate further examined the viability of offering the course and ensuring its quality. After gaining approval in principle, the course went through a period of planning, consultation, and curriculum development. Subsequently, the completed curriculum was referred to and scrutinized by the Internal Validation Panel (IVP). The IVP, composed of an HKU academic (from the cognate HKU faculty), two external specialists, and a HKU SPACE academic (from a different division), convened to consider the document and discuss the proposal with the program team. Approval of the program depended on whether the course met the following criteria:

- The rationale for the program and its aims and learning outcomes are appropriate for the needs of students and their employers;
- The academic standard proposed is appropriate for the level of award;
- The structure and content of the curriculum are satisfactory;
- The proposed academic and administrative staffing arrangements are satisfactory;
- The teaching and learning approach are appropriate, with adequate learner support; especially for these part-time adult learners;
- There is a coherent assessment strategy, with weighting of different assessment tasks and explicit methods and timing of assessment;
- There is a full statement of the regulations for admission, progression, and assessment;
- The necessary library, technological, and any specialist facilities are in place; and
- The management, monitoring, and quality assurance arrangement are clearly stated.

The approval process was completed with the final approval from the school's Board for Continuing and Professional Education and Lifelong Learning. The board was chaired by the vice-chancellor and consisted of senior university members; there was also external representation and School membership. This body examined the recommendations made by the Internal Validation Panel and gave the final approval to conduct the Certificate in Sex Education and the Postgraduate Diploma in Principles in Sex Counseling and Therapy. The whole approval process took one year to complete.

PROGRAM REVIEW

In order to ensure high academic standard and rewarding learning for students, the HKU SPACE has a systematic program-monitoring framework in place that every award-bearing program has to follow according to an independent Quality Assurance Committee.

Feedback from students on their learning experience is a vital part of the program evaluation process. A questionnaire was posted electronically, which the students were asked to complete before taking the final examination for their course. Besides the standard evaluation mentioned earlier, at the beginning of the course, the students were asked to post their opinions of their past experience of learning through the chat room (Ng et al., 2004). The program team addressed problems promptly and monitored, reflected upon, and reviewed the course continuously according to students' feedbacks. The quality of the teaching and the learning outcomes and academic standards of the Certificate in Sex Education were also monitored by an Academic Committee (AC). The AC took into account the feedback from students, teachers, and external examiners and made recommendations on academic content and provision of support to students that were based on the strengths and limitations of the course.

Students' Performances and Course Evaluation

As mentioned above, in order to evaluate the students' perceptions, reactions, and experiences of the course, all students were asked to complete an evaluation questionnaire before taking their examinations. The response rate was 100 percent. The questionnaire consists of five parts, including feedback on the course contents (e.g., whether the course materials covered the stated syllabus), on the Sex Focus seminars (e.g., whether teachers encouraged students to participate in class discussion), on tutors (e.g., whether the tutor usually gave clear and satisfactory answers to questions), and on technical and learning support (e.g., whether the student encountered technical problems in using the chat room), as well as one open-ended question on other opinions. Besides the open-ended questions, all items were measures in a 5-point Likert scale, where 1 was strongly disagree and 5 was strongly agree (Ng, 2004; Ng, Shen, & Ng, 2004).

RESULTS

The Students

There were 27 students in the Certificate in Sex Education course in 2002–2003 and 15 students in that course in 2004–2005. The demographic backgrounds of the students in the Certificate in Sex Education program are summarized in Table 5.3.

The table shows that 42 students participated in the Certificate in Sex Education e-course over the two years it was given (2002–2003 and 2004–2005) with about three-quarters of the students being female and one-quarter male (31 versus 11). The overwhelming majority of students had finished their first degree education, while about 20 percent had postgraduate training. More than half of this group were health professionals (25 of 42), including doctors and social workers, while about 17% were teachers, and about a quarter came from other employment (police, geologist).

For the Postgraduate Diploma in Principles in Sex Counseling and Therapy course, the number of students recruited in the academic year 2004–2005 was 13. Table 5.3 shows that about 60% of those students were male and about 40% were female. With regard to their prior education, about 60% had

Table 5.3
Demographics of Students in the Web-Based Certificate Courses in Sex Education and the Postgraduate Diploma in Sex Counseling and Therapy

Course Total	Certificate in Sex Education		Postgraduate Diploma in Sex Counseling and Therapy
Year	*2002–03*	*2004–05*	*2004–05*
Gender			
Male	9	2	8
Female	18	13	5
Total	**27**	**15**	**13**
Educational Level			
Sub-degree	1	0	0
First degree	20	12	8
Postgraduate/diploma/certificate	3	1	1
Master degree by research	3	1	0
Doctorate	0	1	4
Total	**27**	**15**	**13**
Occupation			
In-service school teachers	5	2	0
Health-care professionals (doctors, nurses)	9	10	10
Social worker	5	1	3
Others (policewoman, geologist)	8	2	0
Total	**27**	**15**	**13**

Note: These are reported in actual numbers.

finished their second degree, and 40% had further training. All the students were health-care professionals (doctors, family planners, or social workers).

A comparison of the students who took the certificate and those who took the diploma course shows that there were more females than males in the former course. More students in the diploma course than in the certificate course had advanced education, and more were involved in health-care jobs, which would be expected, since the diploma course was more advanced than the certificate course and would have attracted students who were more advanced in their careers.

Students' Evaluations of Course Materials and Formats

Altogether, 55 adult learners from different professional fields participated in three courses offered (two certificate courses and one diploma course). On average, half of the students attended 60% or more of the online tutorials and seminars. Of these students, 65.5% received an average grade of C or above for all the assignments and the final examination. Some students' assignments were outstanding, as they considered cultural factors and addressed the current sex education issues of the society. For instance, two students who completed a study on post-SARS reactions were complimented by several teachers as well as by their job supervisors for their initiative in trying to learn new skills in research and for their contemporary concern for the culture. Also, a student who designed leaflets for teenagers about alternative sexual behavior received positive feedback from teachers, as the design was highly appealing to the target population and the project was immediately applicable to the society.

The results of the students' evaluations showed that majority of students agreed that the course materials covered the stated syllabus (84%) and met the learning objectives (78%). They also agreed that the course materials were presented clearly (76%) and in a logical and coherent sequence (79%). In general, students agreed that the level and the work of the modules (69% and 67%, respectively) were suitable and effectively facilitated their learning (75%).

In addition, 57% of the students agreed that the SOUL platform was useful in assisting their learning. Concerning the online tutorial using the chatroom function, 39% of students agreed that the online tutorials were helpful in clarifying course issues with the teachers, and 31% found them helpful in discussing ideas with fellow course mates; however, more than 40% of the students were neutral, and 28% disagreed with the claim that online tutorials facilitated discussions among classmates. Consistent with this, about the same number of students (37.5%) agreed that submitting assignments online was easier, with half of students having no comment on this and only 12.5%

of students rating that they did not find it easier to submit their assignments online. As for the Sex Focus seminars, 36% of the students said they preferred having face-to-face seminars to online chat room discussions in this course compared to 24% who disagreed; about the same proportion as for some of the other questions (39%) were neutral.

Students' Evaluations of Teachers' Performances

Overall, most students rated teachers' performance in facilitating their learning favorably. In terms of online tutorials, 59% of the students agreed that the teachers encouraged the students to participate in the discussion, and 60% said that the tutorials increased their interest in the subject. In addition, a majority of students (67%) agreed that the teachers gave clear and satisfactory answers to their questions during the online tutorials. Considering the teachers' performances during the Sex Focus seminars, more than half of the students agreed that teachers spoke clearly (67%) and that their handouts were useful (63%). A majority (63%) of students thought that teachers gave them clear and satisfactory answers to questions, and more than half of students (64%) agreed that the assignment feedbacks given by the teachers were sufficient. Figure 5.1 and Figure 5.2 show the students' responses on teachers' online tutorials and on Sex Focus seminar performances.

Technical Issues

The ongoing monitoring of the course revealed that a small proportion of students encountered technical problems in using chat rooms. These problems were addressed immediately to minimize the disturbance this problem may have caused to their learning. Indeed, more than half of the students (57%) said that the institutes had provided satisfactory support.

Other Student Comments

There were also some critical reflections about the course. Some students found the course workload too heavy and said that they did not have enough time for study as the schedule was too tight.

Teacher Evaluations of the Course

Feedback from teachers was obtained through unstructured discussions held upon completion of the course. Teachers were asked about their experiences with the course format and about students' performance. All teachers were generally enthusiastic about participating in the course and were

Figure 5.1
Students' Feedback on Teachers' Online Tutorial Performance

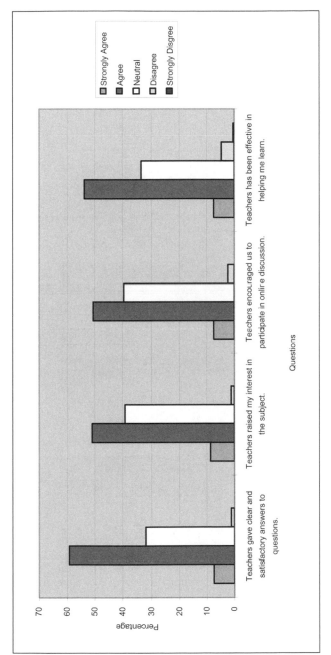

Figure 5.2
Students' Feedback on Teachers' Sex Focus Seminars Performance

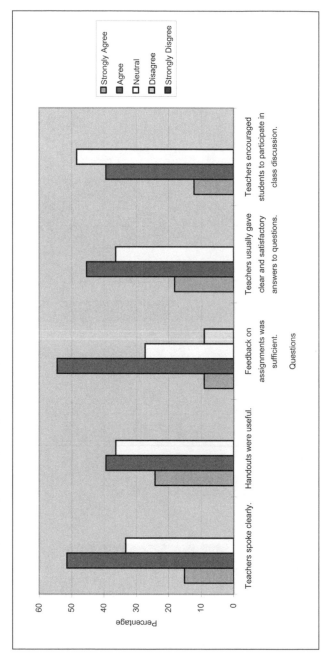

convinced of the value of the e-learning format. However, some frustrations were mentioned regarding technical problems or lack of familiarity with the learning platform. These problems were solved immediately by having support staff assist the teachers or by involving technicians to address the problems. Teachers were impressed with the students' enthusiasm about sex education and with their willingness to work hard.

DISCUSSION AND CONCLUSION

The courses presented in this chapter were pioneer online courses organized in the Asian region that offered high-quality, professional training about sexuality to teachers, social workers, health-care professionals and those who are actively involved in sex education and counseling. Since the course was offered via an e-learning format, students had more control than usual over their learning and study time, which they adjusted according to their particular working schedules. Moreover, with the use of the World Wide Web to deliver the course, geographic restrictions were removed, so teachers and students from all parts of the world were able to participate in the course.

Feedback from the students showed that e-learning courses have an advantage over traditional courses in their ability to effectively utilize global manpower, as most of the teaching is conducted on the Web and is easily accessible worldwide. Additionally, since teachers for the courses were recruited both from Hong Kong and from other countries around the world, problems of inadequate resources and expertise in one region can be overcome. Moreover, the e-learning mode allows students to freely choose their own time and pace of learning, so the courses were convenient, flexible and user-friendly, creating minimal interference with students' daily work.

However, the e-learning courses were not without limitations. While students reported that the computer learning platform was useful, they also faced some technological problems while using the online functions. One proposed solution to the problem is to conduct an orientation session with students and teachers on how to use the learning platform and to explain ways to deal with foreseeable problems.

Feedback from the students also showed that they are still used to the traditional face-to-face type of teaching. Indeed, the in-person presentations, role-plays, and discussions enabled students to practice skills of teaching and counseling and provided an opportunity for them to build a supportive network to help them face the challenge of promoting sex education. Therefore, it is noted that future Web-based course should continue to conduct the majority of lectures and tutorials online but that in-person sessions should also be allocated to facilitate communication among students and between students and teachers.

In addition, student feedback revealed that the schedule was intense and that students were expected to complete a considerable amount of work in a short period of time. To mitigate this problem, the course can be spread out over a longer period of time. Coursework deadlines and assessment dates can also be announced at the beginning of the course, so students can prepare their schedule in advance and better manage their time for coursework, for the independent project and for any required revisions.

A recent study on the provision of sexuality education via the Internet to young people in China supports the idea that the Internet is an effective way to improve awareness of sexual matters and to create more favorable attitudes toward the provision of contraception to the unmarried population (Lou et al., 2006). The study pointed out that sex education is an essential means to promote sexual health and that the Internet is an effective platform by which to carry out sex education. The success of the present courses supports those conclusions.

The present project further provides strong support for the belief that the promotion of globalization in education has been greatly enhanced by advancements in technology. As technological advances emerge, more techniques can be added to the Web-based learning model, including audio and video streaming and other interactive methodologies. Setting up an electronic journal and bulletin can further strengthen communication with past and current students and help attain the aim of life-long learning, which should be a guiding principle in future teaching curricula and projects. Such valuable resources will further facilitate effective teaching-learning outcome for Web-based courses. The potential to globalize the courses described here is significant. Collaborations are being discussed with overseas universities, exploring the possibilities of expanding these courses into regions such as mainland China and other Asia countries where formal professional training in sexuality education is in great demand.

REFERENCES

Belar, C. (2006, January). Distance education is here. *Monitor on Psychology, 37*(1), 40.

Coleman, E. (1996). Evolution of human sexuality course at the University of Minnesota Medical School. In S. Matsumoto (Ed.), *Sexuality and human bonding* (pp. 349–352). Tokyo: Elsevier.

Coleman, E., & Haeberle, E. (1999). *Sexology world-wide.* Hong Kong: World Sexology Association.

Cuthbert, L. (2004). Distance learning: An opportunity and a challenge? In *Review and new perspectives, selected papers from the International Conference on E-education* (pp. 1–4). Macau: Macau Polytechnic Institute.

Family Planning Association of Hong Kong (1997). Youth Sexuality Study. Family Planning Association of Hong Kong, Hong Kong.

Family Planning Association of Hong Kong (2001). Youth Sexuality Study. Family Planning Association of Hong Kong, Hong Kong.

Family Planning Association of Hong Kong (2007). Youth Sexuality Study. Family Planning Association of Hong Kong, Hong Kong.

Haeberle, E. & Gindorf, R. (1993). *Sexology today.* Düsseldorf, Germany: German Society for Social-scientific Sex Research (DGSS).

Hiltz, S. R. (1986). The virtual classroom: Using computer-mediated communication for university teaching. *Journal of Communication, 36,* 2 (Spring), 95–104.

Hiltz, S. R., and Meinke, R. (1989). Teaching sociology in a virtual classroom. *Teaching Sociology, 17,* 431–446.

Hu, P., Kuriansky, J., & Shen, Z. (2003, September). The analysis of American sex therapy training in China. *Chinese Journal of Sexology, 12*(3), 42–44.

Kaimola, K., & Volkama, S. (2000). New approaches to continuing professional education in sexology in Jyaskyla Polytechnic, Finland. In E.M.L. Ng, J. J. Borrás-Valls, M. Pérez-Conchillo, & E. Coleman (Eds.), *Sexuality in the new millennium.* Proceedings of the 14th World Congress of Sexology, Hong Kong, SAR, China, August 23–27, 1999. (pp. 303–306). Bologna: Editrice Compositori.

Kuriansky, J. (1985). Why do they call and how are they helped? A radio call-in psychologist/host's endeavor to go beyond ratings and into research. *Amplifier, 1*(2), 5–7.

Kuriansky, J. (1996). Sex advice on the radio: An overview in the United States and around the world. *SIECUS Report, 24*(5), 6–9.

Kuriansky, J. (2004). *Psychology and the media: New technologies. Symposium presented at the Eastern Association of Psychology,* Boston, Massachusetts, March 12, 2005.

Kuriansky, J., Golia, L., Larsen, E., & Angiola, J. (2005). *An in-depth examination of giving E-advice.* Presentation given at the PsychSoc conference, Columbia University Teachers College, April 15, 2005.

Lee, Y. C. (2000). Sex education in Hong Kong primary schools, a study of teacher beliefs and attitudes. In E.M.L. Ng, J. J. Borrás-Valls, M. Pérez-Conchillo, & E. Coleman (Eds.), *Sexuality in the new millennium* (pp. 279–283). Bologna: Editrice Compositori.

Li, J. (2006). Sex education can't wait. *Beijing Review, 49*(8), 2.

Lou, C. H., Zhao, Q., Gao, E. S., & Shah, I. (2006). Can the Internet be an effective way to conduct sex education for young people in China? *Journal of Adolescent Health, 39*(5), 720–728.

Marega, O. (2005). The challenge to generate and express meaning: can sexual education and e-learning be compatible? Presentation at the XVII World Congress of Sexuality, Montreal Canada, July 10–15.

Ng, E.M.L., Borrás-Valls, J. J., Pérez-Conchillo, M., & Coleman, E. (Eds.) (2000). *Sexuality in the New millennium. Proceedings of the 14th World Congress of Sexology, August 23–27, 1999, Hong Kong.* Bologna: Editrice Compositori.

Ng, M. (1993). Public responses to the sex education series of radio-television Hong Kong. *Journal of Sex Education and Therapy, 19*(1), 64–72.

Ng, M. L. (2001). *A sex education course on the Internet for professionals.* Abstract, 15th World Congress of Sexology, Paris, France. June 24–28, 169.

Ng, M. L. (2004). *The evaluation of a Web-based course for professional sex education in Hong Kong.* Paper presented at the First Asia Pacific Conference of Sexology. Mumbai, India. November 21–24.

Ng, M. L., & Fan, M. S. (1996). Sex education on radio: The Hong Kong and Shanghai experience. In S. Matsumoto (Ed.), *Sexuality and human bonding* (pp. 173–179). New York: Elsevier Science B.V.

Ng, M. L., Ng, T., & Cheung, B. (2004a). Professional sex education through e-learning. In *Review and New Perspectives, Selected Papers from the International Conference on E-Education* (pp. 187–191). Macau: Macau Polytechnic Institute.

Ng, T., Ng, M. L., & Cheung, B. (2004b). *Sex education made possible through strategic use pf alliances and teaching modes. Proceedings of the 3rd Asia-Pacific Conference on Continuing Education and Lifelong Learning Conference.* Perth, Australia: Curtin University.

Ng, T., Shen, S. M. & Ng, M. L. (2004). *Quality assurance of a Web-based sex education.* Paper presented at The 3rd Asia-Pacific Conference on Continuing Education and Lifelong Learning Conference, Curtin University of Technology, Perth, Australia (September 28-October 1). Retrieved January 8, 2009, from http://www.cbs.curtin. edu.au/files/Paper_-_NG_Tina_Mo-Yin_bruce_cheung.pdf

Pan American Health Organization. (2000). Promotion of sexual health, recommendations for action. Proceedings of a regional consultation convened by Pan American Health Organization and World Organization, Antigua Guatemala, Guatemala, May 19–22, 23.

Shefet, O., & Kuriansky, J. (2003). An examination of Internet chat on psychological and sexual subjects: Who chats and why. Paper presented at the annual meeting of the American Association of Sex Educators, Counselors and Therapists. Las Vegas, June 4–8.

Weerakoon, P., & Wong, M. (2003). Sexuality education online for health professionals. *Electronic Journal of Human Sexuality, 6.* Retrieved January 28, 2009, from http:// www.ejhs.org/volume6/SexEd.html

Yen, H. (1996) Sexuality education development—a non-governmental organisation experience in Taiwan. In S. Matsumoto (ed.), *Sexuality and human bonding* (pp. 345–348). Tokyo: Elsevier.

Modules and Chapters Taught in Certificate in Sex Education Course

Module 1: Sex and Health

Chapter 1   Sexual anatomy and physiology
Chapter 2   Concepts of sexual health and diseases
Chapter 3   Sexual practices for health, safe sex, and sexually transmitted diseases
Chapter 4   Contraception
Chapter 5   Sexual function and dysfunction
Chapter 6   Sexual complications in diseases
Chapter 7   Sex and depression

Module 2: Sexual Psychology

Chapter 1   Psychosexual development
Chapter 2   Sexual attraction, intimacy, and desire
Chapter 3   Sexual identity and orientation
Chapter 4   Gender and sex roles
Chapter 5   Sex, interpersonal relationship, and love
Chapter 6   Marital sex
Chapter 7   Sexual psychology of people with different or special needs
Chapter 8   Abnormal sexual psychology

Module 3: Sex and Society

Chapter 1   Sex and culture
Chapter 2   Sex and law
Chapter 3   Sex and religion
Chapter 4   Sex crimes and society
Chapter 5   Sexual equality and sexual rights
Chapter 6   Sociological studies on sex, findings and methodology
Chapter 7   Sex and love in the age of terrorism
Chapter 8   Philosophy of sex

Module 4: Sex and Education

Chapter 1   Promoting sexual health through education: Principles and concepts
Chapter 2   The psychology of sexual health education
Chapter 3   Sexuality education at school: Experiences of different developed countries
Chapter 4   Sexual health education: Program planning, implementation, and evaluation
Chapter 5   Practical skills in sex education
Chapter 6   Question & answer training
Chapter 7   Group techniques in sex education
Chapter 8   Class management in sex education
Chapter 5   Production of sex educational materials
Chapter 6   Group and individual counseling
Chapter 7   Sex education in the family
Chapter 8   Sexual attitude restructuring as in the SAR curriculum

APPENDIX 5.2

Modules and Chapters Taught in the Postgraduate Diploma in Principles of Sex Therapy and Counseling Course

Module 1: Sex and Health

Chapter 1 History of sex therapy and counseling
Chapter 2 Sexual health, sexual functions, and sexual practice
Chapter 3 Sexual anatomy and physiology
Chapter 4 Fertility control
Chapter 5 Safe sex and sexually transmitted diseases
Chapter 6 Sexual dysfunction associated with medical and psychiatric conditions
Chapter 7 Sexual dysfunction associated with mental health problems—depression, etc.

Module 2: Sexual Psychology

Chapter 1 Sexual attraction, intimacy, and psychosexual responses
Chapter 2 Psychosexual development
Chapter 3 Homosexuality: Current theories and treatment
Chapter 4 Sexual variations

Module 3: Sex and Society

Chapter 1 Sex and culture—understanding the patient's context
Chapter 2 Sex and religion
Chapter 3 Sexual politics and legal issues
Chapter 4 Sex in the age of terrorism
Chapter 5 Sexual abuse

Module 4: Sexual dysfunctions and treatment modalities

Chapter 1 Classification, diagnosis, and overview of treatment modalities
Chapter 2 Male dysfunctions and treatment
Chapter 3 Female sexual disorders and treatment
Chapter 4 Critical steps for positive sexual behaviors
Chapter 5 New issues in sexual functioning—G spot and female ejaculation
Chapter 6 Drugs effects on sex

Module 5: Sex Counseling Skills

Chapter 1 Therapeutic roles in helping clients with sexuality issues
Chapter 2 Basic assumptions: PLISSIT model
Chapter 3 The Reassure Model
Chapter 4 Active suppressive and expressive techniques
Chapter 5 Counselling of special groups

Module 6: Sex Therapy Skills

Chapter 1 Sexual desire and promoting couple's sexual relationship
Chapter 2 Assessment, problem formulation, intervention, and making referrals
Chapter 3 Basic sex skills education and safe use of sex aids
Chapter 4 Dealing with the couples versus the individual patient
Chapter 5 Integrating East and West techniques in therapy
Chapter 6 Therapeutic milieu

Chapter Six

SEXUALITY EDUCATION IN VIDEO GAMES: RECOMMENDATIONS FOR THE USE OF VIDEO GAMES TO TEACH HUMAN SEXUALITY ISSUES

M. Scott Gross

Following the release of the Nintendo Entertainment System and the Sega Master System in the mid 1980s, video games have found their way into American homes in vast and ever increasing numbers. According to the Electronic Software Association (ESA), sales of video games reached $7 billion in 2003, nearly doubling sales less than 10 years ago. Furthermore, more than 239 million computer or video games were sold in 2003, or about 2 for every household in America (ESA, 2004). Roughly 58% of computer gamers and 77% of console (game systems in the home) gamers are less than 36 years of age, and about 39% of all players are women, with more women playing computer games than console games (Interactive Digital Software Association [IDSA], 2002). This ever-expanding media form has had little attention paid to it aside from examining the effects that violence in games has on players. However, within the last ten years video games have been the focus of media theorists who have recognized games as having a tremendous impact on society akin to television and film. Unfortunately, unlike in television or film where specific films and shows become icons for many years, new video games are released on a weekly basis, and newer and more advanced systems are also releasing more quickly. Research and content studies of video games are outdated almost as quickly as they are released, with studies done more than five years ago being completely irrelevant to today's gamers (Beasley & Collins Standley, 2002). Furthermore, as with most pop culture targeted towards teens, parents and adults have little understanding of the realm of video games unless they themselves are also players. What do terms like PS2 and

XBOX mean? What's the difference between a Game Boy and a Game Cube? For people who find setting the clock on their microwave or programming their VCR to be difficult, then the task of hooking up a video game system, let alone multiple systems, can be a daunting task. It is not the intent of this paper to offer a general guide to video games, but such a guide would be an excellent source for parents and educators who wish to become savvier with the world of video games. Rather, this paper shall focus on the trends found in video game research and on offering suggestions for further study and suggestions for how video games or images of video games may be used in the classroom to discuss gender, gender roles, and stereotypes about both.

VIDEO GAMES IN THEORY

Many of the theories used to examine video games in the past few years have their roots in television and film theories, and have primarily focused on the issue of violence (Wolf & Perron, 2003). However, theories that have been used to examine the societal effect of television and film such as Agenda Setting and Framing Theories (Kosicki, 1993) and Cognitive Social Learning Theory (Bandura, 1994) can also be used to examine the effects that video games may have on how we view gender and gender roles in our society. Furthermore, theories that examine how we identify with or objectify the characters in video games have much to offer to the study of how we perceive gender based upon how it is portrayed (Mikula, 2003). Video games are also becoming more like movies in the ways that reality is portrayed, and so theories used to study film can more readily be applied to the study of video games (Rehak, 2003). Due to the interactive nature of video games, special attention needs to be paid to the portrayal of the game world since players interact with that world for many more hours (up to 30 to 50 times longer) than they do with the environments portrayed in most movies.

Certainly, video games have been designed within the context of our existing culture, and are therefore influenced by the existing definitions and roles of gender as set up by our society, as well as the stereotypes that also exist within the culture. Video games, however, could very well perpetuate negative or damaging stereotypes or gender roles based upon the images portrayed within them. According to Kosicki (1993), Agenda Setting and Framing Theories put forward that media forms tell people what is important in the world and how to think about those important events. Beasley and Collins Standley (2002) found in their content analysis of 47 randomly selected video games that women are much less likely to appear in video games (13.74% female characters compared to 71.52% male characters [the remaining percentage is made up of characters with indeterminate gender]), and that they are also more likely to be depicted with fewer clothes than males. Furthermore, earlier studies have shown that women are much more likely to be portrayed in subservient roles or the victims of violence in video games than men are (Dietz, 1998). Even when we examine depictions of women in independent or strong roles, they are often held back by the focus of attention on their appearance. Speaking about the main character of the game *Tomb Raider*, Lara Croft, Mikula stated that she "is everything that is bad about representations of women in culture, and everything good . . ." (2003, pp. 79–80). This is but one representation of the many myths that video games portray about gender and sexual orientation. Some others include but are not limited to:

- A woman's beauty is proportional to the size of her breasts, i.e., bigger breasts equals more attractive
- Gay men are comical, flamboyant, and stereotypical
- Lesbian women are highly sexualized and are often used in games to please a heterosexual male audience
- Lingerie or revealing clothing is standard issue uniform for female secret operative or military agents
- Female sexual arousal and killing are often linked; men are cold blooded killers
- Men are leaders, providers, and protectors while women are followers, nurturers, healers, and incapable of protecting themselves
- Women are only interested in clothing and shopping, while men are only interested in sports and cars.

Many games thrive on myth and stereotype as their main forms of entertainment. This is the primary draw of players to the Grand Theft Auto [GTA] series which includes the titles Grand Theft Auto 3, Grand Theft Auto: Vice City, and Grand Theft Auto: San Andreas. These games have been slammed by critics for their glorified depictions of prostitution, organized crime, and violence. Much of the humor in the game is based upon stereotypes about gang life, police officers, gay men, women, and racial backgrounds, and these games have certainly earned their M for Mature ratings. Mature players who have passed beyond adolescence often find the depiction of these stereotypes to be amusing and are able to distinguish them from reality. However, younger players who have yet to develop formal operational thought have trouble distinguishing between fantasy and reality and may play out the fantasy in the real world (Piaget, 1972). This has lead to a number of incidents involving children between the ages of 10 and 14 acting out scenes of violence "like they do in GTA."

With the exception of most sports games and games that are based upon historical events, most games are set within some kind of fantasy world, which is often very different from the real world. However, there are many games that offer a fantasy world that is very much like the real world except for a few cosmetic or fantastical differences. Through repeated viewing and interaction with such games, it is possible that some players may begin to have a skewed perception about the real world is actually like or they more readily buy into stereotypes about the culture (Iyengar, 1991). Therefore, we can assume that repeated consumption of such images described above will lead to a greater acceptance of what is considered appropriate or inappropriate for males and females despite the stereotypical or harmful nature of these scripts.

Cognitive Social Learning Theory (Bandura, 1994) predicts that people will imitate behaviors that are rewarded or not punished. This theory has been used to examine sexual scripting in movies and television shows, but is also particularly useful in examining issues in video games such as violence and interaction between genders (Brown, 2002). A huge percentage of video games include violence, and this violence is often rewarded or at the very least not punished within the video game world. Some critics argue that video games are training players to be good killers while their rivals claim that games are harmless fantasy (Thompson, 2002). Furthermore, many games depict scripts of how to seek sexual gratification or how to find sexual mates (Consalvo, 2003). There are often few negative consequences for mistreating others within the game world and in some cases ill treatment of women is encouraged or rewarded. It should be noted, however, that most depictions of ill treatment of women occur in games that are rated M for mature, which do not represent a majority of video games available. Furthermore, the vast majority of violence laden games have players acting on behalf of forces of social order such as police or fantasy military organizations, with very few games daring to have the player act the role of a criminal or psychopath (Thompson, 2002). Finally, it has been shown that the less teens know about a particular subject area (e.g., gender roles, sexual scripting, appropriateness of violence), the more likely they are to turn to the media to increase their knowledge base, especially if the topic area is sensitive in nature (Jeffres, 1997). Hence, we as educators need to be concerned and knowledgeable about the content of the media that teens consume with special attention paid to video games since they are being consumed by greater numbers of teens for longer periods of time each year.

ADVANTAGES AND DISADVANTAGES OF VIDEO GAME USE IN THE CLASSROOM

Video games have inherent advantages and disadvantages to their use in the classroom, which need to be addressed so that the games and images can best be put to use. This paper focuses on the specific topic of gender, but video games could be used to examine a wide variety of subject areas including violence, racial issues, and sexual scripting.

Advantages

- Video games and video game images are readily available. Games and game systems can be easily rented at little individual cost from local video stores as well as online. Furthermore, many Web sites offer screenshots and background information about specific game titles (see www.gamefaqs.com, www.gamespot.com, and www. ebgames.com). Gaming magazines such as *Electronics Gaming Monthly, Playstation Magazine, PC Gaming,* etc., offer screen-shots, previews of upcoming games, and reviews of existing titles.

- Gaming can itself be an educational experience. Playing video games requires and develops strong hand-eye coordination, and also usually requires strong literacy skills. Furthermore, many games require the player to make decisions important to the game character's life as well as requiring the player to be able to make use of conflict resolution techniques. Cooperative multiplayer games require players to work as a team to complete various tasks which often requires players to engage in real world communication and support.
- Video games, game boxes, and game advertisements can easily be examined in the classroom. The game boxes themselves, as well as the television and printed advertisements, are more or less readily accessible through the Internet, as well as in magazines and can be broken down in order to examine stereotypes using techniques made famous by Jean Kilbourne (1999). With the increasing prevalence of Internet-enabled computers in classrooms, it is going to be even easier to access this information in the very near future directly from the classroom.
- Video games are enticing to young people. Vast numbers of young people already play video games at home, are familiar with a huge number of video game titles, and enjoy them as a cutting edge form of pop-culture media. Video games are something that many teens can identify with (whether they like them or not), and therefore information drawn from them will likely hold more relevance to them.

Disadvantages

- Video games are time consuming. Most games require a time commitment of at least 30 minutes, which is simply not possible in most educational settings especially if the class size is large because each student will not have an opportunity to interact with the game environment. Furthermore, many elements of game play that would be of interest for use in the classroom, such as decisions made by the game character regarding treatment of other characters in the game, require extensive game play and cannot be easily demonstrated in the classroom.
- Video games are constantly changing. I have avoided offering specific titles for use because any that would be suggested are likely to be outdated or unfamiliar to students within two years. Certain games and images will be lasting and can be examined to great effect for many years, but for the greatest impact it would be best to use games that are currently being played by the students in the class.
- Many video games are violent. For good or for ill, violence has become indelibly linked with the video game industry and this is not likely to change any time soon. Some parents and teachers may object to the use of media which in many ways glorifies violence against others. However, this can also be an excellent discussion point with students and parents when discussing appropriate and inappropriate behaviors.

HOW TO USE VIDEO GAMES IN THE CLASSROOM

Staying up-to-date with video games is often a daunting task even for individuals who claim to be aficionados. However, the educator has an excellent resource in his or her students. Questioning the students about what games they are playing and why it can be vitally important in staying on top of what games and images could best be put to use in the classroom. Although most games require a time commitment to play, images and even video of game play can be found on the Internet, either through distribution Web sites, informational Web sites, or fan based Web sites. As with using any media form, it is important to become knowledgeable about the specific games, images, and game play movies that one is to use so as to not be surprised by any of the content that happens to pop up in the middle of a lesson. These images are extremely valuable because they allow the educator to examine and discuss stereotypes about gender and gender roles using a format that is of great interest to many of their students. Video game covers and screenshots can easily be used alone or in conjunction with images from magazines of advertisements or famous people in lessons aimed at discussing the dominant cultures of clothing and body types that exist here in America. Getting students to talk about and discuss what makes one character or person "hot" and others "not" can help them begin to form critical thinking skills about cultural stereotypes.

As mentioned above, one of the easiest ways to incorporate video games into a classroom lesson is to use screenshots or advertisements. Video game advertisements appear in many hobby magazines, teen interest magazines, and video exclusive publications. Using a critical eye to examine trends and the use of imagery in these advertisements can be an eye opening experience and an excellent discussion starter. A review of Jean Kilbourne's work would be beneficial here as she has pioneered the critical examination of video and print advertising. Many of the dangerous innuendo that she discovered in other advertisements applies equally well to video game advertisements. Screenshots and gameplay movies can be used to study depictions of gender and gender roles as well as sexual orientation and treatment of women. Screenshots are easily located on the Internet at commercial sites like www.ebgames. com and at fan sites like www.gamespot.com. Gameplay movies are a little harder to acquire for classroom use, but can be found at the Gamespot site mentioned above and many video games have their own individual sites to promote them. The best source of new titles and information is from students and other gamers; following their leads will help an educator to develop an interesting and informative lesson using media forms that students will readily grasp.

MASSIVELY MULTIPLAYER GAMES AND SUGGESTIONS FOR RESEARCH

This paper has focused specifically on computer or console games that are typically played by a maximum of four players at any given time. However, there are a variety of computer games, and an increasing number of console games, that allow online play with a massive number of individuals from around the world. These are appropriately called Massively Multiplayer

Online Role Playing Games or MMORPGs. These games are a special case because most of the interaction the player has with the game is with the characters or avatars of other human players. These games are an ongoing, living, and sometimes changing fantasy world that offer players the chance to explore relationships and make decisions that are not regularly possible in their daily lives. Such games offer an excellent opportunity for research in communication based upon such factors as the supposed or assumed anonymity of identity in the interaction with others, the assumed or perceived gender of the avatars being interacted with, and acquisition and maintenance of a role of "other." Furthermore, an important factor to many players in such games is the creation of their avatar, or alternate self (Filiciak, 2003; Lahti, 2003). Many factors go into the creation of an avatar, such as race or creature type, gender, body type, facial appearance, and clothing style. Filiciak points out that most players attempt to create an avatar that represents not only how the player perceives him or herself, but also how that player wants to be represented. As such, it would be interesting to examine why players make the choices that they do in avatar creation. Computer labs with networked computers are more available on college campuses, but there also exist gaming establishments that allow many people to play online games together for an hourly cost. Such an environment would be ideal for conducting a student driven experiment in which students create avatars, interact with the others from their group or the world at large, and then report back on why they made the choices they did or why they chose to portray themselves in a specific manner.

There has been some evidence that playing video games causes an increase in dopamine levels in the brain. Dopamine is an important neurotransmitter for experiences of pleasure, reinforcement, and reward, thereby giving rise to a hypothesis that video games may have an addictive component to them. Furthermore, dopamine has been shown to have several sexual effects on the body including increasing sex drive and promoting orgasm in both males and females (Crenshaw & Goldberg, 1996). These effects of dopamine combined with its release during game play could reinforce and strengthen sexual attitudes portrayed in video games as well as explain the large number of sexually titillating images in video games. Further research is needed in these areas to determine if playing video games has a physically addictive component, a habitually addictive component, and determining what role dopamine plays in reinforcing attitudes and values as portrayed in games.

CONCLUSION

I believe it is clear that video games have a lot to offer in the study of culture and society, as well as a lot to teach about areas like gender and gender roles. Use of this material could be helpful in developing critical thinking skills in students and could help them to become more conscientious consumers of electronic media. There is a lot that can be learned from observation of players at play, and from observing the virtual worlds of MMORPGs as they could be considered a microcosm (a rather large microcosm with more than 1,000 players in any given game) of intercultural interaction since players are hailing from all over the world and represent all ages and genders. As a long time player and fan of video games, I find the recent trend of video games that emphasize sexual content to be disturbing in that the images depicted are often unrealistic and could be potentially damaging to the world view of younger gamers who have not developed the critical thinking skills necessary to differentiate fact from fiction, stereotype from truth, or appropriate behavior from inappropriate behavior. Video games are fantasy, and many children are incapable of fully differentiating between fantasy and reality without the intervention of parents or educators. Visual media forms like video games have already been shown to be an incredibly powerful influence on how people perceive the world around them. When coupled with reward systems like higher scores, unlockable secrets, and a powerful neurotransmitter like dopamine, information presented in video games may become more influential than information presented in other forms like TV and movies. Therefore, it is important that the theoretical, academic, and educational study of video games not only continues, but proliferates, so that we may better understand how to use this tremendous media form as well as how it affects our students.

NOTE

"Sexuality Education in Video Games: Recommendations for the Use of Video Games to Teach Human Sexuality Issues," *American Journal of Sexuality Education* 1(1): 51–61. Reprinted by permission of Taylor and Francis.

Available online at http://www.haworthpress.com/web/AJSE? 2005 by The Haworth Press, Inc. All rights reserved.

REFERENCES

Bandura, A. (1994). Social cognitive theory of mass communication. In J. Bryant & D. Zillmann (Eds.), *Media effects: Advances in theory and research* (pp. 61–90). Hillsdale, NJ: Lawrence Erlbaum.

Beasley, B., & Collins Standley, T. (2002). Shirts vs. skins: Clothing as an indicator of gender role stereotyping in video games. *Mass Communication and Society, 5*(3), 279–293.

Brown, J. D. (2002). Mass media influences on sexuality. *The Journal of Sex Research, 39*(1), 42–45.

Consalvo, M. (2003). Hot dates and fairy-tale romances: Studying sexuality in video games. In M. J. P. Wolf & B. Perron (Eds.), *The video game theory reader* (171–194). New York: Routledge.

Crenshaw, T. L., & Goldberg, J. P. (1996). *Sexual pharmacology: Drugs that affect sexual functioning.* New York: W. W. Norton.

Dietz, T. L. (1998). An examination of violence and gender role portrayals in video games: Implications for gender socialization and aggressive behavior. *Sex Roles, 38,* 425–441. doi: 10.1023/A: 1018709905920.

Electronic Software Association (2003). *Top ten industry facts.* Retrieved June 21, 2004 from www.theesa.com/pressroom.html

Filiciack, M. (2003). Hyperidentities: Postmodern identity patterns in massively multi-player online role-playing games. In M. J. P. Wolf & B. Perron (Eds.), *The video game theory reader* (171–194). New York: Routledge.

Interactive Digital Software Association (2003). *Essential facts about the video game industry: 2002 sales, demographics, and usage data.* Retrieved June 21, 2004, from the Electronic Software Association Web site: http://www.theesa.com/EF2003.pdf.

Iyengar, S. (1991). *Is anyone responsible? How television frames political issues.* Chicago: University of Chicago Press.

Jeffres, L. W. (1997). *Mass media effects.* Prospect Heights, IL: Waveland Press.

Kilbourne, J. (1999). *Can't buy my love: How advertising changes the way we think and feel.* New York: Touchstone.

Kosicki, G. (1993). Problems and opportunities in agenda-setting research. *Journal of Communication, 43,* 100–127.

Lahti, M. (2003). As we become machines: Corporealized pleasures in video games. In M. J. P. Wolf & B. Perron (Eds.), *The video game theory reader* (171–194). New York: Routledge.

Mikula, M. (2003). Gender and video games: The political valency of Lara Croft. *Continuum: Journal of Media and Cultural Studies, 17*(1), 79–87. doi: 10.1080/1030431022000049038.

Piaget, J. (1972). Intellectual evolution from adolescence to adulthood. *Human Development, 15,* 1–12.

Rehak, B. (2003). Playing at being: Psychoanalysis and the avatar. In M. J. P. Wolf & B. Perron (Eds.), *The video game theory reader* (171–194). New York: Routledge.

Thompson, C. (2002). Violence and the political life of video games. In L. King (Ed.), *Game on: the history and culture of videogames* (22–31). New York: Universe Publishing.

Wolf, M. J. P., & Perron, B. (Eds.). (2003). *The video game theory reader.* New York: Routledge.

Chapter Seven

SEXUALITY ADVICE FOR TEENS ON THE RADIO: TUNING IN AND TURNING OUT HEALTHY

Judy Kuriansky and Erika Pluhar

The radio has long served as a major source of communication, entertainment, and news coverage in the United States. With its immediate, intimate, and also anonymous interaction between listeners and radio host/broadcasters, the radio has provided a useful means of two-way communication, which has created an open forum for discussion of personal issues. The use of radio specifically to address sensitive relationship topics began over a half-century ago, partly as a result of the "sexual revolution" of the 1960s which opened the floodgates for public discourse about sexuality. The popularity of that subject matter led broadcasters to realize the potential ratings success of programming on that topic, with the result that discussion formats evolved to include advice on intimate life issues. These advice-driven shows that took listener calls about relationships and sexuality questions became extremely popular early in the 1980s (Schwebel, 1982) and continued throughout that decade, when it was estimated that there were at least 50 such radio advice shows throughout the country hosted by mental health practitioners, with the number of listeners ranging from the thousands to the millions (Bouhoutsos, Goodchilds, & Huddy, 1986).

Several such advice programs were prominent in large metropolitan cities on both coasts (Los Angeles and New York) as well as in other large city radio markets (e.g., Boston, Chicago, and Denver). Due to impressive listenership and ratings success, some shows were syndicated across the country. One nationally aired advice show was hosted by a female talk show host, Sally Jesse Raphael, who did not have a professional degree but was nonetheless highly popular among listeners. Other shows were launched with psychologists as hosts but in the early days of this programming few of these hosts were also sex educators, therapists, or researchers. The first author's call-in advice show aired on a major New York radio station, WABC, five nights a week for three hours a night. A similar daily show aired on the opposite coast, on KABC in Los Angeles, hosted by psychologist Toni Grant during daytime hours. Because of the popularity of such programming, some shows were syndicated on radio stations across the country, and one show hosted by psychologist Sonja Friedman expanded from its Detroit radio slot to television (in the era pre-Dr. Phil). While most shows were aimed at an adult audience, a pioneer show in New York on the weekends that offered advice to parents about children was hosted by psychologist Lawrence Balter.

Most of these advice shows focused on general relationship issues and personal problems, although questions about sexuality also arose (Kuriansky, 1985). Growing public interest in discussing sexuality publicly led to shows specifically addressing this issue, notably the *Sexuality Speaking* radio call-in show, hosted by sex educator Dr. Ruth Westheimer. This show began airing in 1980 on Sunday nights on a country music station in the New York market, initially for 15 minutes and then expanding to 2 hours. The show host, trained by well-known sexologist Helen Kaplan, was fondly referred to as simply "Dr. Ruth" and was often quoted for phrases she used, like "Use condoms!," and for her warnings against engaging in sex at too young an age (Hackett, 1982). In subsequent years, Dr. Ruth became a well-known media personality in the United States and abroad, providing information about sexuality—and particularly about safe sex—in many media outlets.

The first author's program, launched the same year as the *Sexually Speaking* show, was initially open to all questions about life issues, but questions about sex became increasingly common. For example, after one caller would discuss a sexual issue (e.g., premature ejaculation or penis size), other listeners would call with similar questions, to the point where, on some evenings, questions were overwhelmingly about sexuality (Kuriansky, 1984). In the 1990s, the author was asked to host a nightly show dealing specifically with questions about sex, love, and relationships. This show, called *LovePhones*, was the first of its kind on the east coast to air on a major FM music radio station (as opposed to an AM talk station) which played music in all parts except for the 2-hour nightly slot—10 P.M. to midnight—given over to the call-in advice program. As with the *Sexually Speaking* show, the show's largest listening audience was composed of young adults, ages 18–24 (a demographic measured by radio ratings), with younger adolescents also listening. The show format took calls and questions from listeners about their love, sex, and relationship problems, answered by the first author with serious professional advice in her role as a licensed clinical psychologist and certified sex therapist. The cohost was a disc jockey at the radio station who was psychologically astute and also had a keen sense of humor; his role was to move the show along and to provide entertainment value to the program as required by the station programmers. A similarly formatted syndicated show (called *Lovelines*) was broadcast from studios in Los Angeles, cohosted by a disc jockey and a medical doctor (an addiction specialist) who gave advice about sex and relationships. A form of this show also aired on MTV.

The *LovePhones* radio show became extremely popular, receiving about 350,000 calls each month and drawing impressively large shares of the radio listening audience—20% of the available audience in its time slot and more than 27% of teens and 20-years-olds in the New York market (Hinckley, 1983). Because of this success, the program was syndicated on stations in many cities around the country, including in major radio market states like Texas, Ohio, and Florida, where the listening audience also blossomed, according to soaring Arbitron ratings (Premiere Radio Networks, 1997). Many articles were written about the popularity and the value of the show, including examples of calls and questions discussed on the air (Austin, 1997; Barnard, 1995; Halperin, 1995; Hinckley, 1983; Pener, 1993; Romero, 1993; Thomas, 1995), even referring to the show's host as "reliable and most of all trustworthy, and always, always [giving] good advice" (Liebenson, 1999). The program also won a Maggie Award from Planned Parenthood Federation of America for outstanding media excellence in coverage of sexuality education, sexually transmitted diseases, and other reproductive health issues (Planned Parenthood Federation of America, 1993). Further, the program was featured on many television shows and in many magazines targeted to teens because of the huge following of young listeners. For example, four teens interviewed the host for an article in *Children's Express,* a news service of youth reporters about youth news. Their article focused on positive messages about sexuality education given on the show, for example, excuses that sex "just happened" are unacceptable because being mature enough for sex means being responsible for your actions. The host was also asked to write Q&A advice columns for magazines with youth readerships, such as *CosmoGirl,* aimed at young females, and *Smug* music magazine aimed at young males.

On some of the radio programs, popular musicians (e.g. Gwen Stefani, lead singer of the music group No Doubt, and Aerosmith lead singer Steven Tyler) whose music was played at other times on the station, served as "honorary love doctors" giving advice about sexuality and relationships (Mundy, 1997). In addition, many promotional events were held in cities around the country, including rock concerts featuring favored bands and evening club events where the call-in host could meet listeners in person and where listeners had an opportunity to ask their questions in person. These aspects of the program made serious messages about sexuality education more appealing to the younger audience.

HEALTH INFORMATION ON THE RADIO

Various organizations have attempted to modify risky or unhealthy behaviors of young people (e.g. smoking and drinking alcohol) by broadcasting information on the radio (Bauman, LaPrelle, Brown, Koch, & Padgett, 1991; Cernada, Darity, Chen, & Winder, 1990). In the United States, a California survey of health professionals found that 56% of the respondents had used radio to reach large numbers of people and to promote community awareness about health messages (Flora & Wallack, 1990). Several reports from around the globe have suggested the importance and usefulness of disseminating health information on the radio (Bosompra, 1989; Clift, 1989). The value of radio as a source of information about another health risk—specifically sexually transmitted diseases such as HIV/AIDS—has been shown in studies of such programs in various countries (Ng, 1993; Pitts & Jackson, 1993; Tauna & Hildebrand, 1993). For example, a program in West Africa that specifically offers sexual health and safer-sex advice on the radio (in addition to community and school settings) shows the value of this medium in communicating with youth (Berlin, 2008; Rubardt, 2007; see chapter 10 in volume 2, and chapter 11 in volume 3 of this set).

TELEPHONE COUNSELING

Radio call-in advice can be considered similar to telephone counseling and hotline services in its mode of communication and lack of face-to-face contact. Case studies, surveys, and some empirical evidence have supported the effectiveness of the latter modes of delivering professional help (Lester, 2002). For example, in one study of telephone counseling, respondents indicated improvement in their work, social life and emotional state, and satisfaction with the counseling they received. The benefits were favorable when compared to those of face-to-face contact (Reese, Conoley, & Brossart, 2002).

AN ABBREVIATED HISTORY OF RADIO CALL-IN ADVICE

Radio call-in programs have been used to disseminate both physical and mental health information. In the radio call-in format, the host receives anonymous calls from members of the listening audience. Within the course of an interaction lasting only several minutes, the caller presents the problem and receives advice that might include factual information, expression of support and compassion, and/or a referral for further assistance (Bouhoutsos, Goodchilds, & Huddy, 1986; Kuriansky, 1996b). The caller's question often provides an opportunity for the host and/or an expert to present a "mini-lecture," intended to increase general knowledge of the topic.

The first example of a psychologically based radio call-in program is credited to the Los Angeles Popenoe Institute of Family Relations in the 1950s (Bouhoutsos, 1988). Similar shows followed, including *The Private Line* with Gil Henry in the 1960s and the *Leon Lewis Show* on WMCA in New York in the 1970s, where the host (not a trained psychologist) themed shows on love and sponsored Date Nights to introduce singles (Baumgold, 1972). *The Feminine Forum* in Los Angeles featured host Bill Balance in the early 1970s talking about love and sex. One frequent guest, psychologist Toni Grant (mentioned earlier), became a favorite of the listening audience and eventually took over as host of the program in 1977.

CONTROVERSY

The medium became popular but also raised controversy, with critics questioning the practice of giving psychological advice over the radio (Lum, 1982). In reaction, professional psychologists (including the first author) formed the Association of Media Psychologists to address these concerns. This group subsequently evolved into the Media Division of the American Psychological Association (www.apa.org/division46). Also, in response to the proliferation of this format, the APA revised its ethical guidelines to allow advice-giving in the media as long as the interaction was not specifically diagnostic and did not constitute psychotherapy (American Psychological Association, 2002; Raviv, Raviv & Yunovitz, 1989).

Such radio talk became a powerful tool for open discussion about sexuality in a very public forum, particularly reaching young people with few other resources to obtain such information. As a result, questions emerged about the impact on adolescents of such public talk and whether sexual activity in this population would increase. Critics opposed to the dissemination of psychological advice over the radio charged that hosts could not provide adequate and beneficial advice given the time constraints and the absence of face-to-face contact; claimed that such programs exploit callers' personal problems for commercial enterprise; and asserted that the public may be turning to such shows for a quick fix and as a replacement for long-term therapy (Rice, 1981; Ricks, 1984; Zussman, 1983). In contrast, supporters of this emerging field of media psychology and specifically of the radio call-in advice format pointed to their value in the field of psychology as a resource for the public, a means of marketing a positive image of psychology, and an opportunity to perform a community service by raising awareness of mental health issues and enhancing well-being through wide-reaching public education (P. Levy, personal communication, March 23, 1993; Ring, 1982; Ruben, 1986; Van Steenhouse, personal communication, March 23, 1993). In fact, surveys showed that these shows presented a positive image of psychologists to the public since listeners perceived the hosts of psychology radio programs as warm, caring, and intelligent individuals who based their advice on research and clinical experience (Bouhoutsos, Goodchilds, & Huddy, 1986; Ricks, 1984). Further, callers were likely to have positive expectations of receiving information and help, since half of the callers to a psychology call-in radio show in one study had already been in face-to-face therapy. Additionally, listeners reported no harm and instead rated the experience as helpful (Bouhoutsos, Goodchilds, & Huddy, 1986). While these listeners reported that they turned to such radio programming rather than to a mental health clinic because of fear of stigma and embarrassment of the latter and the minimal cost and the greater convenience of the former, it has also been suggested that such shows might encourage people to seek profession help by demystifying the field of psychology and therefore offering help to those who would be reluctant to enter the more traditional setting of a therapist's office (Klonoff, 1983).

In response to these issues, training was established by the American Psychological Association to address the challenges and promote approved techniques for delivering psychological advice in the media (Farberman, 2000). The practice of making psychology more available to the public—which had been initiated in a famous 1969 presidential address to the American Psychological Association by George Miller—was continued by APA presidential initiatives that asked psychologists to "give psychology away" by sharing its findings with the general public in ways they could apply to their daily lives (Fowler, 1999).

RESEARCH ON THE VALUE OF RADIO CALL-IN SHOWS

Studies of radio call-in talk shows support the value of the medium. An Australian survey of 100 callers to a variety of call-in programs found that 37% of respondents stated that they had "no one else to turn to" for assistance, and 72% viewed calling the program as their first move toward a solution to their problem (Monaghan, Shun Wah, Stewart, & Smith, 1978). Most participants in another sample viewed radio and television call-in advice shows as accurate representations of the range of problems in peoples' lives and believed it was not an invasion of privacy to discuss personal problems on the air (Najavits & Wolk, 1988). The first large-scale study of such a U.S. radio call-in talk show surveyed 386 listeners, nonlisteners, and callers and found that about half of respondents listened to this type of radio show, an overwhelming majority of listeners (95%) believed that such shows were worth airing, and a similar high number (86%) reported that such shows were useful (Bouhoutsos, Goodchilds, & Huddy, 1986).

Another study represented a pioneer pre-postevaluation of the effect of the interaction on the air between the caller and the adviser by conducting subsequent follow-up interviews. The study focused on callers to the first author's show, named by the station as the *Dr. Judith Kuriansky Program.* Callers were interviewed immediately before and after being on the air and 3 months later. Results showed that 64% of the callers reported feeling better after they had called, 57% said the call was helpful, and 52% stated they would have liked to speak to the host longer. At the 3-month follow-up, callers reported a general increase in psychological well-being, and 83% of the callers who had been given advice on the air reported following this advice.

In an effort to replicate the findings of this study, another study examined a call-in radio show in Denver, hosted by a psychologist, Andrea Van Steenhouse (Bouhoutsos, 1988; A. Van Steenhouse, personal communication, 1993). Results showed that the Denver callers, like those to the show in New York, felt they were helped by calling the program and believed that others could benefit from both listening and calling. Callers to both shows viewed themselves as psychologically healthy, optimistic about their ability to solve their own problems, and loyal listeners to the call-in program.

In a review of the impact of radio call-in shows and hotlines around the world to reach youth, many advantages of such programming were noted (Moch, & Stevens, 1999). In particular, such outlets offered helpful advice to youth on subjects they wanted to know about, including sexual and reproductive health, STIs, masturbation, drug abuse, suicide, sex abuse, and sexual identity. Further, these formats provided confidential, cost-effective access to such information and help. A further advantage of such programming is in raising adult's consciousness about these sexual concerns, problems and behaviors of youth.

DESCRIPTION OF THE PRESENT STUDY

Radio industry ratings and testimonials from teens indicating the popularity of the radio call-in advice show led to media coverage of the program and indicated interest by teens in matters about sexuality, love, and relationship issues (Halperin, 1995; Public News, 1994). Callers reported that the value of listening included increasing their knowledge about sex, improving their decision making about sex (specifically, helping to dissuade them from engaging in sexual activities at a too-young age), alerting them to the consequences of sexual behavior (emotionally and physically and also in terms of the dangers of sexually transmitted diseases), and helping them to navigate relationship problems (choosing healthy partners, developing good communication, avoiding abuse, and handling painful rejections) (Kuriansky, 1996a). Yet, few studies assessed these effects using scientific methods, such as pre-postevaluations and follow-up assessments. This chapter reports the findings of one preliminary study that evaluated the association between the frequency of listening to the radio show and factors like sexual knowledge, behavior, and overall psychological well-being. The results are discussed in the context of the potential contribution of using such media as a valuable, wide-reaching, and cost-effective method for meeting the sexuality education needs of the listening audience.

Questions that were explored included:

Question One: Do adolescents who spend more time listening to a call-in advice show addressing sexuality, love, and relationship issues report learning factual information about these topics, including information about prevention of unplanned pregnancy and sexually transmitted infections (STIs and HIV/AIDS) and safer sex practices?

Question Two: Do adolescents who spend more time listening to a call-in advice show report practicing safer sex, including increased condom and contraceptive use, and choosing sexual partners more carefully compared to those who listen less frequently?

Question Three: Do adolescents who spend more time listening to this type of call-in advice show tend to have a lower frequency of sexual activities than those who do not?

Question Four: Are adolescents who spend more time listening to this type of call-in advice show more able to refuse sexual activity, including resisting peer pressure to have sex and saying "no" to sexual activity, than those who do not?

Question Five: Do adolescents who spend more time listening to such a call-in advice show have higher levels of psychological well-being, including feeling better about themselves and feeling less lonely and less anxious, than those who do not? This question was included because other research has linked radio advice listening to lower levels of emotional distress and also because emotional well-being has been considered a component of comprehensive sexuality education programs.

METHODS

Participants

Participants for this study were obtained from a pool of adolescent listeners to the call-in advice radio show cohosted by the first author. The participants called at their own initiative and spoke to the hosts over the air after first speaking to employees of the radio station (called "screeners"), who answered the phone from a bank of 20 telephone lines and selected calls to be passed on to the hosts for possible airing based on several criteria.[1] Over a 4-month period during 1994, these screeners routinely asked callers if they were willing to participate in a survey requiring that they stay on the line after being on the air.[2] They were reassured that their decision to participate was voluntary and would not affect their chances of being aired and that their privacy would be protected. Once a caller agreed to participate in the study, a screener switched the call to another line and a researcher conducted the interview. If the timing for this interview was inconvenient, the researcher requested the caller's phone number and called back at a scheduled time. The researchers were trained in the use of the questionnaire and administered the questionnaire over the telephone, with a typical interview lasting 30 to 45 minutes. The research interviewers (two males and two females) were all graduate students in psychology from various universities in the New York area who were interested in the field of sexuality and in the use of media in sexuality education.

Measures

The questionnaire consisted of 88 items that elicited information regarding demographics, time spent listening to the radio show and perceived effects of listening to the radio show on positive and negative emotions, knowledge and attitudes about sex, frequency of sexual activity, sexual behaviors, and use of safer-sex practices.[3] Questions had varied formats; including multiple-choice and open-ended questions[4] and questions that asked for responses on a graduated 10-point scale (e.g., "As a result of listening to *LovePhones*, do you feel you know more factual information about sex in general? [1 = not at all; 10 = a lot]"). Questions to determine the level of listening included a multiple-choice question, "How often do you listen to *LovePhones*? [a = almost every night; b = often (2 times each week); c = sometimes (2–3 times each month); d = very occasionally].

The questionnaire was designed by the first author and the team of researchers. In addition, several experts in the field of sexology were asked for their review and comments. These experts were sexuality counselors or educators who belonged to professional organizations or who were known to have conducted research in the sexuality field. An expert in data collection in the broadcasting field was also consulted.

To determine the time spent listening, participants were asked how many months they had been listening to the call-in advice show, how many nights per week they typically listened, and how many hours they listened per show. A single "time spent listening" (TSL) score was calculated for the number of hours participants spent listening to the call-in advice show (converting a continuous measure into a categorical measure). TSL scores ranged from 1 to 3, with 1 = low intensity listening, 2 = moderate intensity listening, and 3 = high intensity listening.

Questions were asked about sexuality and relationships but also about psychological well-being. For example, items were included about self-esteem, mood, and social skills, as these issues were shown to be important in comprehensive sexuality education programs and deemed to influence healthy sexual choices, frequency of behaviors, practices, and decision making.

Sample

The sample used in the present analysis consisted of 120 adolescent callers from the greater New York area (including New York City and areas in

New Jersey and Connecticut, as determined by the broadcast coverage of the station). In terms of their demographics, all participants were between the ages of 15 and 19, with an average age of 17.2 years old. The majority (62%) were female, and 38% were male. About half (56%) were high school students, 23% attended college, and 21% were not in school. Two-thirds of participants reported their race/ethnicity as Caucasian (66%), with 20% reporting themselves as Latinos, 7% identifying as being African American, and 5% identifying as "other." Nearly all participants (91%) had never been married, 2% were living with someone, 2% were engaged, and 5% were married. A majority of the sample lived with a parent (44% lived with both parents, and 33% lived with only a mother). More than half of the sample said they had learned of the radio call-in advice show from a friend or partner, and almost a third learned of the show from listening to the radio station in general. Subjects were not asked about their sexual orientation, although the specific content of some calls to the show addressing homosexuality and transgender issues did reveal the caller's orientation.

RESULTS

To determine which items would be used to assess the constructs of sexual knowledge, sexual behavior refusal, safer-sex sexual practice, and psychological well-being, a factor analysis was conducted on the questionnaire items. The Kaiser-Meyer-Olkin Measure of Sampling Adequacy was .85, indicating that the data were appropriate for factor analysis. Factors were extracted using principle components analysis and then subjected to oblique rotation. The factor structure revealed clusters of items that were judged to reflect knowledge, behavior, and psychological well-being,

These factors were saved as scores, which were used to operationalize the dependent variables.[5] Total scores created by summarizing item scores contain both variance reflecting the construct measured and error variance. Factor scores contain only variance due to the underlying construct.

As a result of the behavior items analysis, several factors emerged. One factor emerged from the analysis of the items expected to measure knowledge; hence, a factor score was created for each participant and saved into the data set to reflect the dependent variable of perceived increase in knowledge associated with listening to the sex call-in advice show. Other factors represent items that reflect safer-sex practices; perceived reduced frequency of sexual activity; participants' perceived ability to refuse sexual activity; and psychological well-being.

On the basis of the factor analysis, the knowledge scale included items about better knowledge about sex and AIDS and about how to have safer sex and solve problems. Items in the scale about safer sex (risk reduction) practices include more frequent use of condoms and other contraceptives; more careful choice of sexual partners, and less frequent sexual activity. Items in the refusal-of-sexual-activity scale include the ability to say "no" to sexual activity and to resist pressure to be sexually active.[6] Items in the psychological-well-being scale include feeling better about oneself and more in charge of life; feeling more comfortable talking about sex; finding it easier to confront someone; feeling like one is not the only person with the problem; feeling more able to control anger; and feeling less shy, lonely, anxious, or sad.

A reliability analysis was conducted to examine the unidimensionality of proposed items with their respective scales. Cronbach's alpha reliability coefficients were calculated for the three scales that contained more than two items. The values for the sexual knowledge, sexual-risk-reduction practices, and psychological-well-being scales were .78, .75, and .80, respectively. Therefore, the reliability was high for the unidimensionality of the proposed items with their respective scales.

The first question suggested that time spent listening would be positively correlated with reported increased knowledge of sexual information. This question was tested with a Pearson correlation between TSL and the knowledge factor. The results show that TSL was significantly correlated with the knowledge factor ($r = .41$, $p < .001$), suggesting a moderately strong positive correlation between time spent listening to the sex call-in advice show and a perceived increase in knowledge about sex. The second research question postulated that reported safer-sex practices would be positively correlated with time spent listening to the sex call-in advice show. The results showed that TSL correlated positively with this safer-sex factor ($r = .49$, $p < .001$). This indicates that there is a moderately strong correlation between listening to the sex call-in advice show and reporting the use of safer sex behaviors.

Research questions four and five also revealed statistically significant correlations. The fourth research question proposed that perceived ability to refuse sexual activity would be correlated with time spent listening to the call-in advice show. The results show that TSL had a positive correlation with this factor ($r = .34$, $p < .001$). This suggests a moderately strong association between listening to the show and feeling more able to refuse sexual activity and to resist peer pressure to have sex. The fifth research question posited that perceived psychological well-being would be positively correlated with TSL. Bivariate analyses revealed a moderately significant positive correlation between TSL and the psychological well-being factor ($r = .39$, $p < .001$).

The third research question was the only research question that did not reveal a statistically significant correlation. This question addressed whether reported reduced frequency of sexual activity would be positively correlated with time spent listening to the call-in advice show. Listening frequency did not correlate to frequency of sexual activity; consequently, frequent listening was not associated in this instance with higher levels of sexual behavior.

Qualitative responses to items in the questionnaire were examined in order to determine their support of the findings. Clarifications and spontaneous comments in response to open-ended questions supported the results reported about the impact and value of listening to the show. For example, in response to the question "Does listening to the show encourage you to have more sex?" two-thirds of respondents confirmed that listening did not encourage them to have more sex and additionally, 57% of respondents specified that "No, it gives them information and encourages them to make their own decisions"; and 10% said, "No, but it gives good information if you are already sexually active." Further clarification of this issue is evident in responses offered to the question "How has listening helped you to say 'no' to sex?" The responses showed that 60% of listeners reported that they were "more assertive and self-confident" about refusing sexual behavior and "more aware of negative consequences" of sexual behavior (39% and 21%, respectively). Of those teens who reported that listening had changed their sexual behaviors, the most common answers were that "I have safer sex" (31.7%) and "I approach sex more seriously" (25.4%). These findings were confirmed by another question that asked about how listening had changed respondents' thoughts, feelings, and attitudes about sex; the most common responses suggested that listeners had become more open about sexuality, had increased information, and practiced safer sex. Responses also referred to feeling better knowing that they are not the only one with their problem.

Ratings on other individual questions about the program were examined to explore their potential relationship to listeners' responses about sexuality and the general impact of the program. These ratings were on a graduated scale of intensity from 0 (not at all) to 10 (an extreme degree). In response to how much they liked hearing about other people's problems, 86.7% of listeners stated that they liked hearing about other's problems to a moderate or extremely high degree (with 65.6% rating this question as a 9 or 10 and an additional 21.1% rating it between 7 and 9). A similarly high number of listeners (89.8%) said they liked listening to the advice, with three-quarters of callers (75.8%) reporting that they found the show exceptionally appealing (giving a rating of 9 or 10) and an additional 14% of listeners reporting that it had strong appeal (with a rating of 7 or 8). With regard to the perceived educational value of the show, nearly 9 out of 10 listeners (89.7%) found the show educational; specifically 73.2% of listeners rated the show as very highly educational (a score of 9 or 10), and an additional 16.5% found it very educational (a rating of 7, 8, or 9). Listeners also found the program very entertaining, with 93.7% of respondents rating this quality higher than 7 (and 80.3% of respondents rating the entertainment value as a 9 or 10). A total of 85.7% of respondents reported that they had recommended the show to others, and 96.8 % said they would do so.

DISCUSSION

The findings demonstrate correlations between the amount of time a group of adolescents spent listening to a radio call-in advice show about sexuality, love, and relationship issues and their reported knowledge of factual sexual information, safer-sex practices, perceived ability to "say no" to sexual activity, and psychological well-being. The correlational findings provide some contradiction to criticism that talking about sex makes young people become more sexually active or engage in risky sexual behaviors. Further, the findings are consistent with former Surgeon General David Satcher's call to action to promote for sexual health and responsible sexual behavior (Satcher, 2001), which maintains that talk about sexuality is a "public health imperative." Further, the findings add support to the suggestion that sexuality education can have a broad positive impact on individuals.

The amount of time spent listening was not associated with reduced frequency of sexual activity at a statistically significant level, nor was it associated with increased sexual behavior, as critics charge. Additionally, time spent listening was associated with safer-sex practices and refusal of sexual behavior at a statistically significant level. In further support of this association, teens' answers to open-ended questions and their specifications in response to questions about how the show has affected their sexual behavior and feelings revealed that a majority reported that, as a result of listening to the show, they were more assertive and confident about saying "no" to sexual behavior and were aware of the negative consequences of being sexually active. In addition, a majority of youth responded that listening to talk about sex on the program did not encourage them to be sexually active but rather gave them helpful information (e.g., that they should wait for the right time, recognize other ways to please, resist peer pressure and choose healthy relationships). Furthermore, respondents reported that they became more aware of sexually transmitted diseases and would be more careful about their sexual health and more likely to practice safer sex. These results are consistent with the authors' vast clinical experience and experience giving advice to teens, coupled with feedback from young listeners, all of which suggest that hearing other callers' questions and the advice given motivates teens to be more careful in deciding whether to engage in sexual activity (for the first time or on subsequent occasions or with any particular partner) and to make healthier choices about partners. In addition, those who are committed to continue being sexually active are also more careful about choosing partners and more likely to practice safer sex. Further studies with rigorous outcome methodology, using objective long-term measures of sexual activity (e.g., the amount and type of sexual activity teens engaged in over a period of time) and control groups, is essential to confirm these important issues.

The relationship between listening to such a show and a decrease in the frequency of sexual activity deserves more intensive research. This would require long-term assessments and measures of sexual behavior beyond subjective self-reports of intentions. Additionally, it would be worthwhile to connect specific publicly discussed messages about sexual behavior with the sexual decision-making of those not already sexually active compared with those already engaging in sex.

The results of this preliminary analysis suggest that a radio call-in talk show can be a useful forum for discussion of sexuality issues that matter to youth. This is important given that teens are at risk for STIs and unplanned pregnancy and suffer general psychological distress over sexual and relationship matters. In this regard, it is important to note that, while the radio show being evaluated did not focus specifically on STIs, such discussions did arise and callers' on-air comments as well as questionnaire responses indicated the usefulness of such discussions and listeners' increased awareness of the risks of such diseases and the importance of being careful about safer-sex behaviors as a result of listening to the program.

Positive correlations found between listening to the sex call-in advice show and sexual behavior and psychological well-being supports the suggestion that such media programming targeted at youth meets several criteria demonstrated for effective comprehensive sexuality education programs. These include not only the presentation of accurate information and knowledge about sexuality, but also the reinforcement of appropriate values about responsible sexual choices, an emphasis on reducing risk taking behavior, and support in building self-esteem and skills in decision making and communication (Kirby, 2001; Kirby et al., 1994). The show also takes a holistic approach, as noted in veteran sexuality educator Michael Carrera's Adolescent Pregnancy Prevention Program in conjunction with the Children's Aid Society, which empowers youth to develop personal goals and the desire for a productive future (http://www.childrensaidsociety.org/youthdevelopment/carrera). The advice given on the show intentionally models problem-solving skills, methods of communication, ways to refuse unwanted sexual relations and advances, and how to practice safer-sex behaviors and offers listeners positive reinforcement for adopting healthy attitudes and behaviors, ending unhealthy relationships and choosing healthy partners. In addition, positive correlations were found in the present study between time spent listening to the advice show and perceived improvement in emotional variables such as feeling less lonely, sad, and anxious as well as between time spent listening and psychological well-being variables such as feeling more in charge, feeling better about oneself, being more able to control anger, and being more able to confront someone about a problem. These associations are important, given that these are the goals of comprehensive sexuality education programs but that few such programs are available. In light of the usefulness of such comprehensive approaches to this subject matter, such a public advice forum can serve as an effective supplement to curricula provided in schools or communities.

While a decrease in sexual activity among already active teens was not shown to be associated with listening to the advice show, it is important to note that neither was listening to this subject matter found to be associated with an increase in listeners' sexual behavior (as critics of sexuality education have asserted). Furthermore, participants did report safer-sex behaviors, showing that even those who continue sexual activity are inclined to become more responsible. These factors considered together strengthen the case for such programming as a tool for prevention and education, as well as a "solution-focused" forum consistent with brief interventions.

IMPORTANCE OF OPEN TALK ABOUT SEXUALITY AND SEXUAL HEALTH INFORMATION AND EDUCATION

The importance of delivering accurate sexual health information to teens and of having open discussions of sexuality is underscored by statistics that show high rates of sexual behavior in youth and associated risks for unplanned pregnancy and sexually transmitted diseases (Centers for Disease Control, 2007), which can in turn lead to other personal, interpersonal, and social problems. Recent studies suggest that sexuality education can effectively reduce adolescent sexual risk behavior if provided before sexual initiation (Mueller, Gavin, & Kulkarni, 2007), with males being 71% and females being 59% more likely to postpone sex until the age of 15 and males being 2.77 times more likely to use birth control. Considering the present advice call-in show as a form of sexual education offers optimism in achieving such outcomes.

The first author's years of experience talking about sex with teens has qualitatively revealed that such talk does not encourage teens who are unsure about engaging in such activity to "go out and try it" but rather makes them more aware of the consequences of their choices (Kuriansky, 1996a). While such talk may not make those who are already sexually active cease all activity, open discussion about sexuality within the context of what constitutes healthy relationships can help such teens to make wiser decisions and, most important, to be more aware of safer-sex practices.

While the United States has been considered a model of openness about sexuality talk, in fact the situation in this country has been complicated when it comes to youth. For example, religious fundamentalists have argued that open talk about sexuality leads to sexual behavior, buoyed by pervasive and explicit sexual content and displays of precocious sexuality in contemporary media and culture (American Psychological Association, 2007; Hedgepeth & Helmich, 1996; Naigle, 2005). Yet, others contend that research has not conclusively established a cause and effect relationship between mass media and adolescents' sexual attitudes and behaviors (Brown, 2002; Escobar-Chavez et al., 2005). This confusing landscape makes decisions about sex challenging for youth. For example, a group of sexuality experts on a study tour who compared American teens and those in industrialized (European) nations found that the former had higher birth rates, began intercourse (at least a year) earlier, used oral contraceptives at lower rates, and had higher rates of HIV infection. These experts suggested that more practical and healthier attitudes toward sex accounted for the fewer problems in European countries (Advocates for Youth, 1999).

In the midst of this debate over sexuality education, teens themselves express a desire for more information and skills related to sexuality and relationships. According to a survey by the Kaiser Family Foundation (2005), 48% of teens 12 to 47 want more information about sexual health from health care providers. At the time this show was airing, it was estimated that only 1 in 10 American youth were receiving comprehensive sexuality education (Hedgepeth & Helmich, 1996). The radio discussions described in the present report represents one means through which the proportion of youth receiving sexuality information can be increased.

VALUE OF THE ADVICE SHOW AND RADIO AS A MEDIUM

The overall results from this pilot study suggest the value of open talk about sexuality in a public forum such as that provided by broadcast media. Qualitative data—in the form of open-ended questions and clarifications to quantitative questions—are currently being further analyzed to explore the relationship between listening and increased self-esteem, healthier relationships, more knowledge about sex and safer sex practice. Ratings on additional items in the questionnaire used in this study reveal positive responses to the radio program and the advice, with nearly 9 out of 10 callers rating that they liked hearing other people's problems and listening to the advice given on the program and found the show educational (as well as entertaining). The first author's experience from decades of giving advice to thousands of radio listeners has revealed that people want reassurance on three related dimensions: that they are normal, that they are not alone in their problem, and that there is hope in the form of help for their problem (Kuriansky, 1996a).

The value of the radio advice show is further indicated by anecdotal reports when listeners meet the host in person. These listeners invariably recall individual callers and the issues raised, as well as report dramatic positive effects that listening to the show had on their lives, for example, helping them feel better about themselves, learn about sexuality, and make healthy choices about their sexual behavior and relationships. Listeners—many of whom are now in their twenties and thirties and in impressive careers (e.g., running for local office, working in finance, banking, and broadcasting and in health-related careers, including two who reported running a nonprofit organization that helps AIDS-infected teens) commented to the host, "You taught me every-thing I know about sex," "I felt so much better about myself listening to the show," "I never could have grown up knowing what I know if it were not for the show," "You are my surrogate big sister whom I trusted so much," "I have a happy marriage because of what I learned from the show and your advice," and "I owe everything I am now in my happy relationships to you and the show." Some listeners have reported wanting to go into the field of sexuality educa-tion as a result of listening to the show and have pursued such career goals and related fields of study involving gender studies and health.

As the show format appeared to approximate the benefits of group counsel-ing, a study was carried out to explore this association (Kopelan & Corbin, 1995). Callers were randomly selected and interviewed after their interaction on the air by researchers using a questionnaire devised by the investigators. The results showed that callers' responses after listening to the show were equivalent to dimensions the researchers predetermined as indicative of group therapy. These include having the ability to try out coping strategies, feeling they were not the only one with their problem, trusting the adviser (therapist), learning from other people, and having a cathartic reaction from both their own sharing as well as from listening to others. Given the reports that listeners like hearing about other people's problems, the researchers suggest that such a program has value as "vicarious learning" where people learn from listening to others' reports of problems, consistent with modeling theory and social learn-ing theory (Bandura, 1977).

Given the popularity of the program, the value of the advice program can be derived, at the very least, from its public airing of sexuality issues and its dissemination of sexuality information, keeping sexuality in the public eye and presenting a positive view of sexuality and healthy models of relation-ships. This is consistent with Agenda Setting and Framing Theories, which maintain that the media tell people what is important in the world and how to think about events (Brown, 2002). The present results support the sugges-tion that media in the United States can be more effectively harnessed as a teaching tool about responsible sexuality and sexual health for young peo-ple, as such media has been used effectively in other countries around the world (Brown & Keller, 2000; Kuriansky, 1996b; Ng & Fan, 1996b). Given that entertainment-education (also called edu-tainment)—which puts socially responsible messages into an entertaining format—has been shown to be an effective model to increase access to and acceptance of knowledge, positive attitudes, and behavior about an issue (Singhal & Rogers, 1999), and given that listeners in the present study rated the program as highly entertaining as well as educational, the current format has considerable potential value in presenting prosocial messages about sexuality.

Other attributes that make the radio advice format valuable as a source of sexuality education for youth include its vast accessibility to young people, availability free of charge, ability to help to those who are not likely to seek therapy, and anonymity, which helps those youth who might be too embarrassed to ask sensitive questions in other settings, including in school. Many young people reported anecdotally that they would listen to the program on their headphones while in bed and under the covers as they were about to go to sleep at night, giving them privacy and freedom from possible parental disapproval. In contrast to the latter, parents often expressed appreciation to the host for permission and encouragement to talk to their teens about private matters discussed on the show. The show further provided an opportunity for young people to talk together about sexuality, which they would not ordinarily do, by providing interesting and even entertaining subject matter. In fact, teens spontaneously reported that they would listen together in "*LovePhones* parties" and would enthusiastically discuss calls heard the night before in school the next day.

The entertainment value of the sexually oriented material has several advantages, not only in holding young listener's attention for important educational messages but also reducing anxiety associated with sexual material. To accommodate young listener's media habits, segments were kept fast paced with compelling topics covering a wide array of subjects. Discussions provided revelations about peer behaviors, evoked emotional reactions (like compassion) and offered teens a model of healthy behavior and communication about sexuality, relationships and other aspects of life.

BRIEF INTERVENTIONS

Critics have charged that brief interactions such as those in these radio calls are not sufficient to create change. However, the present associations shown between listening and positive changes suggest that such brief interactions can be important as a part of larger public health and sexuality education efforts. Research has shown that a brief cognitive-behavioral telephone-based intervention (with training in diaphragmatic breathing and cognitive restructuring) was effective in reducing anxiety in participants who called a mental health emergency hotline (Somir, Tamir, Maguen, & Litz, 2005). Psychoeducational as well as therapeutic interventions have become increasingly brief since the 1970s (Lambert, 2006) in keeping with increasingly limited resources, time, and finances. As a result, mental health practitioners have had to adjust to providing the greatest amount of help in the shortest amount of time, leading to the development of models of brief and specific intervention and advice giving. The three to five sessions required for solution-based therapy (Iveson, 2002) have been reduced to a single session (Cameron, 2007; Talmon, 1990). In one study, a single 2-hour assessment and treatment session of solution-focused single-session therapy (SST) was found to be effective in treating mental health problems for urban children and adolescents, according to parent and clinician outcome measures from baseline to 1 month later (Perkins, 2006). Radio advice has shortened this period of time to interventions averaging 4 to 5 minutes. Such interventions require specific tasks and skills in order to address issues and to provide useful guidance.

MEASUREMENTS

While the assessments here are based on subjective and retrospective reporting, without the advantage of also measuring actual behavior, it has been pointed out by other researchers that simply feeling helped can lead to significant positive change (Brockopp, 2002). In addition, though the present assessment measure has not been scientifically validated, other studies using similar global measures of overall self-reports of improvement based on question formats similar to the present one have been shown to be useful. In one study (Reese, Conoley & Brossart, 2002) where 82% of respondents who had used a telephone counseling service reported improvement in their presenting problem, the effectiveness of the counseling was evaluated by the use of broad self-reports on 10 mental health questions scored on a 5-point Likert scale in the Consumer Reports Annual Questionnaire. For example, measuring Specific Improvement was derived from the question "How much did treatment help with the specific problem that led you to counseling?"; Satisfaction was measured by the question "Overall, how satisfied were you with the counselor's treatment of the problem?"; and Global Improvement was measured by how respondents described their overall emotional state at the time of questioning and at the start of treatment.

LIMITATIONS

The cross-sectional design of the present analysis does not allow establishing a cause-and-effect relationship between time spent listening and factors like sexual behavior and psychological well-being. This is true despite the fact that questions were worded so as to focus respondents on a comparison between how they felt as a result of listening to the show and how they felt before. However, this wording measured participants' perception of the effects of listening rather than actual attitudes and behaviors. While other correlational studies have found relationships between frequency of television viewing and initiation of intercourse in samples of high school students, such cross-sectional analyses in these studies as well as in the present study cannot identify whether sexual content in the programs actually encourages sexual behavior (consistent with Cultivation Theory) or whether youngsters seek out sexual content consistent with their already established interest in sexual behavior (Brown, 2002). The results in the present study did not find a correlation between sexual content and sexual activity. However, more rigorous and longitudinal research with control groups, use of assessment tools with proven reliability and validity and pre-post outcome assessments of behavior is necessary to establish a casual relationship between listening to advice in a radio talk-show format and actual sexual attitudes and practices.

FURTHER STUDY

The outcome of this study reinforces the importance of continued research on the impact of public means of delivering sexuality information. Longer-term follow-up of this sample is possible and would be valuable. Related research in progress involves analysis of questions from readers of newspaper columns seeking advice and from other anonymous forums (e.g., the Internet and question cards submitted before lectures), some preliminary data from which are presented in chapter 5 of volume 2 in this set. Since comparisons of questions in various advice formats would be a valuable contribution to the sexuality education field, other researchers are encouraged to contact the authors.

EVOLVING FORMATS

While several call-in advice shows are currently aired on broadcast media, only one national show—*Loveline*—targets youth and specifically addresses sexuality. A television show, *Sex with Sue,* on which septuagenarian Sue Johannsen discussed sexual aids and responded to viewers' questions, was aired on the WE network, which targets a female audience. Some advice about sex is being increasingly offered on alternative broadcasting systems, specifically through "teleheath" (Baker, 1977), satellite radio, and Internet sites with webcams and podcasts, often with hosts not formally trained in psychology or sexuality education, and some of whom are youth who openly admit their lack of experience or authority on the subject matter.

The call-in advice format as presented in this chapter can serve as a model for college radio stations, which have a built-in youth audience. College radio has been shown to be an important forum to inform listeners about a variety of topics, from academic issues to self-esteem, gender roles, and condom use, with outcome research showing that such programs can even increase condom use (Van Haveren, Blank, & Bentley, 2001). For example, the *Lafeneline Show*, aired in 1999 on the Kansas State University radio station, had the explicit mission to provide sexual education information to the student body, as well as the surrounding community. Such college advisers can be trained by certified sexuality educators. Among other considerations about content and production, the coordinators of that program wondered how to make the show more entertaining while maintaining professional standards. The program presented in this chapter shows that such a combination is possible and is useful to reach a young audience with valuable messages about sexuality and sexual health.

INTERNATIONAL SEX ADVICE

The first author's U. S. radio show was syndicated internationally in Japan, airing live (therefore during daytime hours) so that listeners could call in or fax questions. The fact that listeners did so reveals an interest and a growing openness in Japanese culture toward public discussions about sexuality and questions like those from the American audience (Kuriansky, 1993; 1997; 2000; 2002). Similar questions to those asked on the American radio program were also asked on a hotline service in Shanghai for which the first author consulted (Zhu et al., 2001; see chapter 8 in volume 2 of this set). Such forums are increasingly available in other countries traditionally conservative about public discussion of sexuality and personal matters. For example, a hotline in Yemen focuses on domestic violence (Saleh, Haider, & Bassidiq, 2003) and a radio and internet program available in Iran dealt with a wide range of sexuality issues (see chapter 9 in volume 2 in this set). Studies assessing the impact of a radio show currently airing in the West African nations of Sierra Leone and Liberia in a question and answer format similar to that of the show in the present study have shown that it has had a positive impact on the targeted youth audience (Berlin, 2008; Rubardt, 2007; see chapter 11 in volume 3 of this book set). Cross-cultural studies of such shows can be done to compare the questions, the outcome of the advice given, and the formats used.

CONCLUSION

The present results suggest that listening to an advice show about sexuality issues was correlated with increased knowledge about sex and feelings of self-control, ability to say "no," and increased general well-being. Such findings challenge the assertion that informational and educational talk about sex encourages youth to become more sexually active. In fact, listening to a show that offers advice about sexuality, love, and relationships may help youth make more responsible decisions about sex and relationships and motivate youth to delay sexual activity if they are not already sexually active and to become more responsible about sexual behaviors if they are already sexually active. Participatory radio advice formats targeted at teens can serve as a valuable supplement to sexuality education in schools, the community, and the home. In addition, the anonymity provided by call-in formats provides an opportunity for adolescents to ask questions they might not otherwise address and to learn from listening to discussions of issues presented by their peers. Further, because of the wide accessibility of radio among people of all financial status, such programming has the potential to provide a large youth population with access to high-quality sexuality information. Further research can explore in-depth the impact of such forums on youth sexual behavior and attitudes.

ACKNOWLEDGMENTS

Much deep gratitude is extended to the team and staff at Z100 Radio, including co-host Chris Jagger, program director Steve Kingston, producer Sam Milkman, and phone screeners; to the graduate students who served as interviewers, prepared preliminary reports and assisted in this project with great interest and dedication, including Audrey Sorgen, Brett Allen Kopelan, and Joann Ricovero; and to the students who entered data, including Yi Wang, Rachel Snyder, Ariana Zsuffa, and Vincent Sostre. Special appreciation and honor is expressed to all the listeners and fans of the LovePhones show and to the participants in this study.

NOTES

1. These factors included callers' abilities to clearly verbalize their concerns and the relevance of the content of the call to the subject matter and continuity of the show.

2. Although a precise response rate could not be calculated, reports from screeners indicated that most callers agreed to participate in the study. The few callers who declined to participate were noted as students of high school age who feared their parents' reaction if they knew that the teen had contacted the radio station.

3. Questions assessing safe-sex practices were worded differently depending on whether the participant had prior sexual experience (e.g., "Do you use a condom?" versus "Would you use a condom?").

4. Responses to open-ended questions provide qualitative data that can enhance the understanding of the quantitative results. An example of an open-ended question is "What is the one of the best things you have learned since listening to *LovePhones*?"

5. The advantage of using factor scores as opposed to adding answers on the relevant items is that factor scores reflect a more pure measure of the construct.

6. Because approximately one-quarter of the sample had not yet initiated sexual intercourse (i.e., were virgins) and the safer-sex items asked about actual sexual behavior, participants were instructed to answer these items on the basis of their intentions for the future rather than on actual behavior. To determine whether the factor structure for the nonvirgins was the same as for virgins on the safer-sex items, the sample was split into two groups reflecting these two conditions and the safer-sex factor analysis was repeated. The results showed that the factor structure was identical for both groups, confirming

construct validity for the safer-sex items. Therefore, no separate analyses were conducted for virgins and nonvirgins.

REFERENCES

Advocates for Youth. (1999). *European approaches to adolescent sexual behavior and responsibility.* Washington, DC: Advocates for Youth.

American Psychological Association. (2002). Ethical principles of psychologists and code of conduct. Retrieved December 27, 2008, from http://www.apa.org/ethics/code2002.html

American Psychological Association. (2007). Report of the American Psychological Association Task Force on the sexualisation of girls. Retrieved December 27, 2008 from http://www.apa.org/pi/wpo/sexualization.html

Austin, J. (1997, September 21). Timing of Love Phones' is perfect (Howard take a lesson). *State Telegram.* P. 4.

Baker, B. (1997, June/July). Lights! Camera! Therapy! *Common Boundary, 15*(4), 39–41.

Bandura, A. (1977). *Social learning theory.* New York: General Learning Press.

Barnard, L. (1995, July 7). She's the Dr. Ruth for Gen-Sex. *The State News.* p. 8.

Bauman, K., LaPrelle, J., Brown, J., Koch, G., & Padgett, C. (1991). The influence of three mass media campaigns on variables related to adolescent cigarette smoking: Results of a field experiment. *American Journal of Public Health, 81*(5), 597–604.

Baumgold, J. (1972). Radio therapy: Surrogate Father at night. *New York Magazine, 5*(14), 33–36.

Berlin, L. (2008, February). "Sis Lorpu: Evaluation Report." Talking Drums Studios, Liberia: Search for Common Ground. Internal report for Search for Common Ground.

Bosompra, K. (1989). Dissemination of health information among rural dwellers in African: A Ghanaian experience. *Social Science Medicine, 29*(9), 1130–1140.

Bouhoutsos, J. (1988). Communicating psychology to the public: The media psychology connection. Paper presented at the 24th International Congress of Psychology, Sydney, Australia.

Bouhoutsos, J., Goodchilds, J., & Huddy, L. (1986). Media psychology: An empirical study of radio call-in psychology programs. *Professional Psychology: Research and Practice, 17*(5), 408–414.

Brockopp, G. W. (2002). The telephone call: Conversation or therapy. In D. Lester, Crisis intervention and counseling by telephone (p. 88). Springfield, IL: Charles C. Thomas. Brown, J. D. (2002). Mass media influences on sexuality. *Journal of Sex Research, 39*(1), 42–45.

Brown, J. D. & Keller, S. N. (2000, September/October). Can the mass media be healthy sex educators? *Family Planning Perspectives. 32*(5), 255–256.

Cameron, C. (2007, December). Single session and walk-in psychotherapy: A descriptive account of the literature. *Counseling and Psychotherapy Research, 7*(4), 245–249.

Centers for Disease Control and Prevention. (2007). *Youth risk behavior survey.* Retrieved December 27, 2008, from http://www.cdc.gov/healthyyouth/yrbs/index.htm

Cernada, G., Darity, W., Chen, T., & Winder, A. (1990). Mass media usage among Black smokers: A first look. *International Quarterly of Community Health Education, 10*(4), 347–364.

Clift, E. (1989). Social marketing and communication: Changing health behavior in the third world. *American Journal of Health Promotion, 3*(4), 17–24.

Escobar-Chaves, S. L., Tortolero, S. R., Markham, C. M., Low, B. J., Eitel, P. & Thickstun, P. (2005, July). Impact of the Media on Adolescent Sexual Attitudes and Behaviors. *Pediatrics, 116*(1), 303–326.

Farberman, R. K. (2000). Preparing for media interviews. *Monitor on Psychology, 31*(8). Retrieved January 8, 2009, from http://www.apa.org/monitor/nov00/interview.html

Flora, J., & Wallack, L. (1990). Health promotion and mass media use: Translating research into practice. *Health Education and Research, 5*(1), 73–80.

Fowler, R. (1999). Giving psychology away. *APA Monitor Online, 30*(5). Retrieved January 8, 2009 from http://www.apa.org/monitor/may99/rc.html

Hackett, G. (1982). Talking sex with Dr. Ruth. *Newsweek*, May 3, p. 78.

Halperin, S. (1995). Talkin' sex with Dr. Judy. *Smug Magazine, 1*(4), p.18.

Hedgepeth, E., & Helmich, J. (1996). *Teaching about sexuality and HIV: Principles and methods for effective education.* New York: New York University Press.

Hinckley, D. (1983, Sept 7). Talk on the Wild Side: HTZ's *LovePhones* has the airwaves buzzing with winning blend of sex advice. *New York Daily News*, Entertainment Section, pp. 1, 3.

Iveson, C. (2002). Solution-focused brief therapy. *Advances in Psychiatric Treatment, 8*(2), 149–156.

Kaiser Family Foundation. (2005, January). *U.S. teen sexual activity.* Retrieved December 26, 2008, from http://www.kff.org/youthhivstds/upload/U-S-Teen-Sexual-Activity-Fact-Sheet.pdf

Kirby, D. (2001). *Emerging answers: Research findings on programs to reduce teen pregnancy.* Washington, DC: National Campaign to Prevent Teen Pregnancy.

Kirby, D., Short, L., Collins, J., Rugg, D., Kolbe, L., Howard, M., et al. (1994). School-based programs to reduce sexual risk behaviors: A review of effectiveness. *Public Health Reports, 109*(3), 339–360.

Klonoff, E. A. (1983). A star is born: Psychologists and the media. *Professional Psychology: Research and Practice, 14*(6), 847–854.

Kopelan, B., & Corbin, P. (1995). Similarities between radio call-in advice and traditional group therapy. Master's thesis, Columbia University Teachers College, New York.

Kuriansky, J. (1984). *Sex: Now that I've got your attention, let me answer your questions.* New York: Putnam.

Kuriansky, J. (1985). Why do they call and how are they helped? A radio call-in psychologist/host's endeavor to go beyond ratings and into research. *Amplifier, 1*(2), 5–7.

Kuriansky, J. (1993). *Sex therapy—Dr. Judy responds.* Vols. 1 and 2 (Japanese translation of *Sex: Now that I've got your attention, let me answer your questions*). Tokyo, Japan: Floral Publications, Japan Floral Art.

Kuriansky, J. (1996a). *Generation Sex: America's hottest sex therapist answers the hottest questions about sex.* New York: HarperCollins.

Kuriansky, J. (1996b). Sex advice on the radio: An overview in the United States and around the world. *SIECUS Report 24*(5) (June–July), 6–9.

Kuriansky, J. (1997). *Goodbye my troubles, hello my happiness.* Tokyo, Japan: Magazine House.

Kuriansky, J. (2000). *Let's have happy sex!* Tokyo, Japan: Floral Publications, Japan Floral Art.

Kuriansky, J. (2002), *Love Vitamin.* Tokyo, Japan: Chuokoron-Shinsha, Inc.

Lambert, D. (2006). *Bergin and Garfield's handbook of psychotherapy and behavior change.* San Francisco: John Wiley & Sons, Inc.

Lester, D. (2002). *Crisis intervention and counseling by telephone.* Springfield, IL: Charles C. Thomas.

Liebenson, D. (1999, Summer). The irrepressible coolness of Dr. Judy. *Zone*. pp.42–45.

Lum, S. (1982, March). News and talk stations—solid state radio. Special Radio Report. *Madison Avenue Magazine,* pp. 104–108.

Moch, L. & Stevens, C. (1999, December). Reaching adolescents through hotlines and radio call-in programs. *In Focus. Focus on Young Adults.* Retrieved January 3, 2009, from http://www.fhi.org/NR/rdonlyres/efxl6bhjkkqv37k4jdacchgeslhhl5e2ykmm5lbfkt fldbjdssng5slaeu64ctp5d6qtjiuxdrk37m/hotlinesandradiocallindec99.pdf

Monaghan, J., Shun Wah, A., Stewart, I., & Smith, L. (1978). The role of talkback radio: A study. *Journal of Community Psychology, 6,* 351–356.

Mueller, T. E., Gavin, L. E. & Kulkarni, A. (2007). The association between sex education and youth's engagement in sexual intercourse, age at first intercourse, and birth control use at first sex. *Journal of Adolescent Health, 42*(1), 89–96.

Mundy, C. 1997. Love, American style: On radio and MTV, fans are looking to rock stars for their "professional" advice about sex and relationships. *Rolling Stone,* October 2, p. 28.

Naigle, D. (2005). Literature review of media messages to adolescent females. Paper presented at Program for Educational Communications and Technology, University of Saskatchewan. Retrieved on July 13, 2008, from http://www.usask.ca/education/coursework/802papers/naigle/index.htm

Najavits, L., & Wolk, K. (1988). Giving psychology away: A survey of the uses of media self-help resources. *Amplifier, 4*(3), 3–4.

Ng, M. (1993). Public responses to the sex education series of radio-television Hong Kong. *Journal of Sex Education and Therapy, 19*(1), 64–72.

Ng, M. L., & Fan, M. S. (1996). Sex education on radio: The Hong Kong and Shanghai experience. In S. Matsumoto (Ed.), *Sexuality and human bonding* (pp. 173–179). New York: Elsevier Science B.V.

Pener, D. (1993, May 9). EGOS & IDS; Sex Talk on the Radio With Dr. Judy. *New York Times.* Retrieved January 2, 2009 from http://query.nytimes.com/gst/fullpage. html?res=9F0CEEDD1238F93AA35756C0A965958260&scp=1&sq=degen%20 pener%20judy%20kuriansky&st=cse

Perkins, R. (2006, June). The effectiveness of one session of therapy using a single-session therapy approach for children and adolescents with mental health problems. *Psychology and Psychotherapy: Theory, Research and Practice,79*(2), 215–227.

Pitts, M., & Jackson, H. (1993). No joking matter: Formal and informal sources of information about AIDS in Zimbabwe. *AIDS Education and Prevention, 5*(3), 212–219.

Planned Parenthood Federation of America (1993, November 2). News release: Planned Parenthood honors media excellence at celebrity gala.

Premiere Radio Networks (1997, Spring). Dr. Judy & Jagger's *LovePhones:* Guaranteed success in love. Sales sheet based on Arbitron ratings nationwide. New York: sales office.

Public News (1994). Sex, love and the Surgeon General. Public News, *Houston Newsweekly,* Issue 657, pp. 16–19.

Raviv, A., Raviv, A., & Yunovitz, R. (1989, April). Radio psychology and psychotherapy: Comparison of client attitudes and expectations. *Professional Psychology: Research and Practice, 20*(2), 67–72.

Reese, R. R.,Conoley, C. W. & Brossart, D. F. (2002). Effectiveness of telephone counseling: A field-based investigation. *Journal of Consulting and Clinical Psychology, 49*(2), 235–242.

Rice, B. (1981). Call-in therapy: Reach out and shrink someone. *Psychology Today, 39,* pp. 87–91.

Ricks, J. M. (1984, December). Reach out and shrink someone. *Psychology Today 15*(20), 89–90.

Ring, B. (1982, August 25). The psychological radio call-in program: Its therapeutic value. Paper presented at the American Psychological Association Symposium "Psychologists and the Media." Washington DC.

Romero, D. (1993, January 17). Hotlines sizzle with sex talk. *Daily News City Lights*. p. 3.

Rubardt, M (2007, June). Sexuality and Youth Project (SAY) CARE Sierra Leone: An innovations project of CARE International. Final project evaluation—2007. Internal report to CARE.

Ruben, H. (1986). Reflections of a radio psychiatrist. *Hospital and Community Psychiatry, 37*(9), 934–936.

Saleh, M. A, Haider, S. M., & Bassidiq, A. S. (2003). Manual for the hotline service for psychological aid. Aden, Yemen: Aden University Printing and Publishing House.

Satcher, D. (2006, May 16). *Interim report of the national consensus process on sexual health and responsible sexual behavior.* Atlanta, Georgia: Morehouse School of Medicine Sexual Health Program.

Singhal, A., & Rogers, E.,M. (1999). *Entertainment-education: A communication strategy for social change.* Mahwah, NJ: Erlbaum.

Somir, E., Tamir, E., Maguen, S., & Litz, B. T. 2005 Brief cognitive-behavioral phone-based intervention targeting anxiety about the threat of an attack: A pilot study. *Behavior Research and Therapy, 43,* 669–679.

Schwebel, A. I. (1982). Radio psychologists: A community psychology/psychoeducational model. *Journal of Community Psychology, 10,* 181–184.

Talmon, M. (1990). Single session therapy: Maximizing the effect of the first (and often only) therapeutic encounter. San Francisco: Jossey-Bass.

Tauna, B., & Hildebrand, V. (1993). Reproductive health knowledge and implications: A study in Nigeria. *Early Child Development and Care, 87,* 83–92.

Thomas, C. (1995, June 27). Only ignorance shocks sex "doctor." *Houston Chronicle.* p. 7.

Van Haveren, R. A., Blank, W., & Bentley, K. (2001). *Lafeneline*: Promoting sexual health through college radio. *Journal of College Counseling, 4,* 186–189.

Zhu, H., Kuriansky, J., Tong, C., Xu, X., Chen, J., & Cheng, L. (2001). China Reproductive Health Hotline: Professionals solve problems on sex and emotion." Shanghai: Sanlien Press.

Zussman, S. (1983, February). Dial a love shrink. *Self Magazine,* 98–102.

Chapter Eight

NEW TECHNOLOGIES AND NEW AUDIENCES: OFFERING ADVICE OVER AIRWAVES AND WEBCAMS

Diana Falzone

Providers of sexuality education have come a long way from the sweet aunt or caring older sister to common-sense advisers and professional psychologists who answer people's questions about sexuality and relationships on the broad media platform. This trend has been going on for the past two decades and has recently experienced a resurgence, given the expansion of technology, which makes more outlets available.

This chapter explains the use of those new technologies, which represent the latest evolution of broadcast transmission (in which I am involved in through my role as a communicator to the public of information about sexuality and relationships). I describe how this new technology works, what I do, what the audience wants to know, and essentially how new formats represent an advancement and new opportunities not only for all broadcasters but for sexuality educators around the world. I focus on the two media services for which I host shows: Sirius radio and an exciting new Internet service called Paltalk. Many people are discarding their "terrestrial" (traditional) radios and tuning in to a new pulse via these new and exciting technologies.

SIRIUS RADIO

Sirius is a new satellite radio system that people have to buy to listen to, but it is commercial-free. This format began to take hold a few years ago and now is becoming very popular. There are many channels, and the options have expanded for programming, which ranges from news to music and even includes specialties like cooking. Celebrities like Oprah Winfrey even have their own channels. As there are no controls imposed by the FCC, the talk is uncensored. So, hosts like Howard Stern, the "shock jock," can do his very sex-driven show without controls like the fines like he endured on commercial radio.

The daily show I cohost derives from a very popular magazine called *Cosmopolitan*, most of whose readers are female. The show airs on Cosmo Sirius Satellite Radio on Channel 111 and XM on Channel 162, Monday through Friday afternoons, from 2 P.M. to 5 P.M. EST. The name of the show is *Cosmolicious with Diana*. (My previous show derived from a male magazine and I had a male co-host.) On my show, I discuss topics of the day, which include dating and relationships, pop culture, and politics, and interview celebrities and experts.

As most of the *Cosmopolitan* magazine readers are female, so, too, most of the audience for our show is composed of females, between the ages of 18 and 45. Consequently, many of the calls are from women, and many of them, not surprisingly, want to talk about sex. Many of the questions we address are about sex. The topic of dating is also very spicy and elicits questions about how to get your mate to be more adventurous in the bedroom or how to approach an attractive woman at a bar. Although these topics may sound clichéd, people still want to talk about them and do not know the answers to these questions. For example, they rely on advice from hosts to provide them with the ways in which to win the affections of a perspective partner.

Over the years, I have heard many questions from men about their relationships and sexuality. A talk show format offers an opportunity to truly hear about the sexual problems on people's minds and what worries them. One of the most common questions from male listeners who have called is, "How do I get my woman to participate in a threesome?" As a woman, I usually roll my eyes at such a question, take a deep sigh, and tell them that having a threesome is sometimes better kept a fantasy than acted out in reality, specifically if the man has been in a relationship for a long time. I educate them that many times when a couple has a threesome, feelings of jealously can emerge and sometimes ruin the current relationship. If a couple is set on living out this desire, the partners must give each other boundaries in order to have a good experience. Otherwise, it can ruin the relationship quickly. I also educate them that if the partner is not comfortable engaging in such a threesome, it is not wise to pressure the person. It is that person's choice, and if that person is uneasy, the partner should respect his or her wishes.

Another common question from the male audience is how to have their girlfriends or wives engage in anal sex. Over the past two years, I have discerned, on the basis of accounts from callers, that, ironically, men actually don't always enjoy the sensation of anal sex but instead request this sexual activity because they enjoy breaking what seems to be a societal taboo. As in other situations, I make it clear that both partners need to be consenting, rather than one partner bullying the significant other into agreeing to participate. Otherwise, the experience will be dreadful, and resentment will be fostered.

PALTALK

Technologies have evolved dramatically over the past decade. Each year, new technology is being perfected. In 2007, for example, a new media outlet, www.Paltalk.com, emerged. This medium uses Webcams as a mixture of video and audio, with interactive and log-in capacity. The Paltalk service offers all kinds of daily or weekly news and entertainment programming, with audience participation, which focuses on different topics. My own show specifically focuses on dating and relationships. Through Paltalk, I am able to communicate to an audience all over the world. As spokesperson for Paltalk, I also know that this service represents a significant achievement in technology, one that enables us to have voices all over the planet communicate about important issues via the Internet.

My show on Paltalk is a dating and relationship show called *The Diana Falzone Show* and can be accessed on www.paltalk.com/dianafalzone. The show is live on Thursdays at 11 A.M. EST for an hour and can be seen in every country. On this Paltalk service, people log on to their computers to access the shows. This show reaches a larger audience than my Sirius radio show since I'm broadcasting to many countries, rather than just the United States and Canada. To broadcast, I sit in a room in front of a camera that acts like a Webcam (which people have on their computers). The people can see me on their computers, but I cannot see them. A computer is on my desk. I have a producer who monitors the show and lets me know who has a question.

According to the show's format, sometimes I introduce a topic related to dating and relationships, such as how to find a mate or perhaps a sex topic like swinging, and then I take calls.

Although the media of broadcasting have changed, the tradition of media relationship experts remains the same. I grew up listening to professional psychologist Dr. Judy Kuriansky on her syndicated radio call-in advice show and reading Dear Abby's down-home newspaper advice; these women impacted my life not only personally but professionally. For instance, Dr. Judy is my role model in terms of how to deal with callers when they ask sensitive questions about sex, such as questions related to having been abused or not having orgasm or about penis size or lasting longer. She always offered professional advice based on her years of academic training, and her style was firm, yet she had a softness to which callers responded well. In contrast, I believe that the tough-love approach that TV advice host Dr. Phil uses is more for the camera and less for the good of his guests.

Addressing questions about sexuality from the public heightens my awareness that there is a difference between visiting a psychologist's office and seeking advice on TV or radio. One major difference is that TV and radio are entertainment mediums; therefore, ratings are usually the top priority. In addition, being on a public show is usually a one-time experience. One hour of being counseled by Dr. Phil or being on *Oprah* is not going to fix the core of a problem; it takes time to help mend a conflict. TV or radio shows can only help point a person in a better direction; therefore, they are essentially an educational medium.

MY PERSONAL EXPERIENCE

Over the past few years, I have been branded a "relationship expert" by various media outlets. I have an undergraduate degree with a major in psychology from Eugene Lang College at the New School University; however, I do not claim to be a "psychologist," a profession that requires a state license. As a result, I see myself more as a sexuality educator of sorts. I am giving information to the best of my ability about how people can be helped and what the facts are about a sexual situation. My expertise comes less from books and more from everyday experiences, perhaps like Sally Jesse Raphael, who ruled the airwaves with advice for decades and also had no professional training but who gave common-sense answers people needed. Although I was always fascinated by psychology, I first entered the entertainment business as an off-Broadway actress; from there, I went to TV hosting and then to radio. At the age of 25, my focus has shifted to entertaining my audience at the same time that I try to help listeners with their questions and concerns.

I have been fortunate enough to listen to people's troubles from all over the world, as they share their trials and tribulations related to dating and relationships. It is astonishing to me that a man who lives in Scotland suffers from the same fears about sex as the man who lives in Canada. Doing my Paltalk show has shown me that people all over the world have the same issues about sexuality and relationships. For instance, I received a call from a Spanish woman who had difficulty climaxing during sex because she was insecure about her body. On that same show, I received a call from an Irish woman who had the same exact problem as her Spanish counterpart. Similarly, men from almost every continent have asked what the average penis size is. For some reason, all men seem to feel the need for validation about this concern. They want to have validation from an expert that they are adequate. From these experiences with my callers, I have observed that it is less about the culture one grows up in and more about human nature. Over this time, I have discovered what it means to be a media expert and the responsibility that comes along with that role.

THE RESPONSIBILITY OF BEING AN EXPERT

Those who are considered relationship experts in the media bear a great responsibility. When a caller asks what he should do about a crumbling marriage, I realize that I may be the only person whose advice he seeks, due to financial constraints, limited time, or a fear of sharing his problems with friends, family, or a counselor. Therefore, in the few minutes allotted to each caller, I must be thorough and provide the caller with direct and useful information. At times, this can be a very difficult task. A media expert such as myself—unlike my psychologist counterparts working in offices—does not have the advantage of talking one-on-one at length about the client's concerns. A media expert must be intuitive and instinctive; usually they cannot see the caller and can only sense the pain in the caller's voice, which reveals an urgency and a yearning for answers about a difficult situation.

Critics charge that one should never trust a media relationship expert on television, radio, or the Internet. However, in today's society, it is becoming commonplace to reach out to someone like myself. The majority of the population owns or has access to computers, radios, and/or televisions. A caller has a veil of confidentiality that a client at a therapist's office does not. From my experience, people who are the least likely to go to a psychologist's office are the most likely to call in to a radio or Internet show seeking advice. Therefore, these outlets are offering a service that provides education to a public that might not otherwise get such knowledge about sexuality.

PERSONAL CHALLENGES AND CALLER ETIQUETTE

There are challenges to being in the position of offering education about sexuality publicly. As a female relationship expert, I encounter callers who want not only advice but also a date with me. It can sometimes be uncomfortable when such approaches are made, but, unless the caller is being entirely inappropriate, I try to laugh off the advance. I see the caller's "hitting" on me as confusing the accessibility and comfort they feel while listening to my Sirius Radio show or watching me on my Paltalk show with something more. I remember my program director at my radio station saying, "The listener thinks you're only talking to them." I've found that statement to be true. Unlike psychologists, media experts sometimes reference their personal stories and experiences, which in turn can create a false sense of intimacy between the expert and the listener. Being an expert can be a double-edged sword. You want to be open with your audience, but you do not want to invite them into your life. It is a very thin line that I must walk every day. For instance, a caller said, "Diana, your energy and spirit are so beautiful. I feel a connection between us. You understand me. Please e-mail me so we can take this outside the show." Immediately, I was taken off my guard. One minute, I'm dispensing advice, and the next minute I feel like a girl at a bar being thrown a cheesy pick-up line. Although the caller's comments were intended to be flattering, I had to pay little attention to his advances. My response was simply, "Thank you." Then, as an expert, I had to return to discussing the current topic, which might involve an emotional discussion with a woman who is fleeing from her abuser husband. The caller who made the advance may feel dejected, but I hope he understands that there is a boundary that should not be crossed. The expert must create the wall between herself and her audience.

The biggest challenge I face is trying to always be informative yet entertaining. It is very difficult to help a caller in so few minutes. Many times, I would love to ask a series of questions about the person's current relationship or past experiences, but time does not allow me to do so. At times, I feel like a psychological vending machine: call me up, ask a question, and instantly I'm supposed to give you the fix. It is not that easy, and I worry that I may lead people in the wrong direction because I don't know the details of their relationship. However, I do try to preface each show with the caveat that I am a media expert and not a psychologist; if a caller needs significant advice, I suggest that she or he seek professional help.

Each night my goal is to have fun and to enjoy what I'm doing. I believe that when I have fun at my job, my listeners will have a great time. After all, I'm entertaining my listeners as much as I am informing them. At the end of a show, I want to walk away saying, "I think I gave someone good advice."

CONCLUSION

In conclusion, new technologies are being developed that give a broad audience access to advice and sexuality education. This is possible because of advancements in radio broadcasting and in computer technology that offer not only audio but visual contact through Webcams.

Media experts offer a new source of help in addition to traditional education and counseling; yet, they are not a substitute. Individuals should always seek professional educators and counselors for extended information and help with serious problems; however, for the everyday breakup or makeup, relationship experts can offer a good way to help a listener feel that she is not going through it alone. I always remind my audience to remember to use their best judgment and that, ultimately, "You know yourself and your situation better than anyone. The true expert is you."

Chapter Nine

ETHICAL CONSIDERATIONS IN THE USE OF SEXUALLY EXPLICIT VISUALS AS AN INSTRUCTIONAL METHODOLOGY IN COLLEGE SEXUALITY COURSES

Chuck Rhoades

An examination of the ethics of using sexually explicit materials (SEM) as an instructional methodology in university human sexuality courses begins with an attempt to define such materials. As used here, SEM refers to visual depictions of nudity, which may include the genitals, and depiction of sexual acts involving the genitals, such as anal, oral, and vaginal sex. Steinem (1980, 2003) drew a distinction between *erotica* and *pornography*, characterizing the former as evidencing a mutuality of sexual pleasure and expression that is voluntary and consensual, and that depicts prosocial values such as an acceptance of bodies, emotional warmth and sensuality. She defined pornography as a dehumanizing portrayal of sexual violence and conquest, depicting sexual inequalities, particularly degrading to women, and functioning as a means of social control. While these categories provide more clarity than the "I know it when I see it" definition of Supreme Court Justice Potter Stewart (U.S. Supreme Court, 1964), it leaves the classification of specific materials open to subjective interpretation and debate. Some researchers (McConnell, 1987; Saunders & Naus, 1993) operationalized the definitions through scale development and assessment of differing reactions to materials based on this dichotomy. With the vast amount and wide variety of SEM currently available in various formats, such as videos, DVDs, print, and on-line websites, categorizing commercial products as either pornographic or erotic presents a formidable task.

While erotica and pornography could be examined and discussed as instructional materials in university courses, a third category of SEM is proposed here that would comprise materials developed specifically for educational use. These include SEM developed to achieve specific educational objectives, such as to provide information about sexual behaviors and safer sex practices, to examine emotional reactions to sexual experiences, to identify values related to sexual experience and expression, and to develop comfort and skills in communicating about sexuality issues. These materials are typically developed by, or in consultation with professionals with advanced degrees and specialized training in sexuality, such as those certified by the American Association of Sexuality Educators, Counselors and Therapists (AASECT).

Educational SEM present thematic content consistent with instructional objectives and are often accompanied with suggested discussion questions and learning activities. Materials in this category are frequently used in Sexual Attitude Restructuring (SAR) programs (Rosser, B. R. S., Dwyer, S. M., Coleman, E., Miner, M., Metz, M., Robinson, B. E., & Bockting, W.O., 1995), which are required training for professionals seeking certification as sexuality educators, counselors, or therapists (AASECT Requirements, 2004). Some educators prefer the term, *Sexual Attitude Reassessment* to *Sexual Attitude Restructuring* and these programs may significantly differ in their educational purpose, scope, and choice of materials. During the 1970s, production and use of educational SEM proliferated, notably through the National Sex Forum, originators of the SAR format, and the Human Sexuality Program at New York University.[1]

EDUCATIONAL USE OF SEM

Film historians reported that the first known use of SEM for educational purposes occurred in the pre-World War I era, in the form of social hygiene films designed to portray the effects of what were then known as venereal diseases. These films reputedly depicted live births and close-ups of genitals affected by diseases, as well as images of prostitution and birth control use (Stevens, 1983).

In a historical review of the use of educational SEM, Schoen (2003a) credited Alfred Kinsey with introducing SEM in the 1940s for formal use in research and suggesting their use in education, a concept that faculty member Edward Tyler first implemented when showing a variety of sexual behaviors to his Indiana University students in 1967. The following year, Theodore McIlvenna and associates Laird Sutton and Phyllis Lyon, pioneered the use of SEM in the first structured SAR seminars through the National Sex Forum in San Francisco. As Methodist ministers, McIlvenna and Sutton considered their work integral to their vocation. Lyon, a cofounder of the first international organization for lesbians, the Daughters of Bilitis, brought an important perspective to the development of the methodology. They designed the SAR to guide participants in the examination of attitudes, values, and emotional reactions to sexual issues and behaviors. An important aspect of the SAR process they developed was its length, up to eight days and evenings of audio-visual viewing, personal reflection, and discussion. Not content with commercially produced sex films, Sutton developed a number of films that presented explicit sexual behaviors depicting emotional and relational values useful in SAR programs. The films were produced and distributed through Multimedia, an offshoot of the National Sex Forum (Brecher, 2000). On the east coast, Calderwood, director of the NYU graduate program in human sexuality, the first of its kind in the United States and Schoen, a former student, produced educational SEM through Focus International.

Production and distribution of SEM for educational use peaked in the 1970s and 1980s, with the National Sex Forum, which evolved into the Institute for the Advanced Study of Human Sexuality (IASHS), Focus International, and EDCOA being the major providers of these materials (M. Schoen, personal communication, June 28, 2006).[2] While production of educational SEM has declined since those years, university faculty, sex counselors and therapists, and workshop trainers continue using SEM in their professional work (Dailey, 2003; Robinson, Manthei, Scheltema, Rich, & Koznar, 1999; M. Schoen, personal communication, June 27, 2006; Stayton, 1998; Strair & Bartlik, 1999; Tepper, 1997). The IASHS has continued to utilize the full Sexual Attitude Restructuring Program as a required component of its curriculum, using much of the material and format developed in its original SAR seminars (T. Gertz, personal communication, February 19, 2007).[3] In comparison, professional organizations such as Planned Parenthood and university medical schools, such as the Robert Wood Johnson Medical School, continue to utilize a shorter duration Sexual Attitude Reassessment Program to augment sexuality instruction (Leiblum, 2001).

EDUCATIONAL OBJECTIVES OF SEM USE

Given a history of cultural, legal, religious, and political repression of sexuality and sexuality education in the United States (D'Emilio & Freedman, 1997), the use of SEM continues to garner controversy (Burleson, 1974; Dailey, 2003; Leiblum, 2001; McIlvenna & Lyon, 1975). In addressing these controversies, educators attempted to clarify the goals and rationale for SEM use.

The Sexuality Information and Education Council of The United States (SIECUS), a leading professional organization in the sexuality field, formally endorsed the use of SEM for educational purposes in its Position Statements. It asserted that "(w)hen sensitively used in a manner appropriate to the viewer's age and developmental level, sexually explicit visual, printed, or on-line materials can be valuable educational or personal aids, helping to reduce ignorance and confusion and contributing to a wholesome concept of sexuality" (SIECUS, 1996–2005).

As SIECUS Education Director, Burleson (1974) stated the goals of SEM use as providing information on biological processes, developing comfort in using sexual terminology, and providing a venue for the exploration of emotions and values. Gendel (1973) advocated helping learners develop "sexual self-insight" by relating elements in the materials to their own personal attitudes, while supporting others' examinations of values, attitudes, and emotional reactions. Educational and therapeutic uses of SEM may have overlapping objectives in seeking enhancement of sexual technique and couple intimacy, improvement in body image, increased communication skills, and as adjunct to treatment for sexual dysfunction (Calderwood, 1981; Robinson et al., 1999; Schoen, 2003b). Stayton (1998) explained that SEM use could help train sex therapists to develop comfort and ability to address a range of sexual issues with their clients.

Rhoades (2006) informed students in an undergraduate human sexuality course of the following objectives for the use of SEM:

1. To examine personal attitudes, values, and emotional reactions to a variety of sexual issues,
2. To participate in other students' examination of their reactions,
3. To support and receive support from other students in this process,
4. To gain an integrated understanding of the cognitive, affective, and interpersonal aspects of the sexual issues being examined,
5. To increase comfort and ability to discuss sexual issues,
6. To explore how gender, race, religion, values, and culture affect understanding and responses to SEM, and
7. To establish a common reference for examining sexual issues.

EFFECTS OF SEM USE

Research is lacking on the effects of using SEM as an educational methodology in undergraduate courses. Carrera & Lieberman (1976) studied the effects of using SEM on graduate students (N = 50) in a Human Sexuality course and found that students reported increased understanding and knowledge of differences in sexual expression and increased personal knowledge of their own sexual experience. Schoen (1980) found that sexual experience and levels of sex guilt were associated with undergraduates' attitudes toward viewing SEM, with lower levels of sex guilt and higher levels of sexual experience associated with more positive attitudes and less sexual experience and higher guilt associated with more negative attitudes. Tepper (1997) examined the effects of SEM use for people with disabilities, and found these materials helpful for improving judgments of self-efficacy in the context of a sexuality education or therapy program.

Some researchers (Aja & Self, 1986; Byrd, 1977; Friend, 1987) found that SEM use did not differ from other educational methodologies in achieving information gain and attitude change. Furthermore, Kleinplatz (1997) cautioned that some educational SEM might reinforce myths and stereotypes about gender roles and erotic preferences.

Further understanding of other potential effects may be inferred from research conducted with participants who attended SARs and from clients in therapy. Research on the effects of viewing pornography may also provide some additional areas for consideration.

SAR Seminars

Research on the effects of SEM used for educational purposes comes primarily from studies conducted with participants who attended SAR seminars, the primary component being SEM viewing and discussion. The largest survey, by Rosser et al. (1995) reported on an 18-year study of 7,451 SAR participants, and found that 96.2% rated the SAR seminars as beneficial to them personally, while 1.5% rated the experience as personally harmful. A partial sample of the study (N = 1,237) provided an independent rating of the SEM, with 89.8% rating the materials as helpful and .8% as harmful. In addition, 91% of these participants reported that the SEM were appropriate to their own issues and concerns and 93% reported that SEM were valuable for promoting emotional awareness.

Wollert (1978) reported that SAR participants experienced increased acceptance of their own and others' sexual attitudes, increased understanding of the range of sexual behaviors, and an increased understanding of how attitudes affect sexual values.

SEM Use in Therapy

Evaluations of therapeutic use of SEM have demonstrated beneficial effects such as successful treatment of sexual dysfunction (Amelang & Pielke, 1992; Cole, Chan, Blakeney, & Chesney, 1974; Robinson, Manthei, Scheltema, Rich, & Koznar, 1999; Strair & Bartlik, 1999), and enhanced sexual pleasure and improved intimacy skills (Schoen, 2003). Robinson et al. (1999) found evidence for increased knowledge about sexuality, reduced anxiety, shame, and guilt regarding sexual expression, improved couple communication, successful treatment of sexual abuse survivors, reduced homophobia, and enhanced learning from the modeling of sexual techniques. Vandervoort and McIlvenna (1976) stated that SEM use reduced counselor contact time in conveying information and helping clients to develop more accepting attitudes that served to reduce guilt and shame.

Harmful effects are cited as occurring with lower frequency than beneficial effects in the literature, but include contributing to couples' dissatisfaction with their sex lives (Amelang & Pielke, 1992), and disorientation regarding sexual attitudes and values (Anderson, 1986). Robinson et al. (1999) found evidence that SEM use increased homophobia in some viewers. This study also noted that SEM viewing could trigger memories of past sexual abuse. Therapist misjudgment of client readiness and inadequate preparation for viewing may have contributed to the reported reactions of shock, resentment, and hostility (Robinson et al., 1999).

Effects of Pornography

Although the context for viewing pornographic materials differs substantially from SEM use in college classes, there are reported educational benefits, such as learning erotic scripts and sexual techniques (Attwood, 2005). Money (1988) discussed the potential of incorporating safer sex messages and techniques into pornographic materials as an aid in preventing transmission of HIV and other sexually transmitted infections.

A review of over 20 years of studies on the effects of pornography by Davis and Bauserman (1993) concluded that influences and effects are dependent on a complex interaction of personal predispositions, the situation and context in which the viewing takes place, and the content of the materials. They noted that the most commonly reported effect of viewing pornography was short-term sexual arousal, which did not necessarily carry over to overt sexual behavior, due to factors such as opportunity, the nature of the viewer's affective response to the material, and the viewer's predisposition. They found evidence that repeated exposure tends to increase acceptance of the sexual activity viewed. Concerning aggression, they reported findings that most men who view aggressive pornography do not report acting on that aggression, and that those that do were prone to violence prior to such viewing.

Malamuth (1986) linked viewing pornography to rape-supportive attitudes and found that viewers of sexually violent pornography were more likely to report a history of past sexual violence. Hardy (2004) asserted that pornography presented a misconstruction or distortion of female sexuality that presents women as acquiescent and submissive to male fantasy and desires. Other studies reported that pornography might have negative effects on women's body image and sexual performance (Attwood, 2005) and on men's genital satisfaction and sexual self-esteem (Morrison, Ellis, Morrison, Bearden, & Harriman, 2006).

ETHICAL PRINCIPLES AND SEM USE

In its general principles, the American Psychological Association's (APA) Ethics Code (American Psychological Association, 2002) provides professionals with five ideals that guide professional practice. Applicable to psychologists working as therapists, educators, and researchers, these principles can guide the use of SEM in college and university courses.

Beneficence and Nonmaleficence

Grounded in perhaps the oldest professional proscription (Hippocrates, n. d.) "to do no harm," this principle calls on professionals to aspire to work for the benefit of those with whom they work. Recognizing that educators in the classroom exert power over their students by nature of evaluating them for academic grades, adherence to this principle requires educators to avoid misusing such influence or power. It also calls for creating a classroom environment that accentuates students' emotional safety and enhances the potential for experiencing benefits from viewing and discussing SEM. Educators should identify the intended benefits and potential problems in using SEM and consider these factors in the selection, presentation, and discussion processes. A discussion of such benefits and concerns, including the results of the studies of SEM effects presented earlier should occur with the students prior to showing the first SEM. Educators should identify campus resources for students who may experience relationship problems or whose past traumas are triggered by SEM use.

Fidelity and Responsibility

Instructors have an obligation to establish trust with their students, particularly when such challenging course content and methodology as sexuality is concerned. Providing students with a clear description of class methodologies in the course syllabus and verbally, in the initial class session, begins the process of building trust. The faculty member using SEM should define a format for the use of SEM and incorporate student input into the establishment of group principles that guide how the class operates. These should include issues related to confidentiality, speaking and listening roles in class discussions, and expression of student opinions. Teachers need to assure students that expression of an opinion per se is unrelated to the grade they will receive. The faculty member should also establish an ongoing dialogue with another experienced colleague regarding student response to SEM. Such consultation allows instructors to obtain an informed perspective unattached to the current teacher-student relationship and may serve to enhance understanding on how to meet the professional responsibilities to serve the best interests of the students.

Integrity

With accuracy, honesty, and truth as the elements of this principle, educators should choose SEM that accurately represent the content being studied. Material on lesbian sexuality, for example, should reflect a lesbian perspective and not a heterosexual male fantasy. This further illustrates the preferred use of educational SEM developed for classroom instruction rather than pornography developed for commercial use. Such selection may obviate Kleinplatz's (1997) concern regarding the perpetuation of stereotypes in SEM use. As the SAR program has demonstrated, alignment of instructional methodologies to course objectives cannot only preserve the integrity of the program, but can maximize positive participant outcomes (Rosser et al., 1995). Integrity also involves adhering to the commitments stated in the course syllabus and the established class principles or ground rules.

Justice

This principle speaks to the importance of granting all students an opportunity to achieve the course objectives. As some may be predisposed to be unable to fully benefit from the use of SEM, alternative methods should be made available to them. Student survivors of sexual assault, as noted earlier, may require such consideration. In fairness, instructors should design alternatives to help the students accomplish the same objectives addressed through SEM use, but should not involve undue effort or hardship on the student. For example, assigning the student to view a non-explicit film or to read and respond to a journal article examining the issues addressed in the SEM would be reasonable alternatives. Assigning an entire book to read and review would not be a fair option.

This principle might also be applied to issues of justice of social and political justice that arise from consideration of SEM involving common sexual behaviors, such as oral sex that were subject to legal injunction and to groups experiencing prejudice and discrimination, such as those with same-sex partners. Educators might adhere to this principle by including questions on these issues for discussion following the viewing of SEM.

Respect for People's Rights and Dignity

Respect requires acknowledging the existence of differences in religious perspectives, gender and sexual orientation, and for variations in erotic preferences and affirming the importance of how such differences influence the development and expression of an individual's sexuality. A goal of a human sexuality course is to enhance understanding of these influences. The use of SEM may aid in this process by serving as material to view through the lenses of these different perspectives. Instructor attention to how individual students experience the use of SEM in the classroom begins with helping students to assess their own readiness for such viewing. Such reflection may help eliminate the negative results of SEM use found by Robinson et al. (1999). As stated earlier, it is important for the instructor to allow an alternative educational experience for those who deem SEM based on these differences, and to allow open discussion of reactions to the SEM from various perspectives.

It is also important that the instructor include discussion of perspectives not presented by the students in order to expand the range of potential reactions to the SEM content and to model respect for differences beyond those evident in the class. For example, as Tiefer suggested (1995), gender role restrictions and anti-pornography sentiment serve to inhibit women's openness regarding erotic preferences, such as might occur when verbalizing responses to SEM. Discussing this perspective after viewing a SEM in a class session offers a tangible learning opportunity for students to use their viewing experience as primary source material.

APPLYING APA STANDARDS TO SEM USE

Several areas of the APA Ethics Code (2002) apply to SEM use beginning with Standard 2.01, which requires instructors to be competent and well-trained in selecting, planning for, facilitating, and evaluating the use of SEM. As the AASECT certification requirements state, such training should include the professional's own participation in exploring personal attitudes and knowledge through attending professional training that use SEM, such as a SAR seminar. APA Standard 2.03 states that the instructor should remain cognizant of current research related to SEM use and the issues presented in the materials shown in class. If the instructor is absent from a class session in which showing a SEM was planned, an alternative instructional methodology should be provided for the substitute instructor to present. Delegating such work to another would not necessarily guarantee that the class environment would maintain the levels of trust and safety important for students to learn from the SEM instruction.

Human Relations Standards

Selection of SEM should be made with awareness of APA Standard 3.01 prohibiting discrimination based on characteristics that may be evident in the materials. Instructors should seek to affirm human diversity by selecting appropriate materials that reflect variations in age (such as including both young and older adults), gender, gender identity, race, ethnicity, culture, religion, sexual orientation, disability, socioeconomic status and other areas that enrich students' understanding of how the diversity present in other areas of life also extends to sexuality.

APA Standards 3.02 and 3.03 ban sexual and other forms of harassment of students. Instructors should present SEM and facilitate related discussions in a professional manner, without overt or subtle messages that would indicate a sexual advance to any student. Instructors in sexuality courses should consider clearly stating at the beginning of the course that they condemn harassment behaviors and reject any possibility of sexual intimacies with students, as Standard 7.07 requires.

Informed Consent Standards

As stated earlier, instructors should inform students about the intended use of SEM in writing, such as on the course syllabus, and verbally during the first class session to satisfy the provisions of informed consent. Instructors should include information concerning both potential benefits and potential problems identified in the research and present a clear explanation of the purpose for using the SEM and the procedures to be employed, including the right of students to refuse the SEM instruction and participate in an equitably comparable assignment without penalty to the grade they will receive. Informed consent should be viewed as a process, with the initial discussion of the purpose and procedures of SEM use framed at the start of the course in conjunction with the identification of class operating principles or ground rules.

The creative instructor may enhance the learning during the early phase of the informed consent process by helping students distinguish between consent to participate in SEM instruction and acquiescence to what is on a professor's syllabus, a concept that can then be linked to later topics in the course, such as sexual consent (Muehlenhard, 1996). As the course proceeds, the instructor should revisit the informed consent issue by providing students with information about each SEM before it is shown and allowing students to decide about viewing or choosing alternatives. Informing students about the discussion format following the viewing and obtaining their perspectives should also be considered an aspect of informed consent.

Harm Avoidance Standards and Survivors of Non-Consensual Sex

Consistent with Standard 3.04, special consideration should be made to avoid harm to those students who are sexual abuse/assault survivors. As Kidman (1993a) noted, survivors may experience a range of responses to sexuality education programs, including feelings of shame, guilt, and fear related to their trauma, an inability to stay mentally present during instruction, feelings of isolation, and other reactions may be triggered by recall of the traumatic experiences. While not directly addressing the use of SEM for students who are survivors, Kidman provided guidelines for incorporating this perspective into educational programs. This included the establishment and maintenance of ground rules as boundaries for safety, a policy of "no surprises," which speaks to a detailed and thorough informed consent process, careful choice of language, and the stated assumption that the group has students who are survivors and the potential benefits and risks unique to these students (Kidman, 1993b). Consistently referring to the ground rules prior to each viewing may help allow student survivors to experience a predictable and safe structure, which may minimize the potential for difficulty identified by Robinson, Manthei, Scheltema, Rich, and Koznar (1999).

Privacy and Confidentiality Standards

An agreement as to what constitutes confidentiality needs to be reached in the first class discussion when group principles or ground rules are first discussed, in keeping with Standard 4.01 on maintaining confidentiality. Instructor and students' respective responsibilities to maintain confidentiality should be specified. The instructor should assert that no discussions or assignments in the course require or seek disclosure of personal sexual histories, although individual students may choose to disclose under the terms agreed upon by the entire class, including the instructor, according to the group principles.

Disclosure and confidentiality should be addressed specifically with regard to SEM use. Students may understand their reaction to the materials as related to their experiences and may or may not choose to provide this information in the class discussion. Prior to showing the SEM and certainly prior to the follow-up discussion, the instructor should discuss the reasons for and against disclosure, reinforce the group principles, and provide alternative means of discussing reactions that do not include personal disclosure. These may include posing discussion questions in the third person, such as "how might a person who has experienced this behavior react to negative comments about it?" The instructor may also provide a safer, more comfortable structure for students to disclose (or not) by allowing for paired or small group discussions following the viewing.

Education and Training Standards

Providing students with information on the purpose, procedures, and research on the SEM instructional methodology in the written syllabus and/or supplementary written materials conforms to Standard 7.02's requirements for providing an accurate and current description of course content. To conform to Standard 7.01, instructors need to design and present the SEM sessions to clearly reflect the course goals and objectives. Ensuring that the materials selected and the discussions, learning activities, and information contained in the sessions are consistent with the current knowledge in the field pertains to the importance of maintaining accuracy in teaching, as specified in Standard 7.03. While the instructor may advise students to seek therapy for a variety of reasons during the course, such advisement, including that related to the SEM sessions, should not be presented as a mandate from the instructor, nor should the instructor become the therapist for the student, in accordance with the Standard 7.05 prohibition on mandating therapy as a course requirement. Educational standards related to student disclosure (7.04), performance assessment and grades (Standard 7.06) and the prohibition of sexual intimacies with students (Standard 7.07) have been discussed earlier in this paper. These and other relevant APA standards should be reviewed by instructors as regular tasks in the planning, teaching, and evaluation of courses using SEM.

SUMMARY

Research on the effects of using sexually explicit materials in university undergraduate human sexuality courses is mostly sparse and dated, with past studies lacking the rigor of current research standards. Findings for beneficial effects predominate, while cautionary suggestions appear in the literature, especially with regard to students who are survivors of non-consensual sexual experiences.

In choosing to use SEM, instructors are advised to be mindful of the APA Ethical Principles and adhere strictly to the standards of the APA Ethics Code in order to provide students with a meaningful educational experience in the context of ethical and competent practice.

RECOMMENDATIONS

Based on the research and the application of the APA Ethics Code, the following recommendations are offered as guidelines for the use of SEM in undergraduate human sexuality courses.

1. Only instructors having advanced training in human sexuality and who have experienced SEM use in their training should consider using SEM.
2. Instructors should identify specific goals and objectives in their courses for which SEM may be an appropriate methodology.
3. Selection of SEM for classroom use should occur after careful screening of the media to insure that they relate to the objectives, avoid myths and stereotyping unless these areas are being investigated by using the material, and are clearly connected to the course session and readings. Ideally, the instructor should select SEM in consultation with another faculty member(s) with similar credentials.
4. SEM that depict sexual violence should not be shown.
5. Instructors who plan to show SEM should make this information known to students beforehand, in the course description, syllabus, and/or a supplement to the course syllabus.
6. Instructors should discuss the purpose of using SEM and describe the procedure for viewing and discussion to be used during the class sessions prior to showing the visuals. The instructor should inform students of research findings regarding the potential benefits and potential harm from SEM viewing.
7. Instructors should work with the students to establish class principles or ground rules that address aspects of SEM use, including confidentiality, how differences of opinion will be respected, and options for students to achieve course goals as an alternative to SEM viewing. It should be made clear that viewing SEM is voluntary.
8. The instructor should develop a structure for SEM use that includes preparing students to see the video by describing its contents beforehand, showing

the SEM in an appropriate classroom environment, and allowing ample time to discuss the SEM after it is viewed. Instructors may help students identify their expectations before viewing the SEM so that they may compare their reactions after seeing the material.

9. In the follow-up discussion and class activities, instructors should help students examine and discuss the information presented in the SEM, their emotional reactions to viewing the SEM, and clearly relate the experience to course goals and objectives.

10. Instructors should provide students with frequent opportunities to state their reactions and opinions regarding the use of SEM in the classroom setting. This would include regular review of group principles.

11. Instructors should affirm the normalcy of the range of emotional responses to SEM.

12. Instructors should provide students who do not choose to view the SEM with alternative instruction that helps them achieve the course objectives. Such instruction should be comparable to the SEM instruction in terms of the amount of time and effort required from the student. It should be made clear that the student choice of an alternative to the SEM does not negatively impact grades.

13. Since viewing SEM may evoke strong emotional reactions on the part of some students, the instructor should be available for individual student conferences and maintain a current list of available counselors and therapists for student referrals.

14. Course evaluations should assess student feedback on the use of SEM.

It is also recommended that further research be conducted on the use of SEM in the undergraduate human sexuality course. Research is needed to identify the extent of SEM use in undergraduate sexuality courses, to thoroughly investigate the effects of SEM use on students, and to compare the effects of SEM use and other methodologies on student outcomes. Further research may also help develop a clearer understanding of the effects of SEM use on particular groups of students, such as those who have experienced nonconsensual sex. Specific attention to SEM use in the ethics codes of professional sexuality organizations, such as AASECT and the Society for the Scientific Study of Sexuality (SSSS), may also benefit instructors and students.

NOTES

"Ethical Consideration in the Use of Sexually Explicit Visuals as an Instructional Methodology in College Sexuality Courses," *American Journal of Sexuality Education* 2(4): 5–23. Reprinted by permission of Taylor and Francis.

American Journal of Sexuality Education, Vol. 2(4) 2007. Available online at http://ajse. haworthpress.com. © 2007 by The Haworth Press. All rights reserved.

1. The author was a student in the Human Sexuality Program, obtaining a Master's Degree from New York University in 1982. He has used SEM in teaching undergraduate courses in human sexuality and in professional trainings since 1980.

2. Mark Schoen, Ph.D., is the Director of Sex Education for the Sinclair Intimacy Institute, the largest producer and distributor of educational SEM.

3. Thomas E. Gertz, Ed.D., DACS, is a Professor of Sexology and Director of the Department of Sexual Attitude Restructuring Programs at the Institute for the Advanced Study of Human Sexuality.

REFERENCES

AASECT Requirements for certification. (2004). Ashland, VA: American Association of Sexuality Educators, Counselors, & Therapists. [Electronic version].

Aja, A., & Self, D. (1986). Alternate methods of changing nursing home attitudes toward sexual behavior of the aged. *Journal of Sex Education &Therapy, 12,* 37–41.

Amelang, M., & Pielke, M. (1992). Effects of erotica upon men's and women's loving. *Psychological Reports, 71,* 1235–1245.

American Psychological Association. (2002). *Ethical principles of psychologists and code of conduct.* Washington, DC: AP. [Electronic version]

Anderson, W. (1986). Stages of therapist comfort with sexual concerns of clients. *Professional Psychiatry, Research and Practice, 17,* 352–356.

Attwood, F. (2005). What do people do with porn? Qualitative research into the consumption, use, and experience of pornography and other sexually explicit material. *Sexuality & Culture, 9,* 65–86.

Brecher, E. M. (2000). *The sex researchers: Expanded edition.* San Francisco: Specific Press.

Burleson, D. L. (1974). Use and abuse of audio-visuals in sex education. *SIECUS Report, 2,* 1&6.

Byrd, J. W. (1978). The effects of sexually explicit films on the sexual knowledge, attitudes, and behaviors of college students (Doctoral dissertation, Southern Illinois University). *Dissertation Abstracts International, 38(10-A),* 5933–5934.

Calderwood, D. (1981). Educating the educators. In L. Brown (Ed.), *Sex education in the eighties: The challenge of healthy sexual evolution* (pp. 191–201). New York: Plenum Press.

Carrera, M. A., & Lieberman, S. (1976). Evaluating the use of explicit media in a human sexuality course. *SIECUS Report, 6,* 1–3.

Cole, C. M., Chan, F. A., Blakeney, P. E., & Chesney, A. P. (1974). Participants' reaction to components of a rapid-treatment workshop for sexual dysfunction. *Journal of Sex & Marital Therapy, 6,* 30–39.

Dailey, D. (2003, May). Kansas legislature threatens to drop funding over sexuality course. *Contemporary Sexuality, 37,* 7.

Davis, C. M., & Bauserman, R. (1993). Exposure to sexually explicit materials: An attitude change perspective. In J. Bancroft (Ed.), *Annual review of sex research: An integrative and interdisciplinary review* (Vol. 4, pp. 121–209). Mount Vernon, IA: Society for the Scientific Study of Sex.

D'Emilio, J., & Freedman, E. B. (1997. *Intimate matters: A history of sexuality in America.* Chicago, IL: University of Chicago Press.

Friend, R. A. (1987). The relationship between group cohesion and the development of pluralism in sexual attitudes as a function of the small group component of SAR seminars (Doctoral dissertation, University of Pennsylvania). *Dissertation Abstracts International, 47(7-A),* 2466–2467.

Gendel, E. S. (1973). Use of explicit visual materials in professional education. *SIECUS Report, 1,* 2.

Hardy, S. (2004). Reading pornography. *Sex Education, 4,* 3–18.

Hippocrates. (n. d.). *The oath of Hippocrates.* Retrieved June 27, 2006, from Medword Resources Web site: http://www.medword.com/?hippocrates.html

Kidman, C. (1993a). Non-consensual sexual experience & HIV education: An educator' s view. *SIECUS Report, 21,* 9–12.

Kidman, C. (1993b). Tips for incorporating sexual abuse and non-consensual sex into HIV education and prevention programs. *SIECUS Report, 21,* 11.

Kleinplatz, P. (1997). "Educational" sex videos: What are they teaching? *Canadian Journal of Human Sexuality, 6,* 39–43.

Leiblum, S. R. (2001). An established medical school human sexuality curriculum: Description and evaluation. *Sexual and Relationship Therapy, 16,* 59–70.

Malamuth, N. M. (1986). Predictors of naturalistic sexual aggression. *Journal of Personality and Social Psychology, 50,* 953–962.

McConnell, J. (1987). *Differences in emotional reactions to erotica and pornography.* Unpublished master's thesis, University of Waterloo, ON, Canada.

McIlvenna, T., & Lyon, P. (1975). Use of explicit sex films for adult education. *SIECUS Report, 3,* 5.

Money, J. (1988). The ethics of pornography in the era of AIDS. *Journal of Sex & Marital Therapy, 14,* 177–183.

Morrison, T. G., Ellis, S. R., Morrison, M. A., Bearden, A., & Harriman, R. L. (2006). Exposure to sexually explicit material and variations in body esteem, genital attitudes, and sexual esteem among a sample of Canadian men. *Journal of Men's Studies, 14,* 209–222.

Muehlenhard, C. L. (1996). The complexities of sexual consent. *SIECUS Report, 24,* 4–7.

Rhoades, C. (2006). *Human sexuality course lecture notes.* Unpublished manuscript, University of New Hampshire, Durham.

Robinson, B. E., Manthei, R., Scheltema, K., Rich, R., & Koznar, J. (1999). Therapeutic uses of sexually explicit materials in the United States and the Czech and Slovak republics: A qualitative study. *Journal of Sex & Marital Therapy, 25,* 103–119.

Rosser, B. R. S., Dwyer, S. M., Coleman, E., Miner, M., Metz, M., Robinson, B. E. et al. (1995). Using sexually explicit material in adult sex education: An eighteen-year comparative analysis. *Journal of Sex Education & Therapy, 21,* 117–128.

Saunders, R. M., & Naus, P. J. (1993). The impact of social content and audience factors on responses to sexually explicit videos. *Journal of Sex Education & Therapy, 19,* 117–130.

Schoen, M. (1980a). The influence of sex guilt and sexual experience on attitudes toward sexually explicit behavior as portrayed in visuals (Doctoral dissertation, New York University, 1980). *Dissertation Abstracts International, 41/02,* 544.

Schoen, M. (2003b). *History of explicit sexual health films.* Unpublished manuscript, Sinclair Intimacy Institute, Chapel Hill, NC.

Schoen, M. (Narrator). (2003). *A lover's guide to self-pleasuring* [Motion picture]. (Available from Sinclair Intimacy Institute)

Sexuality Information, & Education Council of the United States (SIECUS). (1996–2005). *Position statements.* New York: SIECUS. [Electronic version]

Stayton, W. R. (1998). A curriculum for training professionals in human sexuality using the sexual attitude restructuring model. *Journal of Sex Education & Therapy, 23,* 26–32.

Steinem, G. (1980). Erotica and pornography: A clear and present difference. In *Take back the night: Women on pornography* (pp. 35–39). New York: William Morrow.

Steinem, G. (2003). Erotic and pornography: A clear and present difference. In R. Baird & S. Rosenbaum (Eds.), *Pornography: Private right or public menace?* Amherst, NY: Prometheus.

Stevens, J. O. (1983). Sex as education: A note on pre-1930 social hygiene films. *Film & History, 13,* 84–87.

Strair, S., & Bartlik, B. (1999). Stimulation of the libido: The use of erotica in sex therapy. *Psychiatric Annals, 29,* 60–62.

Tepper, M. S. (1997). Use of sexually explicit films in spinal cord injury rehabilitation programs. *Sexuality and Disability, 15,* 167–181.

Tiefer, L. (1995). Some harms to women of restrictions on sexually related expression. In L. Tiefer (Ed.), *Sex is not a natural act* (pp. 129–134). Boulder, CO: Westview Press.

U.S. Supreme Court. (1964). *Jacobelis v. Ohio,* 378 U.S. 184. Retrieved June 27, 2006, from Findlaw for Legal Professionals Web site: http://caselaw.lp.findlaw.com/? scripts.getcase.pl?court=US&vol=378&invol=184

Vandervoort, H. E., & McIlvenna, T. (1976). Sexually explicit media in medical school curricula. In R. Green (Ed.), *Human sexuality: A health practitioner's text* (pp. 235–244). Baltimore: Williams & Wilkins.

Wollert, R. W. (1978). A survey of sexual attitude reassessment and restructuring seminars. *Journal of Sex Research, 14,* 250–259.

Chapter Ten

ESSENTIAL INFORMATION ABOUT THE USE OF EROTICA FOR SEXUALITY EDUCATORS

Barbara Bartlik, Sharna Striar, Cynthia Cabral, and Julie Anne Kolzet

This chapter informs the sexuality educator about the breadth of erotic material available to the public and its applications to educating adults about sexual behaviors and relationships. This chapter also serves as a short reference guide to erotic films and literature. It is supported by the authors' combined 30 years of teaching and clinical experience in the field of human sexuality. Since erotica has both educational and clinical utility, several of the ways in which such material can be utilized (e.g., with individuals and in groups) are discussed (Bartlik & Striar, 1998; Striar & Barlik, 1999). Teaching considerations as well as cautions are highlighted. Questions applicable to group discussion are included.

DEFINITION OF TERMS

At the outset, it is necessary to clarify the terms "erotica" and "pornography." Erotica is a modern word used to describe materials that are intended to inspire sexual feelings (Miller, 2002), which includes visual and auditory stimuli in film, Internet formats, literature, photography, sculpture, and painting that are associated mainly with sensually stimulating or sexually arousing images. While the distinction between erotica and pornography is highly subjective, there is some consensus among sexuality professionals that pornography is grounded more in physicality, while erotica places greater emphasis on suggestive or symbolic images of sexual arousal. ("Pornography," 2008).

HISTORICAL OVERVIEW

Until a generation or two ago, most erotica was considered culturally and officially obscene, until Supreme Court decisions in the 1950s and 1960s loosened restrictions. Erotica included a range of items from "naturist," "men's culture" magazines, and "stag" films to once- forbidden literary works by recognized authors like D. H. Lawrence, Henry Miller, and Vladimir Nabokov. By a half-century ago, the era when the existence of such materials was shocking was coming to an end.

Sexually explicit materials have now become deeply embedded in modern-day society, as the Internet, along with television, movies, and magazine articles, continues to desensitize and familiarize the general public to implicit and explicit sexual content. Individuals from all walks of life are stimulated by sexually explicit content on a regular basis and without much effort on their part. Concurrently, the use of erotica has been integrated into and become more a part of "mainstream" life.

Formal sexuality education in American society stereotypically ends at the high school level, with courses about human sexuality offered at the college level usually only as electives. Those who go on to pursue graduate degrees in a sexuality-related profession—such as health or sexuality educator or sex therapist—can access a range of educational opportunities. There is, however, a dearth of educational opportunities for individual adults who are not sexuality professionals to receive ongoing sexuality information and education that can help them learn about their changing bodies and experiences over time and to understand how to diversify their sexual relationships. As a result, it is becoming more commonplace—and more accepted—for adult individuals to turn to erotica for their ongoing sexuality education. However, the sheer profusion of erotica makes it difficult for individuals and couples to select the type most appropriate, pertinent, and desirable for their needs, as well as to be sure it is accurate according to the standards of sexuality educators. Sexuality educators and clinicians also have difficulty in determining—and often are left wondering about—how best to introduce or incorporate erotica into the teaching curriculum and therapy setting. In addition, there is confusion surrounding the ways in which erotica can impact an individual or group.

The authors believe that comprehensive, accurate, and age- and developmentally appropriate information on the subject is limited but needed. A search of the medical and psychological literature revealed a paucity of evidence-based research on the use of erotica as an educational medium. In addition, no case-controlled studies on the implications of erotica in both the classroom and the clinical setting were found. In summary, while there is no shortage of erotica, much of what is available is either inadequate or deleterious to the efforts of sexuality educators or fails to consider clinical and educational applications.

SEXUALITY EDUCATION AND EROTIC MATERIAL: ALFRED KINSEY

Alfred Kinsey, the ground-breaking sex researcher of the 1950s, was among the first to incorporate sexually explicit films into the teaching curriculum (Christenson, 1971). He intended to dispel myths and raise his students' consciousness about the multifaceted concept of sexuality. Kinsey's work was based on the premise that images presented in sexually explicit films normalize different forms of sexual expression and that, through repeated exposure, students would become more comfortable viewing a range of sexually explicit acts. Kinsey's pioneering teaching curriculum is one of numerous ways he informed and advanced the field of sexuality while providing a sound basis and rationale for the ongoing use of these types of materials with adults today.

SEXUALITY EDUCATION: THE SAR MODEL

The Sexual Attitude Reassessment ("SAR," http://www.neihs.org/SAR.html) is a teaching format grounded in the work of Kinsey and his contemporaries and later by many noted sexologists, including the well-known medical team of William Masters and Virginia E. Johnson. The SAR curriculum incorporates explicit films that were made for use in educational settings, as well as in lectures and facilitator-run, small-group discussions.

After viewing a film, participants discuss in a small-group setting the impact of the film on their attitudes, beliefs, and values. These films *usually* are educational films created for this purpose, although, as the original SAR films have become dated, more recent, mainstream erotica has been used. Often, the discussions that result from these films center around an associated topic that has little to do with the material depicted. For example, in some SARs, after viewing many images of genitalia, small groups often end up discussing body-image issues. A video about bisexuality has resulted in discussions about monogamy in relationships, and so on. Because different feelings and reactions can be triggered by these media, they are often referred to as "trigger" films. Through this process, the participants become self-reflective and are encouraged to communicate their feelings about sexuality with others, particularly their partners. They often also assume a more expanded view of sexuality and what it encompasses as they are exposed to different images, relationships, behaviors, and opinions.

Through various teaching modalities, SAR participants become more knowledgeable about why sexual problems develop and the ways in which education and therapy can help. The SAR model promotes an open, direct, and supportive style to help reduce the embarrassment that some individuals feel when learning about sexuality. When teaching human sexuality with support materials in the SAR model, it is often necessary to tailor the course to the values, orientations, sexual issues, and state of readiness of the group.

Some SARs are designed for couples and need additional format alterations and considerations.

SAR workshop participants often work in the education or health care sector. Consequently, they can be more comfortable with the material than early-career professionals. Students who come into contact with individuals with sexuality-related questions and concerns often are encouraged to take the SAR workshop. The SAR model remains one of the cornerstones of sexuality education today, and is required for certification from the American Association of Sexuality for Educators, Counselors, and Therapists (AASECT).

CATEGORIES OF ADULT AND EROTIC FILMS

The SAR is one format for using sexually explicit media that was created with education in mind. There are other educational films about sexuality that can be used in educating adults and adult professionals—and more mainstream erotic films that can be used to do the same.

The selection of films included in this article gives educators and health care providers a sampling of the types of adult films available. Before incorporating erotic films into the teaching curriculum or clinical process, the sexuality professional should have an understanding of the many forms of erotica and the instances in which they can be applied. It should also go without saying that no resource should be used without viewing it first.

INSTRUCTIONAL AND EDUCATIONAL FILMS

Adult films that are didactic in nature can be helpful not only for the general public but also as teaching instruments for professionals in the field of sexuality. These films explore such topics as the proper use of sex toys, how to give a massage, the fundamentals of foreplay, how to masturbate, and the location of the G-spot. These types of films are unique in that they tend to combine erotic content with technical information. Tristan Taormino's *Expert Guide to Oral Sex* (both fellatio and cunnilingus), *Expert Guide to Anal Sex*, and *Expert Guide to the G-Spot* are examples. Additionally, Nina Hartley's *Guide to Oral Sex* includes a comprehensive lesson on female and male sexual anatomy complete with charts and photos.

Sexologist Betty Dodson has played a significant role in promoting women's sexual self-esteem and demonstrating the importance of masturbation to women's sexual satisfaction. Her film *Orgasmic Women: 13 Self-loving Divas* features Dodson discussing the art of self-stimulation along with demonstrations and commentary by 13 women. The film encourages women to be creative when they masturbate and to use vibrators and novel sexual aids. Other films by

Dodson include *Self-loving: Portrait of a Sexual Seminar; Celebrating Orgasm: Women's Private Self-loving Sessions;* and *Viva la Vulva: Women's Sex Organs Revealed.*

The *Better Sex Video Series* is another example of instructional adult films intended for couples who wish to enhance mutual communication skills and learn techniques to improve their sex lives. These films contain demonstrations and interviews with actual couples as well as qualified sex therapists and educators.

"Soft-Core" Erotica

Adult films that depict sexual behavior in a subtle and understated way often are classified as "soft-core" erotica. Films in this category emphasize arousal through sexual suggestion and stimulation and often are devoid of images of aroused genitalia, masturbation, ejaculation, or penetration. These films tend to be plot driven and feature actors with relatively natural proportions. The ways in which these films can be used in the classroom and the clinical setting is discussed in the following section.

Women: Stories of Passion, directed by and starring Elisa M. Rothstein, is a series of short films that exemplify a type of soft-core erotica. The characters in this series act out sexual fantasies of heterosexual and bisexual women. These fantasies include being married to a mobster or a "tough" man, having an affair with a husband's colleague or another forbidden individual, and working as a cop and becoming attracted to the pimp the female cop is supposed to arrest.

Another example of soft-core erotica is the category of Japanese "Pinku Eiga," or pink films. The term was first coined in 1963 by journalist Murai Minoru and is derived from the "pink trade," a term that refers to the Japanese sex industry. These films do not show penetration, genitals, or even pubic hair, as the films evolved in response to Japanese censorship laws (Weisser & Weisser, 1998). Typically, the films are around 1 hour in length, and the eroticism is presented in the context of comedy and/or violence. Moreover, women often are depicted in vengeful and dominant roles. Satoru Kobayashi is considered the pioneer of this genre, directing the film *Flesh Market*, in 1962. Other directors include Teruo Ishii and Tatsumi Kumashiro (Weisser & Weisser, 1998).

Explicit "Hard-Core" Erotica

The term "hard-core" for some erotica emerged in the second half of the twentieth century, following the mainstreaming at that time of "adult" films when productions featured graphic sexual content. Hard-core sexuality films vary greatly both thematically and in terms of graphic content. These films often feature direct shots of engorged genitalia or acts of cunnilingus, fellatio, and vaginal and/or anal penetration.

One of the more recent forms of hard-core erotica to emerge, known as "gonzo" sex films, is derived from the term "gonzo journalism," or journalism that is written in a first-person narrative. Gonzo films stand in sharp contrast with feature films in that gonzo films attempt to place the viewer directly in the scene (Joannides, 2008). Feature films, on the other hand, include some degree of plot, character development, and dialogue (Jensen, 2005). The gonzo films differ from traditional forms of the genre in that they are not scripted movies with a plot and actors playing roles. The emphasis of gonzo sex films is the genitalia, commonly with close-up shots of a vagina and/or penis. Moreover, there is often an interactive element to gonzo erotica, with one or more participants both filming and performing sexual acts. Works by John Stagliano and Tristan Taormino are examples of this genre.

Amateur filmmaking is yet another example of hard-core erotica (Swartz, 2007). This term refers to unpaid actors who perform sex acts in front of the camera. Like gonzo erotica, there is no script, plot, or elaborate sets, as the focus is on the sex acts being performed. Amateur films have become extremely popular with the emergence of digital video and the Internet in the past several years because it is readily available and often free of charge. However, common problems with this amateur material are poor production quality and the brevity of the clips, which are frequently less than ten minutes long. These films tend to feature couples or groups engaging in sexual acts without a storyline.

Female-Friendly Films

Historically, most erotica has been geared toward and made with the desires and fantasies of heterosexual men in mind. Former adult-film actress Candida Royalle now directs and produces a wide-variety of adult erotic entertainment. Royalle's films differ from traditional pornographic films in that they appeal to the sensual sensibilities of women. Films that cater to women integrate sexual activity into a story line rather than place sole emphasis on the sexual activity.

Royalle's *The Femme Series* are erotic films that include conversation, plot, and foreplay. The actors in this series convey to one another in words how they would like to be pleasured. Couples communicate with each other as they would in real life, using humor and offering suggestions. Many of the female characters in this series have breasts of natural portions, rather than unusually large breasts that appear to have implants, as is often the case in pornographic films. Similarly, males in these films often are presented in various states of arousal and with intentions to please their female partners. These approaches and "naturalistic" details are meant to ease men's and women's anxieties about the film they are watching and to help them focus on pleasuring each other.

Gay and Lesbian Erotica

Adult films produced for gay and lesbian viewers are plentiful and diverse. Films by director Kristen Bjorn, one of the first directors to create gay erotic films, are popular among members of the gay community. Noteworthy modern-day adult films directors who produce films predominately for adult homosexual men include Chi Chi LaRue, Wash West, and Steven Scarborough. Comparable producers that cater to lesbians include Fatale Media, Pink and White Productions, and BLEU Productions. A selection of lesbian films features more masculine or "butch" lesbians, as opposed to the "lipstick" lesbians seen in more mainstream erotic "girl on girl" scenes, which usually are created to titillate heterosexual male viewers.

While gay and lesbian adult films traditionally are geared toward gay men and lesbians, many heterosexual individuals enjoy watching these films. The depiction of two or more women engaging in sex acts is a fairly common heterosexual male sexual fantasy because, theoretically and according to surveys, men find this image arousing and nonthreatening. For this reason, woman-to-woman scenes are fairly common in contemporary American and European "mainstream" works, and gay and lesbian erotica often is not considered a separate genre.

Bondage and Discipline, Dominance and Submission, Sadism and Masochism (BDSM)

Activities involving bondage and discipline, dominance and submission, and sadism and masochism are referred to collectively as "BDSM." It is important to note that while many people are uncomfortable with some of the concepts behind BDSM, this form of sex play is quite common (Henkin & Holiday, 2006). BDSM can be classified as a paraphilia, a situational, an elective, and/or a preferred sexual style or practice (Lawrence & Love-Crowell, 2008).

Moreover, BDSM films portray actors engaging in BDSM practices, which may include the incorporation of items such as whips, leather binds, blindfolds, or nipple clamps. Depictions of BDSM activities in films range from mild to intense physical violence. Films in this category may appeal to heterosexual or homosexual couples or groups.

Cultural and Ethnically-Inclusive Erotica

Adult films with ethnic or racial minorities and culturally diverse actors are referred to as "ethnic erotica." Many mainstream erotica actors are Hispanic,

Asian, or African American; however, what differentiates ethnic sexuality films from erotica that simply features actors of actresses of different races is that the placement of ethnic actors is a deliberate choice by the directors. Ethnic erotica is meant to cater to individuals who would like to see members of that particular race or ethnic group performing sexual acts. *Afrodite Superstar* (spelling is deliberate, to refer to the racial element) produced by Candida Royalle, features a predominately African American cast. *Caribbean Heat,* another film by Royalle, features a multiracial cast.

EROTIC LITERATURE

Both men and women turn to erotic literature as a form of sexual stimulation. The erotica that appeals to males, however, often is different from that which appeals to females; differing fantasies of the sexes may be a contributing factor (Coles & Shamp, 1984). Early research suggests that male fantasies typically portray more physical arousal than do female fantasies, while women fantasize more about a person whom they have been with, rather than someone with whom they want to have sex (Coles & Shamp, 1984).

ROMANCE NOVELS

Romance novels are a form of erotic literature. Although romance novels are not necessarily intended for women's use only, they provide a form of sexual stimulation that is consistent with characteristics of most women's fantasies. Women stereotypically prefer fantasies that include feelings, partner response, and extended foreplay. Accordingly, the majority of romance novels contain themes of tenderness and affection and emphasize a couple's first encounter and the process by which they unite. Romance novels tend to be full of sensuous details but do not focus solely on the sexual experience. In this way, the other elements to a relationship are expanded upon. In many novels, one person pines over another, which heightens the desire between them. Moreover, the couple breaks down the barriers that prevent them from being together.

Nancy Friday is an author who has written on the topics of female sexuality and liberation. Several of her books are compilations of women's personal sexual fantasies, including *My Secret Garden* and *Forbidden Flowers*.

The work of Violet Blue, a sexuality educator and blogger, is aligned with that of Friday's. Blue compiles a *Best Women's Erotica* book annually. Similarly, Tristan Taormino, author, columnist, editor, and adult film director, is a co-editor of *Best Lesbian Erotica*. Richard LaBonte has been instrumental in editing or co-editing *Best Gay Erotica*. Betty Dodson's Web site gives many examples of sexual experiences, along with photographs and her own illustrations. She also has published two books describing her open-minded views on sexuality, her personal experiences, and the importance of masturbation, particularly for women.

Playboy magazine can be considered a form of erotic literature popular among heterosexual men. *Playboy* magazine is similar to traditional erotic films in that it stresses variety, lust, and physicality by way of visual representation. *Penthouse Letters* is a series of books that compile the best letters sent to *Penthouse* magazine by readers, most of whom are heterosexual males. Stories in these books describe male sexual fantasies in detail, including graphic descriptions of genitalia and penetration, as well as sexual encounters with different types of women.

Female-friendly erotic literature may be found via the Internet at a number of Web sites, including libida.com. This particular Web site provides listings of erotic and educational books, as well as instructional guides for sexual activities, such as how to masturbate and how to perform cunnilingus and fellatio. The literature is categorized so as to make it is easy to find specific topics.

SOME BENEFITS OF USING EROTICA IN ADULT SEXUALITY EDUCATION

Erotica can be used to introduce a partner to novel and unfamiliar modes of sex play. For example, consider a man who prefers to be dominated during sex but who has a partner who is not comfortable playing the part. The partner may find the dominant role to be distasteful or socially unacceptable. Viewing adult films portraying mild sadomasochistic activities or reading certain erotica books may alter the partner's beliefs, contradicting the notion that these activities are aberrant. With time and increased exposure, the partner may become more comfortable experimenting in the bedroom. This is likely to have a positive effect on the couple's relationship.

Erotica offers the opportunity to expand one's sexual repertoire by showing different lovemaking techniques. This is particularly beneficial for those who are in long-term relationships and who feel the need to reawaken and diversify their sexual activities. In addition, individuals with limited sexual experience gain confidence through greater exposure to varied positions and activities. Several videos borrow from tantric sex and massage techniques. These videos are quite beneficial to persons who feel awkward about touching, as well as to individuals who simply want to enhance their experience. Some examples include Laurie Handler's *Bliss Beginner's Tantra* and Michaels and Johnson's *Tantric Sexual Massage for Lovers.* In addition, Judy Kuriansky's book, *The Complete Idiot's Guide to Tantric Sex,* presents a comprehensive picture of this ancient approach to sexuality that is refreshing, playful, and practical.

Women who are inhibited about asking for what they want can benefit from watching certain adult films. Several of Candida Royalle's films, for example, depict women taking the lead and being assertive about obtaining pleasure the way that they want it. Moreover, heterosexual or bisexual men who have difficulty understanding what a woman tends to like sexually can benefit from watching these films, as selections of Royalle's films convey the many ways women like to be pleasured.

Couples may benefit from incorporating into their relationship the communication techniques and styles of relating exhibited in the resources mentioned earlier, including some of Royalle's films. Her films demonstrate how loving couples relate to each other in a kind and playful way. They also demonstrate how couples communicate effectively when discussing fears and desires about sex and relationships. In addition, Comstock Film's *Real People, Real Life, Real Sex* features romantically involved couples having sex and discussing their relationships. Moreover, a woman who is too exclusively focused on pleasuring her partner can benefit from watching a film in which a woman's desires are considered before her male partner's. Tina Tyler's *Handyman* series features a male actor whose main focus is to cater to the sexual desires of his female partner.

Erotic films may also help individuals who struggle with body-image issues, particularly those films that feature actors and actresses with less than ideal physical characteristics. Women tend to feel more comfortable watching films of this nature because they are less likely to compare themselves to the actors and thus are able to focus on their own sexual experience. In recent years, a proliferation of men with "superhero"-like physiques has been presented in the media. Average men find such displays intimidating and hard to relate to. Royalle's *Fortune Smiles* depicts the thoughts and insecurities both partners can bring into the bedroom at the outset of the couple's first sexual experience. The film models how common sexual concerns can be dealt with in bedroom in a healthy and therapeutic way. Useful in a similar way, adult-film-star-turned-director Nina Hartley's Guide to Seduction features a woman of ample proportions who is not shy about her body and who is adept at pleasuring her partner. Amateur pornography can also be very helpful in this regard for those with low self-esteem, in that the actors are real people.

Erotica also can help to dispel the myth that aging means the loss of one's femininity or masculinity. In particular, films that feature older couples are quite effective in debunking the widespread misconception of asexuality in older years. An example of such a film is the *Better Sex Video: The Couples' Guide to Great Sex over 40*. Vibrating sexual aids are also especially valuable to older individuals or people with disabilities who have diminished sensation and require more intense stimulation.

Some adult films model sexual behaviors that encourage foreplay and de-emphasize genital sex. These films may be of significant benefit for patients with chronic pain or disability; for example, individuals with multiple sclerosis often experience discomfort during sexual behaviors due to muscle spasm and other reasons (McCabe, 2002). Adult films, as well as vibrators, lotions, and lubricants, may enable such individuals to become more aroused prior to or instead of requiring penetration. Since many individuals with chronic pain experience pain relief with orgasm, this is particularly important.

Finally, and quite simply, there are many adults today who have received little to no formal sexuality education. Just because they are of a certain age, there is an assumption that—seemingly by osmosis—they should know how their bodies work and how to pleasure a partner. Far too often, adults are imitating what they see in mainstream sexually-explicit media, which often perpetuate gender role stereotypes, lowered self-esteem, and unhealthy communication and relationships. With the guidance of a trained sexuality professional, these same adults can improve their level of sexual knowledge in a healthy way through the use of the same media.

SEXUALITY EDUCATION VIA THE INTERNET

Internet pornography is available through Web sites, peer-to-peer file sharing, or Usenet newsgroups (Rehmeyer, 2007). Like videotapes and DVDs, the Internet is a preferred channel for distributing sex-explicit materials because it allows people to experience erotica anonymously and with great ease. Moreover, the Internet is a powerful tool through which much knowledge of sexuality now is conferred. The nature of the Internet, however, causes the dissemination of some of the very same misinformation about sexuality that educators seek to dispel. Common misconceptions include these: good sex happens without much effort; sex is only for young and stereotypically "attractive" and able-bodied people; sex is only between a man and a woman; and sex is good only when it is spontaneous and with a partner who is new to a given individual. The authors of this chapter believe that individuals who seek information over the Internet to help cope with their concerns need to have this information contextualized by a trained sexuality professional. This contextualization can be provided within a group educational setting or during a one-on-one intervention.

CAUTIONS ABOUT USING EROTICA IN SEXUALITY EDUCATION

Abuse of erotica can lead to sexual compulsivity and excessive masturbation that can interfere with overall functioning, including professional commitments. For example, one of the authors of this chapter has worked with a student who had difficulty completing his degree because he spent an average of four hours a day watching adult films and visiting pornographic Web sites. Shy individuals who are timid about dating may spend inordinate time on the Internet at the expense of face-to-face relationships. Without practice, their social interaction skills become progressively worse, and they retreat into solitary activity or online relationships, thereby not addressing the problems that interfere with their ability to be intimate in the real world. Additionally, individuals can become so accustomed to the high degree of stimulation and variety provided by some forms of erotica (e.g., Internet, adult films, magazines) that they have difficulty becoming aroused by their partner, who simply cannot compare. For example, the authors have found that some patients who engage in masturbation while watching erotic visual aids can continuously eschew a partner's efforts to have sex, which leads to significant problems in the relationship.

The use of erotica can be viewed by some as a betrayal of a partner. If a person is on sex sites and his or her partner discovers this, or if they are on the sites excessively, the partner may react with shock, anger, or rejection. This often is the case when use of the Internet is coupled with sexual avoidance and communication difficulties. However, once this use is uncovered, the experience can be used as a tool for opening up and enhancing the sexual relationship of the couple, if dealt with effectively. Often, this requires professional assistance.

An industry of outpatient and inpatient treatment facilities, as well as professional education programs, is available that offers advanced training to help individuals and couples deal with issues of sexual addiction. The Meadows, located in Wickenburg, Arizona, is a secular treatment center for addicts, spouses, and families of sex addicts. It also offers training for professionals. The National Council on Sexual Addiction and Compulsivity, located in Atlanta, Georgia, is a secular organization for professionals who work with sexual addiction and sexual trauma.

CONCLUSION

Individuals in the fields of sexuality education and sex therapy can benefit from the use of psychoeducational resources, such as adult films, to help the individuals and couples they serve to have healthy, satisfying relationships, diversify their sexual repertoires, and cope with sexual problems. Erotica can be used to provide factual information on sexual functioning and encourage discussion of values and beliefs around sexual issues. The following questions may be used by sexuality educators when discussing sexually explicit materials with adult audiences.

Discussion Questions about Erotica for Sexuality Educators to Use with Adult Learners

1. Erotica is a very loaded word. What associations does it bring up?
2. What could be the benefits of watching erotic films with a partner? What are the potential drawbacks?
3. What could be the benefits of watching adult films alone? The drawbacks?
4. What kind(s) of adult films do you think would be enjoyable to you? Why?

5. Many people believe that sexually graphic films are antifeminist because they degrade women. What do you think?

6. Adult films depicting older individuals can elicit different types of reactions. Please describe.

7. What type of erotica appeals to women? In what ways could it be different for heterosexual women than for lesbian or bisexual women?

8. What type of erotica appeals to men? In what ways could it be different for heterosexual men than for gay or bisexual men?

Discussion Questions about Internet Sex Sites for Sexuality Educators to Use with Adult Learners

1. What are the potentially beneficial aspects to logging on to Internet sex sites?

2. Are there potentially adverse consequences?

3. Are we becoming more sex positive or negative because of exposure to sex information and behaviors on the Internet?

4. What are your attitudes and opinions about cybersex? Are they different if a person is single rather than in a relationship?

5. Is cybersex cheating? Should spouses or partners know?

6. Eventually, will the Internet take away people's imagination about sex? Is there a benefit to suppressing information?

7. Should the government put controls on sexual content on the Internet? If so, to what extent?

REFERENCES

Bartlik B. & Striar, S. (1998). The use of erotic video in sex therapy. *The American Academy of Clinical Sexologists.* Clinical Monograph Number 7, p. 1–4.

Christenson, C. (1971). *Kinsey: A Biography.* Bloomington: Indiana University Press.

Coles, C. D., & Shamp, M. J. (1983). Some sexual, personality, and demographic characteristics of women readers of erotic romances. *Archives of Sexual Behavior, 13,* 187–209.

Friday, N. C. (1973). *My Secret Garden: Women's Sexual Fantasies.* New York: Simon & Schuster.

Friday, N. C. (1975). *Forbidden Flowers: More Women's Sexual Fantasies.* New York: Simon & Schuster.

Henkin, B. & Holiday, S. (2006). *Consensual sadomachism: How to talk about it and how to do it safely.* Los Angeles: Daedalus.

Jensen, R. (2005, February 26). *Just a john? Pornography and men's choices: A talk by Robert Jensen.* Talk delivered to the Second Annual Conference on the College Male, Saint John's University, Collegeville, MN. This version reflects changes based on comments of conference participants.

Joannides, P. (2008). Paul's sex term of the day. *Psychology Today.* Retrieved July 16, 2008, from http://blogs.psychologytoday.com/blog/you_it/200806/pauls-sex-term-the-day-gonzo-porn

Kuriansky, J. (2004). *The complete idiot's guide to tantric sex* (2nd Ed.). New York: Penguin.

Lawrence, A. A. & Love-Crowell, J. (2008). Psychotherapists' experience with clients who engage in consensual sadomasochism: An aualitative study, *Journal of Sex & Marital Therapy, 34*(1), 67–85.

McCabe, M. P. (2002). Relationship functioning and sexuality among people with multiple sclerosis. *Journal of Sex Research, 39*(1), 302–309.

Millier, E. (2002). Erotica and Pornography. *Encyclopedia of gay, lesbian, bisexual, transgender, and queer culture.* Retrieved July 16, 2008, from http://www.glbtq.com/literature/erotica pornography.html Pornography. *Microsoft Encarta online encyclopedia.* Retrieved July 16, 2008, from http://uk.encarta.msn.com

Rehmeyer, J. J. (2007). Mapping a medusa: The Internet spreads its tentacles. *Science News, 171*, 387–388.

Striar S. & Bartlik, B. (1999, January). Stimulation of the libido—The use of erotica in sex therapy. *Psychiatric Annals 29*(1), 60-62.

Swartz, J. (2007). Purveyors of porn scramble to keep up with Internet. *USA Today.* Retrieved July 16, 2008, from http://www.usatoday.com/techinvestor/industry/2007–06-05-internetporn_N.htm

Weisser, T., & Weisser, Y. M. (1998). *Japanese cinema encyclopedia: The sex films.* Miami: Vital Books, Asian Cult Cinema Publications.

FILM REFERENCES

Adam and Eve Productions (Producer) & Nina Hartley (Director). (2006). *Nina Hartley's Guide to Oral Sex DVD* [motion picture]. Location: Adam and Eve Productions.

Capozzi, M. (Producer) & M. Sabrosa (Director). (2005). *Candida Royalle's Caribbean Heat* [motion picture]. New York: Femme Productions.

Cortes, N. (Producer) & V. Hottentot (Director). (2007). *Candida Royalle's Afrodite Superstar* [motion picture]. Location: Adam & Eve Productions.

Dodson, B. (Producer) & B. Dodson (Director). (2005). *Celebrating Orgasm: Women's Private Self-loving Sessions* [motion picture]. Location: Distributor.

Dodson, B. (Producer) & B. Dodson (Director). (2005). *Self-loving: Portrait of a Sexual Seminar* [motion picture]. Location: Distributor.

Dodson, B. (Producer) & B. Dodson (Director). (2006). *Betty Dodson Presents: Orgasmic Women: 13 Self-Loving Divas* [motion picture]. Location: Distributor.

Dodson, B. (Producer) & B. Dodson (Director). (2007). *Viva la Vulva: Women's Sex Organs Revealed* [motion picture]. Location: Distributor.

Ikeda, I. (Producer) & S. Kobayashi (Director). (1962). *Nikutai no ichiba [Flesh Market]* [motion picture]. Japan: Distributor.

Playboy (Producer) & Elisa Rothstein (Director). (1996–1999). *Women: Stories of Passion* [television program]. New York: Showtime.

Sinclair Institute (Producer) & M. Schoen (Director). (2005). *Better Sex Video Series: Sexploitations Volumes 1, 2, & 3* [motion picture]. Chapel Hill, NC: Sinclair Institute.

Vivid Entertainment (Producer) & T. Taormino (Director). (2007). *Tristan Taormino's Expert Guide to Anal Sex* [motion picture]. Los Angeles: Vivid Entertainment.

Vivid Entertainment (Producer) & T. Taormino (Director). (2007). *Tristan Taormino's Expert Guide to the G-spot* [motion picture]. Los Angeles: Vivid Entertainment.

Vivid Entertainment (Producer) & T. Taormino (Director). (2007). *Tristan Taormino's Expert Guide to Oral Sex—Cunnilingus* [motion picture]. Los Angeles: Vivid Entertainment.

Vivid Entertainment (Producer) & T. Taormino (Director). (2007). *Tristan Taormino's Expert Guide to Oral Sex—Fellatio* [motion picture]. Los Angeles: Vivid Entertainment.

Part III

LEARNING ABOUT SEXUALITY IN UNEXPECTED PLACES

Chapter Eleven

SEXPOS AND SEX MUSEUMS: NEW VENUES FOR AN EDUCATION ABOUT SEXUALITY

Judy Kuriansky

Let sexuality bask in the sunshine with the opening of heart. Let the time of sexual taboo pass...sexuality relevant to the quality of human life (and) to the progress of human civilization.

From the pamphlet of the Wuhan Sexuality Museum

Sex sells. Education, unfortunately, doesn't. But the proliferation of sex exhibitions and museums in cities around the world is proving that a marriage of the two can be profitable as well as pedagogical. While built as businesses and tourist destinations that require entertainment value to thrive, such attractions can also serve as an important medium for education about sexuality. This chapter describes a sampling of these venues and discusses their role in sexuality education. Of course, all visitors will have a personal experience—which may be only passively educational—but the potential lessons about history, culture, and practices are vast. For example, many museums are worthy of visits by classes on sexuality education. This chapter is meant to serve as a "tour guide" and inspiration for sexuality educators to encourage the public—and themselves—to use these venues as resources and to view exhibits with a different—that is, more active and educational—eye. For example, one sex educator took a group of sexuality expert colleagues on a "sexuality education tour" of ancient Greek art at New York's Metropolitan Museum of Art, describing statues and paintings in the context of that culture's sexuality practices and beliefs. Even the most seasoned sexuality experts in the group found the experience edifying and saw the exhibits from a new perspective. This chapter intends to inspire that reaction.

SEX MUSEUMS

Despite taboos about sex in many cultures throughout the ages, people of all ages throughout the world are fascinated by the subject of sex. So it is no surprise that there are sex museums all over the world. But, while many people may come to sex museums curious about what they will see, a visit offers much more in the way of education, with insight into the culture and history of sex and displays that equal a university course—and even professional training—in sexuality education. Items in these museums prove that the wish for better sex, the worship of objects for better sex, and even the fear of sex are as ancient as they are modern.

Most sex museums offer erotic paintings, drawings, clothing, literature, sculptures, artifacts, and objects. But, while some exhibits may seem racy, they are hardly pornographic—even when it is *about* pornography from an historical point of view. Some museums have faced controversy in a repressive society but have managed to thrive and offer visitors a valuable view into their culture's long history, like those in South Korea and China (Kuriansky, 2007; Ruan, 1991). Some have struggled over inadequate funding yet flourish thanks to gift store sales (implying that the public can be attracted more to items than to instruction); for example, on a recent visit to Berlin's sex museum, only a few visitors paid the small fee to view the exhibits on the upper two floors of the building, while dozens of locals and tourists crowded the gift shop well into the late open hours of the evening. Museums' names alone show a varied attempt to appeal, from Miami Florida's World Erotic Art Museum, which emphasizes its paintings collection, to China's Museum of Sex Culture, which clearly promotes its historical perspective. Finding a museum of eroticism is not surprising in a city known for sensuality, like Paris, or for sexual permissiveness, like Amsterdam. But sex museums in traditionally repressive China and the once-behind-the-Iron-Curtain Czech Republic are real signs of increasing worldwide openness about sexuality.

Sex Museums in China

A collection of Chinese sexuality artifacts and contemporary education aides for family planning and reproductive health are on display at a special exhibition in a district of the capital city of Beijing, China. This *Exhibition of Sexual and Reproductive Health* is the result of years of work by respected Chinese sexologist Xiao-nian Ma. The exhibition is exceptionally distinctive in that it is supported by multiple professional organizations (e.g. the Beijing Shijingshan District Family Planning Association, the district Beijing Science and Technology Association and the Beijing Sexuality Education and Research Association) and endorsed at the local and also highest levels of government. In fact, Premier Wen Jiaboa pointed out in his *Report on the Work of the Government*, announced at the National People's Congress, that this exhibition provides the people with "information, consultation and services of sexual and reproductive health with the purpose to facilitate civilized and advanced sex, sexual harmony and perfection for everyone, every couple and every family, and to improve people's life quality" (Beijing Shijingshan District Family Planning Association, Beijing Science and Technology Association Shijingshan District & Beijing Sexuality Education and Research Association, 2007).

Newly married couples in the district are meant to visit the exhibit as part of a course they attend in reproductive health (called the New Married School) given by the Population and Family Planning Committee of Science and Technology. The course helps them prepare for compatibility (called harmony in China) in their relationship. Public visits can also be arranged by appointment.

Professor Ma has been the vanguard of sex education in China, having published many books on the subject, conducted an Internet survey, and hosted radio and television shows answering questions about sex from people of all ages and educational levels (Ma, 1990, 2003a, 2003b, 2003c, 2003d, 2003e, 2004a, 2004b; Ma & Yang 2005a, 2005b). Also a medical doctor, Ma started learning about sexuality in the early 1980s while studying in Britain and reading about Masters and Johnson's work that motivated him to research ancient Chinese books on sexual matters. Growing up in a sexually repressive era spurred his fascination with shifts in sexual attitudes over different dynasties. During the Cultural Revolution, Ma's post to provincial areas exposed him to ethnic minority peoples less inhibited and troubled sexually than mainstream Chinese. These experiences led Ma to pursue evidence of cultural changes regarding sexuality in efforts to help people understand their cultural roots and to appreciate contemporary increasing openness. "There is no reason why people cannot have access to knowledge about sex and permission to have a healthy relationship," says Ma (personal communication, October 23, 2008).

Encased in the 77 display counters at the museum are dozens of posters and over 1,000 items divided into 6 parts that read like a syllabus in sexuality education: ancient sex worship, sexual physiology, sexual psychology, sexual ethics, sexual harmony, and reproductive health. Peoples in antiquity believed in supernatural powers of sex and procreation that led to the worship of sexual organs to facilitate fertility that in turn led to portrayals of enhanced sizes of male genitalia. Because animals were associated with humans, the male phallus was symbolized and depicted as a bird (based on similar head and neck movements) and as a lizard, snake, and turtle. Carvings of sex positions on caves, animal bones, or ivory served as primitive sex education tools, with double fish, frogs, or dragons foretelling human blessings of fertility and reproduction. Couples cherished figurines symbolizing the male in pursuit of their wish for a boy child. Other lessons in the exhibits are consistent with contemporary sexuality education teaching. For example, anatomy charts trace early, middle, and late stages of adolescent development (e.g., growth in genital size and increases in pubic hair in both males and females) and posters outline Freudian stages of development from oral attachment to the controlling anal stage; the phallic stage where children may experiment with genital play; Oedipus and Electra stage of attachment to the opposite-sex parent; and later stages of curiosity about the sex (specifically accompanied by boys' embarrassment about spontaneous erections). In addition, masturbation is presented as a normal activity (for self-consolation or arousal); homosexuality is traced from early dynasties when it was not condemned nor exclusive of marriage; and out-of-the-ordinary behaviors (transvestism, sadomasochism, and fetishes) and lessons in sexual ethics (like incest taboos) are tracked over time; and myths are debunked (with some equivalent to American advice like, that sexual activity is acceptable in later stages of pregnancy, with doctor approval).

Early efforts at sexuality education throughout history are portrayed in sexual education tools. For example, depictions of sex positions printed on scrolls or hidden in porcelain fruits (strawberries, bananas, and peaches) were placed in the bottom of dowry trunks to be discovered by newly married couples and laid out on the bed to mimic.

Gender rights are traced from eras of severe imbalance (men freely had sex with multiple females to preserve virility while women were subjected to chastity belts and foot-binding) to times when European influences spurred changes in marital law that, by the 1950s, insured more rights for women, obligations of men, and a focus more on love than ownership. Exhibits on reproductive health show how this trend has continued, especially in contemporary times as insurance against disease and HIV/AIDS and as promotion of healthy family life.

Another museum tracing sex culture in China presents valuable lessons on sexuality education over time. Nestled in a quiet city outside Shanghai, the collection of some 1,500 items is owned by a Chinese sociologist (now in his 70s) who collaborated on a survey about Chinese sexual behavior undertaken at the time of the student reform uprisings in China (Liu, Ng, Zhou, & Haeberle, 1997). The effort has been compared to pioneer surveys of the American sex researcher in the 1950s, Alfred Kinsey (Burton, 1990).

The collection has been shown at conferences worldwide, from Korea and Japan to Australia and America and even at public events like the sexpo in the repressive society of Singapore (described below) (http://www2.hu-berlin.de/sexology/CSM/index.htm; Liu 2000a, 2000b, 2000c). Items on display include examples of phalluses of every size, shape, and material (e.g., in wood, stone, jade, and gilded gold) and objects for sex practice (e.g. "sex sticks" which the minority Miao people knock together when a female desires intercourse). The founder and co-organizer say that "Understanding sex culture helps people appreciate their past but also understand the impact of tradition on modern life" (Liu, 1994) and that, "Preserving and showing our rich tradition and sex culture carries forward sex education" (H. Hu, personal communication, November 19, 2005).

On display in the section about women and marriage, including prostitution, is a sex chair in which a woman reclines and lifts her leg on the elongated arm to welcome a lover. Paintings display images of multiple women pleasuring one man or of courtesans in all positions using strap-ons and dildos (although usually not for pleasure as is common contemporary practice, but to stay chaste after their husband died or to satisfy urges while men were otherwise engaged).

Also educational for modern-day visitors are displays of ancient sex practices derived from neighboring countries. Tantric sex from India is represented by statues of two figures embracing, in practices being revived and taught by Western sexologists today (Kuriansky, 2004).

Once located upstairs from a famous department store on the busiest shopping and strolling street in Shanghai, the museum previously encountered resistance from city officials who objected to an advertisement on the pedestrian mall using the word "sex," and so moved to a more outlying district. Locals were often shy to visit, consistent with traditionally reserved Chinese demeanor, but foreigners are more enthusiastic, as one young British couple said, "We never expected such sexual things from this repressive country." The museum is now set in gardens in a suburb of Shanghai where it is a tourist attraction. Increasingly, other sex culture museums have opened in various provinces of China, including Hubei, Shaanxi, and Wuhan.

Prague

The academic nature of Chinese culture collections contrasts with more sensational displays at Prague's *Sex Machines Museum*, with its three floors of hundreds of mechanical erotic appliances, just off the busiest tourist square in the center of town (www.sexmachinesmuseum.com). The feather-masked showgirl mannequin perched atop a pleasure contraption, slick techno videos, and futuristic wall paintings in the museum entrance prompted one tourist to perfectly observe, "This is like a sexual Disneyland."

Upstairs, amid an array of pelvis constrictors and other apparatuses, is an antimasturbation machine. This gadget reveals the repressive attitudes toward, and the restrictions imposed on, acts of self-pleasure that every sexuality educator knows has troubled men and women of all ages. In this particular gadget, a ring was placed on a boy's penis. This ring would switch a contact and sound a bell in the parents' room if the boy had an erection, alerting them to come to his room to stop the practice. A young male visitor to the sex museum was observed to cringe over this display.

Other restraints aimed at self-pleasuring, like chastity belts from the 1500s and 1800s, used in Germany and France, are reminders of how many young people today have anxiety about masturbation, the myths about the act, and the problems that come from being told the act is "bad" or punishable.

Other gadgets tout the practice, like a lubricated ring for men, placed around the penis to transmit an electrical current to stimulate an erection, and, for women, an antique crank-operated wood and steel vibrator resembling a can opener with interchangeable heads to stimulate the clitoris (note, that every sexuality educator today knows that wood should not be used for this purpose because of the dangers of splinters). A wide range of modern-day examples of vibrators, clitoral stimulators, dildos, strap-ons, and anal insertions—found in most sex shops—are also on display, along with erotic clothing and accessories that all sexuality educators would recognize as part of modern-day bondage and discipline, like handcuffs, nipple clips, and rubber and latex clothing. Other machines are still used in contemporary sex clubs, like a table with a phallus-like object sticking out from a spring board and meant for insertion.

Items demonstrate the creative extent to which people go to devise gadgets for sexual stimulation, like a chandelier with a G-spot stimulator. Curios include a Japanese walking stick with erotic engraving and an opening for the man to urinate into without taking off his clothes. Some items were patented but never manufactured.

In a small auditorium at the back of the first floor, erotic subtitled films from the early 1900s play on a screen. The flickering images of sex acts (e.g., gentlemen paddling ladies' plump bottoms) are a stark contrast to the female-friendly erotic entertainment now offered by companies like Femme Productions that are purchased publicly and used in sexuality education to reinforce the empowerment of female sexuality.

Most sexuality education courses include a component that teaches about prostitution—a practice common to most every culture, and therefore worthy of a place in a sex museum. The Prague collection shows sandals worn by Greek prostitutes with nails on the bottom that spell out "follow my steps" to advertise the owner's services; a red throne with a hole for clients' pleasure to view the prostitute's private parts; and a glass platform so that the patron can eliminate on a person positioned underneath (considered a philiac sexual activity).

Despite the racier fare, the Italian owner and businessman who started the museum, Oriano Bizzocchi, wants his museum to be seen not as pornographic or exploitative but as entertaining and pleasing. As he says (personal communication, 2004), "I enjoy finding and presenting strange and funny erotic objects to make people smile about what man has invented for sexual pleasure."

New York

The United States is known for its 1960s sexual revolution, but, as every American sexuality educator who supports a comprehensive approach knows, factions from ultra-conservative and religious groups have been adamantly critical and repressive. While New York City might seem a mecca for openness about sexuality, suppression has affected even this cosmopolitan city. For example, the New York Museum of Sex (*MOSEX* at www.museumofsex.com) faced hurdles when it was deemed ineligible for government funds and for not-for-profit status by New York State, thus forcing it to raise private money for the millions required to open. Founder Daniel Gluck, who has a background in computers and fine arts, started the museum using profits from the sale of his dotcom company. Expensive to run, the museum now is supported by private investors, as well as profits from sales in the gift shop and fees for admission and seminar events. The owners are applying for approval as a cultural institution in order to qualify for federal funding.

The museum clearly has educational objectives and hosts events (of various kinds) more than other sex museums. Noted sexologist June Reinisch is the executive vice president of scientific affairs and director of acquisitions and new exhibitions at the museum, and also has credentials as director emeritus and senior research fellow at the famous Kinsey Institute for Research in Sex, Gender, and Reproduction. Reinisch (personal communication, August 23, 2008) says, "We are focused on being simultaneously both educational and entertaining, while presenting a wide range of exhibitions related to human sexuality. Our curators are popular culture, social and art historians as well as scientists and scholars from the many other academic specialties that relate to sexuality. One of our unique contributions as an institution is that we work to integrate scholarly expertise with some of the very hippest design talent from both sides of the Atlantic whose firms have joined us in an effort to meld cutting edge information with entertainment and art."

Many professionals well known in the sexology field have given speeches and done book signings at the museum. These include San Francisco sexologist Marty Klein, introducing his new book *America's War on Sex,* and Beverly Whipple, who holds offices in many sexuality organizations, including as Secretary General of the World Association of Sexology and past president of the American Association of Sexuality Educators, Counselors and Therapists (AASECT) and of the Society of the Scientific Study of Sexuality (SSSS). Whipple discussed her books, *The Science of Orgasm* and *The G Spot and Other Discoveries about Human Sexuality.* Other evening seminars have more racy than academic; guests have included a dancer teaching burlesque moves and a stripper and nude magazine model teaching "The Art of the Female Orgasm" with explicit directions about the clitoris, pelvic muscles, and even anal pleasure. A workshop—repeated by popular demand—described basic how-tos of BDSM (bondage and discipline, domination and submission, and sadism and masochism) with a New York dominatrix teaching how to choose and wear leather and latex clothing and how to use spanking techniques, whips, and other tools.

The museum also supported an outdoor panel in June 2007—the Free Sidewalk Sex Clinic—where sexperts sat at a long table on the sidewalk outside the museum at its location on the fashionable Fifth Avenue, offering passerbys free sex advice and a chance to buy their books. The panel included transgender expert Veronica Vera, author of *Cross Dress for Success*, who runs the Academy for Boys Who Want to Be Girls; performance artist Annie Sprinkle; bisexuality expert Elizabeth M. Stephens; author Barbara Carrellas; and Candida Royalle, pioneer producer of female friendly *Femme* erotic films and author of *How to Tell a Naked Man What to Do.*

Like many museums, *MOSEX* raises needed funds from its store and from sales of books, films, and curios, and also from benefit events with a sexuality theme and intended to be entertaining. For example, an amateur comedy night was organized by Weill Cornell Medical College psychiatrist and sex therapist Barbara Bartlik and held at a downtown comedy club on December 6, 2006, where real sexologists (including myself) volunteered to give "their best five minutes on sex" drawing from their experiences as sexuality professionals (B. Bartlik, personal communication, November 21, 2006). My routine featured humorous accounts of questions people have asked me on my radio show. Another amateur performer was Betty Dodsen, famous for her books on masturbation (*Sex for One*) and her sessions at which she teaches groups of women how to be orgasmic. At another benefit—attended by *MOSEX*'s Reinisch with sexologists Joy Davidson, Candida Royalle, Veronica Vera, and hard-core vintage porn star Vanessa delRio—noted burlesque pin-up Dita Von Teese performed her striptease act, guests were offered Pure Romance sex toys, and an auction was held of sex-related items (a night on the town with Scottish actor and producer Alan Cumming of *GoldenEye* and *Cabaret* fame; a night at the penthouse suite of the midtown Goth and fetish Night Hotel; and a walk-on role in Royalle's next film which drew the highest bid of $2,000).

Special exhibits in the museum are curated with great care and as such are worthy of a class visit as part of a sexuality program on American and foreign sex culture. One past exhibit about Asian erotic art showed the extreme pursuit of pleasure captured in erotic art in Japan during the wildly sexual Edo period (the city of Edo is now called Tokyo) from 1600 to the 1860s. Even today, a section of Tokyo called the "floating district" is devoted to the "pink trade" (sex trade). Other exhibits have explored the objectification of the naked male body, from the ancient Greeks' and Romans' adulation of young athletes to more modern examples of muscle men, like World Wrestling Federation performers, rock stars, rappers, and Hollywood actors revered for their six-pack abdomens. A "kink" exhibit had a unique twist: visitors were invited to "please touch" items made of leather, silk, and latex, to encourage an understanding of sensuality and the value of touch in sex. The no-holds-barred show explored unusual fantasies, fetishes, and kinky sex, like "macrophilia" (where partners use costumes); sploshing ("messy fun" where partners spread food on each other); mudlarking (using mud); and body expansion (donning inflatable suits). On display were diapers and bibs used in infantilism play and brushes used to groom ponies in "ponyplay."

The permanent gallery features sex-related machines, advertisements, and art related specifically to the field of sexuality in New York, and an interactive project called "Mapping Sex in America," where visitors can use a computer to enter personal sex-history information—anonymously—and access an archive of American sex customs and practices. Users can also log on to the Web site at www.museumofsex.com to contribute a personal story.

Listening to visitors reveals how much the experience is about sexuality education, that is, what they are learning and how they are using what they see to communicate to each other about sexuality issues they might not otherwise share. At the MOSEX exhibit about female pin-ups (seductive photos of women, popular during World War II to entertain soldiers), a young man was overheard saying to his female companion, "I've seen a few things I'd like to try out. Are you game for a few poses from the good old days?"

Another museum in New York worthy of a visit for a valuable education is the Rubin Museum of Art, which has a comprehensive collection of Himalayan art, some of which is related to tantric practices. The museum holds professional development sessions to help teachers and educators of all levels to use the museum's educational resources, programs, and exhibits in their work (www.rmanyc.org).

Indiana

The Kinsey Institute for Research in Sex, Gender, and Reproduction, located in Indiana and named after famous American sex researcher Alfred Kinsey, has an art gallery and varied exhibits from its vast collection of 7,000 artifacts, art, and photography from the United States, Europe, South America, Africa, and Asia, covering more than 2,000 years of history. Leading sex researcher and psychologist Julia Heiman, director of the Institute, says, "Alfred Kinsey is known as a pioneer sex researcher who contributed invaluably to education of the public about sex by starting public discussions about previously taboo subjects. The Institute and our exhibits keep up that tradition" (J. Heiman, personal communication, August 19, 2008). Open only a few hours weekdays (other museums are often open seven days a week), the institute has had exhibits on sex in the movies, with posters, publicity stills, and press kits for Hollywood, independent, and adult heterosexual and homosexual films to show how sex has been used throughout the history of movies to sell tickets. An exhibit titled "Women of Pleasure" showed how women were depicted in eighteenth- and nineteenth-century European erotic art and literature.

Florida

Sexuality educators often have their own collection of books, art, or other materials related to the field that they may use for research or in classes but only rarely turn into a public venture. Some private citizens without formal sexuality training develop an interest in sex culture and have impressive collections. Such is the case of a former New Jersey housewife, millionaire grandmother and art connoisseur and collector, Naomi Wilzig, who has arguably the largest private collection of erotic art in the United States. Recently, she realized her dream to found a sex museum to share with the public her collection of many original and one-of-a-kind items. The museum—the World Erotic Art Museum (www.weam.com)—offers an historic trip through time that is educational in its classifications of art from various eras and parts of the world, covering vast time periods, including biblical art, art related to Greek mythology, Asian artifacts, African ancestral art, pre-Colombian and South American art as well as more modern European, nouveau/deco, surreal, folk, and contemporary art. One of her valued sculptures comes from the 1971 Stanley Kubrick movie classic *A Clockwork Orange*. Potential lessons from this collection—as at many museums—can center on the repression of sexuality at different periods of time on different occasions; for example, the collection shows works by photographer Robert Mapplethorpe, criticized for his sexually-charged imagery, as well as works of other artists who once sought anonymity for fear of public reprisal.

"This was my dream to build this museum," says Wilzig (personal communication, May 11, 2008). "It is important to me not only to present high-caliber art but also to perform an educational service. Half the purpose of the museum is to reveal what has been done in history regarding sexuality and why it has been done and to go beyond sex used in ancient times as fertility incentives. My intention is always about showing the beauty of erotic art, but there is an important educational value to every piece, as it shows the history of the period and the mores and values of the people throughout time."

Wilzig's personal story is also one of overcoming repression about sexuality. Her conservative husband did not approve of her new hobby (the European refugee and Auschwitz survivor she had married had become the head of a commercial bank after striking it rich investing in various oil stocks). This, and her own private sexual shyness—emanating from an orthodox background as the daughter of a cemetery owner—made her hide for years behind a pen name, "Miss Naomi." When her husband passed away, she found new freedom for her interest in sexuality and her art expertise and endeavors and finally opened her museum in fashionable South Beach in Miami. Yet, like other founders of sex museums, she faced a struggle with local authorities and was initially denied acceptance by public officials and landlords who refused to allow her in their communities or buildings.

Wilzig credits her eldest son with piquing her interest when he asked for her help furnishing his apartment with something risqué. She found Japanese prints and a piece of art depicting a threesome sex act. Her interest took off from there, leading to collections featured in her elaborate table top books, *Forbidden Art; The World of Erotica, Visions of Erotica, Erotic Secrets, Erotic Treasures,* and *Erotic Wonders.* She says, "My goal is that we learn that we are all sexual beings; that the erotic tendency is the spark of life; and that we accept our own bodies as good and natural. It upsets me that kids are allowed to see violence, which is so much unhealthier than seeing the nudity of the body in art, which is natural and healthy. Art to me is healthy sex education."

Wilzig's commitment to education is recognized by local professors, who note the value of the exhibits as a complement to what students are being taught in human sexuality courses. Several professors (at Miami Dade, Barry University, and Florida International University) require their classes to visit the museum. Proud of this, Wilzig says, "I feel it is important that students as well as the general public see that erotic art created throughout the ages reflects natural life and that issues of sexuality in the art not be hidden away but bring to light what real people think about and need to learn about."

London

Like the sex museums in Prague and New York, the London sex museum is located in the center of its host city, in popular Piccadilly Circus. The museum is the brainchild of a Frenchman who is a Harvard Business School graduate who became an investment banker and sought out an advisory team of sexuality experts to set up his project. This board included well-known British sexologist, psychiatrist, and gender identity expert Kevan Wylie, general secretary of the European Federation of Sexologists and president of the International Scientific Committee for the World Association for Sexual Health. The establishment has an academic-sounding name: *Amora—The Academy of Sex and Relationships,* which can serve to emphasize an educational angle and to extinguish attacks of pornography. But unlike other museums focused on historical material, London's offering is geared toward contemporary sexual experience with brightly colored pink, red, and yellow tunnels, halls and rooms that house interactive exhibits aimed to enhance sensual experience in "seven zones of love" (www.anoralondon.com). Visitors can learn about attraction with tips, 3-dimensional graphics and computer programs to compose their ideal partner and understand body language. Another room offers opportunities to enhance foreplay skill, (e.g. to perform a sexy striptease, expand kissing techniques, give a sensual massage and play erotic food games). A sensory tunnel lays out the stages of the sexual response cycle; another room explores tantric sex and the Kama Sutra with models that help visitors locate the G-spot and prostate gland; an exhibit of fantasy and fetish equipment includes a test of skills using a paddle; and a "well-being room" has lessons on sexual dysfunctions and various methods of contraception and ways to avoid STIs. To go along with its display on women's orgasm, the museum has even named a women's response to relate to the museum name: Amorgasm. A lounge also serves cocktails with various aphrodisiac-like ingredients.

Berlin

Walls have come down in more ways than one in Berlin, where the *Beate Uhse Erotic Museum* is one of the top 10 tourist attractions. The museum is a shrine to reproductive rights activist Beate Uhse—called the Queen of Rubber Willy—who fought many legal battles in Germany for sexual freedom. While the museum's expansive ground floor is abuzz with customers buying all sorts of sex toys, the upper exhibit floors were quiet on the author's two recent visits. The two-story rooms cram in a mélange of displays of clashing cultures, eras, and materials, with Japanese Shunga erotic prints mixed in with a 1980 painting of a vagina, not far from a nineteenth-century corseted mannequin, across from ancient Chinese silk paintings of sex positions, catty corner to a life-size figure of Marilyn Monroe beckoning in her famous pose with pursed lips and up-flying skirt. A life-size model of *Latin Lover* and 1920s silent screen star Rudolph Valentino rotates not far from a small replica of the Indian goddess Radhika, around the corner from rows of toy bears encased in glass and packaged in costumes, some dressed like a dominatrix. Aficionados of Asian culture will recognize tourist reproductions of the sex carvings from the Khajarahu temples in India, drawings on Ola leaves, and Ben Wa balls (meant to be inserted in the vagina for stimulation). Also on display and perhaps new to sexuality educators who have "seen it all" were Indonesian stabbing weapons (Keris) thought to have supernatural powers, including the power to bewitch women.

The visit also presents valuable lessons about German sexuality pioneers not covered in other museums (which makes sense given that the museums in each city emphasize their local culture). These include Magnus Hirschfield, a German-Jewish physician, sex researcher, and early gay rights activist around the turn of the century. Called the "Einstein of Sex" and often caricatured in the press as an expert on sexual manners, he catalogued varieties of sexuality, coined the word "transvestism," and even developed a theory of a third "intermediate" sex between men and women. He also campaigned for women's rights to abortion. A lesser known figure in sexuality is German illustrator Heinrich Zille, who drew many erotic pictures of real people. Also illuminating is information about the museum founder, Beate Uhse-Rotermund, a Margaret Sanger-type pioneer of birth control in post–World War II Germany. While selling door-to-door after the war, she learned of women's unhappiness being pregnant and poor, so she wrote a pamphlet about the rhythm method to teach women about their fertile days. She sold this "Pamphlet X" through a mail order company, which became so successful that she soon was selling condoms and marriage guides. In 1962, the one-time pilot-turned-sexuality-entrepreneur opened the first store in the world selling sexuality-related items (referred to as the "specialty store for marital hygiene"), which blossomed into a multimillion-dollar business. Facing controversy as did many sexuality pioneers, by 1992, Beate had been indicted many times on grounds of immorality.

Much of the art from this museum, and the one in Amsterdam, is reproduced in the elaborate tabletop books by Hans-Jurgen Dopp (2000, 2001).

Paris

No review of sex museums would be complete without mention of Paris, a city known as a sensual cultural center. Besides its six floors of art and artifacts, the most significant lessons at the Museum of Eroticism (*Musée de l'Erotisme*) relevant to sexuality education are the two floors of exhibits about the world of prostitution and brothels, appropriate given the museum's location in a nineteenth-century former cabaret townhouse in the Pigalle district—the epicenter of Paris sex shops, strip clubs, and the famous Moulin Rouge cabaret. Particularly illuminating are drawings and descriptions of famous artist Toulouse Lautrec, the French artists who was physically deformed and immersed himself in end-of-the-twentieth-century Paris decadent lifestyle, which he documented in his art. The upper floors of the museum have revolving exhibits of mainly contemporary art; a 2008 exhibit of Japanese erotica depicted young girls restrained, suspended, and self-mutilating, and as dolls, dogs, or dead (Vanilla Gallery, 2008). One print (particularly disturbing to the author) showed a teenage schoolgirl on her knees in front of a male standing above her inserting a pistol in her mouth.

Other Sex Museums

Some host locations for sex museums are expected given their reputation for openness, like Copenhagen, Denmark (with its "Museum Erotica") and Amsterdam, whose erotic museum in the city's red-light district has five floors of erotic art, artifacts, and a screening room showing pornographic cartoons. Spain also hosts museums in two cities: Barcelona and Madrid.

But not all museums make it. *The National Museum of Erotica* opened in Canberra, Australia, in March 2001—at the same time as the *National Museum of Australia*—but closed a few years later. Launched by the Eros Foundation (appropriately named), it was a project of the Eros Association, a national adult retail and entertainment think tank. Eros publisher Robbie Swan explained, "It was in the wrong place"; but it may be reopened sometime, perhaps in the more popular city of Sydney (Woodburn, 2006).

Finding Sexuality-Related Treasures

Curators admit that it takes years and much effort to develop collections, by hounding antique markets; purchasing from dealers and discovering treasures while on journeys in foreign lands. Indian psychiatrist and sex therapist Prakash Kothari has a valued collection made up of some items friends have gifted him, knowing his interest in ancient Indian sexuality culture. While traveling in Nepal, the author has found many out-of-the-way shops in cramped alleyways with replicas of tantric statues of Shiva and Shakti stored on dusty shelves (varieties of which are sold in fancy shops in New York City for high prices). A small shop in an outlying town also yielded cards with scenes from the Kama Sutra painted on rare tree leaves (treasures that seemed unnoticed by many other passers-by). Sex educators around the world may have items that can be of future historical interest; for example, mine include audiotapes of years of my radio call-in advice shows dating back to 1980, with examples of answers addressing questions by callers of all ages about all kinds of sexuality and relationship problems. Sexuality educators are encouraged to review their own work for its historical significance in the field.

Nature's Sex Museums

Nature itself provides sexuality education, as it does in China, where an exhibit opened in a southern province (Guangdong) where the Danxia Mountains are shaped like sexual organs, with a phallic-shaped large stone with a vagina-like cave and breast-shaped rocks. The site is often called a "garden of natural nudity" by the Chinese and is also described as a geopark (defined as a territory that encompasses one or more sites of scientific importance, not only for geological reasons but also by virtue of its archaeological, ecological, or cultural value). Themed exhibition areas have names like "Sex in Waters and Mountains," "Sex in Phallism," "Sex in Chinese Characters," and "Sex and Literature." The China Sexology Association has sponsored a seminar there as an endorsement of the educational value of the site and to highlight the shift from sexual repression to greater sexual openness in the country.

SEXPOS

Sexpos are sexuality-related exhibitions open to the public and held in public venues either indoors or outdoors or a combination of the two. Host cities include major metropolises like New York and Los Angeles but also in cities like Denver, Colorado, Toronto, Canada, and Melbourne, Australia. Many booths are commercial advertisements for sexuality-related products—everything from sexy lingerie, DVDS, books, clothing and jewelry, sex toys, and condoms to health products like vitamins and nutrition supplements, products called aphrodisiacs, and even romance services like promoters for travel destinations. Vendors try to get as much attention as possible, for example, by featuring pole dancers demonstrating vibrating condoms and having scantily clad females demonstrating retraining devices on large plastic mattress pads.

But not all displays are commercial businesses; some are presented by NGOs promoting safer sex and HIV/AIDS testing. The entertaining and educational elements make such events a combination of a trade show and sexuality education conference. Yet the main draw for crowds seems to be the entertainment from attention-grabbing and often sensational performances, and once drawn in, attendees also enjoy the education.

Examples of entertainment are sexy fashion shows like the Dreamgirls Fashion Show and the Miss Axquisite Top Model Show, where you can purchase a photo session with beauty queens; contests on a large stage to see which couple can demonstrate the greatest variety sex positions in the allotted time; and live performances, like comedy acts including a "Sex in the Lion City" troupe and Singapore's "No.1 drag queen, comedian and stand-up comic," Diva Kumar. Racier offerings are often set apart for special entrance, limited to adults at least 18 or 21 years old.

The often weekend-long events have schedules packed with activities, much like a professional convention, with booths on an exhibit floor and even speeches on a main stage or lectures held in smaller rooms that are promoted as educational. These range from presentations on sensational topics given by product pitchers (for example, women modeling bikinis during a talk about which suits Asian or Western bodies better) to serious speeches on topics like infertility, HIV/AIDS testing, and treatment of sexual problems given by highly credentialed professional sexuality educators, therapists, or physicians (even if they are there to promote their services or a product for which they serve as spokesperson). For example, one lecturer at the Singapore Sexpo was a local professor, Ganesan Adaikan, from the OB-GYN department of National University Hospital, with a long list of professional credentials including as a diplomate of the American College of Sexology, a certified and prize-winning clinical sexologist for his work on the physiopharmacology of penile erection and pharmacological treatment, president of the Society for the Study of Andrology and Sexology and the Asian Federation of Sexology and president-elect of the International Society for Sexual and Impotence Research.

To support these events financially, pharmaceutical companies often dominate the lectures with their spokespersons. These companies sidestep a hard sell of their products by searching out respected sexologists and educators to hire for their campaign and by designing presentations that are purposefully educational. For example, Pfizer supported a speaking tour for Australian sex educator and counselor Rosie King to lecture on results of a study supported by Pfizer and formed into a lecture on the "Secret to Better Sex," with the message focusing on how individual well-being can be improved through balanced sexual health. As another example, Bayer engaged Dr. Teoh Seng Hin, an obstetrician and gynecologist and a member of the Singapore Planned Parenthood Association, to give a presentation called "A Couple's Solution to Erection Difficulties," describing erection difficulties linked to serious diseases like diabetes, high blood pressure, high cholesterol, and depression and giving tips on maintaining intimacy.

Sexpos can be mainstream or slanted toward the adult industry. A sold-out 3-day festival held in London in 1997 proved that porn, fetish, and fantasy could be received well by the public, as it was approved by the vice squad and attracted thousands of visitors. Following on that success, a similar event was held in New York. The show—*Erotica USA 99, Erotica Romance with Adventure*—described its goals as (1) to create a venue where retail merchants could display and sell their products at a socially acceptable but titillating event, and (2) to design an event for the mainstream public that would both excite and entertain them in a comfortable environment that they would be happy to bring a date to (Erotica USA, 1999). Exhibitors aim for the public to purchase merchandise that they might be reluctant to enter a shop on a public street to buy. The expositions are often held in a city's major exhibit hall; the one in New York was held at the mainstream Jacob Javits Center. Advertised as the "world's leading exposition of Romance, Adventure, and Sensuality," the event featured mostly adult fare—videos, magazines, comics, Internet sites, piercings, erotic dancers, adult performers, and a Fetish Village designed as an ancient Arab bazaar. Even in that context—as is typical of sexpos—some seminars, coordinated with the New York Museum of Sex, were offered by noted experts and authors about sexuality and on topics from Viagra to lasting love.

The Singapore Sexpo

Singapore, a city/state/country known for its conservatism, caning, and fines for chewing gum and displays of affection in public, hosted its first sex exposition just a few years ago. The first 3-day weekend event in 2005 featured many lectures for the $12 entrance fee, addressing the theme "Let's Talk about Sex" with titles like "The Art of Lovemaking" and "The Feng Shui of Sex" and "Harmony in Relationships" (Kuriansky, 2005b). In the 59 booths, exhibitors showed their wares of lingerie and condoms and advertised various workshops and services, including talks on "serious" subjects like sperm banks and sperm freezing (given by an infertility specialist, Dr. Christopher Chen, credited for delivering the world's first in-vitro triplets) and vaginal rejuvenation (given by an American surgeon noted for the procedure who was introducing it to Eastern countries). But serious education about sexuality was also available, including at the booth sponsored by the government Ministry of Community Development and Sports where information about AIDS was distributed, and in "privacy booths" where people could sign up for a private session of on-site advice from experts.

Despite the commercialism, the organizers claimed to have a serious interest in public education. The two young businessmen who founded the expo recognized the new market potential in a country loosening its tight hold on sexuality—and invested about half a million dollars for the Sexpo's launch. Kenny Goh, a 35-year-old father-of-two and an accountant by training (as is his wife) who is currently director of a medical diagnostics company that produces HIV, hepatitis, and malaria test kits, got the idea over coffee with associates and modeled his more sanitized version on Australian adult-lifestyle exhibitions running since 1996.

Goh explained his interest in sexuality education and in fostering greater openness about sex as an outgrowth of his own childhood experiences, growing up with parents who never talked to him about sex, as is typical of sex-shy Chinese families. His wife had a similar youth and was supportive of his venture, though friends looked at him a little askance when he told them about his idea (K. Goh, personal communication, November 19, 2005). Like sex museum founders, Goh encountered resistance not only from some members of the public but from officials—a challenge familiar to sexuality advocates. Goh and his partner, Robin Lim, had to convince officials that the event would be respectable and not violate any laws. Some medical centers concerned about their reputation declined to participate until they saw how his first venture turned out.

The partners had to get approval for all their exhibits from the police Licensing Unit and from the Ministry of Community Development, Youth and Sports. Officials were adamant that no obscenity, nudity, bestiality, pedophilia, promiscuity, or content about homosexuality, sadomasochism or "unnatural acts" be shown. Also taboo were penis rings, inflatable sex dolls, or anything resembling sexual parts of real people. Topics were selected in consultation with doctors and the Health Promotion Board.

Official acceptance of the Sexpo was a major step in the city-state's relaxing its social controls, which already was evident by allowing table dancing in bars, the sale of some women's magazines, and the airing of TV's *Sex and the City* series. Nevertheless, government officials were still wary and came to inspect the exhibit prior to its opening. According to their ruling, some items had to be removed, for example, dildos shaped like a real genital organ had to be replaced with cartoon-like vibrators shaped like firemen or Santa Claus. Another enforced change: the word "sex novelty" had to be used instead of "sex toy." In another concession to the authorities, promoters of the dietary supplement Argimax blackened out all references to "sex" on the box, which now reads like this: "a scientifically formulated and patented supplement designed to support (sexual) health," conforming to the rule that claims about health are allowed by the Health Sciences Authority but specific claims about sex are not permitted.

Videos have become an integral part of sexuality education material with some being educational (see chapter 10, volume 4 in this set), but others are X-rated. Producers of the latter aim to get their products folded into a more mainstream context to increase sales, but X-rated videos were disallowed at the Singapore Sexpo. One promoter said that he "hoped to be the first in this market when it opens up" (B. Christensen, personal communication, November 19, 2005).

The public seemed receptive—about 9,000 people showed up the first day. Attendance was helped by holding the event in a publicly acceptable venue— a major exhibition center of Singapore (called SUNTEC City) that housed family fare in adjoining rooms. Faces in the crowd ranged from retirees to hip young couples, and there were even some parents cradling infants.

The outer public area was open to all, with exhibits like an NGO "Action on AIDS," specifically geared toward sexual health education and information about STIs and prevention. Other exhibitors nearby advertised beauty services, and a travel company promoted "classic love tours" in exotic locales like a 6-star Bali retreat (the Pita Maha Resort and Spa) with private riverside pools and villas, which its representative, Pande Sutawan, eagerly described as having been designed by a member of the local royal family. A designated "romance pavilion" consisted of booths promoting dating clubs (JustDate.com, Two to Tango, and Wow-Her.com) that are services in line with the Singaporean government's goal of increasing the number of marriages as a way to boost the birth rate and the population. In fact, the government had just recently sponsored a 2-day seminar about dating services and singles' needs with lectures by New Yorker Lisa Clampitt, the founder of the New York-based Matchmaking Institute who described her service and their training and certification; dating experts from England and Korea; and the author addressing challenges facing the dating industry (Kuriansky, 2005a). The author and the British expert also gave presentations to a group of invited young men and women about dating (Kuriansky, 2005c). According to results from the

Durex Global Sex Survey (2005), Singapore could use dating and sexuality education, considering its rank among the last of 41 countries surveyed about behavior like the number of times couples have sex. On average, Singaporean couples reported having sex 79 times a year, compared to the French who topped the list at 137 times a year.

The subject of some talks at the Singaporean Sexpo 2006—like the expo held in that city the year before—included mainstream topics, like "Astrology, Love, and Sex," about the desires and fantasies associated with each Zodiac sign, and "Body Odor and Your Relationship," as well as a considerable number of educational opportunities. Again, more academic center-stage presentations—sandwiched between flashy events such as a sexy lingerie show—had content that was equivalent to a graduate class in sexuality. That was the case in the presentations of two American experts hired by the company producing Zestra, a feminine arousal fluid. They were nurse practitioner Susan Kellogg-Spadt, who has a long list of credentials, including certification from Planned Parenthood Federation of America, an associate professorship in human sexuality at Widener University, and a Ph.D. in human sexuality from the University of Pennsylvania, and her cofounder of the Pelvic and Sexual Health Institute in Philadelphia, Dr. Kristine Whitmore, a professor of urology and an OBG-YN. In their education-intensive presentations about female sexuality and sexual pain, they reported diagnoses and treatment protocols and gave statistics—that 35% to 50% of women report sexual concerns and that 16% of American women and 26% of Asian women have sexual pain disorders. They reviewed the causes of these disorders—including inadequate lubrication or yeast vaginitis, urogenital and muscular disorders, vulvar vestibulitis syndrome, and chronic pain of bladder origin—and described the impact of these conditions on women's intimate lives. Their talk titled "Female Sexual Desire and Motivation" reviewed a circular model of female sexual function as a basis for botanical and other interventions to maintain sexual desire. In another presentation on the topic "Female Sexual Arousal and Orgasm," they explained that an estimated 20% of women experience distress over a lack of lubrication and genital engorgement during sexual intimacy; offered physiologic indices of female sexual excitement, plateau, orgasm, and resolution; explored the biologic and psychological factors that contribute to arousal disorders in women; and described behavioral and pharmaceutical interventions.

Other presentations at the Sexpo, which might be on the scientific program at a professional conference for sexuality education, were on topics like "Prostate Trouble and Treatment—Any Connection to Erectile Dysfunction?" "Infertility," "Sex and Pregnancy," and "Andropause—Implications for the Aging Male and the Need for Safe Sex Practices" (a presentation by the government Health Promotion Board itself). Andropause was defined as the depletion of male sex hormones—equivalent to the effect of menopause in women—occurring in men between the ages 40 to 45 when career, marital life, and parenting are important issues. The psychological, interpersonal, social, and spiritual implications were explored, as well as the pros and cons of testosterone replacement.

Appeals for sexuality education were evident in presentations sponsored by the Health Promotion Board titled "Talking to Your Children about the Birds and the Bees (Sex Education for Parents)," which was listed in the program as a "parent education program." This interactive talk with games, exercises, and role play aimed to teach parents how children can be easily misled by incorrect or partial information and to promote the importance of parents' being aware of their own mistaken beliefs about sexuality before they educate their children. The presentation also described the verbal and nonverbal cues parents give when communicating about sexuality with their children and how to create open safe spaces for children. The program listing promised, "At the end of the session, parents will walk away with tips on talking to their children about sexuality issues, as well as resources to guide them in doing so."

Other Health Promotion Board presentations were clearly consistent with themes in comprehensive sexuality education. A talk titled "Enhancing Your Sexual Relationship (Safe Sex and Enhancement of Sexual Relationship)" presented innovative ways to add spice in the bedroom while emphasizing how a safe and healthy sex life contributes to healthy living and a healthy relationship. Another presentation dispelled myths and misconceptions about human sexuality and highlighted how intimacy helps couples bond and results from good communication.

While the topic of fantasy was evident in events meant to titillate and tease, even this subject matter was also presented in an "educational" way. For example, the "Temptation Nite" put on by Action for AIDS stressed that having unprotected sex in casual or multiple-partner relationships increases the risk of contracting HIV/AIDS. The program listing said, "Remember: Safe sex doesn't mean it's any less pleasurable."

Educational talks about tantra and tantric sex are becoming more common at sexpos, consistent with the increasing popularity of the topic in the public and the increasing number of practitioners and teachers of this topic throughout the world and presentations on the subject at professional sexuality conferences (Barratt, Braveman, Kuriansky & Yarian, 2005; Kuriansky & Simonson, 2005; Valentine & Heumann, 2008; Yarian & Anders, 2008). The author gave one such presentation on the main stage (Kuriansky, 2005b), and businessman Radha K. Govind and his business partner (representative of a trend toward teachers who are not traditionally trained in sexuality education) gave another presentation on the topic, titled "Kama Sutra—The Art of Love Making." The two men, who discovered the value of the practices in their own life and left the "hard cold world of business to spend time in more pleasure and enlightenment [for themselves and others]" (R. Govind, personal communication, November 19, 2005), instructed the audience about the ancient Indian manual of lovemaking and ways to improve sex and intimacy using the five senses, while promoting their DVDs (*Love and Intimacy the Tantric Way*) and weekend workshops (called *The Really Fun Connection*). A Malaysian newspaper reporter wrote that how he learned two new things: that the male's most sensitive zone is the raphae, which is a ridge through the midline of the scrotum, and (humorously) that many of the positions in the Karma Sutra are impossible (Golingai, 2005).

Even a seasoned sexuality educator can always learn something new at sexpos (Kremb, 2005). New sex toys are usually presented (such as straps to achieve the "windshield wiper position"), consistent with the public's ever increasing interest in such novelties (LaFerla, 2009). New supplements are also introduced, like juice from alligators or Tongkat Ali, a product that had been presented as effective for male sexual enhancement at a scientific sexuality meeting in Asia.

On the whole, visitors seemed pleased with the event, although some commented that they wanted to see things that were more surprising, that they would never see anywhere else. Yet, the organizers considered the event a success. It even helped improve Goh's own marriage, as he said, "My wife and I talk about sex, but doing this work has made us even more comfortable."

The Denver Sexpo

In contrast to the sexpo in Singapore, organizers of the sex exposition in Denver, Colorado were not as restricted by government officials. Thus, for example, exhibitors included vendors of erotic films of all varieties, as are commonly available in the United States. The producer, who has launched adult entertainment events, defended the need for spicy offerings. "If I called this *The Love and Romance Show*, no one would come," he said. "People come to shows like this for the spark and to satisfy their curiosity."

But like the Singapore event, the Denver sexpo offered fare similar to that in Singapore, with body painting, condom displays with attention-grabbing pole dancers, sexy-clothing vendors, lingerie fashion shows, burlesque strippers and belly dancers (redheads, brunettes, and blonds), and booths displaying dildos and condoms. Also like that in Singapore, the Denver event mixed educational offerings with entertainment—a disappointment to a few attendees who voiced desire for more unusual and out-of-the-ordinary experiences rather than educational talks. On the schedule were lessons on kissing and a panel of men (from the local Sexual Healers and Educators Guild of tantra practitioners) who gave tips about overcoming premature ejaculation and shared experiences with prostate massage (one man told the audience,

"It gives me a different type of pleasure and helps me have multiple orgasms"). At a more explicit panel, a man described the need to be vulnerable to a female partner and to create a "trusting space" for her and then demonstrated a G-spot (yoni) massage, showing the audience how to move the hands and fingers. Many in the audience considered it a useful lesson in sex.

CULTURAL FAIRS

Sex culture fairs have been increasingly held in cities in China. Hong Kong sexologist and psychiatrist Emil Ng who has co-organized these events, says, "Chinese people have always known the importance of sex education because of the one-child policy and because they are not hindered by the religious right" (personal communication, October 23, 2008). The first-ever "Sex Culture Festival" in Hong Kong was held in 2006 (www.fotop.net/cbenc/06god02?). Up to 50,000 visitors came to the outdoor "carnival" on a major road in the bustling city transformed into a pedestrian mall, with entertainment, games, drama, movies, forums, and more than 40 booths. Half of these booths were sponsored by government agencies or NGOs providing sex health services or education; by sexuality-rights groups (e.g., advocates for homosexuals and prostitutes); and by Hong Kong and Chinese TV stations, which introduced sex education programs. The other half were sponsored by commercial companies, including drug firms (e.g. Pfizer, Organon); holistic health distributors; health centers; companies selling blow-up dolls or supplements like Zestra; and artists promoting their erotic art. Activities at the indoor exhibition—attended by about 3,000 people a day—were more explicit and largely for "adults only." Speakers at the week-long event included district officers, in a show of government support, but also expert sexologists from other regions, like mainland China, Macau, and Taiwan, and sexuality experts from the China Sexology Association, as well as noted American sexologist Beverly Whipple, representing the World Association of Sexology. Professor Ng, from the Department of Psychiatry of Hong Kong University, notes that visitors' reactions were positive and that a good balance was achieved between educational offerings and recreational ones, which were not too explicit, although he noted that the expo was also criticized by some attendees for being "too conservative" (E. Ng, personal communication, March 14, 2006).

A sex culture festival has been held annually for several years in Guangzhou, China (a city about two hours from Hong Kong by train). In 2008, the Asia Adult Expo (as it is called) together with the first Hong Kong-Macau Sex Cultural Festival, was also launched in Macau, a city known as Asian's Las Vegas (for its gambling). As in other sexpos, the events featured hundreds of exhibits and a range of offerings from entertainment (e.g. lingerie fashion shows, pole dancing, and penis painting) to more serious educational experiences, for example, in-person Q&A sessions with professional sexology experts. The events were co-sponsored by adult industry associations with the region's respected sexuality education organization, the Hong Kong Sex Education Association, as well as the Family Planning Association of Hong Kong, among others. Founder and current vice president of the Hong Kong Sex Education Association Emil Ng explained (personal communication, October 23, 2008) that the games and carnival atmosphere draw people and as a result they also hear the messages about healthy sexuality education. "These events have been very successful in China and prove the importance of sexuality education and the positive acceptance and interest of the public for these valuable messages," Ng said. The veteran sex educator explained that holding the sex culture festivals every year is important to build public awareness, so that—as he hopes—"eventually the whole city will talk about what they are learning" and "hopefully the whole world will have sex cultural fairs so all people will know the value of sexuality education."

CONCLUSIONS

Many events that cater to the public but address sexuality themes must strike a balance between entertainment and education. While some efforts face criticism from visitors that they are not sensational enough, organizers often have to be sensitive to the local political climate and government regulations. Yet, museums and expositions are flourishing, even in parts of the world that once were repressive about the subject of sexuality. These venues are proving to be commercially viable but also to be a unique opportunity for the public to be exposed to potential learning about sexuality if they choose to view the experience from a serious, pedagogical point of view. Sexuality educators can learn from these exhibitions, can participate in the events as expert sources of information, and can even create new ways to use these venues as educational opportunities and help the public process the experience through the lens of sexuality education.

REFERENCES

Barratt, B, Braveman, S., Kuriansky, J. & Yarian, D. (2005, May 14). *Tantra in the office practice of sex therapy.* Panel at the annual meeting of the American Association of Sex Educators, Counselors, and Therapists, Portland, Oregon.

Beijing Shijingshan District Family Planning Association, Beijing Science and Technology Association Shijingshan District & Beijing Sexuality Education and Research Association. (2007). *Exhibition of Sexual and Reproductive Health* Beijing, China: Beijing Shijingshan District Family Planning Association, Beijing Science and

Technology Association Shijingshan District & Beijing Sexuality Education and Research Association.

Burton, S. (1990, May 14). China's Kinsey report. *Time*, p. 58.

Dopp, H-J. (2000). *Das Erotik Museum in Berlin.* London, England: Parkstone Press, Ltd. (in German).

Dopp, H-J. (2001). Venus-tempel: Das sex-museum in Amsterdam. New York: Parkstone Press, Ltd. (in German).

Durex (2005*). Global sex survey results.* Retrieved January 8, 2009, from http://www.durex.com/cm/gss2005result.pdf

Erotica USA (1999). *Printed materials.* New York: Erotica USA.

Golingai, P. (2005, November 27). Still no sex, they're Singaporean. *The Star.* Retrieved January 9, 2009, from http://thestar.com.my/news/story.asp?file=/2005/11/27/life focus/12657407&sec=lifefocus

Kremb, J. (2005). Mit Dr. Judy auf der sexpo. Retrieved January 9, 2009, from http://www.spiegel.de/panorama/0,1518,386190,00.html

Kuriansky, J. (2004). *The complete idiot's guide to tantric sex.* 2nd edition. New York: Penguin Group.

Kuriansky, J. (2005a). Challenges facing the matchmaking industry. Panel sponsored by the Ministry of Community Development, Youth and Sports, at The Partner Connection, Matchmaker's Trade Seminar, Raffles City Convention Center, Singapore, November 11.

Kuriansky, J. (2005b). Harmony in relationships. Presentation at the Sexpo Exposition, Singapore Expo Hall, November 19.

Kuriansky, J. (2005c). If you met the man of your dreams, would you recognize him? Speech at the Singles Forum, organized by the Ministry of Community Development, Youth and Sports, Raffles City Convention Center Auditorium, Singapore, November 12.

Kuriansky, J. (2007). Eros in the Red Dragon: The open door to sex in China. In M. S. Tepper & A. F. Owens (Eds.), *Sexual health: Moral and cultural foundations* (Vol. 3, pp. 243–278). Westport, CT: Praeger.

Kuriansky, J., & Simonson, H. (2005, May 13). *A theoretical introduction to tantra.* Workshop at the annual meeting of the American Association of Sex Educators, Counselors, and Therapists, Portland, Oregon.

LaFerla, R. (2009). *Toy story, the adult version.* Retrieved January 9, 2009, from http://www.nytimes.com/2009/01/08/fashion/08TOYS.html?_r=4&ref=todayspaper

Liu, D. (1994). *The mystery of sex culture in ancient China.* Oakland, CA: Hua Wen Books, Co.

Liu, D. (2000a). *Chinese sex artifacts over 5,000 years.* Hong Kong: Ming Pao Publications Limited.

Liu, D. (2000b). *Illustrated hard book of Chinese sex history* (2 vols.). Changchun, Ji Lin Province, China: Times Literature and Art Press.

Liu, D. (2000c). *Sex Culture Object. China and the World.* Ningxia Hui Autonomous Region, P.R. China: Ningxia People's Publishing House.

Liu, D., Ng, M. L., Zhou, L. P., & Haeberle, E. (1997). *Sexual behavior in modern China: Report on the nationwide survey of 20,000 men and women.* New York: Continuum Press.

Ma, X. (1990). *Male sexual dysfunction—impotence.* [video] Beijing, China: Beijing Senior Education Video & Audio Publishing House (in Chinese).

Ma, X. (Ed.). (2003a). *Adolescence and sexual health.* Beijing, China: Scientific Publishing House. (in Chinese).

Ma, X. (Ed.). (2003b). *The counsel of andrology.* Beijing, China: Scientific Publishing House. (in Chinese).

Ma, X. (Ed.). (2003c). *The counsel of femalology.* Beijing, China: Scientific Publishing House. (in Chinese).

Ma, X. (Ed.). (2003d). *The counsel of infertility.* Beijing, China: Scientific Publishing House. (in Chinese).

Ma, X. (Ed.). (2003e). *The counsel of sexual problems of aging.* Beijing, China: Scientific Publishing House. (in Chinese).

Ma, X. (2004a). *The modern sexual medicine* (2nd Ed.). Beijing, China: People's Military Medicine Publishing House. (in Chinese).

Ma, X. & Yang, D. (2004b). *The study of sexuality.* Beijing, China: Chinese Population Publishing House. (in Chinese).

Ma, X. & Yang, D. (2005a). *Report of an internet sexual health survey of Chinese men.* Beijing, China: Guang Ming Daily Publishing House. (in Chinese).

Ma, X. & Yang, D. (2005b). *Report of an internet sexual health survey of Chinese women.* Beijing, China: Guang Ming Daily Publishing House. (in Chinese).

Ruan, F. F. (1991). *Sex in China.* New York: Plenum Press.

Vanilla Gallery (2008, April). Japon erotica, la nouvelle generation. Tokyo, Japan: Vanilla Gallery.

Valentine, S. & Heumann, S. (2008, June 27). Beyond tantra 101: deepening tantra practices. Workshop presented at the annual meeting of the American Association of Sex Educators, Counselors, and Therapists, New Orleans, Louisiana.

Woodburn, R. (2006). Posting by Rob Woodburn, May 25, 11:01 P.M. Retrieved April 12, 2007, from http://blogs.smh.com.au/travel/archives/2006/05/whatever_turns_1.html

Yarian, D. & Anders, S. (2008, June 26). *A gentle introduction to tantra: An experiential tantra.* Pre-conference workshop at the annual meeting of the American Association of Sex Educators, Counselors, and Therapists, New Orleans, Louisiana.

Chapter Twelve

SEX EDUCATION IN ADULT RETAIL STORES: POSITIONING CONSUMERS' QUESTIONS AS TEACHABLE MOMENTS

Debby Herbenick and Michael Reece

Sexuality education remains a highly controversial issue in the United States, with both the type (i.e., abstinence only until marriage and abstinence based) and the timing of such programs being hotly contested topics among policy-makers, religious groups, advocacy organizations, educators and parents (e.g., Irvine, 2002). The debate related to it has largely focused on children and adolescents, and the sexuality education that they do or do not receive in public schools, leaving sexuality education for adults a largely untouched subject.

When sex education for adults has been discussed, it has primarily been within the context of interventions that focus on groups of adults "at risk" for sexually transmitted infections (STI) and HIV/AIDS (e.g., men who have sex with men, injection drug users) or education for healthcare workers (e.g., Solursh et al., 2003). There is strikingly little research on sexuality education for adults in the general population, even though the United States continues to struggle with a high incidence of STI (Centers for Disease Control, 2003).

While these adult-oriented educational efforts related to prevention, testing and treatment strategies for STI and HIV/AIDS are important to our nation's public health, previous writings suggest that adults have had (Pomeroy, 1960) and continue to have (e.g., Reinisch and Beasley, 1990) questions about a much broader and more diverse range of sexuality topics. The fact that adults have such questions—particularly in the context of their enormous consumption of medications, supplements and devices marketed for the enhancement of genital functioning and sensation—points to the need for sex educators and sexual health professionals to consider mechanisms that enable them to be responsive to the sexuality education needs of adult populations.

Previous research has indicated that many of the mechanisms through which adults learn about sexuality are passive in nature, such as television, social standards, movies and art (Addison, 2002). More recently, some professionals in the field have questioned whether our attention would better be spent on more active means, such as the Internet (Johnson-Vickberge, Kohn, Franco, & Criniti, 2004), books, classes, and other ways that adults explore their sexual interests. To that end, professionals remain challenged to explore innovative and effective ways of delivering such forms of sexuality education.

In the United States, many adults are engaged in such sexual exploration through the venues of the nation's adult retail industry. While exact figures as to the scope and magnitude of the industry are difficult to obtain, estimates would suggest that millions of adults in the country turn to it for products of a sexual nature (PBS Frontline, 2002; Michael, Gagnon, Laumann, & Kolata, 1994). While many adults learn about sexuality through passive means, it may be that those who seek the products and services offered by this industry are among those who would be appropriate for more direct interventions, given that they are making efforts to explore their sexual interests through their patronage of the industry. As a result, it may be reasonable to consider whether this industry is in a position to be responsive to the sexuality education needs of its consumers. Should the industry be in such a position, sexuality education and sexual health professionals working with adults may find its venues to present unique opportunities for partnerships that help to further enhance the sexual literacy of society.

While many adults will access the adult retail industry through its Internet-based outlets, others continue to obtain its services and products by visiting its physical retail stores, such as adult bookstores and sex shops. These stores have long been in operation in the United States, yet they often face stigma in the communities where they conduct business, and may be challenged by legal or policy decisions that regulate their operation (e.g., American Civil Liberties Union, 2002) and survival. Perhaps as a result of this stigma and the complexities associated with a store's existence in some communities, educators and public health professionals might have overlooked the potential for these adult retail stores as a partner in their efforts to educate adults about sexuality, regardless of the extent to which they may refer individuals to these stores for products they often recommend for therapeutic or educational purposes, such as vibrators or vaginal dilators (Wilmoth & Spinelli, 2000; Davis & Hutchison, 1999; Hage & Karim, 1998; Heiman, LoPiccolo, & LoPiccolo, 1976).

It is possible that many consumer-employee interactions within these stores may be limited to the exchange of products and money. However, it may also be the case that these consumer-employee interactions also include the exchange of sexuality-related education and information; yet researchers simply have not documented such a phenomenon.

As in any retail establishment, questions about products are to be expected. Adult retail establishments exist specifically to sell sexuality-related products, and it therefore makes sense that the process of answering even some of the most basic product questions (e.g., What does that do?) might include the exchange of sexual health information, whether intended or not. The products that adult retail stores sell include those that are traditionally associated with public health, and the prevention of sexually transmitted infections (e.g., condoms, latex dams and lubricants), as well as products associated with education (e.g., informational books and sexually explicit videos, DVDs and magazines), the relief of sexual problems or dysfunction (e.g., vibrators), and sexual pleasure (e.g., cock rings and dildos); categories which are clearly not mutually exclusive.

Given this, the employees of these stores may be routinely answering questions similar to those asked of other more institutionalized, sexuality-related professionals, such as public health educators (e.g., how to use a condom for disease prevention), sex educators (e.g., how to use a vibrator or whether herbal aphrodisiacs work) or sex therapists (e.g., how to have an orgasm or delay ejaculation). To that end, consumers may be providing employees with "teachable moments" or opportunities to provide sexuality information when they pose such questions. By responding to these questions, employees may be serving as de facto sex educators.

Virtually no literature to date has examined the nature of the questions posed by individuals during their interactions with adult retail employees. However, given the vast number of adult retail outlets in the United States and the millions of individuals who turn to them for products of a sexual nature, a better understanding of consumer behaviors within these stores may provide valuable insights into the contributions that these stores make, or have the potential to make, to the sexual lives of consumers and the communities in which they are situated.

STUDY BACKGROUND AND PURPOSE

In a previous study (Reece, Herbenick, & Sherwood-Puzzello, 2004), we articulated the characteristics of adult retail stores and their employees that we perceived to be supportive of their ability to serve as a sexual health resource for adults in their communities. However, we argued that although these stores and their employees may possess characteristics supportive of this role, they would only be able to maximize this potential if presented with the opportunity to do so by their consumers. While there is inherent value in simply understanding the types of questions that individuals ask when visiting adult retail stores, it is also important to document the extent to which consumers of adult retail stores presented the employees of those stores with opportunities to provide education on a range of sexuality-related topics.

Based upon the results of the previous study, we hypothesized that consumers of adult retail stores would frequently ask questions that, by their nature, introduced "teachable moments" during which employees would be able to provide sexual health education, information, or advice. To assess whether these "teachable moments" for adult sexuality education exist within the venues of the adult retail industry, it is necessary to understand the kinds of questions that consumers ask adult retail employees. The purpose of the present study was to better understand: (1) how often adult retail store employees are asked questions related to certain sexual health content areas; (2) whether the frequencies of these questions are associated with employee or store characteristics; and (3) the types of questions most frequently asked of adult retail store employees.

Should it be the case that the adult retail consumers present opportunities for education through their interactions with employees of adult stores, adults who frequent these venues may benefit by the development of effective collaborations between sexuality education and health professionals, and those who operate and work within the venues of the adult retail industry. These collaborations could focus on identifying and implementing the mechanisms that will facilitate the delivery of sexuality information to adults that is accurate, developmentally appropriate, and that is considerate of, and appropriate for, the business orientation of the industry's venues.

METHODS

Participant Recruitment

Participants were recruited from adult retail stores, with physical storefronts in the United States, that were identified during searches of national erotica guides and Internet telephone directories. Internet-only retail outlets and wholesale warehouses were excluded. These searches resulted in the identification of 448 adult stores in 45 states and Washington DC that appeared to meet study criteria. Research assistants telephoned the stores to request a manager's assistance with the distribution of the study instrument to each store's employees. Of the identified stores, 17.6% ($n = 79$) were no longer in business or did not meet study inclusion criteria (i.e., during the recruitment call, there was an indication that they did not sell products that were sexual in nature or did not have a storefront), and 23.9% ($n = 107$), research assistants were not able to talk with a manager within three calls, and so they were excluded from the pool of potential stores. This resulted in 262 stores that met eligibility and where a discussion with the manager was held.

Of these stores, 71.4% (n = 187) agreed to participate in the study and 28.6% (n = 75) refused participation. At each participating store, the manager provided the researcher with an estimate of the number of employees who routinely had contact with consumers. A package containing research packets for each employee (research packets included a recruitment letter, an informed consent statement, the study survey, and a postage-paid return envelope) was sent via mail to each manager along with a letter asking that the packets be distributed to employees using the store's routine process for distributing mail or other internal materials. All study protocols were approved by the Institutional Review Board of Indiana University-Bloomington.

Of the 187 stores whose managers agreed to participate, 43% (n = 80) had at least one employee return a completed survey resulting in a total of 294 completed surveys. The mean within-store response rate was 52.4%, calculated as the within-store proportion of surveys returned from each of these 80 stores. It is impossible to know whether each employee in the 187 stores actually received the research packet, making it impossible to calculate a true participant response rate. Based on the total number of research packets mailed to the 187 stores, the estimated individual employee response rate was 18.5%. However, the estimated rate is conservative and dependent upon two assumptions: (1) that the estimated number of employees provided by the manager at each store during the recruitment call was accurate, and (2) that the manager actually distributed research packets to employees as agreed upon.

Measures

The study instrument included 89 items and has been described in detail in previous work (see Reece, Herbenick, & Sherwood-Puzzello, 2004). For the analyses described in this paper, items included those related to the types and frequency of questions asked by store consumers and their associations with store and employee characteristics.

It is important to note that items on the study instrument were created based upon the authors' conceptualization of constructs relevant to the research questions. There were no identified measures from previous research for which reliability and validity for the constructs had been established and for those that were designed for use with this specific participant population. To assess the validity of the measures, items were reviewed by five individuals with doctoral level training in sexual health research, and revised based upon feedback obtained from these individuals. Additionally, the study instrument was reviewed for its legal appropriateness and employee sensitivity by corporate leadership at two large adult retail chains.

Consumer Questions

Two measures were used to assess the frequency and type of questions asked by consumers. To assess the frequency with which consumers asked questions related to a broad range of sexual health issues, participants were asked to indicate how often they were asked: how to use condoms; how to select condoms for disease or pregnancy prevention; how to select condoms that maximize sensation; how to use lubricants; how to select lubricants for disease or pregnancy prevention; how to select lubricants that maximize sensation; how to prevent pregnancy; how to prevent HIV or STI transmission; how to select a toy that will maximize pleasure; and how to select a stimulating video or magazine. These were measured using a four-point nominal scale, and for analyses were collapsed into "not often" (e.g., never or a few times a month) or "often" (a few times a week or a few times a day).

The study instrument also included an open-ended item that asked participants to list the three questions that they were most frequently asked by consumers. As there has been limited research on the types of consumer-employee interactions in adult retail stores, this item was included to assess the extent to which consumers asked sexuality-related questions, but also in order to better understand the full range of questions presented by adult consumers.

This open-ended item resulted in the collection of 806 questions. The questions were subsequently coded independently by the first author and an independent judge, who then met together to come to consensus on the categorization of questions. This resulted in the coding of the questions into 14 categories that best reflected the primary nature of their content, including, videos/DVDs, magazines and books; lubricants; vibrators and dildos; penis pumps and cock rings; sexual practices and relationship advice; genital functioning (e.g., erectile function, ejaculatory control, vaginal sensation); nitrites (head cleaners, poppers); arcade/viewing booths; condoms and dental dams; other toys and enhancement items; questions related to the utility of a product (e.g., Does this really work?); miscellaneous store questions (e.g., prices, use of bathroom, store hours); requests for recommendations about things to do (e.g., clubs to go to or finding prostitutes) or personal questions (e.g., Are you single?); and general miscellaneous questions. While the majority of questions were coded into just one category, some questions addressed two distinct topics and were therefore counted in more than one category. For example, the question, "Which lubricant or video head cleaner is best?" was coded in both the lubricant and nitrite product categories.

In order to avoid confusion between the two items related to consumer questions, the former will be referred to as "pre-defined question types" and the latter will be referred to as the "most frequently asked questions."

Employee Characteristics

For the analyses presented here, participant-specific measures included demographics; comfort in responding to consumer questions about sexual health topics (not at all, somewhat or very comfortable); and the length of time spent working within the adult retail industry. The latter was collapsed into two categories (greater or less than two years).

Store-Related Characteristics

Store-related characteristics included the majority-type consumer served (combined into predominantly gay/ lesbian/bisexual, predominantly heterosexual and "about even" with regard to sexual orientation) and the population size of the city in which the store was located. Population size categories were collapsed into more than or less than one million, as specified by the US Census Data for the year 2000, or with data provided by government web pages of cities for which the US Census Data were unavailable. The stores were located in 61 cities and 28 states.

RESULTS

Results are presented according to the following sets of analyses: (1) participant characteristics, (2) comparisons of pre-defined question type by employee characteristics (gender, time in the industry, and comfort answering question types) with store characteristics (geographic size and majority type consumer served), and (3) descriptive information related to the most frequently asked question categories reported by participants. For the purpose of this study, participants were included in analyses only if they responded to this item with at least one "frequently asked question," resulting in a final sample of 273 employees from 80 adult retail stores. For each of the question categories, examples of the questions provided by participants are included.

Participant Characteristics

Of the 273 participants included in these analyses, the majority were men (65.1%, $n = 177$), 33.8% were women ($n = 92$) and 1.1% ($n = 3$) were identified as transgender or transsexual. Most of the participants, 77.2% self-identified as White ($n = 210$), 10.3% as Hispanic ($n = 28$), 5.1% as Black ($n = 14$), 4.8% as Asian or Pacific Islander ($n = 13$), and the remaining participants identified as "other." More than half (54.0%) identified their sexual orientation as heterosexual ($n = 147$), 25.7% as homosexual ($n = 70$), 15.1% as bisexual ($n = 41$), and 5.1% as questioning or other ($n = 14$).

Nearly half of the participants, 47.3% ($n = 129$), reported having worked professionally within the adult industry for more than two years, including

13.2% who reported more than ten years experience (*n = 36*). *The average age of the participants was 34.67 (range = 18–70; SD = 12.26).*

Store Characteristics

More than half the stores (55.3%) were located in cities with a population of less than one million. Regarding the employees' perspectives on the sexual orientation of their stores' consumers, the largest percentage of participants, 38.5% (*n* = 105), indicated that their store consumers were mostly heterosexual, 28.5% (*n* = 78) reported that their consumer base was "about even" (heterosexual and gay/lesbian), 19% (*n* = 52) reported that their consumers were mostly gay, and 5% or less indicated that their consumers were exclusively gay, lesbian, or bisexual or that they were unsure of the sexual orientation of their consumers. For analyses in this paper, these categories of majority consumer type were collapsed into predominantly heterosexual, predominantly gay/lesbian/bisexual, and "about even."

Pre-Defined Question Types

Most participants reported regularly (a few times a day or a few times a week), being asked how to select a sex toy to maximize pleasure (73.2%) or how to select a stimulating video or magazine (71.1%). Participants also often reported being asked how to select a lubricant (46.3%) or condom (34.2%) to maximize sensation, or how to use a lubricant (30.3%). A smaller percentage of participants reported regularly being asked about products related to disease and pregnancy prevention or how to use a condom. Table 12.1 provides

Table 12.1
Percentage of Participants Who Report Being Asked Question Types a Few Times a Week or a Few Times a Day (*n* = 273)

Question Content	*n*	%
How to select a toy to maximize pleasure	200	73.2
How to select a stimulating video or magazine	194	71.1
How to select a lubricant that maximizes sensation	123	46.3
How to select a condom that maximizes sensation	93	34.2
How to use a lubricant	80	30.3
How to select a condom for disease/pregnancy prevention	27	9.9
How to select a lubricant for disease/pregnancy prevention	25	9.4
How to prevent HIV/STD transmission	15	5.6
How to use a condom	12	4.4
How to prevent pregnancy	9	3.4

an overview of the proportion of participants who reported that they were frequently asked the predefined questions (see Table 12.1).

Associations with Employee Characteristics

Chi-square analyses were used to examine the pre-defined question types in relation to participant characteristics only among stores that sold the relevant product. For example, only employees who reported that their store sold lubricants were included in analyses pertaining to being asked questions about lubricants.

Employee Gender

Significantly more women than men (89% vs. 71%) reported being asked questions about selecting sex toys to maximize pleasure, $X^2 (1, N = 252) = 10.36$, $p = .001$. No other significant differences were found when the question type was considered by gender.

Length of Time in the Industry

Participants who had worked for more than two years in the industry were significantly more likely to report being regularly asked questions about preventing HIV/STD transmission than those who had worked in the industry for less time [9% vs. 2%, $X^2 (1, N = 270) = 5.75, p = .016$]. The length of time in the industry was not significantly related to the regularity of other predefined question types.

Comfort Answering Questions

Participants who indicated that they were not at all comfortable answering questions about these pre-defined question types were compared with those who indicated that they were somewhat or very comfortable. Those who expressed comfort answering questions about selecting lubricants that maximize sensation were significantly more likely to indicate receiving such questions on a frequent basis [49% vs. 14%, $X^2 (1, N = 255) = 6.53, p = .011$]. Similarly, those who indicated comfort answering questions about selecting sex toys to maximize pleasure were significantly more likely to report that such questions were regularly asked of them [80% vs. 39%, $X^2 (1, N = 253) = 12.76, p = < .001$]. Comfort answering other types of questions was not related to the regularity with which they were reported as being asked.

Associations with Store Characteristics

Population Size

Participants whose store was located in a city with a population of at least one million were significantly more likely (48% vs. 27%) to indicate that questions about selecting condoms that maximize sensation were regularly asked,

X^2 (1, N = 255) = 11.99, p = .001. The size of the geographic area was not significantly related to the regularity with which other question types were asked.

Majority Type Consumer Served

Participants from stores whose consumers were perceived to be mainly gay, lesbian and bisexual were significantly less likely to report being regularly asked about selecting sex toys to maximize pleasure than those stores whose consumers appeared to be "about even" in terms of sexual orientation [67% vs. 86%, $X2$ (2, N = 243) = 7.29, p = .026]. Of the employees who worked in stores with a predominantly heterosexual clientele, 78% reported that they were regularly asked this question type, though it was not significantly different from the other two categories of consumer sexual orientation.

However, participants from stores with a predominant gay, lesbian or bisexual clientele were significantly more likely to report being regularly asked about selecting condoms for disease/pregnancy prevention (19%) than stores with a mostly heterosexual clientele (8%) or those with an "about even" clientele (7%), X^2 (2, N = 243) = 6.48, p = .039.

Most Frequently Asked Questions

When asked to list up to three questions most frequently asked by consumers, participants reported questions dealing with a wide range of topics. Questions about DVDs/videos/books/magazines, toys and enhancement items, lubricants and vibrators/dildos were among those most frequently asked. Table 12.2 provides an overview of the categories into which the three most frequently asked questions were organized and the frequency with which participants reported being asked questions in each category.

The most frequent topic to be reported by participants dealt with the selection of DVDs/videos/books/magazines. As many as 56.8% (n = 155) of the participants reported this as one of the most frequently asked questions. These questions commonly took the form of a request for an employee's perception of its quality (e.g., What's your best video? or Is this a good magazine?) or their advice on selecting a video for couples (e.g., What is a good video to view as a couple?); for sexual partners (e.g., What is a video my wife will like?"), or for female viewers (e.g., What are the best movies for women?). These questions were sometimes specific to a request for media that contained a certain actor.

Forty-one percent of the participants (n = 112) reported questions about toys and sexual enhancement items aside from those listed in other categories (e.g., Spanish fly, anal beads, bachelorette party gifts, etc.). This diverse group of questions once again included many that asked for an employee's recommendation about what they perceived to be the best, most popular or their

Table 12.2
Questions Most Frequently Asked of Adult Store Employees (*n* = 273)

Question Category	Number of Participants Reporting	
	n	%
DVD/video/book/magazine	155	56.8
Other toys/enhancement items	112	41.0
Lubricants	89	32.6
Vibrators/dildos	66	24.2
Store questions	65	23.8
Things to do/personal	44	16.1
Penis pumps/cockrings	38	13.9
Arcade/viewing booths	32	11.7
Genital functioning/sensation	30	11.0
Do people buy that/does it work	28	10.3
Nitrites	19	7.0
Sex practices/relationship advice	19	7.0
Condoms/dental dams	16	5.4
General misc.	3	1.1

personally most favorite toy. However, there were also many questions that asked specific information about a product (e.g., Can this toy be used for anal sex? and What do butt plugs do?), or its use within a relationship (e.g., What sex toy should I use to introduce variety into a relationship?).

Approximately one-third of the participants (32.6%, *n* = 89) listed questions about lubricants among those most frequently asked. Similar to questions about film and reading materials, questions commonly requested employee recommendations for the best, most popular or most widely used lubricant, while others asked for specific information (e.g., Is this the best lube for this condom?, How effective is nonoxynol-9?, or What's better, oil-based or water-based lubricant?).

Nearly one-quarter of the participants reported questions about vibrators or dildos (24.2%, *n* = 66), as being among those most frequently asked. As with other question categories, questions in this category often asked for recommendations as to the "best" or "most popular" vibrator or dildo, as well as finding one with certain characteristics (e.g., size or volume).

While less common, participants did report questions related to genital sensation (e.g., Do you have any creams to make my vagina tighter/more sensitive?, What can I use to last longer?), relationships with family members (e.g., How do I come out to my parents?), and intimate relationships (e.g., How to spice up the marriage?, How can I get good sex and romance back into my relationship?).

DISCUSSION

This study sought to better understand the types of information routinely sought by consumers of adult retail stores during their interactions with employees, in order to assess the potential for these questions to present opportunities for adult-focused sexuality-related education. To understand this, we explored associations among the regularity of questions asked about pre-defined sexual health topics with characteristics of the employees to whom they were asked and the characteristics of the stores in which they worked. We also analyzed the nature of questions that store employees perceived as those most frequently asked, in order to gain an understanding of the broad nature of questions that adult retail employees receive.

Many of the current efforts for educating adults about sexuality deal primarily with disease- or pregnancy-related aspects of sexual behavior. This is inconsistent with the calls by some to ensure that sexuality-related interventions are less focused on negative outcomes and more consistent with the manner in which individuals construct their sexual lives (Reece & Dodge, 2004; Di Mauro, 1996). The findings of this study suggest that there may be potential for working with the venues of the adult retail industry in order to implement such interventions by focusing not only on the prevention of infection or unintended pregnancy, but also being responsive to the broad range of questions and concerns about sexuality held by adults.

Based on the types of questions reported by the study participants, it is apparent that consumers of adult retail stores are asking questions that provide a unique opportunity for the dissemination of sexuality education to adults. On the surface, these questions may appear to be simple requests for information related to a particular product that a store may sell. However, by reconceptualizing these questions and the potential responses to them by store employees, professionals in the sexuality education and sexual health fields may realize that there is a unique opportunity for engaging with this industry to enhance the availability of accurate information available to sexually active or sexually interested adults.

The four pre-defined question types most commonly reported as being asked by adult retail consumers were all framed within the context of sexual pleasure, stimulation or sensation. This indicates the importance of sexual pleasure in consumers' lives, supports the notion that adults have questions about sexuality, and appears not only to provide opportunities for store employees to educate consumers about sexual enhancement, but also to simultaneously provide information about the prevention of infections or unintended pregnancy.

For example, in responding to questions about sex toys, an employee could be responsive to the consumer's interest in sexual enhancement, and also educate the consumer about sex toy hygiene, an important factor in reducing the risk of infection. When responding to questions about condoms or lubricants, an employee might provide information about their correct use, the appropriate lubricants to use with condoms, or certain features related to both products that are designed to enhance sexual enjoyment. Table 12.3 provides examples of some of the most frequently reported questions and suggestions for being responsive to the educational opportunities that they present.

There was a great deal of consistency in the types of questions across the 80 stores from which participants were recruited. These stores represented 61 U.S. cities of varying geographic location and size. This indicates that the potential for engaging with this industry may be widespread.

There were some differences in the types of questions reported as being most frequently asked, when considering the characteristics of the store employee receiving the questions. Women more often reported being asked about selecting a sex toy to maximize pleasure. Considering the plethora of toys marketed for women, and that questions often solicited a personal recommendation, perhaps consumers assume a female employee may have used a sex toy herself and may therefore be particularly well suited to answer that question.

The finding that employees who had worked in the industry for two or more years were more likely to report being asked questions about HIV/AIDS may be reflective of regular consumers becoming familiar with the employee over time and thus becoming more comfortable about asking health-related (or even stigmatizing) questions about infection. Alternatively, perhaps seasoned employees develop an air of professionalism or confidence that makes consumers feel more comfortable asking such questions. Should sexual education and sexual health professionals develop training for employees of the adult retail industry, it might be useful to explore whether their frequency of being asked specific types of questions subsequently increases.

The degree to which employees expressed comfort answering questions about selecting lubricants for sensation and sex toys for pleasure was significantly related to reports of being asked questions about each of these. The reason for this difference is unclear, but perhaps employees who are comfortable discussing lubricants or sex toys are more likely to initiate conversations about these topics or to approach consumers while they are browsing such products.

It is also unclear why more employees reported being asked questions about selecting condoms based on sensation in cities with a population greater than one million. This could be related to the large amount of HIV prevention messages that have been targeted to individuals living in cities with large populations (and often higher corresponding HIV prevalence). While the message of important condom use may have been successfully received by individuals

Table 12.3
Examples of How Adult Retail Store Employees Can Respond to Consumers'
Questions as "Teachable Moments"

Question Example	Considerations	Examples of Responses
"What's the best lube?"	• Activity lubricant will be used for • Whether latex condoms will be used • Potential for irritation • Whether lubricant will be used in the water • Cross-sell with condoms	"This lube is our best selling lube, probably because it's water-based and is safe to use with latex condoms, plus it's not too sticky. However, there are lots of great options, let me show you some . . ."
"What's your most popular vibrator?"	• Activity vibrator will be used for • Preferred size, noise level, source, material • Cross-sell with a lubricant, sex toy cleaner, a book about incorporating toys into sexual play and perhaps even condoms (for hygiene)	"We sell vibrators designed to stimulate the clitoris, g-spot, vagina, penis and anus. Some have one speed and others have multiple settings. Some run on batteries and others are plugged into the wall. Which ones sound interesting to you?"
"Do penis pumps really work?"	• Consider what consumer means by "work" (e.g., penis enlargement or sexual pleasure) • Cross-sell with a lubricant, sex toy cleaner, and condoms (if sharing toy with a partner)	"I'm not aware of any research that suggests they could make a man's penis longer or wider. However, some men like to incorporate them into self-masturbation or sex with a partner. We also sell some books that discuss everything from penis size to creative sex play for men over here (indicates books)."
"Why don't you sell condoms with nonoxynol 9?"	• Briefly discuss current thinking regarding nonoxynol-9 and STI/HIV risk • Suggest other in-stock condoms and their features • Cross-sell with appropriate lubricants	"We stopped carrying them because some health organizations suggested that they may irritate the genitals, and may increase the risk of getting an infection. However, we do carry a great range of condoms of various sizes and textures, and some lubricants over here."

in these cities, it may still be the case that individuals actually select condoms based on a particular brand's or type's properties to enhance the sexual experience, such as being made of a particular material, having a certain texture, or those that result in a better fit and feel. While the consumer may be seeking a condom for its properties related to pleasure, these questions provide an excellent opportunity for the employee to ensure that the consumer has considered their needs with regard to the prevention of infections or pregnancy, thereby serving as a solid example of where these consumer-employee interactions can be of critical importance.

Although employees less often reported being regularly asked questions about selecting condoms specifically for disease or pregnancy prevention, it is perhaps not surprising that employees from stores with a predominantly gay, lesbian, and bisexual clientele more often reported such questions. This may reflect the disproportionate number of messages related to condoms for disease prevention that have been targeted at men who have sex with men, making this topic more salient among these communities.

Our initial interest in this notion of consumer-employee interactions as teachable moments was driven by our interest in their potential to make available opportunities for the delivery of information that would help consumers make more informed health-related decisions. However, as we developed our understanding of the potential for these stores to serve as a more comprehensive sexuality-related resource, we realized that it would also be important for these interactions to result in the sale of the store's products if we were to effectively partner with this industry. Also realized was that the mutual goals of profit and education did not have to be in conflict with one another. On the contrary, while profit and education may appear to be entirely different goals, consumer-employee interactions offer the potential for education and profit to co-exist, and even support one another. Given the business nature of the adult retail industry, realizing that education and profit not only could exist, but must co-exist, is crucial should we proceed to develop interventions that would meet the needs of each entity.

The adult retail industry remains highly regulated in some U.S. communities. Therefore, it is important to note that the various outcomes associated with answering questions, such as education, communication modeling and influencing consumer comfort, may only be possible in situations where employees are able to freely discuss sexuality with adult consumers. For example, in states where laws regulate the kind of information an employee can provide to a consumer about certain sexuality products, or the extent to which a product can even be acknowledged for its sexually intended purposes, the effectiveness of consumer-employee exchanges may be limited. Sexuality education professionals who find themselves engaged with this industry will need to develop a solid understanding of the local regulations pertaining to this industry's outlets in order to assess the extent to which such an educational role for venues in their community is possible. However, as we understand the potential for this industry to contribute to the sexual literacy of adults in communities, and document this through more research, it may be the case that such regulations can be altered to support such interventions.

The results of this study suggest that consumers routinely ask a variety of questions of adult store employees. It is our assertion that these interactions present teachable moments that, if acted upon, could support both health and business outcomes. However, for this to occur, it may be necessary for sexuality education and sexual health professionals, in collaboration with adult retail businesses, to more closely understand the nature of these interactions, reconceptualize our perceptions of the likely outcomes of such interactions, and document outcomes that follow collaborative efforts, such as training or other interventions.

ACKNOWLEDGMENTS

The authors wish to acknowledge the contributions of the managers and employees of the participating adult stores, and the assistance of Robert Gilchrist, Dana Chianello, and the other members of the research team who were invaluable in the process of store and participant recruitment; and Amanda Tanner who assisted with coding. The authors also wish to express their gratitude to the reviewers of earlier versions of this manuscript for their suggestions.

The authors are grateful for financial support for this project provided through the William L. Yarber Professorship, awarded to the second author.

NOTE

"Sex Education in Adult Retail Stores," *American Journal of Sexuality Education, 2*(1), 57–75. Reprinted by permission of Taylor and Francis.

American Journal of Sexuality Education, 2(1) (2006). Available online at http://ajse. haworthpress.com. © 2006 by The Haworth Press, Inc. All rights reserved.

REFERENCES

Addison, N. (2002). What are little boys made of, made of? Victorian art and the formation of gender. *Sex Education, 2(2),* 171–182.

American Civil Liberties Union (2001). ACLU Sues Rhode Island Town for Saying "Never On Sunday" to Adult Video Store. Retrieved online on July 24, 2005 from: http://www.aclu.org/FreeSpeech/FreeSpeech.cfm?ID=9160&c=84

Centers for Disease Control and Prevention (2003). Sexually Transmitted Disease Surveillance. Atlanta, GA: US Department of Health and Human Services. Retrieved online on July 24, 2005 from: http://www.cdc.gov/std/stats/toc2003.htm

Davis, G. D. & Hutchison, C. V. (1999). Clinical management of vulvodynia. *Clinical Obstetrics and Gynecology,* 42(2), 221–233.

Di Mauro, D. (1996). Sexuality research in the United States. In J. Bancroft (Ed.), *Researching Sexual Behavior* (pp. 3–8). Bloomington: Indiana University Press.

Hage, J. J. & Karim, R. B. (1998). Abdominoplastic secondary full-thickness skin graft vaginoplasty for male-to-female transsexuals. *Plastic & Reconstructive Surgery,* 101(6), 1512–1515.

Heiman, J., LoPiccolo, L., & LoPiccolo, J. (1976). *Becoming orgasmic: A sexual and personal growth program for women.* Englewood Cliffs, NJ: Prentice Hall.

Irvine, J. M. (2002). *Talk About Sex: The Battles Over Sex Education in the United States.* Berkeley, University of California Press, 2002.

Johnson Vickberg, S. M., Kohn, J. E., Franco, L. M., & Criniti, S. (2003). What teens want to know: sexual health questions submitted to a teen web site. *American Journal of Health Education,* 34(5), 258–264.

Michael, R. T., Gagnon, J. H., Laumann, E. O., & Kolata, G. (1994). *Sex in America: A Definitive Survey.* Little, Brown and Company.

PBS Frontline. American Porn. Interview Dennis McAlpine. Retrieved on October 23, 2002 from: http://www.pbs.org/wgbh/pages/frontline/shows/porn/interviews/mcalpine.html

Pomeroy, W. B. (1960). An analysis of questions on sex. *Psychological Record,* 10(3), 191–201.

Reece, M. & Dodge, B. (2004). A study in sexual health applying the principles of community-based participatory research. *Archives of Sexual Behavior,* 33(3), 235–247.

Reece, M., Herbenick, D., & Sherwood-Puzzello, C. (2004). Sexual health promotion and adult retail stores. *The Journal of Sex Research,* 41(2), 173–180.

Reinisch, J. M., & Beasley, R. (1990). *The Kinsey Institute New Report on Sex: What you must know to be sexually literate.* New York: St. Martin's Press.

Solursh, D. S., Ernst, J. L., Lewis, R. W., Prisant, L. M., Mills, T., Solursh, L. P., Jarvis, R. G., & Salazar, W. H. (2003). The human sexuality education of physicians in North American medical schools. *International Journal of Impotence Research,* 15, (Supp. 5): S41–S45.

Wilmoth, M. C., & Spinelli, A. (2000). Sexual implications of gynecologic cancer treatments. *Journal of Obstetric, Gynecologic and Neonatal Nursing,* 29(4), 413–421.

Part IV
LOOKING AHEAD TO THE FUTURE

Chapter Thirteen

THE FUTURE OF SEXUALITY EDUCATION IN THE TWENTY-FIRST CENTURY AND BEYOND

Elizabeth Schroeder

This four-volume set has taken readers on a long, sometimes challenging journey from the past through to the present of sexuality education. As we have read, the models and approaches for sexuality education is affected by many contextual factors, not the least of which is the decade in which it is offered. Sexuality education has been and continues to be affected by who is providing it, the professional preparation that person has (or has not) received specifically around being a sexuality educator, the person's own experience with sexuality in general, and the medium through which the sexuality education is being provided. It has been and will continue to be framed by the political and religious beliefs of the administrators in a given school district, of the politicians who decide budget allocation for federal, state, and local dollars, of the parents and adult caregivers of young people, and of religious and other community leaders whose voices carry great power within their communities. Further, sexuality education has been and will continue to be affected (some might argue, thwarted) significantly by the media, restricted mercilessly by the time constraints of school-based curricula that attempt to cover a vast array of topics over a school year, and either supported or denounced based on people's comfort level about sexuality.

This chapter offers a summary of lessons learned from this four-volume set, and a vision for the future of sexuality education.

LESSON ONE: SEXUALITY EDUCATION NEEDS MORE SUPPORT

Research has shown that nearly all American adults (93%) believe that sexuality education should be taught in high schools, with 84% supporting its teaching at the middle school level (Bleakley, Hennessey & Fishbein, et al., 2006). Why, then, is providing sexuality education at schools or through community-based organizations often met with such resistance? The answer is that support given through polls and statistics does not always play out in practice. Nowhere is this support needed more than in the funding of sexuality education programs.

Currently, there is no federal funding in support of comprehensive sexuality education. Opponents of comprehensive programming argue that Title X Family Planning money is used for sexuality education, but this is not the case. Family planning organizations receiving funding may offer some education in clinics, but the sexuality education programming being offered throughout the United States through other community-based organizations, at schools, and by individual practitioners receives zero federal funding. This must change. In addition to fiscal support, the support for sexuality education must also be professional (more and more national and international organizations are supporting the need for sexuality education, but we need more), and political (funding research-based, medically-accurate programming). The field also needs much more support from reasoned adults—especially parents and other adult caregivers—for the expertise of sexuality educators to prevail over the opinions of fear-spreading organizations and individuals. Most teachers believe that a wide range of sexuality-related topics, including contraception, correct condom use, sexual orientation, and more, should be taught before the end of high school; they have found, however, that sexuality education is being taught much less frequently and too late in students' academic careers (Darroch, Landry & Singh, 2000).

As sexuality educators, we are experts in our field. Yet time and again, our expertise is trumped by a lone parent or small group of parents who do not "like" the content of our lessons—age-appropriate, life-enhancing or even life-saving though this content may be. Time and again, school- and community-based administrators give in to their fear of conflict and kowtow to a vocal minority of parents and adult caregivers who are in denial about their children's sexuality and uncomfortable with young people knowing about sexuality. These parents and caregivers have the right to opt their child out of a given lesson on any given day—yet instead of adhering to a policy that is designed to apply to all learners, they choose instead to make their protest public, and take action—to go to the media, to raise a fuss, and to, effectively, bully school administrators into dropping the topic altogether rather than deal with opposition. In no other topic area are parents and politicians given more power than sexuality education. So where are those 93% of supportive adults?

Over the past few years, I was witness to a community-based controversy in a small suburban area that involved the use of a family diversity instructional video in elementary school. Although 50% of parents surveyed supported the use of the video in elementary school, and 50% opposed its use, the video was removed from the curriculum—even though the school district had an opt-out policy, and even though the vast majority of teachers and administrators in the school district supported the use of the video.

Lesson learned: The squeaky wheels get the grease.

Lesson learned: Parents who are well-organized make an impact. Moreover, parents who oppose comprehensive sexuality education are extremely well-organized. They are single-issue focused. They are relentless. On the other hand, parents who support comprehensive sexuality education—consistent with research about those who agree versus disagree with causes—don't contribute in ways they would like—writing letters, appearing at school board meetings, and so on. This must change. If the majority of people in the United States support comprehensive sexuality educator, they need to take action with the same passion as the opposition does. And sexuality educators need to elicit and wisely use their support.

LESSON TWO: WE NEED TO STOP COMPETING WITH EACH OTHER

No organization can be all things to all people. This is why so many youth-serving organizations specialize in one particular area; there are organizations helping rape and sexual assault survivors, organizations that provide a range of health-related services, organizations offering support to young people in foster care, organizations providing sexual and reproductive health, and so on. Because sexuality is such a vital topic when working with young people, many organizations are trying to incorporate sexuality-related issues and discussions into their programs. Why recreate the wheel? The sexuality education field has become so fragmented, that even some non-sexuality organizations are spending more time competing with other agencies for money, they don't see the many opportunities for collaboration available on local, state, and national levels. In this tight economy, organizations will sometimes even create a sexuality "education" intervention in order to qualify for a particular funding stream—when in reality, they may not be the best entity for providing this type of education. As I write this, I am struck by a memory of watching the Christmas classic, *Miracle on 34th Street*. At one point during the movie, a woman brings her daughter to meet Santa Claus at Macy's, where the daughter asks Santa for a specific gift, and Santa agrees. Once the daughter has moved to the side, her mother asks Santa why he guaranteed a gift that she'd already spent hours hunting down and could not find. Santa replies that she should try a competing department store, Gimbels—and the woman tells the store manager that she plans to shop at Macy's more frequently. The point is that the customer-centered approach that resulted in a sale for another store also resulted in repeat, ongoing business from this customer moving forward.

The sexuality education field must follow the same principle. A sexuality education organization that is asked to provide a training on homophobia reduction, for example, should consider whether they have the expertise on staff, or whether they should use outside experts for a given topic. Schools that assign the teaching of human sexuality education to a newer, less experienced, or otherwise less-prepared educator should, instead, consider partnering with some local sexuality experts, inviting them to come in and offer some of the lessons. These experts can, in turn, help prepare the school staff for future questions that will likely come up once the sexuality experts leaves, to ensure self-sustainability of the intervention.

LESSON THREE: SEXUALITY EDUCATION NEEDS TO BE TAKEN MORE SERIOUSLY

One of the greatest ironies for many sexuality educators is how ubiquitous and explicit sexuality messages are portrayed in the media, yet how frightened so many school administrators, parents, and others are for trained, professional sexuality educators—who have dedicated their careers to ensuring that people of all ages have access to accurate, skills-building information—to teach the actual facts. How is it that there is a television program on swinging and polyamory, but the school district mentioned above rejected the use of an educational video about family diversity because among the diverse family structures portrayed were families with same-sex parents and heterosexual parents did not want their children to know these types of families exist? How is it that middle-schoolers are learning about sexual relationships by watching *Cat House* on HBO, yet teachers are restricted from teaching the same middle-schoolers about puberty? The answer lies in two inherently problematic issues with which sexuality educators have been dealing for decades: the first is that sexuality education has not been taken seriously as a valid discipline, and the second is that when it is taken seriously, it is usually within the context of avoiding infections, pregnancy, or, to the most dramatic extent, even death—instead of within the context of creating sexually healthy individuals.

What is clear is that sexuality education remains undervalued as a topic to be addressed in the school curriculum, when there is no better potential opportunity for providing sexuality education than in a classroom setting where trusted adults see and create ongoing connections with young people on a daily basis over a long period of time. Yet sexuality education is so undervalued it is not even present in national testing requirements. In the vast majority of school districts in the United States, sexuality education is taught as part of the health curriculum. Yet health is a topic for which there is no standardized test. Is it no wonder, therefore, that in this recent era of "No Child Left Behind," young people in the United States are being left behind left and right. If sexuality were seen and valued as a topic and discipline in the school curriculum, perhaps there would no longer be just over 800,000 pregnancies among young women between the ages of 15 and 19 in the United States every year (Ventura, Abma, Mosher & Henshaw, 2004). If sexuality education were seen as a serious part of the curriculum, perhaps we would not continue to see nearly 3 to 4 million new cases of sexually transmitted infections (STIs) among young people each year. How is it that math and science are much more important than teaching a young person about their health; more important than learning how to treat another person with respect; more important than building the self-esteem that will help them to believe that they can and should make healthy decisions about sexuality? When we consider that the younger a person is when she or he engages in a sexual relationship, the more likely the experience is to be negative, coercive, and/or result in a pregnancy and/or STI, and that homophobia and transphobia continue to run rampant from as young as elementary school, how can we dare say that focusing exclusively on academics means that no children will be left behind? Unless sexuality education is a formal part of the curriculum, taught by educators who are comfortable with, and adept at, teaching the topic, all young people in schools today will be left behind.

What this means is that there needs to be significantly more pre-service and professional development for educators who plan to be providing sexuality education, whether in school- or community-based settings. Additionally, there needs to be significantly more pre-service and professional development for medical and other health professionals, and for therapists and sex therapists, who will be providing sexuality information and education through their one-on-one interactions with clients and patients. Furthermore, the topic of sexuality must be addressed from a developmental and normative standpoint, rather than focusing exclusively on sexual dysfunctions, assault survival, and so-called "deviancy" as too many programs do.

LESSON FOUR: SEXUALITY EDUCATION NEEDS TO DEFINE "EFFECTIVENESS"

Throughout this series, authors struggled with how they, and/or the relevant research to date, define "effective" sexuality education. What makes sexuality education effective? What are its goals and objectives? Is it only about pregnancy and STI prevention? Those are easy statistics to measure, but how those results come about has to do with many other sexuality-related issues, such as gender and gender roles, self-esteem, confusion about physiology, and more.

It is easy to measure increases in knowledge, but much more challenging to measure increases in self-esteem and the effects of those increases on sexual decision-making and attitudes. How, therefore, can effectiveness be defined and measured? Would sexuality education be seen as effective if homophobia and sexual orientation and gender-based hate crimes were eradicated? That certainly would be an outcome behind which many sexuality educators would be able to stand. Yet that does not encapsulate the full scope of sexuality education.

One solution: instead of trying to define effectiveness for sexuality education in general, effectiveness can be defined for each sub-topic or sub-component of sexuality education. For example, how a social worker in a retirement community defines the effectiveness of her HIV prevention workshop with the senior citizens there would be different from how a fourth grade teacher defines the effectiveness of his or her instructional unit on family diversity. What this means is that every educational intervention needs clearly-worded goals and objectives, and that through these goals and objectives the effectiveness of that intervention will be defined and can be measured. Consequently, publishing data with these setting-specific criteria will help determine which types of interventions within distinct aspects of sexuality education are effective, and, therefore, the circumstances under which sexuality education as an entire discipline can also be seen as effective.

LESSON FIVE: SEXUALITY EDUCATION NEEDS A MAKE-OVER

A metaphor I have used with some of my colleagues when referring to sexuality education today is approaching it in the same way one might approach painting a house. There are only so many times a person can apply coats of paint to a house before the house has to be sanded down to its original wood and a fresh coat of paint applied. Sexuality education desperately needs to be stripped down to its original wood. We need to be clear on what we hope to accomplish, and on what we can't. We need to stop fighting among ourselves as professionals about whether it is best to provide abstinence-only vs. comprehensive programs and listen to what the predominant, science-based research tells us—whatever that may be. We need to ensure that the people who are providing sexuality education are not fresh-out-of-college educators who are learning on the job, but educators who receive both pre-service and on-the-job training on sexuality education content and the skills for providing this content in ways that resonate with young people. They need to be taught the importance of maintaining professional boundaries when providing sexuality education, whether in a group setting or individually, and that sexuality education is a professional discipline, not an opportunity to share one's own personal experiences.

Included within this makeover is a paradigm shift away from curricula and programs that speak exclusively to girls and relegate them to the role of moral gatekeepers in different-sex sexual relationships because boys are incapable of doing so. We must focus on the unique needs and learning styles of boys, as well as those of girls. We must also equalize the type of education provided to learners of all ages by recognizing what the research tells us about learning styles and cultural norms, while at the same time being consistent in the equality of responsibility for sexual decision-making, sexual health, and sexual relationships, regardless of the gender(s) of the people in a given relationship.

Also included in this makeover should be the paradigm shift to move away from sexuality education being taught as its own subject exclusively, and instead to move toward integrating sexuality information, themes, and subjects throughout the entire school curriculum. English and literature classes should discuss sexuality-related themes in the materials being studied—in coordination with the sexuality education instructor so that the learning in both classes can be reinforced. In math, students would learn math and sexuality together if, for example, a homework assignment was to create a budget for having a baby as a teenager. Foreign language classes can use a sexuality-related theme as a topic of discussion, simultaneously offering an affective learning experience for students and an opportunity to strengthen their language skills. And so on. There are many books and articles available about "integrated school health" with other topics. But rather than integrating sexuality just into school health, it should be spread across the entire curriculum. To do so would take some work and professional development for instructors and administrators alike—but the outcomes of doing on young people's sexual development could be exceptionally positive and healthy.

Finally, we must significantly increase our efforts to help parents and adult caregivers to respond to questions and have open, comfortable discussions with their children about sexuality. If the topic is going to be addressed in even more detail at school—as well it should be—then parents and caregivers need to be given the support they need to reinforce the content at home and to contextualize the facts within their own values and belief systems.

LESSON SIX: SEXUALITY EDUCATION NEEDS TO BE MORE DIVERSE IN ITS CONTENT AND PEDAGOGICAL APPROACH

Every profession is filled with its own biases, and sexuality education is no different. Heterocentrism and bi-gender approaches pervade the information provided. How often does an educator teach about relationship issues using such language as, "in a relationship, is it the guy's responsibility to…or the girl's?" How often do educators offer an individual lesson about nonheterosexual sexual orientations, and then teach the remaining lessons toward male–female interactions? How often do educators refer to "LGBT" issues, only to ignore bisexual and transgender individuals? It is imperative that sexuality educators learn to always be thinking of "the other," whomever that "other" may be, and to use language and examples that include more than the power majority—heterosexual, white, able-bodied, and so on.

Diversity does not only refer to sexual orientation, of course. So many curricula and lessons are developed using a middle class, white, suburban orientation. While they certainly can be adapted for use in urban and rural communities, programs are needed that can be used in various settings—or, at the very least, recommendations need to be provided in curricula about how to adapt them for use with specific populations. No one curriculum will fit all learners, so there is much work to be done in this area.

Diversity also refers to age group. With so much advocacy for beginning sexuality education at kindergarten, for example, there is a dearth of materials to help educators be able to do so in age- and developmentally-appropriate ways. In addition, sexuality education does not—or, I should say, it should not—stop once a person completes college. If, as SIECUS advocates, sexuality is a lifelong process, there needs to be more resources for teaching adults about sexuality during various life-stages. Currently, sexuality education for adults is offered within the context of resolving a relationship issue or sexual dysfunction, rather than reinforcing previously-learned lessons or helping adults to understand the changes in functioning, desire, and needs as one journeys through each decade of one's life.

Similarly, there is very little being done for adults in mid- and later-life. Recently, SIECUS published a manual edited by veteran sexuality educators Peggy Brick and Jan Lunquist titled, *New Expectations*. In our ageist society, where youth is valued above all, the assumption that one ceases to become a sexual being upon reaching a particular age is perpetuated by a lack of information and education geared specifically toward adults in mid- and later-life. This must change.

Diversity also pertains to developmental and physical ability. One of the greatest travesties in our educational system today—in general, not just pertaining to sexuality education—is the extent to which young people with developmental challenges are peppered throughout classes with a varying level of support made available to them. When it comes to sexuality education, young people are grouped by age, not developmental functioning, which can range from severely limited to highly functioning. Developmental issues, whether learning disabilities, attention deficit or sensory integration issues, autism, or any others, not only influences the manner in which young people and adults understand sexuality, but also the manner in which their more higher-functioning counterparts learn as well. Sexuality education must be targeted—and provided—specifically to young people of different developmental levels, not to a hodgepodge of learners who are thrown together because there isn't sufficient time or space in a school environment to allow for separating the groups.

Sexuality education must also include individuals with physical challenges, who often, depending on the severity of the disability, are asexualized by the general public in the same way as individuals who are aging. Educational interventions should be made with parents of young people with disabilities at early ages; they should be made with young adults to help them navigate and negotiate healthy relationships; and they should be reinforced on an ongoing basis throughout an adult's life to help normalize the concept that everyone has a right to enjoy one's sexuality in healthy, consensual ways.

LESSON SEVEN: SEXUALITY EDUCATION MUST TEAM UP WITH THE MEDIA

In addition to teaching young people how to analyze and deconstruct media messages, sexuality education as a field must recognize the omnipresence and power of the media and, instead of railing against the myriad ways in which it makes working as a sexuality educator challenging, find ways of allying with the media.

In addition to the examples in this series, there have been organizations that have met with and served as consultants to television programs watched by individuals of varying age groups. Meetings with producers and directors from various soap operas, for example, resulted in the 1990s with storylines having to do with teen pregnancy, same-sex adult couples, a teenage girl coming out to her mother as lesbian, and much more than the stereotypically lurid sexual encounters between characters on many of these programs. Young people are learning about various aspects of sexuality through so-called "reality" television shows, ranging from sensationalized shock shows like *Jerry Springer* to MTV's *A Shot At Love with Tila Tequila*. These programs, although they often portray sexuality in exploitative and unhealthy ways, are teaching young people more frequently than formally school- or community-based sexuality education. Sexuality educators must work within this system to help portray more healthy examples of sexual health and relationships.

CONCLUSION: ONE VISION OF THE FUTURE

In 2001, Advocates for Youth, a national nonprofit organization based in Washington, DC that focuses on helping young people make informed decisions about their sexual and reproductive health, sponsored a sexuality education summit in Washington, DC. At this summit, sexuality educators Dr. Elizabeth Casparian, Dr. Eva Goldfarb and I offered a workshop on sexuality education advocacy for professionals from around the United States. As part of that workshop, we created a guided imagery that we read to participants of one proposed vision of the future of sexuality education.

The following is a slightly adapted version of that guided imagery, offering a view of what a positive school-based sexuality education future might look like:

> Picture yourself at a point in the future. You are working as a sexuality educator in a public high school in a community of your choosing. The community you choose for this fantasy does not matter, since age-appropriate sexuality education is required across the country for all K-12 students. The state you choose for this fantasy also does not matter because there is a standardized sexuality curriculum used nationwide, one with clear instructions for adapting the curriculum for use with any student population. This curriculum's primary goal is to create sexually healthy adolescents and adults—not just to reduce the spread of STIs and teen pregnancy. It was evaluated nationwide over a 10-year period, using an unprecedented sample size and methodologies that focused on the long-term effects of the curriculum on creating sexually healthy adolescents and adults.
>
> In your office, you look proudly on your framed certification, which you were mandated to earn before becoming a sexuality educator. It made sense to take this certification right after you graduated from your teacher training courses, since you took an entire year of human sexuality during your last semester there.
>
> One of the nicest aspects of your teacher training program was having some of the other faculty members you currently work with—the math, French, English, and social studies teachers, to name a few—in your human sexuality course with you. They, and all teachers, regardless of the topic they teach, are required to take a human sexuality course as part of their pre-service training. Federal law now requires that any youth-serving professionals must receive some basic sexuality information and education pre-service, and ongoing professional development about the same. This makes your job much easier, since themes related to sexuality are interwoven throughout the school curriculum in all subjects. In addition, part of the school curriculum focuses on life skills and job placement for noncollege bound and college bound students.
>
> You open your date book, and see that your afternoon will be spent meeting with the gay-straight-bi alliance. You need to plan the presentation the group will be making at the national conference of GSB alliances, since all 50 states will be represented there. This evening, you have your weekly sexuality education and communication programs for parents. You wonder whether you can begin to offer them more than once a week, since they are so well-attended!
>
> The newspaper open on your desk has a headline, "Comprehensive Sexuality Education Funding Renewed at Record Levels." This funding, which has been in effect for decades now, provides generous support to programs nationwide that provide comprehensive, life-enriching sexuality education programs. There is a photograph of the United States President and the bi-partisan committee that has ensured that this act is reintroduced and refunded every year. You flip your date book open again, reminding yourself to attend the monthly meeting of sexuality education advocates, which is coordinated by a statewide nonprofit organization.
>
> On the way to your classroom, you pass the school's health resource room, where education, health exams, and condoms are offered. Across the hall is the school's federally subsidized in-school daycare program that allows teen parents to attend school. All schools actively encourage teen parents to return to school and graduate, and you're particularly proud of your school's 100% return rate. Teen parents are

asked to speak about their experiences in the school's sexuality education classes, and already there has been a decrease in teen pregnancy in your school district.

In front of the school's main office, you drop your reimbursement forms in for the 3-day professional development program you attended last week. You still have 12 more professional development days left for the school year. Only teachers who are interested in and equipped to teach sexuality education actually teach it—but because there are so many teachers on staff who are equipped to teach sexuality education, your class is always covered on your professional development days. You return from each program you attend, as your colleagues do, excited to present what you learned to your fellow teachers and administrators in order to determine how the new material can be integrated throughout the curriculum.

You reach the classroom, which is filled with 20 students—the maximum number of students allowed in any classroom nationwide. The energy is high as you take your supplies out of the classroom desk and begin the day's lesson.

This guided imagery represents only one area of sexuality education, school-based programming. But it addresses some key components of what many educators believe would make this type of programming more successful, and that reflect the lessons learned from this four-volume series. These include: Prepared educators. Liberal funding for sexuality education and for professional development support for sexuality educators. School- and community-wide support. Parents and adult caregivers who participate in programs that enable them to reinforce what their children learn at school and that allow school professionals to reinforce parental values in the classroom. Small classrooms and sufficient time in which to address the information that needs to be addressed. A curriculum with a clear goal defining and then evaluating its effectiveness. Inclusive programming.

I do not think that this vision of the future is an impossibility—and I would venture to say that some of the authors in this book series agree with me. If the sexuality education field hones its goals and objectives, if organizations work together and if the field focuses on mentoring and growing its cadre of professionals in school-, community-, and clinic-based venues, this vision could become a very powerful reality.

REFERENCES

Bleakley, A., Hennessey, M. & Fishbein, M. (2006). Public opinion on sex education in U.S. schools. *Archives of Pediatrics and Adolescent Medicine, 160*(11), 1151–1156.

Darroch, J. E., Landry, D. J. & Singh, S. (2000). Changing emphases in sexuality education in U.S. public secondary schools, 1988–1999. *Family Planning Perspectives, 32*(5), 204–211, 265.

Ventura, S. J., Abma, J. C., Mosher, W. D., & Henshaw, S. (2004). Estimated pregnancy rates for the United States, 1990–2000: An update. *National Vital Statistics Reports 52*(23), 7. Hyattsville, MD: National Center for Health Statistics.

APPENDIX: REFERENCES FOR FURTHER INFORMATION ABOUT SEXUALITY EDUCATION

Lauren A. Antonecchia and Maria D. Ramirez

The following is a listing of resources that can be used to acquire additional information about issues addressed in this book series. The list is divided by type of resource, including membership and resource organizations, Web sites, journals, articles, sexuality education institutions, curricula, books, newsletters, magazines, videos/DVDs, film companies, sex museums, additional print resources, and innovations in the area of human sexuality education, with a brief description of each resource. Please keep in mind that this list is not comprehensive and that new resources will continue to become available over time.

MEMBERSHIP ORGANIZATIONS

Membership organizations give educators, counselors, and therapists the opportunity to pursue shared interest and discuss common concerns dealing with human sexuality and sexual health. Membership organizations further provide research and support that allow professionals to be better prepared in the field of human sexuality. Member groups exist for individual countries (e.g., the China Association of Sexology, South African Sexual Health Association, Associacion Argentina de Sexologia y Educacion Sexual, Indian Association of Sex Educators, Counselors, and Therapists) or for regions (e.g., the European Federation for Sexology, the Asia-Oceanic Federation for Sexology).

American Association of Sexuality Educators, Counselors, and Therapists (AASECT)
PO Box 1960
Ashland, VA 23005–1960
P: 804-752-0026

The American Association of Sexuality Educators, Counselors, and Therapists (AASECT) is a not-for-profit, interdisciplinary professional organization.
Web site: http://www.aasect.org

American School Health Association
7263 State Route 43
PO Box 708
Kent, Ohio 44240
P: 330-678-1601
F: 330-678-4526
E-mail: asha@ashaweb.org
Unites many professionals working in schools who are committed to safeguarding the health of school-aged children.
Web site: http://www.ashaweb.org

International Society for the Study of Women's Sexual Health (ISSWSH)
Two Woodfield Lake
1100 E. Woodfield Road, Suite 520
Schaumburg, IL 60173
P: 847-517-7225
F: 847-517-7229
Provides opportunities for communication among scholars, researchers, and practitioners about women's sexual function and sexual experience; supports the highest standards of ethics and professionalism in research, education, and clinical practice of women's sexuality; and provides the public with accurate information about women's sexuality and sexual health.
Web site: http://www.isswsh.org

Society for Sex Therapy and Research (SSTAR)
409 12th St., S.W., PO Box 96920
Washington, DC 20090–6920
P: 202-863-1644
Composed of a broad range of professionals who have clinical or research interests in human sexual concerns. SSTAR's goals are to facilitate communications among clinicians who treat problems of sexual function, sexual identity, and reproductive life and to provide a forum for exchange of ideas between those interested in research in human sexuality and those whose primary activities are patient care.
Web site: http://www.sstarnet.org

Society for the Scientific Study of Sexuality (SSSS)
PO Box 416
Allentown, PA 18105–0416
P: 610-530-2483
F: 610-530-2485
The oldest professional society dedicated to the advancement of knowledge about sexuality. SSSS holds annual conferences each year with presentations about the latest research and science about sexuality.
Web site: http://www.sexscience.org

Healthy Teen Network
1501 Saint Paul St., Ste. 124
Baltimore, MD 21202
P: 410-685-0410
F: 410-685-0481
The only national membership network that serves as a leader, a national voice, and a comprehensive educational resource to professionals working in the area of adolescent reproductive health—specifically teen pregnancy prevention, teen pregnancy, teen parenting, and related issues.
Web site: http://www.healthyteennetwork.org

World Association for Sexual Health (WAS)
Tezoquipa 26
Colonia La Joya
Delegacion Tlalapan
Mexico D.F. 14000
Mexico
WAS has worked in promoting sexual health for all. Sexual health is not a goal for clinicians only. Sexual health is the crystallization of our common goal. Sexuality education has the objective to facilitate sexually healthy lives of those who are being educated. Interventions in clinical sexology have the goal of restoring sexual health. Sex research, although objectively driven, has as its justification the creation of knowledge that supports others to attain and maintain sexual health.
Web site: http://www.worldsexology.org

RESOURCE ORGANIZATIONS

The main goal of this section is to provide a variety of different resources pertaining to human sexuality. Resource organizations make valuable information available without cost to professionals and all those who are interested in gaining more knowledge in this field.

Advocates For Youth
2000 M Street NW, Suite 750
Washington, DC 20036
P: 202-419-3420
F: 202-419-1448
Dedicated to creating programs and advocating for policies that help young people make informed and responsible decisions about their reproductive and sexual health. Advocates provide information, training, and strategic assistance to youth-serving organizations, policymakers, youth activists, and the media in the United States and the developing world.
Web site: http://www.advocatesforyouth.org

Centers for Disease Control and Prevention National Prevention Information Network
P.O. Box 6003
Rockville, MD 20849–6003

P: 1-800-458-5231

The CDC National Prevention Information Network (NPIN) is the U.S. reference, referral, and distribution service for information on HIV/AIDS, viral hepatitis, sexually transmitted diseases (STDs), and tuberculosis (TB). NPIN produces, collects, catalogs, processes, stocks, and disseminates materials and information on HIV/AIDS, Viral Hepatitis, STDs, and TB to organizations and people working in those disease fields in international, national, state, and local settings.

Web site: http://www.cdcnpin.org/scripts/index.asp

Gay Men's Health Crisis
119 West 24 Street
New York, NY 10011
P: 212-367-1000

An example of a community-based organization, which provides information and services, committed to the fight against AIDS and homophobia. Operates a hotline in Spanish and English.

Web site: http://www.gmhc.org

Girls Incorporated
120 Wall Street
New York, NY 10005
P: 212-509-2000

Girls Inc. develops research-based informal education programs that encourage girls to master physical, intellectual, and emotional challenges. Major programs address math and science education, pregnancy and drug abuse prevention, media literacy, economic literacy, adolescent health, violence prevention, and sports participation.

Web site: http://www.girlsinc.org/girls-inc.html

Health & Science Advisory Board
HSAB.org, LLC
7765 Lake Worth Rd., Suite 341
Lake Worth, FL 33467

The Health and Science Advisory Board is an interdisciplinary team comprised of more than 40 leading academics, educators, theologians, therapists, and medical professionals worldwide. The HSAB's mission is to provide practitioners, educators, and consumers with information and resources related to sexuality, health, and human relationships.

Web site: http://www.hsab.org

Kaiser Family Foundation
2400 Sand Hill Road
Menlo Park, CA 94025
P: 650-854-9400

Provides data and information on vast array of health issues, including HIV/AIDS and teen sexual activity and pregnancy.

Web site: http://www.kff.org

National Education Association Health Information Network
1201 16th Street NW

Washington, DC 20036
P: 202-822-7570
NEA HIN's mission is to improve the health and safety of school personnel
and students by providing the school community with vital and timely health
information that will increase teacher and education support professional (ESP)
quality and student achievement.
Web site: http://www.neahin.org

Planned Parenthood Federation of America
434 West 33rd Street
New York, NY 10001
P: 212-541-7800
Health Center Hotline: 1-800-230-PLAN
The official gateway to the online Planned Parenthood community and to a wealth
of reproductive health and rights information, services, and resources.
Web site: http://www.plannedparenthood.org

The Guttmacher Institute
120 Wall Street
New York, NY, 10005
P: 212-248-1111
F: 212-248-1951
A nonprofit organization focused on sexual and reproductive health research, policy
analysis, and public education.
Web site: http://www.guttmacher.org

The Women's Sexual Health Foundation
PO Box 40603
Cincinnati, Ohio 45240-0603
The Women's Sexual Health Foundation (TWSHF) is a nonprofit corporation
that supports a multidisciplinary approach to the treatment of sexual health issues
and serves as an educational resource for both the lay public and health care
professionals.
E-mail: info@twshf.org
Web site: http://www.twshf.org/

WEB SITES

These Web sites—as well as many of those organizations already listed—
present useful information for individuals and professionals as well as specific
cultural groups. Through these Web sites all those interested will gain a better
understanding of human sexuality and where they can go to meet their specific needs dealing with all matters of human sexuality.

Advocates for Youth
Dedicated to creating programs and advocating for policies that help young people
make informed and responsible decisions about their reproductive and sexual

health. Advocates for Youth believes it can best serve the field by boldly advocating for a more positive and realistic approach to adolescent sexual health.
http://www.advocatesforyouth.org

Ambiente Joven
Dedicated to the Young Latino/a Gay, Lesbian, Bisexual, and Transgender community in the United States with the goal of providing information about sexual health.
http://www.ambientejoven.org

American Psychological Association
Scientific and professional organization that represents psychology in the United States. References for books, articles, films and videos, organizations, and health information, pertaining to all fields of psychology, including human sexuality.
http://www.apa.org

American Social Health Association (ASHA)
Offers a wealth of information about health, focusing on sexually transmitted diseases.
http://www.ashastd.org/

Answer
A national organization dedicated to providing and promoting comprehensive sexuality education to young people and the adults who teach them. Includes a teen-to-teen sexuality education initiative that features the SEX, ETC Web site and magazine, and a nationwide training programs for youth-serving professionals.
http://answer.rutgers.edu
http://www.sexetc.org

The Birds and Bees Project
Provides comprehensive reproductive health information to youth and adults with specific areas of activity, including Internet-based education, classroom-based education, and community outreach. The message in all materials is positive, respectful, developmentally appropriate, and aims to compliment the education and values that people receive from their families and communities.
http://www.birdsandbees.org

The Body: The Complete HIV/AIDS Resource
The Web's largest source of information on HIV and AIDS. Read and listen to the latest news, research, and resources on HIV prevention, testing, and treatment.
http://www.thebody.com

CDC's Division of Adolescent and School Health (DASH)
Seeks to prevent the most serious health risk behaviors among children, adolescents, and young adults.
http://www.cdc.gov/HealthyYouth/index.htm

Children of Lesbians and Gays Everywhere (COLAGE)
The only national and international organization in the world specifically supporting young people with gay, lesbian, bisexual, and transgender parents.
http://www.colage.org

Education Training Research Associates (ETR) Resource Center for Adolescent Pregnancy and Prevention (ReCAPP)
Non-profit health education promotion organization known for state-of-the-art programs, professional training, and research in the area of adolescent pregnancy prevention as well as for publications and clearinghouse services. ReCAPP provides practical tools and information to effectively reduce sexual risk-taking behaviors.
http://www.etr.org/recapp/

Family Pride Coalition
Dedicated to advance the well-being of lesbian, gay, bisexual, and transgender parents and their families through mutual support, community collaboration, and public understanding.
http://www.familypride.org

The Gay, Lesbian, and Straight Education Network
The largest national organization of parents, educators, and students working to end homophobia in K–12 schools.
http://www.glsen.org

Gay Men of African Descent
Developing leadership among black gay men to address issues that they face including homophobia, isolation, discrimination, and invisibility. This mission is accomplished through trainings, social marketing campaigns, community forums, advocacy, and direct client services.
http://www.gmad.org

Go Ask Alice! Columbia University's Health Q&A Internet Service
Question and answers on many topics, with a health focus. From Columbia University's Health Education Program, with a searchable database.
http://www.goaskalice.columbia.edu

Human Rights Campaign
Works for lesbian, gay, bisexual, and transgender equal rights by lobbying the federal government, participating in election campaigns, mobilizing grassroots actions in diverse communities, and educating the public about GLBT issues.
http://www.hrc.org

Intersex Society of North America
Devoted to systemic change to end shame, secrecy, and unwanted genital surgeries for people born with an anatomy that someone decided is not standard for male or female.
http://www.isna.org

My Sistahs
Created by and for young women of color to provide information and offer support on sexual and reproductive health issues through education and advocacy.
http://www.mysistahs.org

The National Campaign to Prevent Teen and Unplanned Pregnancy
Seeks to improve the lives and future prospects of children and families and, in particular, to prevent teen pregnancy and unplanned pregnancy among single, young adults. Supports a combination of responsible values and behavior by both men and women and responsible policies in both the public and private sectors.
http://www.teenpregnancy.org

National Gay and Lesbian Task Force
A national organization that advocates for the civil rights of GLBT individuals. Building the grassroots power of the lesbian, gay, bisexual, and transgender (LGBT) community by training activists, equipping state and local organizations with the skills needed to organize broad-based campaigns to defeat anti-LGBT referenda and advance pro-LGBT legislation, and building the organizational capacity of our movement.
http://www.ngltf.org

The National Latina/o Lesbian, Gay, Bisexual, & Transgender Organization
This site is designed to build and strengthen the national network of Latina/o GLBT community based organizations. Information on over 170 affiliated organizations nationally.
http://www.llego.org

National Sexuality Resource Center
The National Sexuality Resource Center gathers and disseminates the latest accurate information and research on sexual health, education, and rights in the United States. The Web site has a news feed about sexuality, sexual health, and gender issues; rotating slideshows about topical issues; and links to *American Sexuality* (targeted to consumers), the *Journal of Sexuality Research and Social Policy* (empirical research), and the University Consortium for Sexuality Research and Training (online networking tool for researchers).
http://www.nsrc.sfsu.edu

Outproud
Serves the needs of GLBT young men and women by providing advocacy, information, resources, and support. Goal is to help queer youth become happy, successful, confident, and vital gay, lesbian, and bisexual adults.
http://www.outproud.org

Renaissance Transgender Association
Support and information for transgendered individuals. Provides comprehensive education and caring support to transgendered individuals and those close to them. This is accomplished through offering a variety of carefully selected programs and resources focused on the factors affecting their lives.
http://www.ren.org

Sex, Etc.
Web site by and for teens; teens and parents can submit questions to a sexuality expert and receive a personal response. A program of Answer at Rutgers University (see previous entry).
http://www.sexetc.org

SexEDLibrary
A highly acclaimed and comprehensive online sex-ed resource by SIECUS (the
Sexuality Information and Education Council of the United States) for educators,
counselors, administrators, and health professionals seeking the latest in human
sexuality research, lesson plans, and professional development opportunities.
http://www.sexedlibrary.org

Sexuality Information and Education Council of the United States (SIECUS)
Develops, collects, and disseminates information; promotes comprehensive
education about sexuality; and advocates the right of individuals to make
responsible sexual choices.
http://www.siecus.org

Talking with Kids about Tough Issues
A national initiative by Children Now and The Kaiser Family Foundation to
encourage parents to talk with their children earlier and more often about tough
issues such as sex, HIV/AIDS, violence, alcohol, and drug abuse.
http://www.talkingwithkids.org

Teenwire
The Planned Parenthood Federation of America Web site for teens, staffed
by professionals who are dedicated to providing the information you need on
relationships and sexuality.
http://www.teenwire.com

Transfamily
Homepage includes many resources for family members of transgender persons. A
Trans 101 written with children of Trans people in mind.
http://www.transfamily.org

Transproud
OutProud's home on the Web for transgender youth. Includes resources and
information, including news, questions and answers, related links, message board,
support, referrals, and more.
http://www.transproud.com

JOURNALS

Professionals can submit research, reviews, commentar, and other contributions. Some countries have journals open to worldwide readership and submissions (e.g., the *British Journal of Sexual Medecine*) or in local language (e.g.,
the *Chinese Journal of Human Sexuality*). These publications provide current
research, practice methods, and information on a plethora of human sexuality
material.

American Journal of Sexuality Education
Editor: William J. Taverner, MA

Publisher: Taylor & Francis
This peer-reviewed journal provides sexuality educators and trainers at all skill levels with current research about sexuality education programming and "best practices," sample lesson plans, reports on curriculum development and assessment, literature reviews, scholarly commentary, educational program reports, media reviews (books, videos, Internet resources, and curricula), and letters to the editor.
Web site: http://www.tandf.co.uk/journals/titles/15546128.asp

The Canadian Journal of Human Sexuality
Editor: Alex McKay
Quarterly peer-reviewed academic journal focusing on the medical, psychological, social, and educational aspects of human sexuality.
Web site: http://www.sieccan.org/cjhs.html

Electronic Journal of Human Sexuality
Editor: David S. Hall, PhD
To disseminate knowledge about all aspects of human sexuality to the widest possible international community at moderate cost.
Web site: http://ejhs.org/

Journal of LGBT Youth
Editor: James T. Sears, PhD
Publisher: Haworth Press
Covers the latest international perspectives on the issues that impact GLBT students and educators.
Web site: http://www.haworthpress.com/store/product.asp?sku=J524&sid=0HEW LLMQK2BF9HJ7AM27SKKVD1TQ6VH4&

Journal of GLBT Family Studies
Editor: Jerry J. Bigner, PhD
Publisher: Haworth Press
The *Journal of GLBT Family Studies* is the first journal to address family issues and concerns important to GLBT individuals and their families of origin, as well as families formed in adulthood.
Web site: http://www.haworthpress.com/store/product.asp?sku=J461

Journal of Psychology & Human Sexuality
Editor: Eli Coleman, PhD
Publisher: Haworth Press
Encompasses clinical, counseling, educational, social, experimental, psycho-endocrinological, and psycho-neuroscience research devoted to the study of human sexuality. It fills an existing gap in the psychological literature by specifically covering issues in the field of sexual science.
Web site: http://www.haworthpress.com/store/product.asp?sku=J056

The Journal of Sex Research
Editor: Cynthia A. Graham, PhD
A scholarly journal devoted to the publication of articles relevant to the variety of disciplines involved in the scientific study of sexuality. *JSR* is designed to stimulate

research and to promote an interdisciplinary understanding of the diverse topics in contemporary sexual science.
Web site: http://www.sexscience.org/publications/index.php?category_id=439

Sex Education: Sexuality, Society and Learning
Publisher: Routledge
An international refereed journal concerned with the practice of sex education and its underpinnings from various disciplines.
Web site: http://www.tandf.co.uk/journals/carfax/14681811.html

Sexuality Research and Social Policy
Editor: Gilbert Herdt
Official online journal of the National Sexuality Resource Center, publishes multidisciplinary state-of-the-art empirical research on sexuality, theoretical and methodological discussions, and implications for U.S. and international policies regarding sexual health, sexuality education, and sexual rights in diverse communities. Also includes brief research and conference reports, white papers, book, film, and other reviews, along with guest editorials and commentaries.
Web site: http://nsrc.sfsu.edu/sexuality_research_social_policy

SEXUALITY EDUCATION HIGHER EDUCATION INSTITUTIONS

Below are examples of undergraduate and graduate programs that focus on or result in a degree in fields most directly related to human sexuality. These are recognized institutions throughout the United States and Canada. Most colleges have courses, if not degrees, in subjects like Women's Studies and Gender and Sexuality, which can be found by searching on the web or at sites like http://userpages.umbc.edu/~korenman/wmst/programs.html. Programs of such study also exist in other parts of the world.

Undergraduate

California State University-Northridge
Undergraduate Interdisciplinary Minor in Human Sexuality
18111 Nordhoff Street
Northridge, CA 91330
P: 818-677-4830
F: 818-677-4778
Web site: http://www.csun.edu/~sr2022/minor.ht

New York University
Undergraduate Program in Gender and Sexuality Studies
Center for the Study of Gender and Sexuality
41 East 11th Street, Seventh Floor
New York, NY 10003
Phone: 212-992-9540

Fax: 212-995-4433
E-mail: gender.sexuality@nyu.edu
Web site: http://www.nyu.edu/csgs/

Ohio State University
Interdisciplinary Minor in Sexuality Studies
Graduate Interdisciplinary Specialization in Sexuality Studies
186 University Hall
230 North Oval Mall20
Columbus, OH 43210
P: 614-292-1882
F: 614-292-8666
E-mail: humanities@osu.edu
Web site: http://sexualitystudies.osu.edu

San Francisco Sate University
Undergraduate Minor / Graduate Program in Human Sexuality Studies
1600 Holloway Avenue
San Francisco. CA 94132
P: 415-405-3570
F: 415-405-0411
Web site: http://hmsx.sfsu.edu

University of Iowa
Undergraduate Interdisciplinary Program in Sexuality Studies
120 Schaeffer Hall
Iowa City, IA 52242
P: 319-335-2633
F: 319-335-2439

University of Minnesota
Undergraduate Program in Gender, Women, and Sexuality Studies
Minneapolis, MN 55455
E-mail: gwss@umn.edu

University of Pennsylvania
Undergraduate Program in Gender, Culture, and Society
(Specialization in Sexuality Studies)
411 Logan Hall
249 South 36th Street
Philadelphia, PA 19104–6304
P: 215-898-8740
Web site: http://www.sas.upenn.edu/wstudies/

Graduate/Professional Training

The American Academy of Clinical Sexologists
Ph.D. Program in Clinical Sexology

3203 Lawton Road, Suite 170
Orlando, FL 32893
P: 407-645-1641
Web site: http://www.esextherapy.com

Answer
Online Professional Development Programs
Rutgers University
41 Gordon Road, Suite C
Piscataway, New Jersey 08854–8067
P: 732-445-7929
F: 732-445-7970

California State University, Northridge
College of Social and Behavioral Sciences
Human Sexuality Program
Center for Sex Research
18111 Nordhoff Street
Northridge, CA 91324

Columbia University School of Public Health
Center for Gender Sexuality and Health
Graduate Degree in Sexuality and Health Allan Rosenfield Building
722 West 168th Street
New York, New York 10032
P: 212-305-5656
E-mail: ph-admit@columbia.edu
Web site: http://www.mailman.hs.columbia.edu/sms/programs/sexhealth-track.html

Curtin University of Technology
Graduate Program in Sexology/Doctoral Program in Sexology/Forensic Sexology
School of Public Health
P: +61 (08) 9266 7819
F: +61 (08) 9266 2958
E-mail: enquiry@health.curtin.edu.au
Web site: http://www.publichealth.curtin.edu.au/html/areasofstudy_s.htm

Engender Health
Online Self-Instructional Mini-course on Sexuality and Sexual Health
440 Ninth Ave. New York, NY 10001
P: 212-561-8000
E-mail: info@engenderhealth.org
Web site: http://www.engenderhealth.org/pubs/courses/

The Fogel Foundation
Human Sexuality Institute
Continuing Education, Training Programs and Workshops in Human Sexuality
7920 Old Georgetown Road
Bethesda, MD 20814

P: 301-907-8777
Web site: http://www.thefogelfoundation.org

HIV Center for Clinical and Behavioral Studies
Postdoctoral Behavioral Science Research Training Program in HIV Infection
1051 Riverside Drive, Unit 15
New York, NY 10032
P: 212-543-5969
F: 212-543-6003
Web site: http://www.hivcenternyc.org/training/nrsa.html

Indiana University/Kinsey Institute for Research in Sex, Gender, and Reproduction
Graduate Program in Human Sexuality
Bloomington, IN 47405
P: 812-855-8853
E-mail: kinsey@indiana.edu
Web site: www.kinseyinstitute.org

The Institute for Advanced Study of Human Sexuality
Graduate/Doctoral Programs in Human Sexuality
1523 Franklin Street
San Francisco, CA 94109
P: 415-928-1133
F: 415-928-8061
E-mail: registrar@iashs.edu
Web site: http://www.iashs.edu

The Magnus Hirschfeld Archive for Sexology
Online Courses in sexual health, offered not-for-credit, covering the topics of
Human Sexual Anatomy and Physiology, Human Reproduction, Physical Problems
in Females and Males, Sexually Transmitted Diseases, Sexual Dysfunctions and
Human Sexual Behavior. These open access curricula in sexual health are offered in
Spanish, German, English, Hungarian, Mandarin, and Yugoslavian.
Web site: http://www2.hu-berlin.de/sexology/index.html

Masters and Johnson Institute
Trauma, Dissociative Disorders and Sexual Compulsivity Programs
River Oaks Psychiatric Hospital
1525 River Oaks Rd. West
New Orleans, LA 70123
P: 504-734-1740
For program information: 1-800-598-2040

Medical College of Wisconsin
Postdoctoral Fellowship Program in HIV Behavioral Research
Center for AIDS Intervention Research (CAIR)
Department of Psychiatry and Behavioral Medicine

2071 North Summit Avenue
Milwaukee, WI 53202
P: 414-955-7700
F: 414-287-4206
Web site: http://www.mcw.edu/display/docid215.htm

Universite du Quebec, Montreal
Graduate Program in Sexology
Département de sexologie
P: 514-987-3504
F: 514-987-6787
Web site: http://www.regis.uqam.ca/prod/owa/pkg_wpub.affiche_prog_desc?P_
prog=3713

University of Arkansas
Graduate/Doctoral Programs in Health Science
Program in Health Science
HP 326A
University of Arkansas
Fayetteville, AR 72701
P: 501-575-5639
F: 501-575-6401
Web site: http://www.uark.edu/depts/hepoinfo/

University of Guelph
Graduate and Doctoral Programs in Family Relations and
Human Development
50 Stone Road East
Guelph, Ontario, N1G 2W1
Canada
P: 519-824-4120 ext. 56321
Web site: http://www.family.uoguelph.ca

University of Hawaii at Manoa, John A. Burns School of Medicine
Department of Anatomy and Reproductive Biology
1951 East-West Road
Honolulu, HI 96822
P: 808-956-7131
F: 808-956-9481
Web site: http://www.jabsom.hawaii.edu/Grad_Physiol

University of Kansas
Women, Gender, and Sexuality Studies
1440 Jayhawk Blvd., Rm. 213
Lawrence, Kansas 66045- 7574
P: 785-864-4012
Web site: http://www.womensstudies.ku.edu/

University of Minnesota Medical School
Postdoctoral fellowships in Human Sexuality and Behavioral Medicine
Department of Family Medicine and Community Health
1300 So. Second St., Suite 180
Minneapolis, MN 55454
P: 612-625-1500
F: 612-626-8311
Director: Eli Coleman, Ph.D.
Web site: http://www.med.umn.edu/fm/phs/home.html

University of Sydney
Graduate Program in Sexual Health
(Distance/Flexible Learning Option)
East Street, PO Box 170
Lidcombe, NSW 1825
Australia
Web site: http://www.usyd.edu.au/sexualhealth/

University of Utah
Doctoral Program in Clinical Psychology with research in Human Sexuality
Department of Psychology
380 S. 1530 E. Room 502
Salt Lake City, Utah 84112
P: 801-581-6123
F: 801-581-5841

University of Washington
Center for AIDS and STD
Training/Graduate Certificate / Research in AIDS and STDs
325 9th Ave, Campus Box 359931
Seattle, WA 98104
P: 206-744-4239
F: 206-744-3693
Web site: http://depts.washington.edu/cfas/training/index.html#2

University of Waterloo
Program in Sexuality, Marriage, and Family
200 University Avenue West
Waterloo, Ontario, Canada N2L 3G1
P: +1 519-884-8110
E-mail: smf@sju.uwaterloo.ca
Web site: http://www.ucalendar.uwaterloo.ca/ARTS/smf.html

Widener University
Graduate Program in Human Sexuality Education
One University Place
Chester, PA 19013–5792
P: 610-499-4372
E-mail: humansexualityprogram@widener.edu
Web site: http://www.widener.edu

University of Wisconsin
Doctoral Training in Sexuality Research
Department of Sociology
University of Wisconsin
1180 Observatory Dr.
Madison, WI 53706–1393
P: 608-262-4357
F: 608-262-8400

CURRICULA

These training programs offer material to help educators in teaching areas of human sexuality. Such education programs provide full lesson plans and activities that build on sexuality information, interpersonal skills, and decision making, as well as problem solving and life skills.

Abstinence: Pick and Choose Activities for Grades 7–12
Written by Michael Young, PhD, and Tamera Young
ETR Associates, 1996
Santa Cruz, CA
Includes 40 abstinence activities, enhances students' self-esteem, builds interpersonal skills, develops decision-making skills, teaches valuable life-planning skills, and includes background information, step-by-step procedures, and student activity sheets.

Be Proud! Be Responsible!
Select Media
An education program emphasizing HIV prevention that consists of eight one-hour modules that include group discussions, videos, games, brainstorming, experiential exercises, and skill building. The program has been successfully tested among young African American adolescents.
For more information:
P: 1-800-707-6334
Web site: http://www.etr.org/recapp/programs/proud.htm

Becoming A Responsible Teen (BART)
ETR Associates
An education program focusing on HIV prevention that consists of eight 1 1/2- to 2-hour sessions that include group discussions, role plays, and activities focusing on creative problem solving and extending learning beyond the classroom. The program uses an Afro-centric approach.
For more information:
P: 1-800-321-4407
Web site: http://www.etr.org

Carrera Program
Developed by noted sexologist Michael Carrera with the Children's Aid Society. The Adolescent Pregnancy Prevention Program is a nationally recognized teen

model that addresses seven components of life skills. The program has been shown to be highly successful in reducing teen pregnancy and improving teen school performance and is being implemented in school curricula.
For more information:
P: 212-949-4800
Web site: http://www.childrensaidsociety.org/cas/teenpreg.html

¡Cuidate!
This HIV-prevention curriculum is tailored for use with Latino adolescents. Its goals are to (1) influence attitudes, beliefs, and self-efficacy regarding HIV risk reduction, especially abstinence and condom use; (2) highlight cultural values that support safer sex practices; (3) reframe cultural values that might be perceived as barriers to safer sex; and (4) emphasize how cultural values influence attitudes and beliefs in ways that affect sexual risk behaviors. It consists of six one-hour modules delivered over consecutive days. The program is recommended for urban Latino youth ages 13–18.
For More Information:
Antonia M. Villarruel at the University of Michigan School of Nursing
400 N. Ingalls, Suite 4320
Ann Arbor, MI, 48109–0482
P: 734-615-9696
E-mail: avillarr@umich.edu

Educating about Abortion
Peggy Brick & Bill Taverner
Planned Parenthood of Greater Northern New Jersey
A compilation of 9 student-centered lessons. Includes 16 interactive worksheets, plus a special resource for pregnant women: Unsure about pregnancy? A guide to making the right decisions.
Web site for this and other PPGNNJ resources: http://www.ppgnnj.org/edu/index.php?sub=books

F.L.A.S.H.: Family Life and Sexual Health Grades 5–6, 7–8, 9–10, and 11–12
Elizabeth Reis
Seattle-King County Department of Public Health:
Comprehensive sexuality education curriculum addressing such issues as physical development, promotion of sexual health, prevention of disease, affection, interpersonal relationships, body image, and gender roles.
Order online: http://www.metrokc.gov/health/famplan/flash

Focus on Kids
ETR Associates
An education program emphasizing HIV prevention that consists of eight sessions that provide facts about HIV prevention and emphasize skills development with regard to communication, decision making, and condom use. The program uses an Afro-centric approach.
For more information:

P: 1-800-321-4407
Web site: http://www.etr.org

Get Real About AIDS
Sociometrics
An education program with 14 one-hour sessions including group discussions,
lectures, public service announcements, role-plays, and videos.
For more information:
P: 650-949-3282
Web site: http://www.socio.com/srch/summary/pasha/paspp01.htm

Making Connections: Identifying the Links Between Body Image and Sexual
Health
ETR ReCAPP Web site, 2001
Through small group work, discussion, and brainstorming, participants discuss the
connection between negative body image and risky sexual behavior. Ages 12–18.
Web site: http://www.etr.org/recapp/freebies/freebie200111.htm

Making Smart Choices About Sex
Eva S. Goldfarb, PhD, and Elizabeth Schroeder, EdD, MSW
The foundation of this three-session abstinence curriculum for adolescents
is that postponing sex is a positive, life-enhancing decision. Topics covered
include: reasons for postponing sex, setting goals, making healthy choices,
and effective communication. Each kit contains the curriculum, 30 interactive
CDs, 30 homework packets, and 30 pre- and post-tests. For grades 7 and 8 (or
younger).
Call 877-603-7306 for information on Product Preview and Training.
Web site: http://www.metrix-marketing.com/dbID/90.html

The New Teaching Safer Sex
Peggy Brick and Colleagues
This manual is designed to provide young people with opportunities to acquire
the knowledge, attitudes, and skills they need to practice safer sexual behavior. It
consists of 21 skill-based lessons targeted to adolescents and young adults. The
lessons can also be used for training teachers, counselors, and parents. Lessons
cover topics such as abstinence, STDs, communication skills, HIV/AIDS, and
condoms.
Planned Parenthood of Greater Northern New Jersey
196 Speedwell Ave.
Morristown, NJ 07960
P: 973-539-9580
F: 973-539-3828
Web site: http://www.ppgnnj.org

Open Minds to Equality: A Sourcebook of Learning Activities to Affirm Diversity
and Promote Equality
Editors: Nancy Schniedewind and Ellen Davidson

This is a practical book for teachers for building multicultural, gender-fair classrooms and for teaching students about both discrimination and approaches to equality. Grounded in theory but fully accessible to teachers, the book's first two chapters explain the need for equitable classrooms, and the remaining chapters provide activities with full-size worksheets for use with children. This is a "teacher-friendly" book that opens teachers' and students' eyes, hearts, and minds to equality.

Our Whole Lives: Sexuality Education for Grades K–1
Barbara Sprung
8 sessions, 1 hour each
Unitarian Universalist Association
Supports parents in educating children about birth, babies, bodies and families. Following a Parent Meeting and Parent/Child Orientation, the eight class sessions engage children with stories, songs, and activities and include a weekly HomeLink—a homework project for parents and children to do together. Promotes dialogue between parent and child. Appropriate for use in classroom and home settings.
Web site: http://www.uuabookstore.org

Our Whole Lives: Sexuality Education for Grades 4–6
Elizabeth Casparian, PhD, and Eva Goldfarb, PhD
Unitarian Universalist Association
8 sessions, 1 hour each
Participants learn about and discuss the physical and emotional changes of puberty. Participants will read *It's Perfectly Normal* by Robie Harris and examine topics such as values and sexuality, communication, and decision making. Each session includes a HomeLink—a homework activity for parents and children to complete together. Note: This program is designed for use with either a grades 4–5 group, a grades 5–6 group, or with one of the three grades separately.

Our Whole Lives: Sexuality Education for Grades 7–9
Pamela M. Wilson
Unitarian Universalist Association
25 sessions, 1 1/2 hours each
Presents a comprehensive approach to human sexuality in an age-appropriate manner. Based firmly on the values of respect, responsibility, justice, and inclusivity, this program helps young people apply these values to their behavior and provides them with information and skills they can use throughout life. Includes a comprehensive parent orientation.
Web site: http://www.uuabookstore.org

Our Whole Lives: Sexuality Education for Grades 10–12
Eva S. Goldfarb and Elizabeth M. Casparian
Unitarian Universalist Association
12 sessions, 2 hours each
Using a comprehensive approach, this program helps senior-high youth gain the knowledge, life principles, and skills they need to express their sexuality in

life-enhancing ways. Includes a parent orientation. Adaptable for classroom, after school, or youth group settings.
Web site: http://www.uuabookstore.org

Positive Encounters: Supporting Healthy Contraceptive and Safer Sex Decisions
Amy Vogelaar
These two volumes provide information, values clarification activities, and exercises to help adults have "positive encounters" that support the healthy decision—making of youth. The first volume is a manual on how to provide a training work shop for professionals about having positive encounters with youth. The second is a guidebook that complements what is learned in the workshop and can serve as a desk reference for professionals who work with youth.
Planned Parenthood of Greater Northern New Jersey
196 Speedwell Ave.
Morristown, NJ 07960
P: 973-539-9580
F: 973-539-3828
Web site: http://www.ppgnnj.org

Positive Images: Teaching Abstinence, Contraception, and Sexual Health
Peggy Brick and Bill Taverner
This manual focuses on prevention behaviors as well as the developmental, social, emotional, interpersonal, historical, cultural, and cross-cultural forces that shape healthy behavior change. Intended as a supplement to existing curricula, the manual includes 29 activities for middle school, high school, and college-age groups.
Planned Parenthood of Greater Northern New Jersey
196 Speedwell Ave.
Morristown, NJ 07960
P: 973-539-9580
F: 973-539-3828
Web site: http://www.ppgnnj.org

Project SAFE (Sexual Awareness for Everyone)
This gender- and culture-specific behavioral intervention consists of three sessions, each lasting three to four hours. Designed specifically for young African American and Latina women ages 15 through 24, it actively involves participants in lively and open discussion and games, videos, role plays, and behavior modeling. Discussions cover abstinence, mutual monogamy, correct and consistent condom use, compliance with STI treatment protocols, and reducing the number of one's sex partners. Each participant is encouraged to identify realistic risk reduction strategies that she can use in the context of her own life and values.
For more information or to order, contact:
Sociometrics, Program Archive on Sexuality, Health & Adolescence
P: 1-800-846-3475
F: 650-949-3299
E-mail: pasha@socio.com
Web site: http://www.socio.com

Reducing the Risk (RTR)
A sex education curriculum, including information on abstinence and contraception. In 16, 45-minute sessions, it offers experiential activities to build skills in refusal, negotiation, and communication, including that between parents and their children. Designed for use with high school students, especially those in grades 9 and 10, it is recommended for use with sexually inexperienced, urban, suburban, and rural youth—white, Latino, Asian, and black. For more information or to order, contact:
Sociometrics, Program Archive on Sexuality, Health & Adolescence
Phone: 1-800-846-3475
Fax: 650-949-3299
E-mail: pasha@socio.com
Web site: http://www.socio.com
Or:
ETR Associates
P: 1-800-321-4407
Web site: http://www.etr.org

Streetwise to Sex-Wise: Sexuality Education for High-Risk Youth
Steve Brown and Bill Taverner
This manual is intended as a supplement to a sexuality education curriculum and focuses on issues of particular concern to high-risk teens. It consists of 25 lessons broken up into two series: one for young teenagers ages 9–13 and one for older teenagers ages 14–19. Topics addressed include communication and decision-making skills, contraception, STDs, sexual orientation, and sexual abuse.
Planned Parenthood of Greater Northern New Jersey
196 Speedwell Ave.
Morristown, NJ 07960
P: 973-539-9580
F: 973-539-3828
Web site: http://www.ppgnnj.org

Wise Guys/"Jovenes Sabios" (Spanish Version)
Family Life Council of Greater Greensboro
A 13-session male responsibility curriculum for young adolescent males.
For more information:
P: 1-800-333-6890
Web site: http://www.greensboro.com/family/wiseguys.htm

BOOKS

This list is a selection of books that provide information as well as storytelling on all aspects of human sexuality. These books allow readers to examine issues pertaining to specific age groups, topics, and cultures. In addition to providing access to understanding human sexuality and its impact, these books provide a way for adults to talk about uncomfortable topics with children and young adults in ways that are informative and easier to talk about.

The Adonis Complex: The Secret Crisis of Male Body Obsession
Harrison G. Pope Jr., Katharine A. Phillips, and Roberto Olivardia
Free Press, 2000
This interesting and provocative book describes a form of obsession in which otherwise healthy men become absorbed by compulsive exercising, eating disorders, body-image distortion, and ultimately, abuse of anabolic steroids.

Beyond Dolls & Guns: 101 Ways to Help Children Avoid Gender Bias
Susan Hoy Crawford
Heinemann, 1996
This easy-to-read guide gives anyone concerned about children practical and simple suggestions to challenge the gender bias pervasive in most communities. Includes a section on current research on girls and boys and a bibliography of nonsexist children's and adult reference books.

Beyond the Big Talk: Every Parent's Guide to Raising Sexually Healthy Teens from Middle School to High School and Beyond
Debra Haffner
New Market Press, 2002
Examining issues ranging from physical development to peer pressure to youth culture, the book is arranged by grade level and explores issues especially relevant to particular age groups and offers solid advice and resources to parents, who will greatly appreciate her candor.

Bodies and Biases: Sexualities in Hispanic Cultures and Literatures
Edited by David William Foster and Roberto Reis
University of Minnesota Press, 1996
Looking at a wide range of cultural practices and artifacts, including television, popular music, and pornography, this book addresses representations of sexual behavior and collective identity, homosexuality, and ideologies of gender in historical and contemporary Hispanic culture. Topics include cross-dressing on the seventeenth-century Spanish stage, gay life in Cuba and Mexico, a butch-femme reading of Peri-Rossi's Solitario de amor, pornography, and queer and lesbian spaces. Reflecting a diversity of sociological, literary, and psychological theoretical underpinnings, *Bodies and Biases* is a fascinating analysis of sexuality in the context of Hispanic literature and culture.

Boys Will Be Men: Raising our Sons for Courage, Caring and Community
Paul Kivel
New Society Publishers, 1999
Drawing on his decades of experience as a social activist and his antiviolence work with men and teens, Kivel challenges the traditional training boys receive and urges

parents to raise sons to be critically thinking, socially invested men and agents of change in a violent world.

"But How'd I Get in There in the First Place?": Talking to Your Young Child about Sex
Deborah Roffman
Perseus Press, 2002
Young children ask questions about sex, sexuality, conception, and birth that can be embarrassing or uncomfortable for parents. This book's guidance can put even the most awkward parents at ease, giving them the skills to talk confidently with young children about these important but delicate issues.

Caution: Do Not Open Until Puberty! An Introduction to Sexuality for Young Adults with Disabilities
Rick Enright
Devinjer House, 1995
This book attempts to break the silence that seems to prevent an open discussion of sexuality with disabled adolescents and their families. Also recommended for professionals and parents looking for a nonthreatening and humorous way to discuss sexuality with children and adolescents.

Changing Bodies, Changing Lives
Ruth Bell
Random House, 1998
Packed with information on sex, the body, sexual harassment, and relationships. Teens' personal stories about these topics are used throughout the book.

The Complete Idiots Guide to Dating
Dr. Judy Kuriansky
Alpha Books, 3rd edition, 2003
Dating never gets easier. Here's time-tested advice for everyone from first-daters to those who have been around the block. Loaded with information on how to meet interesting people, break the ice, keep conversations going, and find the relationship of your dreams.

The Complete Idiots Guide to a Healthy Relationship
Dr. Judy Kuriansky
Alpha Books, 2nd edition, 2002
Offers advice that is relevant and useful to anyone in any relationship. Dealing with more than one aspect of relationships, the book covers all the bases: what constitutes a healthy relationship, how to keep the passion alive, and how to overcome obstacles to a long-lasting relationship. New chapters on relationships in the new millennium, including content on managing long-distance relationships and relating in the Internet age, are included in this second edition.

The Complete Idiots Guide to Tantric Sex
Dr. Judy Kuriansky
Alpha Books, 2nd edition, 2004

Comprehensive guide to the increasingly popular practices of tantric sexuality. Includes all the basics and more advanced practices about sacred loving and enlightenment, as well as unique chapters on adaptations for all ages, stages, and types of relationships and techniques for healing, better health, and peace.

Continuum Complete International Encyclopedia of Sexuality
Robert T. Francoeur, PhD, and Raymond J. Noonan, PhD, Editors
The Continuum International Publishing Group, New York and London, 2004
Written by more than 200 leading sexologists in their respective countries and cultures, each lengthy entry explores such areas as heterosexual relationships, children, adolescents, adults, gender-conflicted persons, unconventional sexual patterns, contraception, sexually transmitted diseases, AIDS, sexual dysfunctions, and therapies. It also includes sexual issues for older persons and physically and mentally challenged individuals.

The Facts of Life . . . and More: Sexuality and Intimacy for People with Intellectual Disabilities
Leslie Walker-Hirsch, M.Ed., FAAMR (editor)
Brookes Publishing Co., 2007
This book gives teachers, caregivers, and direct support professionals the information they need to educate people with disabilities about sexuality and help them make the best possible choices throughout their lives. Also includes interviews that show how couples with disabilities handle the joys and challenges of their relationships. It assists people in managing risks associated with sexual activity and uses behavior interventions to encourage appropriate sexual expression.

Families Like Mine: Children of Gay Parents Tell It Like It Is
Abigail Garner
HarperCollins, 2004
Abigail Garner was five when her parents divorced and her dad came out as gay. Growing up immersed in gay culture, she now calls herself a "culturally queer" heterosexual woman. This is a deeply personal book about gay parenting, from the perspective of grown children raised in these families.

Family Book
Todd Parr
Two Lives Publishing, 2003
Family favorite Todd Parr celebrates all kinds of families, including LGBTQ: "Some families have two moms or two dads . . ." Simple drawings of people, pets, and other animals are perfect for kids ages: 2 and up.

Flight of the Stork: What Children Think (and When) About Sex and Family Building
Anne C. Berstein
Perspective Press, 1996
Provides parents with some insight on how children come to understand sex and reproduction. This understanding of child development will help adults

communicate better with children about the origin of families as well as the origin of babies. The revision also deals with such twenty-first-century topics as assisted reproductive technology, donor insemination, and surrogacy.

Free Your Mind
Ellen Bass and Kate Kaufman
Harper Perennial, 1996
A practical resource guide that helps LGBT youth and their allies understand, accept, and celebrate their sexual orientation; overcome obstacles; make healthy choices about relationships and sex; and participate in the gay and lesbian community. Bass and Kaufman weave together their professional experience with the immediate voices of dozens of gay and lesbian youths.

Gay and Lesbian Parenting
Deborah Glazer and Jack Drescher
Haworth Medical Press, 2001
A guide for lesbian and gay parents.

Generation Sex
Dr. Judy Kuriansky
Harper Books, 1996
Unique collection of thousands of questions from young people about sexuality and relationships and the author's advice. Based on questions from teens, college students, and Gen-Exers, who called an extremely popular radio advice show, this extensive collection covers an extremely broad range of topics, including attraction, virginity, body image, fantasy, common concerns, and unusual behaviors, providing an invaluable way to know about the worries, problems, and practices of young people that persist to modern times.

The Go Ask Alice! Book of Answers: A Guide to Good Physical, Sexual, and Emotional Health
Columbia University's Health Education Program
Henry Holt & Company, Inc., 1998
Provides straightforward, nonjudgmental, comprehensive answers to the toughest, most embarrassing questions teens (and adults) have about their sexual, emotional, and physical health. Inspired by Columbia University's award-winning and hugely popular Q&A Web site, this essential book is packed with answers to questions initially posed online. A thorough list of resources is included, providing telephone numbers and Internet addresses for related health organizations, as well as directions for where to look on the Go Ask Alice Web site for more information on the immense variety of subjects.

Growing a Girl: Seven Strategies for Raising a Strong, Spirited Daughter
Barbara Mackoff
Dell Publishing, 1996
Identifies seven specific strategies designed to help parents strengthen their daughter's individuality, self-esteem, and independence. Strong examples and

suggested approaches within these seven strategies give readers the opportunity to employ the strategies immediately.

It's Not the Stork: A Book about Girls, Boys, Babies, Bodies, Families and Friends
Robie H. Harris
Candlewick Press, 2008
From the expert team behind "It's Perfectly Normal" and "It's So Amazing!" this is a book for younger children about their bodies—a resource that parents, teachers, librarians, health care providers, and clergy can use with ease and confidence.

It's Perfectly Normal: Growing Up, Changing Bodies, Sex and Sexual Health
Robie Harris
Candlewick Press, 1996
Providing accurate, unbiased answers to nearly every imaginable question, from conception and puberty to birth control and AIDS, this book offers young people information to make responsible decisions and to stay healthy.

It's So Amazing!: A Book about Eggs, Sperm, Birth, Babies, and Families
Robie II. Harris
Candlewick Press, 1999
This creative book uses bird and bee cartoon characters to present straightforward explanations of topics related to sexual development.

My Body, My Self For Boys (3rd ed.)
Lynda Madaras and Area Madaras
Newmarket Press, 2007
Features detailed coverage, in age-appropriate language, of the body's changing size and shape, the growth spurt, the reproductive organs, voice changes, romantic and sexual feelings, puberty in the opposite sex, and much more. Filled with activities, checklists, illustrations, and plenty of room for journal jottings, plus lots of personal stories in which boys share their concerns and experiences about growing up. For ages 10 and up.

My Body, My Self For Girls (3rd ed.)
Lynda Madaras and Area Madaras
Newmarket Press, 2007
Features detailed coverage, in age-appropriate language, of the body's changing size and shape, the growth spurt, the reproductive organs, menstruation, romantic and sexual feelings, puberty in the opposite sex, and much more. Filled with activities, checklists, illustrations, and plenty of room for journal jottings, plus lots of personal stories in which girls share their concerns and experiences about growing up. For ages 10 and up.

Period
JoAnn Loulan and Bonnie Worthen
Book Peddlers, 2001
Covers questions about puberty and menstruation. The authors emphasize the positive and use diagrams to familiarize readers with the inner workings of their

bodies, including what happens during menstruation. A question-and-answer format in the last three chapters allows girls to locate easily the information they seek. A parent's guide bound into the back suggests how to begin a conversation about puberty and what to cover.

Raising Boys: Why Boys are Different—and How to Help Them Become Happy and Well-Balanced Men
Steve Biddulph
Celestial Arts, 2008
Australia's best-known family therapist and parenting author looks at the most crucial issues that happen in the male's lifetime, from birth to manhood, and offers instruction on the warm, firm guidance that boys need in order to become happy, well-balanced men.

Sexual Etiquette 101 . . . and More
Robert Hatcher, Shannon Colestock, Erika Pluhar, and Christian Thrasher
Bridging the Gap Communications, Inc., 2002
A crash course on sexuality, this book for college students contains stories, resources, ideas, and other valuable tools to help successfully navigate the often confusing world of relationships and sexuality. This book aims to provide information to help prevent the possibly negative and harmful side of sexuality, to be able to enjoy the pleasurable and beautiful side of sexuality, and to make the right decisions.

Sexuality Education: What Adolescents' Rights Require
Nova Publishers, 2007
This book explores adolescent changes and challenges by examining the extent to which we may foster adolescent development in ways that respect and foster adolescents' basic rights to relationships they deem appropriate, fulfilling, and worthy of protection. It also explores those changes and rights from a view that acknowledges the need to respect the rights of others, that recognizes that adolescents' rights are not for them alone.

Sexuality Education Across Cultures: Working with Differences
Janice M. Irvine
Jossey-Bass, 1995
Cultural differences affect sexuality education. This book includes information on approaching the topic with different cultures and gaining an understanding of the diverse perspectives of sexual speech. Examples of how to develop culturally appropriate education programs are also included.

Third Base Ain't What it Used to Be
Logan Levkoff
New American Library, 2007
Brings parents up to date on the world that their kids are living in: what their slang means, what myths and stereotypes they are learning from friends, and how pop culture is affecting how they make decisions. Arranged by topic, it includes

common questions that children and teens have asked the author and offers tips and talking points for tackling these issues in your own home.

The "What's Happening to My Body" Book for Boys (rev. 3rd ed.)
Lynda Madaras with Area Madaras
Newmarket Press, 2007
To help boys realize they are not alone in their concerns about masturbation, body hair, growth spurts (or lack thereof), female puberty, voice changes, perspiration, shaving, and sexuality, this classic guide is written in a down-to-earth, nonjudgmental style and filled with answers to the many questions boys have as their bodies begin the transformation into adulthood. The third edition has been revised to include more detailed discussion of penis size (the authors get more questions about penis size than all other topics combined); updated information on acne treatment; expanded sections on eating right, exercise, steroid abuse, and weight training; important facts about STDs, AIDS, and birth control; and more.

The "What's Happening to My Body" Book for Girls (rev. 3rd ed.)
Lynda Madaras with Area Madaras
Newmarket Press, 2007
Straight talk on the menstrual cycle, reproductive organs, breasts, emotional changes, puberty in boys, body hair, pimples, masturbation, and all the other fun, scary, and interesting things that go along with growing up. Filled with anecdotes, illustrations, diagrams, and honest, sensitive, nonjudgmental information for the young girl, the revised edition also addresses the new scientific facts about when a girl actually begins puberty (earlier than previously thought), advice on "female athletic syndrome," eating disorders, unwanted attention because of early development, and information on eating right, exercise, AIDS, STDs, birth control, and more.

NEWSLETTERS

Newsletters are an important resource because they make available relevant issues and research in a brief manner while offering support to those interested in the field of human sexuality. Newsletters also provide information on upcoming events and conferences dealing with human sexuality.

Contemporary Sexuality
American Association of Sexuality Educators, Counselors, and Therapists
(AASECT)
P.O. Box 1960
Ashland, Virginia, 23005–1960
P: 804-752-0026
F: 804-752-0056
The monthly voice of the Association. The newsletter discusses contemporary and relevant issues through lead articles; provides a summary of significant

contemporary issues, legislation, and policy related to the field; and lists AASECT-approved and -sponsored continuing education workshops.
Web site: http://www.aasect.org

The Kinsey Institute Newsletter—Kinsey Today
E-mail: Kinsey@indiania.edu
Web site: http://www.kinseyinstitute.org/newsletter/

The Sexual Health Network (TSHN) Newsletter
3 Mayflower Lane
Shelton, CT 06484
Dedicated to providing easy access to sexuality information, education, support, and other resources.
Web site: http://www.SexualHealth.com

SIECUS Newsletter
Newsletter for the Sexuality Information and Education Council of the United States.
Web site: http://www.siecus.org

MAGAZINES

These magazines offer useful information about human sexuality to stay up to date with the latest information, research, and issues in the field of human sexuality.

American Sexuality Magazine
National Sexuality Resource Center
San Francisco State University
835 Market St, Suite 517
San Francisco, CA 94103
P: 415-817-4525
F: 415-817-4540
E-mail: nsrcinfo@sfsu.edu
Web site: http://nsrc.sfsu.edu/MagWebpage.cfm

Sex, Etc.
Answer
Rutgers University
41 Gordon Road, Suite C
Piscataway, New Jersey 08854–8067
P: 732-445-7929
F: 732-445-7970
Web site: http://www.sexetc.org

VIDEOS/DVDS

Videos and DVDs about sexuality provide educators in the field of human sexuality a tool for their own learning, as well as for making learning interesting and visual for others. These visual aides can be useful in various contexts, including in the classroom, and in public and professional presentations. Through documentaries and animated videos those who watch will be able to gain the knowledge they would often find in the pages of books, journals, and textbooks. Information, as well as personal stories and experiences, can help learners relate to issues, and can leave a lasting memory.

Girls: Moving Beyond Myth
Produced by: Susan Macmillan
This documentary focuses on the sexual dilemmas and difficult life choices young girls face as they come of age in contemporary American culture. Challenging long-held myths about girlhood, the film draws on the insights of girls themselves to explore and shed light on their actual lived experience as they navigate our increasingly hypersexualized society.
http://www.mediaed.org/videos/

In Our Own Words: Teens and AIDS
Family Health Productions, Inc., 1995
Boston, MA
P: 978-282-9970
Denial can lead to disease. Teens infected with HIV through unprotected intercourse discuss denial, condoms, postponing sex, and how alcohol affects decision making. With discussion guide. 20 minutes. Available in Spanish. Recommended for grades 5 through 12, parents, and other caregivers.
http://www.abouthealth.com/h_products.htm

The Power of Girls: Inside and Out
Family Health Productions, Inc., 2003
Boston, MA
Strong connections help young people make healthy choices. These girls discuss how they dealt with bullying, eating disorders, early sexual activity, and deep loss by talking with friends, parents, or other caring adults. With discussion guide. 20 minutes. Recommended for grades 5 through 12, parents, and other caregivers.
http://wordscanwork.com/products/productsservices.html

Raising Healthy Kids: Families Talk About Sexual Health
Family Health Productions, Inc., 1997
Boston, MA
P: 978-282-9970
Communication about sexual health begins at birth. These parents and young people tell how they discuss sexual health. Experts offer insight and skills to help families start and continue these conversations. Includes discussion guides. Recommended for parents and other caregivers.
http://www.abouthealth.com/h_products.htm

Speak Up!: Improving the Lives of GLBT Youth
Media rights
Copyright 2001

Gay, lesbian, bisexual, and transgender (GLBT) students and their allies face unique challenges of violence and harassment in schools. *SPEAK UP!* explores what these students and their allies have done to transform their schools into safer and more welcoming environments. Interviews with students, parents, teachers, administrators, and national activists highlight not only the need for transformation, but offer resources and advice for those actively working for change. http://www.mediaed.org/videos/MediaGenderAndDiversity/SpeakUp

Talking About Sex: A Guide for Families
Planned Parenthood Federation of America, 1996
New York
An animated video designed to educate children about the basics of sexual relations, including puberty, relationships, contraception, and abstinence. Includes a guide for parents as well as an activity book for children. For ages 10–14.

Teens & Sex in Europe: A Story of Rights, Respect & Responsibility
Narrated by Mariette Hartley
Advocates for Youth, 1998
Provides a fascinating glimpse into the sexual health attitudes of Dutch, German, and French teens and their parents and into the attitudes of government officials, educators, and health care providers.

FILM COMPANIES

Some film companies specialize in producing visual aides that can help educators in their own learning and with presentations, as well as help individuals and couples gain knowledge and skills about sexuality. These companies offer a variety of products for these purposes.

Access Instructional Media
1750 N. Sierra Bonita Ave.
Hollywood, CA 90046
P: 1-800-772-0708 (toll free; to order)
Online superstore. Offers couples-friendly instructional erotica videos.
E-mail Dr. Michael Perry: mepsexdoc@aol.com
Web site: http://www.sexualintimacy.com/home.htm

Alexander Institute
15030 Ventura Blvd., Suite 400
Sherman Oaks, CA 91403
P: 888-270-6510 (toll free; to order)
P: 818-508-1296
F: 818-508-9076
Produces the most critically acclaimed sexuality video series for couples and singles who want to enhance their sex life. World-renowned sex therapists, educators, and best-selling authors developed these erotic and informative series.

E-mail: sales@alexander-institute.com
Web site: http://alexander-institute.com

Femme Productions
A unique collection of "female-friendly" films made with a women's perspective, voice, and pleasure in mind, following story lines and fantasies that appeal to women, and also provide positive female role models, but can be enjoyed by men. The company also offers sexuality-related toys and aides. Founded by a woman. Intended for use by individuals 18 or older.
Web site: http://www.candidaroyalle.com/catalog.html

Sinclair Institute Library
402 Millstone Drive
Hillsborough, NC 27278
P: 1-800-865-9165
F: 1-800-794-3318
Sinclair Institute has earned its reputation as a trusted source for couples seeking greater intimacy, variety, or passion in their sex lives. They offer a wide range of videos and DVDs, which have been produced on a vast array of topics about sexuality. In addition, they sell sexual aids designed to enhance sex and intimacy, including adult toys, videos, massagers, educational products, and sexy clothing for both men and women. Sinclair Institute selects only top-quality products to sell in a discreet and comfortable Web environment.
E-mail: cservice@sinclairinstitute.com
Web site: http://www.sinclairinstitute.com

Vivid-Ed
The sex education imprint of Vivid Entertainment produces videos that cover a range of topics in human sexuality, from anal sex and G-spot stimulation to fellatio and bondage. Vivid-Ed videos offer useful information and explicit techniques' taught by experts, demonstrated by enthusiastic performers, and presented with sensuality.
Web site: http://www.vivid-ed.com/index.php

SEX MUSEUMS

Sex museums provide entertainment and education about the history, development, and cultural significance of human sexuality throughout the world and about the particular culture and country they are set in. Permanent, and sometimes rotating, exhibits include erotic art, artifacts, clothing, and diverse historical and modern-day objects related to sexuality, often in multimedia displays, and that vary in the degree to which they are geared to serious study. Most museums also have a retail boutique or store of items for purchase related to the exhibits, as well as books and various sexuality-related aides and items.

USA, New York: Museum of Sex
233 Fifth Avenue

New York, NY 10016
P: 212-689-6337
Web site: http://www.museumofsex.com

USA, Florida: World Erotic Art Museum
1205 Washington Ave.
Miami Beach, Florida 33139
P: 866-969-WEAM (9326)
Web site: http://www.weam.com

USA, Nevada: Erotic Heritage Museum
3275 Industrial Road
Las Vegas, Nevada 89109
P: 702- 369-6442
Web site: http://www.eroticheritagemuseum.com

USA, California: The Erotic Museum Hollywood
6741 Hollywood Blvd.
Hollywood, CA 90028
P: 323-GO-EROTIC (463-7684)
Web site: http://www.theeroticmuseum.com/them/

Denmark: Erotica Museum
Købmagergade 24
1150 København K, Denmark
P: +45 3312 0311
Web site: http://www.museumerotica.dk

Netherlands: The Sex Museum Amsterdam
Damrak 18, Amsterdam
1012 LH Amsterdam
P: +31 0 20 622 8376
Web site: http://www.sexmuseumamsterdam.nl

France: Musée de l'érotisme de Paris
72, boulevard de Clichy
75018, Paris, France
Web site: http://www.musee-erotisme.com

Spain: Museo de Erotic in Barcelona
Rambla, 96
08002, Barcelona, Spain
P: +34 93 318 98 65
Web site: http://www.erotica-museum.com

England: Amora Academy of Sex and Relationships
13 Coventry St.

London W1D7DH, England
Web site: http://www.amoralondon.com

Germany: Beate Uhse Erotik–Museum
Joachimstaler Str. 4
10623 Berlin Charlottenburg
P: +49 886 06 66
Web site: www.beate-uhse.ag

Czech Republic: Sex Machines Museum
Melantrichova 18–11000 Prague 1
P: +420 227 186 260
Web site: http://www.sexmachinesmuseum.com

China: The Chinese Sex Culture Museum
Tongli Town
Jiang Su Province 215217
China
E-Mail: hongxia508@hotmail.com
Web site: http://www2.hu-berlin.de/sexology/CSM/index.htm

Japan: Beppu's Hihōkan Sex Museum
338–3 Shibuyu Kannawa
Beppu City, Oita Prefecture
P: 0977-66-8790
Web site: N/A

INNOVATIONS

Contemporary times are characterized by technology and new innovations. The following resources represent innovations in the field of human sexuality that allow people to get personalized information, and also to come in touch with others through the Internet and communicate about issues relating to human sexuality.

Internet Sexuality Information Services, Inc. (ISIS)
This nonprofit has been an innovator in the field of sexual health promotion and disease prevention online. Their most well-known project is an e-card service for people to notify their partners of potential exposures to sexually transmitted diseases. Called **inSPOT** (http://www.inspot.org), the site exists in the United States, Romania, and Canada and is being translated into Spanish and French. Recipients of the e-cards can click back to the site to get local testing referrals and disease treatment and prevention information. **SexINFO** (http://www.sextext.org), a short message service (SMS) text-messaging service on mobile phones to inform low-income youth about sexual health and resources. Users type in a code and get a menu of frequently asked questions and answers about HIV, STDs, unintended

pregnancies, and sexual activity, together with one or two local youth-friendly resources.
Web site: http://www.isis-inc.org

Kinsey Confidential Podcast
An opportunity to ask questions and have them answered by experts in sexual health and behavior from the Kinsey Institute at Indiana University.
Web site: http://www.kinseyconfidential.org/podcast/

INDEX

ABOUT THE EDITORS AND CONTRIBUTORS

EDITORS

Judy Kuriansky, PhD, is a clinical psychologist and sex therapist and educator, international trainer, author, and journalist. She is on the adjunct faculty in the Department of Counseling and Clinical Psychology at Columbia University Teachers College and Columbia University College of Physicians and Surgeons, visiting professor at Peking University Health Sciences Center and honorary professor in the Department of Psychiatry of the University of Hong Kong. A diplomat of the American Board of Sexology and fellow of the American Academy of Clinical Sexology (AACS) and awarded the AACS Medal of Sexology for Lifetime Achievement, she is a veteran sexuality educator and therapist, working with individuals, couples, and groups across the country and the world. A past board member of the American Association of Sexuality Educators, Counselor and Therapists (AASECT) and a cofounder of the Society for Sex Therapy and Research, she has authored hundreds of articles in professional journals and mass-market publications about sexuality and sexual health.

As a pioneer of Internet advice and radio call-in advice, "Dr. Judy" has given sexuality and relationship advice in many formats and forums to thousands of men and women of all ages for decades. She has led innumerable workshops across the United States and the globe and developed unique approaches to teaching about safer sex and relationship enhancement, integrating Western and Eastern techniques, which have been presented nationally and internationally from China and Japan to India, Israel, Iran, Austria, and Argentina. In the early days of the developing field of sexuality, she served on the committee determining the first sexuality diagnostic criteria for the American Psychiatric Association's *DSM-III* and evaluated the Masters and Johnson techniques. She has also written advice columns for decades in many mass market publications like *Family Circle Magazine, CosmoGirl, Chicago Triune's Womanews, Single Living, King Features newspapers,* the *South China Morning Post,* and the *Singapore Straits Times, China Trends Health Magazine, Bottom Line Women's Health* newsletter, and the *New York Daily News* Web site. Her commentary about sexuality and relationship issues is quoted in many print sources from newswires to abc.com to *In Touch* magazine. She has developed numerous Internet educational Web sites on topics such as women's issues, healthy aging, and overcoming blues in the bedroom. Her own Web site is www.DrJudy.com.

A former feature television reporter for WABC-TV and CBS-TV and host of CNBC'S *Money and Emotions,* she has been a guest commentator on innumerable TV news and talk shows including *Oprah, Larry King,* and *CNN Headline News' Issues* and *Showbiz Tonight;* has hosted TV specials on topics like "Teens and AIDS" and "No Secrets" about child sex abuse; and has been featured in media from *People* magazine to the *New York Times.* A Fellow of the American Psychological Association and board member of the Peace division, cofounder of the Media Division and Committee of International Relations representative for the Society for Humanistic Psychology, she has expanded help to individuals' relations to intercultural relations, consistent with her philosophy that "peace within leads to peace between people and then peace between nations."

She collaborates extensively with colleagues worldwide, including in China doing trainings for health professionals and helping develop a family planning and reproductive health hotline, and Japan. She has presented her work about sexuality at World Association of Sexology conferences in Rio, Hong Kong, and Sydney, Australia, Asia-Oceanic Conferences on Sexology, and for the China Association of Sexology. At the United Nations, she is the main representative for the International Association of Applied Psychology and the World Association for Psychotherapy and serves on the executive committee of the Committee on Mental Health. A former advisory board member of Planned Parenthood, she is currently on the advisory board and the head of psychosocial programs for U.S. Doctors for Africa and is a member of the executive committee of the section on disasters of the World Association of Psychiatry in association with the Iberoamerican Ecobioethics Network for Education, Science and Technology and the UNESCO Chair in Bioethics. Her books on resolving conflict include *Terror in the Holy Land* and *Beyond Bullets and Bombs: Grassroots peace building between Israelis and Palestinians.*

At Smith College she was a Sloan Foundation Science Research Grant awardee and received her EdM in counseling psychology from Boston University and her PhD in clinical psychology from New York University. She was awarded two Maggie awards for her work with adolescents, as well as a Freedoms Foundation award and a STAR award for individual achievement in radio from American Women in Radio and TV (AWRT), and the first AWRT International Outreach Award.

Besides her professional accomplishments, she is in a band called the Stand Up for Peace Project, which performs at peace summits around the world, including recently at the International Peace Summit with the Dalai Lama in Hiroshima. Her many books about sex and relationships include *Generation Sex: America's Hottest Sex Therapist Answers the Hottest Questions about Sex, The Complete Idiot's Guide to Dating, The Complete Idiot's Guide to A Healthy Relationship,* and *The Complete Idiot's Guide to Tantric Sex,* as well as books originally published in Japan and China. She helps others get their work published in her role as a series editor for two Praeger books' series: Practical and Applied Psychology and Sex, Love, and Psychology.

Elizabeth Schroeder, EdD, MSW, is an international trainer, consultant, and author in the areas of sexual health and sexuality education, curriculum development, teacher training, and counseling. She has provided trainings as well as conference workshops and keynote addresses throughout the United States and overseas to thousands of youth-serving professionals and young people.

Dr. Schroeder is currently the Executive Director for Answer, a national organization based at Rutgers University that is dedicated to providing and promoting comprehensive sexuality education throughout the United States. Known worldwide for their award-winning Web site, "Sex, Etc." (www.sexetc. org), Answer also provides much-needed professional development for teachers and other youth-serving professionals (http://answer.rutgers.edu).

Dr. Schroeder was the cofounding editor of the *American Journal of Sexuality Education,* a journal that provides not only the most cutting-edge research in sexuality education, but also "lessons from the field" as well as lesson plans. In addition to many articles, she is coauthor of several curricula, including "Making SMART Choices: A Curriculum for Young People," and "Being Out, Staying Safe: An STD Prevention Curriculum for LGBQ Youth," both with Dr. Eva Goldfarb. She has edited the 5th, 6th, and 7th editions of *Taking Sides: Clashing Views in Controversial Issues in Family and Personal Relationships,* and authored chapters in *Health Counseling: Applications and Theory* and *The Continuum Complete International Encyclopedia of Sexuality.* She was also proud to contribute a lesson on lesbian and gay issues and aging for *New*

Expectations: Sexuality Education for Mid- and Later Life, coedited by Peggy Brick and Jan Lunquist.

Dr. Schroeder has taught courses on human sexuality, health counseling, curriculum development, and teaching methods at Montclair State University and has been a guest lecturer at other colleges and universities. She also served as the Associate Vice President of Education and Training at Planned Parenthood of New York City, where she worked to establish their training institute for teachers and other youth-serving professionals. Before that, she was the Manager of Education and Special Projects at Planned Parenthood Federation of America, where she coordinated the production of their multiple award-winning video kit for families with adolescent children, *Talking About Sex: A Guide for Families.*

Dr. Schroeder has lent her expertise to Web-based sexuality education initiatives as an expert on the Sex, Etc. Web site, a Web site by teens, for teens. In addition to responding to questions through the "Ask the Experts" section, Dr. Schroeder answered questions and provided counseling during moderated live chats. She has also provided sexuality education for adults by writing articles and responding to e-mails for http://www.sexualhealth.com.

Elizabeth Schroeder has been honored with the Schiller Award by the American Association of Sexuality Educators, Counselors, and Therapists for her approaches to teaching Internet safety to adolescents, and the Mary Lee Tatum Award, given to "the person who most exemplifies the qualities of an ideal sexuality educator." She has been recognized by the Society for the Scientific Study of Sexuality as an "Emerging Professional" in sexuality education and research, and back in 1999, she was given the national Apple Blossom Award, which recognized a Planned Parenthood Education or Training Director who has "risen quickly to the forefront with new ideas, energy, and commitment."

Dr. Schroeder has served as Chairperson of the Sexuality Information and Education Council of the United States (SIECUS) Board of Directors and on numerous local, state, and national task forces and committees. She earned an EdD with a specialization in Human Sexuality Education from Widener University and a Master's Degree in clinical Social Work from New York University.

CONTRIBUTORS

Lauren A. Antonecchia, BS, is currently a second year Psychological Counseling EdM student at Teachers College, Columbia University. Presently is working on a participatory action research project with a New York City public high school and completing a one year internship with the counseling department at a Westchester County high school. She plans to go on to be a high school counselor and is interested in human sexuality education, with a focus on adolescent behavior.

Kriss Barker, MPH, is Vice President for International Programs at Population Media Center (PMC), through which she has assisted production teams throughout the world to develop entertainment-education serial dramas using the Sabido methodology for behavior change communication. Overseeing the management of PMC programs in more than 20 countries worldwide, she has also authored several publications on the Sabido methodology.

Barbara Bartlik, MD, is an Assistant Professor of Psychiatry in the Departments of Psychiatry and Obstetrics and Gynecology at the Weill Cornell Medical College. A graduate of Albert Einstein College of Medicine, she trained in psychiatry at New York University Medical Center, and in sex therapy with noted sexologist Helen Singer Kaplan, MD, PhD. Dr. Bartlik is also a part-President of the Women's Medical Association of New York City and hosts radio shows on sexuality.

Jane D. Brown, PhD, is the James L. Knight Professor in the School of Journalism and Mass Communication at the University of North Carolina, Chapel Hill. She has studied the role of the media in adolescents' health behaviors for more than 30 years. Co-editor of *Sexual Teens, Sexual Media: Investigating Media's Influence on Adolescent Sexuality,* she serves on the Trojan Sexual Health Advisory Committee and the Research Advisory Group for the National Campaign to Prevent Teen and Unplanned Pregnancy.

Cynthia Cabral graduated from Barnard College, Columbia University, with a BA in psychology. She currently works as a Research Coordinator at Weill Cornell Medical College and as an intern for Dr. Barbara Bartlik. She is working toward her PhD in clinical psychology.

Amanda Calvo is a history major at Smith College with a concentration in Middle East studies. She is a features staff writer for the *Sophian,* a campus independent newspaper and has written several articles on current events for the digital newspaper *Clave Digital* in the Dominican Republic.

Bruce Cheung, PhD, is Senior Program Director of the College of Life Science and Technology at the School of Professional and Continuing Education at Hong Kong University and is responsible for introducing IT and e-commerce into HKU SPACE programs. With more than 20 years' experience in education technology and applied artificial intelligence, Dr. Cheung has been involved in numerous research projects on adult continuing education that exploit advanced technologies such as artificial intelligence and datamining. He specializes in strategic planning and design, the application of technology, and pedagogical consultation.

Diana Falzone is a talk show host for *Cosmolicious with Diana*, on Cosmo Radio Sirius XM and a spokesperson for Paltalk, where she hosts a dating and relationship show called *The Diana Falzone Show*. She is also the host for *Date Night with Diana* on Fox News iMag and appears regularly on *Red Eye* on Fox News, *The Strategy Room* on Fox News.com where she guest hosts, and other television shows, including *The Morning Show with Mike & Juliet*, where she serves as a relationship expert. She also writes a weekly advice column for Military.com.

Yvonne K. Fulbright, PhD, is a sexologist and sexuality educator who has written several books, including *The Hot Guide to Safer Sex*. A popular media resource, she is the "sexpert" columnist and sex expert for foxnews.com, a member of BottomLine Women's Health Magazine's Advisory Board, and the sex expert for Comcast's Dating on Demand, SexualHealthGuru.com, and cherrytv.com. She is also a professor of human sexuality at Argosy University and a postdoctoral fellow at the University of Iceland.

M. Scott Gross, MEd, is the former manager of Teen PEP/Teen Council Co-Coordinator, HiTOPS, in Princeton, New Jersey. He earned his master's degree in sexuality education from Widener University in Pennsylvania.

Debby Herbenick, PhD, is a Research Associate and Lecturer in the Department of Applied Health Science at Indiana University. She is also the Associate Director of the Sexual Health Research Working Group at Indiana University, a collaborative of faculty and students conducting research on contemporary issues related to sexuality. Her primary research interests are related to the adult retail industry and the promotion of sexual health, women's sexuality and genital health.

Sarah N. Keller, PhD, is an assistant professor of Communication and Theater at Montana State University-Billings, studying the role of media in health behavior change, with a focus on adolescent sexual health. Dr. Keller has developed a service learning curriculum that has produced three social marketing campaigns, a curriculum that allows her to apply her professional experiences in overseas entertainment education and health communication campaigns with Population Communication International, USAID, and Family Health International.

Julie Anne Kolzet, MA, is studying clinical psychology in the doctoral program at Albert Einstein College of Medicine, Yeshiva University. She earned her MA in counseling psychology from New York University and attended the University of Colorado at Boulder for her undergraduate work.

Judy Kuriansky, PhD, is a clinical psychologist, sex therapist and educator, and international trainer on the adjunct faculty at Columbia University Teachers College and Columbia University's College of Physicians and Surgeons. A visiting professor at Peking University Health Sciences Center and honorary professor in the Department of Psychiatry of the University of Hong Kong, she is a Fellow of the American Psychological Association and main United Nations representative for the International Association of Applied Psychology. Past board member of AASECT, she was awarded a Medal of Sexology for Lifetime Achievement from the American Academy of Clinical Sexology. A veteran radio talk show advice host and TV commentator, and pioneer of "media sexology," she has authored many books, including *Generation Sex* and *The Complete Idiot's Guide to Tantric Sex*. She writes advice for Bottom Line Women's Health newsletter and at her Web site www.DrJudy.com, and helps others get their books published as a Praeger series editor for the Practical and Applied Psychology and Sex, Love, and Psychology series.

Emil Man-Lun Ng, MD, is the Associate Director of the Hong Kong University Family Institute. Formerly, he was Professor of Psychiatry and Coordinator of the Human Sexuality Course at the Faculty of Medicine at the University of Hong Kong, head of the Sex Clinic at Queen Mary Hospital, and in charge of the training program in psychotherapy and sex therapy at the Hospital Authority of Hong Kong. He is the Founding President of the Hong Kong Sex Education Association and the Asian Federation for Sexology and was awarded the Gold Medal in Sexology from the World Association for Sexual Health.

Tina Mo-Yin Ng, PhD, has been involved in the area of mental health for 30 years, and counseling is one of her specialties. She has more than 20 years' experience as an educator in Australia and Hong Kong and has received several grants to develop Web-CT learning packages.

Erika Pluhar, PhD, EdS, is a licensed professional counselor, a certified sexuality educator and a certified sex therapist providing individual, couple, and sex therapy in private practice in Atlanta, Georgia. She also teaches graduate courses in human sexuality at the Rollins School of Public Health at Emory University and at the Georgia School of Professional Psychology at Argosy University. Dr. Pluhar currently is serving a 3-year term on the National Advisory Council at the Center of Excellence for Sexual Health at the Morehouse School of Medicine.

Maria D. Ramirez, MA, is obtaining her masters degree in Psychological Counseling at Teachers College, Columbia University. She has an internship at New Rochelle High School as a school counselor and is involved in Participatory Action Research involving middle school students.

Michael Reece, PhD, MPH, is Assistant Professor and the William L. Yarber Professor of Sexual Health in the Department of Applied Health Science at Indiana University. He also serves as the Director of the Sexual Health Research Working Group at Indiana University and was a postdoctoral fellow at the Bloomberg School of Public Health at Johns Hopkins University. His primary research interests are related to the mental health consequences of HIV infection and the delivery of community-based sexual health interventions.

Chuck Rhoades, MA, is a sexuality and education consultant for CERES Associates. He also serves as an adjunct faculty member at the University of New Hampshire.

Eric Jay Rubenstein, MBA, founded Sex Week at Yale University during his sophomore year. Since graduating from Yale, Eric earned a Master of Business Administration degree from Temple University with a concentration in international business. He remained intimately involved in the planning of the 2006 and 2008 iterations of Sex Week at Yale and continues to work closely with Yale students to plan future iterations on the event. Currently, he currently lives in Houston, Texas, where he works as a commodity trader.

Elizabeth Schroeder, EdD, MSW, is the executive director for Answer, a national sexuality education organization housed at Rutgers University in New Jersey (http://answer.rutgers.edu). She is an award-winning sexuality educator, author, and consultant who has worked with thousands of youth-serving professionals and teens throughout the United States and overseas. A regular presenter at national and international conferences, she has written extensively about sexuality, counseling and training issues, and appears frequently in the media as a sexuality expert, with particular expertise in parent-child communication about sexuality and sexual orientation issues. Dr. Schroeder is the cofounding editor of the *American Journal of Sexuality Education,* a past Chairperson of the Sexuality Information and Education Council of the United States' Board of Directors, and has served as an adjunct professor at Montclair State University. Dr. Schroeder earned her Doctorate in human sexuality education from Widener University and her Master's degree in clinical social work from New York University.

Shir-Ming Shen is an Associate Professor in the Department of Statistics and Actuarial Science at the University of Hong Kong. She also worked in the School of Professional and Continuing Education of the University of Hong Kong (HKU SPACE) in curriculum planning and teaching quality control.

Yee-Lun (Eilean) So, PMP, MSc, has participated in a number of sexuality education projects, including video-editing, publishing organization booklets and organizing sexuality education events. An English major, she helped to proofread translated course documents and articles. She is also a volunteer with the Hong Kong Sex Education Association and is dedicated to contributing to the promotion of healthy sexuality lifestyles.

Sharna Striar, RN, PhD, a certified sex therapist and psychotherapist in private practice in New York City, earned her doctorate from the University of Michigan. Her postdoctoral fellowship in the Human Sexuality Program was directed by Dr. Helen Singer-Kaplan at Weill Cornell Medical College. She was an associate in Dr. Singer-Kaplan's practice and the Project Director of a research study on Kaplan's patient population that spanned more than 20 years. She is the Dean of Nursing at International University for Graduate Studies, St. Kitts, West Indies.

Wing-Yan (Winnie) Yuen, MA, is a researcher at Hong Kong University Family Institute. Her research interests include sex education, adolescent gambling and public stigma. She is also the course officer of the Web-based sex education course offered by the University of Hong Kong and Macau Millennium College. A committee member of Hong Kong Sex Education Association, she has been involved in several public sex education projects in Hong Kong and in Macau.